Psychiatric Drug Withdrawal

Peter R. Breggin, MD conducts a private practice of psychiatry in Ithaca, New York, where he treats adults, couples, and families with children. He also offers consultations in the field of clinical psychopharmacology and often acts as a medical expert in criminal, malpractice, and product liability suits. His professional website is www.breggin.com.

A lifelong reformer in the field of mental health, Dr. Breggin has been called "The Conscience of Psychiatry." He and his wife Ginger recently founded the Center for the Study of Empathic Therapy (a nonprofit organization; 501c3), which holds an annual conference of leading figures in the field who critique biological psychiatry and offer empathic psychosocial approaches (http://www.EmpathicTherapy.org).

> Dr. Breggin's weekly talk radio show, "The Dr. Peter Breggin Hour," is live and archived on the Progressive Radio Network. He blogs on the Huffington Post. Also follow Dr. Breggin on his public Facebook page and follow him and his wife Ginger on Twitter: @GingerBreggin.

Dr. Breggin is the author of more than 40 peer-reviewed scientific articles and more than 20 mass market and professional books. His two most recent books are *Brain-Disabling Treatments in Psychiatry: Drugs, Electroshock, and the Psychopharmaceutical Complex* (2008) and *Medication Madness: The Role of Psychiatric Drugs in Cases of Violence, Suicide, and Crime* (2008).

Earlier books include *Toxic Psychiatry* (1991), *Talking Back to Prozac* (1994, with Ginger Breggin), *Talking Back to Ritalin* (revised, 2001), the *Antidepressant Fact Book* (2001), and the *Ritalin Fact Book* (2002). *The Heart of Being Helpful* (1997) deals with how to help people through psychotherapy and other human services and *Reclaiming Our Children* (2000) examines the Columbine High School shooting tragedy and addresses the needs of America's school children.

Dr. Breggin's background includes Harvard College, Case Western Reserve Medical School, a 1-year internship and a 3-year residency in psychiatry, including a teaching fellowship at Harvard Medical School. After his training, he accepted a 2-year staff appointment as a full-time consultant at the National Institute of Mental Health (NIMH). He has taught at several universities, including the Johns Hopkins University, Department of Counseling and most recently, State University of New York (SUNY) Oswego in the Department of Counseling and Psychological Services.

He founded a scientific journal, *Ethical Human Psychology and Psychiatry* and is on the board of others, including the *International Journal of Risk and Safety in Medicine*.

He has testified before Congress, addressed numerous federal agencies, acted as a consultant to the Federal Aviation Agency (FAA), and given hundreds of seminars and conferences for professionals. His views have been covered in nearly all of the major media from *Time, Newsweek, Wall Street Journal,* and *New York Times* to *Oprah, 20/20, Nightline, 60 Minutes,* and dozens of network and cable news shows.

Dr. Breggin's reform work has brought about significant changes within the profession. In the early 1970s, he conducted a several-year-long successful international campaign to stop the resurgence of lobotomy and newer forms of psychosurgery. His reform efforts and his testimony in the Kaimowitz case in Detroit led to the termination of lobotomy and psychosurgery in the nation's state mental hospitals, National Institutes of Health (NIH), the Veterans Affairs (VA), and most university centers. A public education campaign surrounding his 1983 medical book, *Psychiatric Drugs: Hazards to the Brain,* led the Food and Drug Administration (FDA) to require a new class warning for tardive dyskinesia in 1985. In the 1990s, he was the single scientific expert for more than 100 combined Prozac suits against Eli Lilly and Company. In 1994, his public education campaign led the NIH to reform some of its research policies and to end the Violence Prevention Initiative, a potentially racist program aimed at studying the genetics and biology of inner-city children. His work initiated the reform that led to the FDA's recognition of numerous adverse reactions caused by the newer antidepressants. The FDA warnings in 2004 about suicidality in children and young adults and about a dangerous stimulant profile involving agitation, akathisia, hostility, aggression, and mania, closely followed the language of observations made and publicized by Dr. Breggin over the prior 10 years.

Psychiatric Drug Withdrawal

A Guide for Prescribers, Therapists, Patients, and Their Families

Peter R. Breggin, MD

SPRINGER PUBLISHING COMPANY
NEW YORK

Springer Publishing Company, LLC
11 West 42nd Street
New York, NY 10036
www.springerpub.com

Acquisitions Editor: Sheri W. Sussman
Production Editor: Joseph Stubenrauch
Composition: Absolute Service, Inc.

ISBN: 978-0-8261-0843-2
e-book ISBN: 978-0-8261-0844-9

13 14 15 / 5 4

Library of Congress Cataloging-in-Publication Data

Breggin, Peter Roger, 1936-
  Psychiatric drug withdrawal : a guide for prescribers, therapists, patients, and their families / Peter R. Breggin.
    p. ; cm.
  Includes bibliographical references and index.
  ISBN 978-0-8261-0843-2 — ISBN 978-0-8261-0844-9 (e-book)
  I. Title.
  [DNLM: 1. Psychotropic Drugs--adverse effects. 2. Substance Withdrawal Syndrome—prevention & control. 3. Risk Assessment. 4. Substance Withdrawal Syndrome—therapy. WM 270]

  615.7'88—dc23
                                    2012026397

Printed in the United States of America by Gasch Printing.

*For my wife Ginger Breggin,
a partner beyond all expectations and imaginings*

Contents

Foreword

I was honored when asked to write the foreword for Dr. Peter Breggin's new book *Psychiatric Drug Withdrawal: A Guide for Prescribers, Therapists, Patients, and Their Families*. Dr. Breggin was an early hero of mine when I read his 1994 book *Toxic Psychiatry* about the significant physiological and emotional dangers of prescribing psychiatric medications and the ethical issues associated with the psycho-pharmaceutical complex particularly for vulnerable populations such as children, women, and the homeless. Breggin's work had a profound impact on my practice and teaching when I began my part-time private practice as a psychoanalyst and prescriber, and a full-time educator and director of a graduate program to prepare advanced practice psychiatric nurses. *Toxic Psychiatry* became required reading for my psychiatric nurse practitioner students.

Since then, Breggin has introduced several new terms into the current lexicon, including medication spellbinding (*intoxication anosognosia*). This term refers to the belief by people taking psychiatric drugs that these neurotoxic substances are actually making them better, when in fact, the false euphoria and artificial sense of relief from anxiety or dysphoria are an iatrogenic medication induced disability. The chronic brain impairment that results from long-term use of psychiatric medication is cited as the most important cause of the current escalating epidemic of psychiatric disability. Intoxication anosognosia literally means the person does not recognize medication intoxication in oneself and may even feel better temporarily. The medications essentially produce a chemical lobotomy and the person does not have true access to his or her feelings and hence does not know what he or she does not know.

Psychiatric Drug Withdrawal provides the answer to *Toxic Psychiatry*. Breggin not only presents compelling evidence about the dangers of long-term use of psychiatric medication, he also provides a solution by outlining a compassionate, detailed plan for helping the patient withdraw from these toxic substances. Breggin's book is a breath of fresh air in the dominant biological paradigm of psychiatry. Monetary incentives from pharmaceutical companies in tandem with managed care practice guidelines have conspired to value psychiatric medication as *the* solution to mental health problems. Pharmacology textbooks focus on the pharmacokinetics and pharmacodynamics with few suggestions offered about how to stop medication, except to titrate and/or to switch to a new psychiatric medication to accomplish discontinuation. There are few if any resources or protocols that guide the prescriber in withdrawing the patient sanely and safely from psychiatric medication.

Breggin's person-centered collaborative approach is holistic and context-driven in contrast to the current biomedical reductionistic symptom-oriented approach that is based on a descriptive approach of specialized knowledge that treats individuals as members of a diagnostic group. Diagnostic groups tell us little about the person sitting in front of us. Those practicing in the biomedical model might diagnose the person who seeks help as "a 22-year-old male with schizophrenia" while those practicing from a holistic approach would know the same person as "a young man who isolates from his peers, lives with his parents, and is terrorized by voices that call him names." The latter respects the uniqueness and complexity of the person while the former tells us nothing about that individual.

Prescribers who wish to practice holistically and are eager to learn about the patient are often thwarted by the realities of current clinical settings. There is little time to develop a therapeutic relationship, to listen to the person's story as the process unfolds, and to understand the context of the person's life with patients scheduled every 15 minutes. The prescriber is marginalized to the role of manipulator (of neurochemicals at receptor sites) while the therapist, if involved at all, is relegated to the role of enforcer (to ensure patient compliance). This approach leaves both the prescriber and the therapist frustrated and often overrides clinical judgment and common sense. Breggin's new book reaffirms the primacy of relationship and presents an empathic relationship-oriented, person-centered framework for treatment that involves collaboration between the prescriber, the therapist, the patient, and the family or significant other.

Perhaps Breggin's approach heralds a shift toward a new hopeful paradigm for mental health care as it aligns with recent research on the brain. Neuroimaging studies dissolve the dichotomy that psychotherapy is the treatment for psychological–based disorders while medication is prescribed for biological-based disorders. Both psychotherapy and medication have been found to change the function and structure of the brain. These outcome studies in tandem with epigenetic research on the crucial role of experience in determining genetic expression challenge simplistic reductionistic thinking as compelling evidence is presented that it is our subjective experience that affects the brain.

Peter Breggin's *Psychiatric Drug Withdrawal: A Guide for Prescribers, Therapists, Patients, and Their Families* is a timely and extremely important addition to the literature in psychopharmacology. This book is much needed and should be read by all psychiatrists, psychologists, nurses, therapists, patients, and their loved ones. In contrast to the current treatment model where the therapist plays little or no role in medication management, the therapist's role is central to the successful withdrawal of the patient from psychiatric medication. Indeed, a collaborative, relationship-centered approach is key, where power is shifted from what the prescriber wants to honoring the patient's wishes. This is a must read for every prescriber and will change the way you practice forever.

Kathleen Wheeler, PhD, APRN, FAAN
Professor
Fairfield University
School of Nursing
Fairfield, Connecticut

Preface

Psychiatric medications are not only dangerous to take on a regular basis, but they also become especially dangerous during changes in dosage, including dose reduction and withdrawal. *Psychiatric Drug Withdrawal: A Guide for Prescribers, Therapists, Patients, and Their Families* is intended to provide the latest up-to-date clinical and research information regarding when and how to reduce or to withdraw from psychiatric medication.

This book describes a *person-centered collaborative approach* and is intended as a guide for the entire collaborative team. The team includes *prescribers* (psychiatrists and other physicians, physician's assistants, and nurse practitioners) and *therapists* (social workers, psychologists, counselors, marriage and family therapists, occupational and recreational therapists, nonprescribing nurses, and others). It also includes the *patient* and the patient's *family* or significant others.

The guide begins with reviews of adverse drug effects that may require drug reduction or withdrawal. It then discusses withdrawal effects for specific drugs to familiarize clinicians, patients, and families with these problems. However, no book can substitute for informed professional guidance during the withdrawal process. It cannot address the nuances of an individual case or cover all the possible hazards of taking or withdrawing from psychiatric drugs. Health professionals, patients, and their families are urged to inform themselves

Although this book focuses on medication reduction and withdrawal, the person-centered collaborative approach is also a model for helping children, dependent adults, adults who are emotionally or cognitively impaired, and the elderly, as well as those going through psychiatric medication withdrawal. It's the soundest approach whenever the individual needs more guidance and help than what is available in one-to-one autonomous psychotherapy.

from as many sources as possible, and patients are encouraged to seek the best possible professional guidance in deciding whether or not to withdraw from psychiatric medication and how to go about it.

Because it presents a person-centered collaborative approach that involves patients and their families, the information needs to be user friendly to nonprofessionals. Therefore, generic names will sometimes be interchanged with or accompanied by familiar trade names.

I have written this book for the spectrum of prescribers, including those who have a much more favorable view of psychiatric medications than I do. Therefore, at times I make recommendations for dose reduction or the use of minimal medication when in my own practice I would not be using medication at all. I continue to believe and to practice on the principle that psychiatric medications do more harm than good, and in my own practice, I rely upon individual, couples, and family therapy without starting patients on psychiatric drugs (see Breggin, 2008a and 2008b).

Acknowledgments

My wife Ginger Breggin played a central role in my motivation to write this book. She perceived a great need for it through thousands of communications to us, many through our websites and social media. Ginger also drew my attention to and obtained many of the most recent research studies relevant to the book.

In 2010 Ginger and I formed a new 501c3 nonprofit organization, the Center for the Study of Empathic Therapy, and in 2011 we held our first annual conference (www.EmpathicTherapy.org). Her work in making all this happen, and our feedback from Center participants and conference attendees, made us especially aware of the need for a book on psychiatric drug withdrawal aimed not only at prescribers but also therapists, patients, and their families.

One of Ginger's most recent projects was the development of www. ToxicPsychiatry.org as a current news and resource library for cutting-edge issues in the field of mental health. The reader can find many of the articles in this book in the archives of the website.

Our office assistant Melissa McDermott has added immeasurably to our lives, including freeing Ginger up to handle so many areas of our professional work together. I also want to thank Ella Keech for making our lives easier around the office. Both bring spiritual sunshine into the office.

My research assistant Ian Goddard continues to provide original insights along with his careful searches of the scientific literature. He makes my books better.

I published my first book with Springer in 1979—more than three decades ago.

I've now worked on several books with Sheri Sussman, Executive Editor, Springer Publishing Company. She is simply the best! I want to thank her and the entire team at Springer.

A number of friends and colleagues were kind enough to review the manuscript in whole or in part in order to comment or to offer a prepublication endorsement. It is quite extraordinary that they took time out of their busy personal and professional lives in order to do this. They include Bertram Karon, PhD, Sarton Weinraub, PhD, Frederick Baughman, Jr., MD, Douglas C. Smith, MD, Stuart Shipko, MD, Charles L. Whitfield MD, Piet Westdijk, MD, Terry Lynch, MD, Fred Ernst, PhD, Wendy West Pidkaminy, LCSW-R, Tony Stanton, MD, Melanie Sears, RN, MBA, Gerald Porter, PhD, Kathryn Douthit, PhD, LMHC, Robert Foltz, PsyD, Joanne Cacciatore, PhD, LMSW, FT, Douglas W. Bower, RN, LPC, PhD, Todd DuBose, PhD, and Timothy Evans, PhD. The first eight—Bert, Sarton, Fred, Doug, Stuart, Charles, Piet, and Terry—also gave me helpful feedback on specific aspects of concern that I asked them about.

Thank you, all!

Introduction: Hazards of Psychiatric Drug Withdrawal

Why are psychiatric drug withdrawal problems so common and often so difficult to overcome? Because the brain adapts to all psychoactive substances, the abrupt withdrawal from any psychiatric drug can produce distressing and dangerous withdrawal reactions. Even medications commonly thought to be free of withdrawal problems, such as lithium, can produce potentially dangerous reactions when they are stopped.

By means of a variety of biochemical reactions, the brain attempts to overcome the primary effects of any psychoactive substance. For example, many antidepressant drugs have been tailored in the laboratory to suppress the removal of the neurotransmitter serotonin from the synapse in the brain. This impact was expected to increase the amount of serotonin in the synapse and perhaps in the overall brain. But the brain quickly compensates through several biochemical mechanisms that can dampen and even reverse this intended drug effect (Breggin 2008a). Similarly, many antianxiety drugs enhance the activity of the neurotransmitter gamma-aminobutyric acid (GABA), but once again, the brain reacts by suppressing or even reversing the drug effect.

When these antidepressants or antianxiety drugs are stopped, the brain can be slow to recover from its own biochemical adjustments or compensatory effects. In effect, the brain cannot immediately keep up with the removal of the drug. This can produce distressing and dangerous withdrawal effects.

When a patient has been taking a psychiatric medication for several months or more—or even for a mere few weeks in the case of benzodiazepines—the brain becomes especially slow to react to the withdrawal of the drug, causing potentially more long-lasting, hazardous, and even life-threatening adverse reactions.

Psychiatric drugs also cause directly damaging effects. As several chapters of this book will document, all psychiatric drugs that have been examined have proven to be toxic to neurons or severely disruptive of normal brain function. These harmful effects may be partially masked by the blunting of emotions and judgment and medication spellbinding (see Chapter 9) that is associated with all psychiatric drugs. When the drug dose is reduced or the drug is stopped, the individual becomes more aware of the deficits, and others may notice them as well. At times, it may be difficult to distinguish withdrawal effects from direct toxic effects, even after the medication has been stopped for many months. It becomes difficult to determine if the individual is experiencing a lasting withdrawal effect because of the brain's own compensatory mechanisms or a more direct toxic effect.

UNIQUE PROBLEMS ASSOCIATED WITH DRUG WITHDRAWAL

Withdrawal from psychiatric drugs commonly causes emotionally jarring biochemical changes in the brain. The physical disruption of mental processes during withdrawal can severely impair the patient's judgment and self-control. In the extreme, severe depression, mania, psychosis, violence, and suicidality can occur during drug withdrawal. The withdrawal process can also elicit many psychological fears about managing life with fewer drugs, lower doses of drugs, or no drugs at all. In addition, concerned or fearful friends and relatives may complicate the drug withdrawal process by directly interfering or by the contagion of their anxiety and other negative emotions. Although the person-centered collaborative approach emphasizes the positive involvement of families in helping the patient withdraw, families can also generate many painful emotions and fears that can stymie the patient's withdrawal attempts.

In addition, psychiatric drugs commonly cause chronic brain impairment (CBI) with cognitive dysfunction, emotional instability, apathy or indifference, and anosognosia (the inability to recognize these dysfunctions). As the medication is reduced, and the brain and mind are no longer so impaired, individuals become more aware of their mental deficits, superimposing additional anxiety and despair on the withdrawal process.

These, and other factors that will be discussed, produce a more complex situation than routine medication treatment. In routine treatment, when the brain is exposed to the same dose of a psychoactive substance on a daily basis for a considerable period, the individual tends to stabilize—that is, to settle into a steadier biochemical and emotional state. The prescriber and the client can be lulled into a sense of safety regarding taking the medication. But if doses are skipped or changed, the brain may be unable to adjust in sufficient time to prevent a withdrawal reaction. Drug withdrawal is therefore more complex and more acutely dangerous than the routine prescription and use of psychiatric drugs. More care, more attention, and more specialized knowledge are required than during the routine administration of the same drug.

These cautionary observations are not intended to discourage withdrawal from psychiatric drugs. The long-term effects of psychiatric drugs on the brain and mind present the most serious hazards of all.

THE RELUCTANCE TO WITHDRAW PATIENTS FROM PSYCHIATRIC DRUGS

Because it is complicated, time consuming, risky, or contrary to their philosophy or training—many healthcare providers do not feel comfortable withdrawing their clients or patients from psychiatric drugs. Very few have the experience to feel confident in how to go about withdrawing from psychoactive medications. As a result, many potential patients have difficulty finding professional supervision and support when they wish or need to reduce the dose or number of their psychiatric medications or to stop them entirely. These individuals may feel compelled to stop their medications on their own without professional help, sometimes with tragic results. Others continue to use their medications despite increasing adverse effects, often with equally or more tragic results.

Because withdrawal from psychiatric drugs can be so difficult, the safest and more effective approach requires a team effort—a person-centered collaborative approach that includes the prescriber, therapist, patient, and the patient's family or support network. This person-centered approach focuses on the client's mental status, needs, feelings, and wishes during the withdrawal process. This person-centered approach is consistent with the practice of contemporary medicine and also provides the safest and most effective approach.

Most prescribers are usually limited in the amount of time they can spend with each patient. These prescribers can provide better services if they work with a therapist who sees the patient more often and can develop more understanding and rapport with the patient and family. Because psychiatric drug withdrawal is so potentially hazardous, the patient's family or social network also needs to be involved to support and to help monitor the patient. The therapist rather than the prescriber will usually be in the best position to coordinate the prescriber, the patient, and the patient's family or friends.

Because it uses a person-centered collaborative approach, *Psychiatric Drug Withdrawal* can and should be read by the entire team. This includes **prescribers**, such as nurse practitioners, primary care physicians, pediatricians, internists, physicians' assistants, and psychiatrists. It includes **therapists**, such as nonprescribing nurses, clinical social workers, clinical psychologists, counselors, marriage and family therapists, and occupational and recreational therapists. And finally, it includes **patients** and their social network of **family** and **friends**. All these potential members of the collaborative treatment team effort should find this book useful regarding understanding and assessing medication effects, observing and reporting adverse effects during treatment or withdrawal, informing or reminding patients and their families about the risks associated with these drugs and the benefits of withdrawing from them, and providing guidance and support during difficult medication withdrawals.

The Center for the Study of Empathic Therapy

The Center for the Study of Empathic Therapy, Education, and Living is a nonprofit organization (501c3) founded by Peter R. Breggin, MD and Ginger Breggin for professionals and nonprofessionals who want to raise ethical and scientific standards in psychology and psychiatry. It provides a community and network for like-minded people who wish to support empathic, caring approaches to therapy, education, and living.

The center continues Dr. Breggin's 40-year reform efforts as "The Conscience of Psychiatry." Find us at http://www.EmpathicTherapy.org. This new organization carries forward the decades of work launched by Dr. Peter Breggin in his first nonprofit International Center for the Study of Psychiatry and Psychology (ICSPP; http://www.icspp.org) in 1972.

The board of directors and advisory council of the Center include more than 60 professionals in many fields spanning psychology, counseling, social work, nursing, psychiatry and other medical specialties, neuroscience, education, religion, and law, as well as concerned advocates and laypersons. Everyone is welcome to become a general member of this innovative and forward thinking organization.

The Center for the Study of Empathic Therapy provides a free e-newsletter. The latest news, research, and a scientific resources library can be found on the Center's related website, http://www.ToxicPsychiatry.org.

The Center holds annual conferences that are among the most scientifically informed, innovative, and inspiring. For many professionals and advocates, they are life changing. Families, advocates, and the general public are also encouraged to attend. Empathic relationship can be the basis of a wonderful, healing, and thriving life.

Join us at http://www.EmpathicTherapy.org.

Related Books by the Author

College Students in a Mental Hospital (1962; jointly authored by C. Umbarger, J. Dalsimer, A. Morrison, and P. Breggin)

Electroshock: Its Brain-Disabling Effects (1979)

Psychiatric Drugs: Hazards to the Brain (1983)

Toxic Psychiatry (1991)

Beyond Conflict (1992)

Talking Back to Prozac (1994; coauthored by Ginger Breggin)

Psychosocial Approaches to Deeply Disturbed Persons (1996; senior editor)

The Heart of Being Helpful: Empathy and the Creation of a Healing Presence (1997)

The War Against Children of Color: Psychiatry Targets Inner City Children (updated 1998; first published 1994; coauthored by Ginger Breggin)

Reclaiming Our Children (2000)

Talking Back to Ritalin, Revised Edition (2001; first edition 1998)

The Antidepressant Fact Book (2001)

Dimensions of Empathic Therapy (2002; jointly edited by Ginger Breggin and Fred Bemak)

The Ritalin Fact Book (2002)

Your Drug May Be Your Problem, Second Edition (2007; first edition 1997; coauthored by David Cohen)

Brain-Disabling Treatments in Psychiatry, Second Edition (2008; first edition 1997).

Medication Madness: The Role of Psychiatric Drugs in Cases of Violence, Suicide, and Crime (2008)

Endorsements

Today many psychologists, nurses, social workers, and counselors are struggling with how to help adults and the parents of children who are over-medicated or who wish to reduce or stop taking their psychiatric drugs. Dr. Breggin's book shows non-prescribing professionals, as well as prescribers, how to respond to their patients' needs in an informed, ethical, and empowering fashion.

> *Sarton Weinraub, PhD*
> Clinical Psychologist
> Director, New York Person-Centered
>   Resource Center
> New York, New York

I don't know anywhere else to get this information, at least not compiled in this easy-to-understand way. This book is the culmination of Dr. Breggin's lifetime of work, and it is chock-full of facts, practical recommendations, and wisdom from experience working with children and adults. His person-centered approach is a breath of springtime air for those tens of millions of people who have tried "treatment as usual" and not been helped, and wonder what to do now. Daily, people come to my office after having tried pills, more pills, newer pills, different pills, and pill combinations, with no real relief, or things have gotten worse. Now they are on medicines and they can't get off, or they are afraid to try. Those people need answers. Breggin has answers.

> *Douglas C. Smith, MD*
> Psychiatrist
> Former Clinic Director
> Juneau, Alaska

Peter Breggin has written a unique, brilliant, and comprehensive book that every mental health professional should read and "prescribe" to their patients and families! Dr. Breggin is a true pioneer in identifying the dangers of psychiatric drugs, being the first to warn us decades ago that treatment of the mentally ill would devolve to the shameful status it reveals today. Professional and lay populations everywhere have come to recognize that we are a dangerously over-medicated society, urgently in need of a fix, and Dr. Breggin's new book provides an intelligent way out of this quagmire.

Fred Ernst, PhD
Professor of Psychology
University of Texas–Pan American
Edinburg, Texas

In this exceptional, easy-to-read, highly informative and thought provoking book, Dr. Breggin continues to be the conscious of psychiatry and leading expert in the field of psychiatric drug withdrawal. This groundbreaking work will empower patients, their family members, and mental health professionals. It is a must have for all those wanting the most accurate, up-to-date information regarding collaborative, empathetic, effective, and safe psychiatric drug withdrawal.

Wendy West Pidkaminy, LCSW-R
Adjunct Professor of Social Work,
   Syracuse University
Syracuse, New York

Our culture has increasing need of a new language to counteract and clarify the ascendant role of psychotropic medication in our society. Peter Breggin has provided us with that language. In *Psychiatric Drug Withdrawal* he has created a truly concise and eminently practical guide for evaluating the effects of psychotropic medications and finding ways to withdraw from them. It is a superb summary of the knowledge he has collected over a lifetime. This is invaluable knowledge for those clients of all ages who have ended up addicted to these medications. The guidelines in this book can lead to the recovery of their lives.

Tony Stanton, MD
Adult and Child Psychiatrist
Private Practice, Poulsbo, Washington

This much-needed book and guide to psychiatric medication withdrawal is clearly written and easy to understand. As people become more empowered and able to inform themselves about the effects of pharmaceuticals, practitioners will be called upon to wean their patients off of damaging medications. This book will provide that guidance. Thank you Dr. Breggin for having the courage to oppose conventional psychiatric thinking and the caring to improve the quality of life for individuals who are ready to experience their own innate healing instead of reaching for a pill to mask the symptoms.

> *Melanie Sears, RN, MBA*
> Author, *Humanizing Health Care*
> and *Choose Your Words*
> Albuquerque, New Mexico

Dr. Peter Breggin has written an invaluable reference for mental health professionals and laypersons alike who are seeking a way out of dependency on psychiatric drugs. He describes the many dangers of psychiatric medication in straightforward research-based and contextually nuanced terms. Most helpfully, he articulates a method of empathic, person-centered psychotherapy as an alternative to the prevailing emotionally and system disengaged drug-centered approach. In this book, Dr. Breggin systematically outlines how to safely withdraw a patient from psychiatric medication with rich case examples drawn with the detail and sensitivity to individual and situational differences that reveal not only his extensive clinical experience, but his clear, knowledgeable, and compassionate vision of a more humane form of treatment. In this volume, Dr. Peter Breggin has again demonstrated that he is a model of what psychiatry can and should be. This is an indispensable text for both mental health trainees and experienced practitioners seeking a practical alternative to the dominant drug-centric paradigm.

> *Gerald Porter, PhD*
> Vice President for Academic
> Affairs School of Professional
>   Psychology at Forest Institute
> Springfield, Missouri

The field of mental health counseling is rooted in principles and practices informed by empathy and client empowerment. Using these core elements of counselor education as guiding principles, Dr. Breggin challenges the status quo of psychiatric practice and provides practitioners with an alternative vision that raises both controversy and consciousness. This book underscores the counselor's ethical imperative to be informed, critical professionals in regard to psychiatric "evidence-based" treatments. Amidst the swell of public resistance to the growing use of psychotropics, Dr. Breggin's bold work bolsters the ability of counselors to contribute to the professional discourse that surrounds the complex decisions clients make concerning their journey toward healing and wellness.

Kathryn Douthit, PhD, LMHC
Chair & Associate Professor
  Counseling & Human
  Development
Warner Graduate School of
  Education & Human Development
University of Rochester
  Rochester, New York

Dr. Breggin has again created an invaluable resource for both treatment providers and treatment recipients. His authoritative knowledge of these issues creates a position of confidence for clinicians, while empowering those individuals and families receiving care. The writing style is great. It offers "chunks" of information—clear, concise, and you don't need to read the whole chapter to get valuable information, making it a handy reference. This important contribution to the field will create a powerful ripple-effect, aimed at ultimately improving the treatment outcomes for those in need of compassionate and effective treatment.

Robert Foltz, PsyD
Assistant Professor, Department of
  Clinical Psychology
Chicago School of Professional
  Psychology
Chicago, Illinois

A pill is a poor substitute for human connectivity and compassion, and Dr. Breggin's new book is the first step toward understanding the insidious nature of foregoing the call to comfort one another during times of hardship. Some sufferings cannot be fixed with a magic wand, or magic mantra, or magic pill. I urge everyone to read this book, slowly and mindfully.

There is, perhaps, no more important message for those who wish to help heal and those who desperately seek such healing.

Because a pill is a poor substitute for human connectivity and compassion, this book provides insight and guidance to empower therapists who are willing to play a much greater role in helping their patients make decisions about taking, and not taking, psychiatric drugs, without the fear that they have to enforce "medication compliance."

Joanne Cacciatore, PhD, LMSW, FT
Bereavement Trauma Specialist
Assistant Professor, Arizona State
    University
Clinical Director and Founder
    MISS Foundation
Tempe, Arizona

This is a warning. Your psychiatric medicines are dangerous. Further, withdrawal from the medications can trigger horrendous consequences, additional psychiatric symptoms, and even death. In *Psychiatric Drug Withdrawal: A Guide for Prescribers, Therapists, Patients, and Their Families*, Dr. Peter Breggin addresses very important issues regarding the use of psychiatric medicines, and the termination of these medications. Counselors, social workers, psychologists, and psychotherapists will find Dr. Breggin's material helpful for understanding the adverse drug effects, feeling empowered in helping adult patients and the parents of child patients make decisions about medications, for monitoring their patient's drug experience, and in assisting families concerning the issues of patient withdrawal from medications.

Douglas W. Bower, RN, LPC, PhD
Athens, Georgia

The psychodynamic and medical issues critical to stopping psychiatric medications are explained. Dr. Breggin provides a novel and comprehensive blueprint for prescribing doctors, therapists, and patients to join in a collaborative effort to stop taking psychiatric medications. It is a book that patients, therapists, and physicians will all want to read.

Stuart Shipko, MD
Psychiatrist in Private Practice
Pasadena, California

This is such an important book. Describing the problem of withdrawal from psychiatric drugs in detail, and providing clear advice regarding how to deal with this problem, as Peter has done so well in this book, is long overdue. For decades, the belief system that is mainstream psychiatry has denied the existence of withdrawal problems from the substances they prescribe so widely. In reality, withdrawal problems with psychiatric drugs is a common occurrence. Because of psychiatry's reckless denial of this real and common problem, millions of people worldwide have not had the support and care they desperately need when attempting to come off psychiatric drugs, often been erroneously advised that these problems are confirmation of the existence of their supposed original so-called "psychiatric illness." Dr. Breggin's book is therefore both timely and necessary.

> *Terry Lynch, MD*
> Physician and Psychotherapist
> Limerick, Ireland
> Author of *Beyond Prozac: Healing*
> *Mental Suffering Without*
> *Drugs and Selfhood: A Key to the*
> *Recovering of Emotional Well*
> *Being, Mental Health and the*
> *Prevention of Mental Health*
> *Problems*

As a physician who specializes in addiction medicine and drug withdrawal and written widely on them, I recommend Dr. Breggin's book to every health professional who deals with anyone taking psychiatric drugs. He gives highly useful information and reasons for stopping or avoiding them. It's an excellent one-stop source of information about psychiatric drug effects and withdrawal. Prescribers, therapists, patients, and families will benefit from this guidebook.

> *Charles L. Whitfield MD*
> Atlanta, Georgia
> Best-selling author of *Healing the*
> *Child Within*, and recently *Not*
> *Crazy* and *Wisdom to the Know*
> *the Difference*

This is a needed book. Thoughtful clinicians, including psychiatrists, other prescribing physicians, clinical psychologists, social workers, and other therapists, frequently think their patients should be withdrawn from psychiatric medication, but they are not sure. In addition, they do not know the best way to help the patient to safely withdraw from psychiatric medication.

They are often afraid of the disapproval of their professional colleagues. Nonmedical therapists may feel they have no right to question the judgment of their medical colleagues about medication. Nonpsychiatrist physicians may feel they should not discontinue the medication unless it is requested by the original prescriber, usually a psychiatrist. Psychiatrists may feel that if they withdraw their patients from psychiatric medication they will be resented by colleagues who almost never withdraw their own patients.

Psychiatric medication is sometimes helpful in the short run, but if continued becomes a problem, and eventually a disaster. For a few patients it becomes a disaster right away.

The first part of the book is a careful and relatively complete description of the reasons why one should consider psychiatric drug withdrawal or dose reduction and when. Included are detailed discussions of antipsychotics (neuroleptics), antidepressants, stimulants, benzodiazepines and other sedatives and opiates, and lithium and other mood stabilizers.

The second part of the book is a detailed description of the best way to withdraw from psychiatric drugs, taking into account the specific drug or multiple drugs, the length of usage, and the characteristics of the individual patient. Case histories are presented of simple and of complex cases of withdrawal. This is information not previously available anywhere.

Withdrawal is best handled by the prescriber, therapist, patient, and one or more family members, working together as a team. Prescribers rarely see patients often enough and long enough to have a detailed knowledge of withdrawal effects without information from the others. Therapists are more likely to know about adverse drug effects, including withdrawal effects, especially if they are looking for them. Patients are likely to report symptoms if they think their therapist and their prescriber want to know. However, one common side effect and withdrawal effect of psychiatric medication is a lack of awareness of symptoms ("medication spellbinding" or intoxication anosognosia). That is why a family member can be useful in pointing out and describing obvious symptoms of which the patient seems unaware.

The most heartening chapter is on children and teenagers. Most children and teenagers can be withdrawn with relative ease and safety, if their parents are cooperative. Withdrawal from stimulants is easily accomplished with children and teens diagnosed with ADHD if sensible family therapy and possible consultation with the child's teachers are provided. Not only will they be off the medication, their troubling symptoms will also be gone. Of course, it would have been better to provide family therapy without medication from the beginning.

Children and teens diagnosed with bipolar disorders also readily respond to family therapy and withdrawal of medication. "Manic" symptoms in children and teens are almost always a side effect of antidepressants or of stimulants. Children diagnosed with autism need help in relating and medication impairs their learning to relate. They are able to respond to efforts by parents and others to relate to them once they are off medication. Children and teens, whatever their diagnosis, even after prolonged exposure to multiple drugs, respond to family therapy and a team approach and usually can be withdrawn easily if they have a stable family.

Peter Breggin has more experience in safely withdrawing psychiatric patients from medication than any other psychiatrist. In this book he shares his lifetime of experience. All of our patients deserve the benefit of our obtaining that knowledge.

> *Bertram Karon, PhD*
> Professor of Psychology
>   Michigan State University
> Author, *The Psychotherapy of*
>   *Schizophrenia*
> Former President of the Division of
>   Psychoanalysis of the American
>   Psychological Association
> East Lansing, Michigan

In his new book, *Psychiatric Drug Withdrawal: A Guide for Prescribers, Therapists, Patients, and Their Families*, Dr. Breggin takes on a subject and practice that draws both anxiety and hope from all parties: withdrawing from psychiatric medication with the goal of avoiding medication-induced chronic brain impairment. His person-centered principles of respect, concern, empowerment of individual choice, providing as much comfort as possible during withdrawal, encouraging a supportive environment, and careful attunement to clinical monitoring, provide the necessary conditions for the journey of withdrawal to be an experience of personal transformation. At the same time, Dr. Breggin's lifelong career in this field mitigates against a naïve and Pollyannaish romanticism of this process. He explicitly, and regularly, addresses the dangerousness of sudden and unsupervised withdrawal and, instead, encourages a collaborative approach centered on the utmost respect for a patient's choice and pace in this journey, while very sensitively discerning and weighting the damage that could be done without withdrawal in relation to the discomfort of the withdrawal. Dr. Breggin equalizes the authority of all parties in this process, thus dethroning the dictatorship of the prescriber, but not excluding him or her.

I have been waiting for a text like this one to recommend to numerous families that come to me distressed and vulnerable to authoritative voices that box them into the false dilemma of either taking medications that have severe side effects for themselves or for their children, or being tagged as medically noncompliant and/or neglectful. Dr. Breggin should wear a large "B" on his chest and a cape as this text is a crime-fighting text that will certainly contribute to expanding options for countless individuals seeking liberation from chemically induced violence.

What is also very important here is that Dr. Breggin's person-centered approach is not a militant enforcer of withdrawal, which would merely adjust chairs on the same sinking ship. On the contrary, he emphasizes that attunement to the patient means encouraging autonomy, responsibility, decision making, and pacing are vital to a successful experiences of withdrawal, a stance quite different than what has typically been the case to date. Again, this isn't an argument of polarization of patients against prescribers, but an invitation to a collaboration of *shared* power in mutual dialogue about how to handle suffering in life.

Most importantly, Dr. Breggin notes that "The best way to avoid psychiatric drugs is to forge ahead with creating a wonderful life." We do this through the power of intimacy and love, which can alter more than brain chemistry; it can alter how we are with each other in the world in more communal ways, thus nullifying the need for medications to orchestrate our lives. In Dr. Breggin's book, the possibility of liberation has come.

Todd DuBose, PhD
Associate Professor, Chicago School
of Professional Psychology
Chicago, Illinois

Peter Breggin shows us the wave of the future. The polluting of our mind and souls goes beyond the Gulf Oil Spill. Dr. Breggin gives us the vision to see the damage and the tools to start the cleanup.

Timothy D. Evans, PhD
Private Practice, Tampa, Florida
and Executive Director
Florida Adlerian Society

CHAPTER 1

A Person-Centered Collaborative Approach to Psychiatric Drug Withdrawal[1]

A person-centered collaborative approach to drug withdrawal requires a trusting relationship between the patient and healthcare providers. Out of respect for the patient and to minimize fear and anxiety, the patient must feel in control of the process or at least an equal partner in it. This requires the clinician to share information and to collaborate with the patient regarding every aspect of the withdrawal process, including what to expect with each dose change up or down. The clinician's empathy for the patient, along with a commitment to honest communication and patient empowerment, lies at the heart of the person-centered approach.

The client's mental status and feelings are the most sensitive barometers of how the withdrawal process is progressing. The prescriber must bring an empathic, positive, and encouraging attitude toward the client that places great emphasis on the client's self-evaluation and feelings and encourages the client to voice concerns and to describe the subjective experience of withdrawal.

In difficult cases, the patient will need a person-centered collaborative team effort involving the prescriber, a therapist or counselor, the patient, and the patient's family or social network. The family or friends not only can provide emotional support; they may also be able to help with monitoring. Patients often fail to recognize when they are

---

[1]The term "withdrawal" will be used instead of the more recent term "discontinuation," which is euphemistic and distracts from the seriousness of the problem. Similarly I will often use the term "addiction" rather than the euphemistic "dependence."

undergoing a dangerous withdrawal reaction, including violent or suicidal impulses, and so the involvement of significant others can be lifesaving. This book can be used as a collaborative guide for prescribers and therapists, as well as for patients and their support network.

Twenty percent of adult Americans were taking psychiatric drugs in 2010—15% of men, and 26% of women (Medco, 2011). Antidepressants were by far the most commonly used by both sexes, although antipsychotic drugs were markedly on the rise among men. Prescriptions for psychiatric problems in all adults rose 22% in the decade.

It has become very easy for individuals to find clinicians who will prescribe psychiatric drugs or refer them to other professionals for medication. But it remains very difficult for patients to find help in reducing or withdrawing from psychiatric drugs. Lack of peer support and training are among the reasons why clinicians often feel uncomfortable responding to the patient's desire or need for medication reduction or withdrawal.

Many clinicians, including both prescribers and therapists, have no training and little experience in lowering doses or stopping psychiatric drugs. Some are not aware of the growing number of reasons why patients should avoid staying on these chemical agents for long periods.

To help patients through the sometimes difficult, frightening, and hazardous process of drug reduction or withdrawal, clinicians need to become fully engaged with patients and their families or significant others who can provide support and at times join the treatment team. The process begins with communicating respect and value for the people who seek help from us. It further requires our own personal commitment to offering genuine help based on good science, honesty, the patient's needs and desires, and partnership in decision making. This collaborative relationship is what is meant by the person-centered collaborative approach.

RELATIONSHIP BETWEEN PRESCRIBERS AND THERAPISTS

In facilities and private practice, many different professionals can prescribe psychiatric medications, including psychiatrists, nurse practitioners, physician assistants, family doctors, internists, neurologists, pediatricians, and even medical specialists such as surgeons, obstetrician/gynecologists, and dermatologists. These prescribers can benefit their patients by working closely with their therapists (see Chapter 12 of this book).

> Prescribers and therapists working in facilities and private practice should cooperate to ensure that medicated patients receive proper monitoring and a maximum opportunity for recovery and overall improvement in their quality of life.

Therapists who work with medicated patients are also found in facilities and private practice, including nurses, social workers, clinical psychologists, counselors, family and marriage therapists, occupational therapists, and school psychologists. These therapists can also benefit their patients by working closely with their prescribers.

In the past, prescribers sometimes felt it was sufficient to write psychiatric prescriptions for patients whom they would see briefly and on widely spaced occasions. Therapists in turn were expected to urge their patients to comply with their prescriptions for psychiatric drugs without conducting their own independent evaluations. This situation is changing, with the realization that psychiatric drugs carry considerable hazards and require more serious monitoring than prescribers by themselves can usually provide.

> Prescribers and the clinicians with whom they work have begun to realize that the use of prescription drugs is far too hazardous and complex to be monitored by the prescriber alone. Informed and diligent therapists can also contribute to the patient's understanding and decision making concerning medication and provide important feedback or consultations to prescribers.

Suicidality, violence, and other serious short-term hazards have been documented for several classes of psychiatric medication. Long-term exposure to psychiatric drugs has proven to be far more dangerous than originally anticipated, including medication-induced obesity, diabetes, heart disease, irreversible abnormal movements, and an overall deterioration in the patient's clinical condition and quality of life.

As a result, Food and Drug Administration (FDA)-approved labels for psychiatric drugs and good clinical practice now call for a degree and intensity of monitoring that is beyond the capacity of most prescribers regardless of the setting in which they work. Fifteen-minute medication checks conducted at widely spaced intervals are especially insufficient to monitor the patient's condition for any potential adverse drug effects or to maximize the patient's potential for recovery and growth. Prescribers need the help of other clinicians to ensure the safest and most effective use of medications.

Therapists can no longer assume that a prescription, once written, should be continuously taken by the patient and that their professional role is limited to encouraging or monitoring compliance. Nurses on psychiatric wards and in private practice, as well as other clinicians, are commonly in a better position to evaluate the patient's needs, wants, and clinical condition than

> Prescribers and therapists, as well as patients and their families, must work closely with each other to ensure the safest and most beneficial use of psychiatric medications.

the prescriber. The informed prescriber will need and want feedback and guidance from key professionals who work more closely with the patient.

Wholehearted collaboration is needed among prescribers, therapists and other clinicians, patients, and their families. Especially when a decision has been made to attempt medication reduction and withdrawal, the team needs to work together to make sure that the patient's needs and desires are being met as safely and effectively as possible.

THE PERSON-CENTERED COLLABORATIVE APPROACH

Recently, a graduate student in my class on Empathic Therapy and Counseling expressed her personal concerns to the group of fellow students. She felt that she no longer needed her psychiatric medications and worried that they were flattening her emotions and impairing her memory. She then explained in heartfelt tones, "I've been taking benzodiazepines and antidepressants for 10 years—since I was 14 years old. I've grown up on these drugs. I am terrified—terrified!—of ever trying to withdraw from them."

I responded to her, "Many people share your fears. In working with your prescriber, the key for you is to feel in charge of the withdrawal. You must feel empowered to control the rate of drug withdrawal and especially to go as slowly as you need. Then, if you feel you're going too fast, you and your prescriber can stop the withdrawal or even pull back to your previous dose. If the process feels under your control, you won't be so terrified, and your chances of success will be greatly increased."

My attitude—more than my words—will communicate to my students or patients whether or not I am genuinely interested in and truly care about them and their viewpoints. Person-centered drug withdrawal calls on the clinician to express many human qualities, including empathy, honest communication about the dangers of staying on psychiatric drugs and the dangers of withdrawing from them, and a respectful relationship that empowers the patient to make decisions and to manage his or her own life.

> Empathic relationship lies at the core of person-centered medication withdrawal, which includes (a) empathy with genuine caring and understanding, (b) honest communication about medication issues, and (c) an empowering respect for the patient's viewpoint, wishes, and needs.

EXPLORING THE PATIENT'S FEELINGS

When a patient explores or considers the possibility of psychiatric drug withdrawal, the prescriber should explore the patient's fears and anxieties about the withdrawal process. As much as patients may desire to stop taking psychiatric medications or to reduce the doses, they almost always feel apprehensive about the process. They may fear that they cannot live without the medication—a subject that will be addressed in a separate chapter. Even more commonly they will have fears about withdrawal reactions.

Many individuals have experienced severe withdrawal reactions after temporarily running out of medication or after abruptly trying to stop the medications on their own. Too often, a prescriber has reacted to a request for medication withdrawal by precipitously stopping one or more psychiatric drugs, resulting in a severe withdrawal reaction. Most attempts to reduce or stop medication are initiated by the patient or even the patient's family, and far fewer are initiated by the prescriber. It is hoped that this book will help prescribers and therapists place greater importance on reducing or stopping medications while also providing a safer and more effective person-centered approach to the process.

Fear and anxiety not only prevent many people from asking to be reduced in dose or withdrawn from psychiatric drugs, fear and anxiety also are a major cause of failure during the withdrawal process. These fears should be explored and taken seriously. They must be addressed before making a shared decision to start psychiatric drug withdrawal, and they must be addressed throughout the process.

Terry Lynch, MD, is an experienced psychotherapist in Limerick, Ireland, who often helps individuals to withdraw from psychiatric medication. He observes that "realism" is required in approaching psychiatric drug withdrawal:

> There are times when I am not prepared to enter into a drug reducing process if I feel the person's expectations remain unrealistic despite having been advised of the realities, or if the person is not prepared or ready to embark on this process. This doesn't happen very often, but it does happen. (T. Lynch, personal communication, 2012)

In my experience, lack of a supportive family or social network is the most difficult impediment to proceeding with an especially difficult psychiatric withdrawal. Another is lack of self-determination on the patient's part.

Therapists are increasingly taking responsibility for empowering their patients to take greater control over their psychiatric medication. Sarton Weinraub, PhD, psychologist, and director of a mental health clinic in New York City, finds that subservience to healthcare providers often stymies the individual's desires to reduce or withdraw from psychiatric medication. In what Dr. Weinraub calls "medical disempowerment," he finds that "individuals prescribed psychiatric medication often have not been given an unbiased assessment of the side effects or the benefits of other options, which can lead to medical disempowerment" (personal communication, 2012). He explains, "Often, medical disempower involves a self-destructive belief in the necessity of involving an authoritarian medical expert in order to recover." Dr. Weinraub has demonstrated that patients can be encouraged and educated to take charge of their own medical treatment and that many prescribers will respond positively when they know the patient has the dedicated support of an informed therapist.

> To allay fear and anxiety and to respect their self-determination, individuals withdrawing from psychiatric medications should feel in charge of the decision to withdraw and in charge of the pace of the taper. When needed, this encouragement can come from a therapist, as well as from a prescriber.

Respect for the patient's decision to pursue, or not to pursue, psychiatric drug withdrawal is key to initiating and continuing the process. Monitoring the individual's feelings and emphasizing his or her control over the rate of withdrawal lies at the heart of the person-centered approach to psychiatric drug withdrawal.

The person-centered approach requires the prescriber and/or the therapist to be willing and even eager to remain aware of the patient's needs, to be readily available at all times, and to pay close attention to what the patient or client feels during the withdrawal process.

In emergencies, the prescriber may have to convince the patient that a more rapid withdrawal must be undertaken. Sometimes this will require 24-hour observation by family or friends, or hospitalization. However, even in emergencies, the prescriber and therapist must take the time to enlist the individual's cooperation and to maintain trust.

> There will be exceptions to a "go slow" policy when, for example, a psychiatric drug is causing severe or life-threatening adverse effects. However, even in emergencies, the prescriber or the therapist must work closely to enlist the patient's cooperation and to offer emotional support, guidance, and relevant information during a rapid and potentially uncomfortable withdrawal. In some cases, hospitalization will be needed to conduct a very rapid withdrawal.

This very brief introduction to therapeutic aspects of the drug withdrawal process will be elaborated in Part II, Chapters 10–18, of this book. The following Chapters 2–9 examine many of the medical reasons why prescribers, clinicians, patients, and their families need to be alert for adverse drug reactions that require drug reduction or withdrawal.

AN APPROACH TO HELPING PATIENTS IN NEED OF ADDITIONAL SUPPORT OR GUIDANCE

The person-centered collaborative approach was developed to help individuals who need more guidance, monitoring, or emotional support than most patients in an outpatient practice. Although applied in this book to people undergoing potentially difficult withdrawal from psychiatric drugs, it is also the best approach to helping children, dependent adults, and adults who are emotionally or cognitively impaired, and older adults. Whenever the individual can benefit from more guidance, supervision, or help than available in one-to-one autonomous psychotherapy, the person-centered collaborative approach is ideal.

KEY POINTS

- Empathy, honest communication, and patient empowerment lie at the heart of the person-centered approach.
- Patient fear and anxiety are a major cause of failure during psychiatric drug withdrawal.
- The individual must feel in charge of the decision to begin the withdrawal and then to continue the process.
- The individual must feel in control of the rate or timing of withdrawal. Unless faced with a very serious adverse reaction, such as tardive dyskinesia or mania, the pace of the withdrawal should stay within the patient's comfort zone. If a faster taper is needed and encouraged, it should be done in a person centered and collaborative manner.
- When prescribers are too busy or otherwise unable to provide sufficient monitoring, psychotherapy, or counseling during the withdrawal process, the prescriber should work closely with an informed therapist or counselor. Therapists and other clinicians should take the opportunity to reach out to prescribers to help them in monitoring and in understanding the patient's needs and desires.
- Even small dose reductions (less than 10%) can sometimes cause serious withdrawal reactions.
- It is important to provide detailed information to the patient about the withdrawal process and then to conduct the process in a collaborative manner that emphasizes the patient's decision making and control over the process. This can help to reverse "medical disempowerment."
- Because individuals undergoing psychiatric drug withdrawal need emotional support and are often unable to recognize when they are experiencing a withdrawal reaction, such as suicidal or violent impulses, a support network of friends and family can be very helpful, and sometimes lifesaving, in the collaborative process. It is preferable, and sometimes necessary, for the patient to permit collaborating

friends or family to contact the prescriber or therapist if they grow concerned. In difficult cases, someone close to the patient should be directly involved in the withdrawal process with office visits and phone contacts.

- In the person-centered approach, the patient's response to each step of drug reduction will determine the rate of reduction. Therefore, it is not possible to predetermine how long a medication taper and withdrawal will take.
- At all times, the prescriber and the therapist must offer hope and encouragement. Few things are more important in successful withdrawals than the positive attitudes of the healthcare providers.
- The person-centered collaborative approach is not exclusively for psychiatric drug withdrawal. It is the best approach whenever the individual needs extra support, monitoring, or guidance, including children, dependent adults, adults who are emotionally and cognitively impaired, and older adults.

PART I

Reasons to Consider Psychiatric Drug Withdrawal or Dose Reduction

CHAPTER 2

Cautions in Assessing the Risks Associated With Psychiatric Drugs

Psychiatric medications can cause so many known adverse reactions that it is impossible for the clinician, patient, or family to remember or to keep track of them all. Furthermore, there are bound to be many serious but as yet unknown adverse effects from almost any psychiatric medication, especially from long-term or polydrug use.

Because psychiatric drugs fundamentally alter neurotransmission in the brain, an infinite number of adverse reactions take place within the brain and mind on a daily basis during exposure to any psychiatric drug, but nearly all are undetectable by our present methods of evaluating the brain and mind.

When medication combinations are used, drug interactions— both known and unknown—further complicate the difficulty of remaining aware of all possible adverse drug reactions. In addition, as documented in this chapter, the Food and Drug Administration (FDA), the pharmaceutical industry, and the medical profession often fail to identify long-term harmful drug effects.

Awareness of the brain's vulnerability to known as well as undiscovered adverse effects should especially caution the treatment team, patients, and their families about the psychiatric medication effects, especially on a long-term basis.

The brain is an extraordinarily complex organ whose basic functioning is very poorly understood. There are hundreds of millions of neurons, some having up to 10,000 connections with each other. Many neurons produce or receive more than one neurotransmitter. We have not yet discovered most of the brain's neurotransmitters, and we continue to identify new subtypes of the ones we have identified. We once thought that neurotransmitter receptors exist solely in synapses. We now know they can be found on the nerve trunks themselves. We used to think astroglia had little to do with neurotransmission, but now we know that they do. To this day, we don't understand the underlying organizing principles of brain function, or how it relates to or generates mental function. Astrophysics is a much less complex and better grounded field than human neuroscience.

It becomes foolhardy to speak or to practice as if we have a good idea about how any psychiatric drugs truly impact the brain in the short run, let alone after years of exposure. Add multiple drugs at once, and we enter the world of speculation and experimentation regarding potential adverse effects on the brain and mind and on the remainder of the body as well.

The human brain and mind are subtle, complex, and potentially fragile, and they develop, grow, and change throughout the individual's life. We cannot anticipate or minimally evaluate the potentially harmful impact of giving psychoactive drugs to children, adults, or older adults. There is no way to ascertain, particularly in the case of children and younger adults, how the quality of their mental lives might have been reduced or might be reduced in the future by exposure to psychiatric drugs. These and a multitude of other considerations should make us very cautious in regard to prescribing psychiatric medications and especially so long-term.

A ROSE BY ANY OTHER NAME

In recent years there has been a growing trend to identify drugs according to the conditions that they are being used to treat rather than by their pharmacological category or characteristics, including their impact on the brain. A long-standing problem, for example, has been the identification of metoclopramide (Reglan) as an antinausea drug rather than as a neuroleptic drug being used to treat nausea. Many unfortunate cases of tardive dyskinesia (see Chapter 4) have resulted from the poorly informed prescription of this dangerous drug.

The problem has become particularly serious regarding the identification or naming of neuroleptics in psychiatry when they are being used to treat something other than schizophrenia. Quetiapine (Seroquel) is a so-called atypical neuroleptic with many adverse effects associated with the older neuroleptics, such as tardive dyskinesia, as well as additional adverse effects more closely associated with the atypicals, such as diabetes. Yet, patients are commonly told that Seroquel is a "sleep aid" or "bipolar drug," in effect misleading them into believing that they are not taking a neuroleptic or antipsychotic drug. Neuroleptics approved for antidepressant augmentation, such as aripiprazole (Abilify), are similarly being called "antidepressants" in a misleading fashion.

This euphemistic naming of drugs not only misleads patients and their families; it also lulls the prescriber and clinician into a false sense of security and makes it increasingly impossible for patients and families to identify the class to which a drug belongs, and hence the risks associated with it.

Sometimes the FDA-approved trade names for drugs are changed depending on the condition being treated, as in the treatment of premenstrual dysphoria with Sarafem (Prozac) or the treatment of nicotine addiction with Zyban (Wellbutrin). The profession and the public are likely to be misled into believing that these drugs do not carry all the risks associated with antidepressants, including suicidality and mania.

Clinicians need to identify drugs by their pharmacological classification, not by their treatment function, and to be clear with themselves and with their patients when identifying the medications and their pharmacological properties, including adverse drug effects.

DOES FDA APPROVAL INDICATE A HIGH DEGREE OF SAFETY?

Too much faith can be placed in premarketing clinical trials as a method of detecting adverse drug reactions. In the 1990s, the FDA (1995) began an educational campaign to warn professionals about the limits of premarketing testing and the importance of the postmarketing spontaneous reporting system (SRS, now called MedWatch). As a part of that campaign, the FDA distributed a dramatic white on black poster with the following point emblazoned on it:

When a drug goes to market, we know everything about its safety. Wrong.

The FDA's June 1995 publication, *A MEDWatch Continuing Education Article*, replicated the poster. In addition, the FDA made the following points in a section subtitled "Limitations of Premarketing Clinical Trials":

Short duration—effects that develop with chronic use or those that have a long latency period and are impossible to detect

Narrow population—generally doesn't include special groups (e.g., children, elderly) to a large degree and is not always representative of the population that may be exposed to the drug after approval

Narrow set of indications—those for which efficacy is being studied and don't cover actual evolving use

Small size (generally include 3,000–4,000 subjects)—effects that occur rarely and are very difficult to detect.

Many other experts have made similar points (Kennedy & McGinnis, 1993; Kessler, 1993). Paul Leber (1992), then director of the FDA's Division of Neuropharmacological Drug Products, addressed additional limitations of premarket testing, which include the following:

1. The patients and volunteers in the study are not likely to represent a true sample of the people who will be treated once the drug is marketed.
2. The studies are quite brief.
3. There may be differences in postmarketing dosing.
4. The "unique combination of concomitant illness, polypharmacy, and compromised physiological status" of real-life patients treated after the drug is approved cannot be anticipated.

Leber (1992) warned that testing done for FDA approval "may generate a misleadingly reassuring picture of a drug's safety in use."

Leber (1992) concluded, "In sum, at the time a new drug is first marketed, a great deal of uncertainty invariably remains about the identity, nature, and frequency of all but the most common and acutely expressed risks associated with its use."

DRUG COMPANY SUPPRESSION OF CRITICAL DATA

The FDA does not conduct clinical trials on its own. It relies on research produced, monitored, and financed by the pharmaceutical companies. I have documented the far-reaching negative consequences of the FDA's dependency on data generated by drug companies (Breggin, 2008a; Breggin & Breggin, 1994). Even severe and relatively obvious adverse effects that commonly show up after only a few doses—such as akathisia (psychomotor agitation) caused by antipsychotic and antidepressant drugs—may not be discovered or reported by drug companies for years or decades (Breggin, 2006c). For example, the manufacturers of fluoxetine (Prozac) and paroxetine (Paxil) fought for years against admitting that these drugs could cause suicidality, systematically hiding and misinterpreting their own data to enhance the safety profile of the medications (Breggin, 2006a, 2006b, 2006c; Breggin 2008a; Breggin & Breggin, 1994).

> Because very severe and even life-threatening adverse drug reactions often do not surface or gain serious recognition for many years and even decades, prudence would lead to caution about prescribing psychiatric medications or taking them for many years.

When unanticipated risks such as suicide, violence or death begin to surface in clinical trials, they are often overlooked, ignored, or even systematically hidden by the pharmaceutical companies who sponsor, conduct, and analyze the clinical trials (Breggin, 2008a; Breggin & Breggin, 1994).

RELYING ON FALSE OR MISLEADING INFORMATION

In addition to fundamental problems in the initial testing of psychiatric drugs, prescribers continue to rely more heavily on the advertisements in journals than on the scientific articles ("Drug Advertising in the Lancet," 2011; Spurling, Mansfield, & Lexchin, 2011). But even the articles themselves cannot be trusted as fraud and retractions become more common (Naik, 2011). Many biological psychiatric publications show "strong biases" (Ioannidis, 2011, p. 773) and many are ghostwritten by the drug companies (Stern & Lemmens, 2011). Data about adverse drug effects often go unpublished, whereas unduly positive reports are often ghostwritten by the drug companies to be published under the names of well-known experts in the field (Stern & Lemmens, 2011).

> Because of the overall influence of the psychopharmaceutical complex over prescribers and clinicians (Angell, 2004; Breggin, 1991, 2008a), it is important to present this summary overview of the hazards of psychiatric drugs with special emphasis on problems that may require dose reduction or withdrawal.

EXAMPLES OF DELAYED RECOGNITION OF SERIOUS PSYCHIATRIC DRUG ADVERSE EFFECTS

Nefazodone (Serzone) was an antidepressant brought to the market by Bristol-Myers Squibb in 1994. Some countries discontinued its use in 2003 because of severe liver damage. Then in 2004, a decade after its introduction, following many consumer lawsuits, the company discontinued selling the drug under its brand name in the United States. (FDA, 2004).[1]

Pemoline (Cylert) was a stimulant used to treat attention deficit hyperactive disorder (ADHD) in children that was first marketed in 1975. In October 2005, after 3 decades of use, the FDA "concluded that the overall risk of liver toxicity from Cylert and generic pemoline products outweighs the benefits of this drug," and it was withdrawn from the market (FDA, 2005).

Chlorpromazine (Thorazine), the first antipsychotic drug, flooded the state mental hospitals worldwide in 1954–1955. However, it took nearly 20 years before the profession began to recognize that antipsychotic drugs were causing a disfiguring and sometimes disabling movement disorder called tardive dyskinesia in more than 50% of these long-term state hospital patients (Crane, 1973). After adding a weak warning in the early 1970s, the FDA did not press the drug companies to upgrade warnings about tardive dyskinesia until 1985 when it was embarrassed by publicity

---

[1]The FDA tightened warnings for the generic form, but did not require the drug to be withdrawn from the market.

surrounding the publication of my book *Psychiatric Drugs: Hazards to the Brain* (Breggin, 1983).

As another example of delayed recognition of adverse effects, triazolam (Halcion) is a very potent, short-acting benzodiazepine used as a sleeping medication that was approved by the FDA in 1982. Over the years, a mountain of evidence accumulated indicating that triazolam has an even greater potential than other benzodiazepines to produce memory loss and a range of psychiatric adverse reactions including paranoia, suicide, and violence (reviewed in Breggin, 2008a, pp. 324–336). Eventually, the drug was completely banned in several countries, including Great Britain in 1991 (Asscher, 1991; Brahams, 1991). A decade after the drug began to be widely used, the FDA increased the warnings for triazolam (FDA, 1992) without withdrawing it from the market.

> Because of the many risks, known and unknown, associated with psychiatric drug exposure, the healthcare provider or patient should approach the use of any psychiatric drug with caution and judicious concern and make every effort to limit the dose, the combination of drugs, and the time of exposure with an eye to withdrawing from the drug as soon as feasible.

For decades, I have been writing and educating the health professions and the public about the risks of suicidality, violence, and overstimulation from the newer antidepressants (e.g., Breggin, 1991, 1992, 2001a, 2002a, 2008a, 2008b; Breggin & Breggin, 1994). It took more than a decade, until 2004–2005, before the FDA issued warnings and made label upgrades that closely parallel and seem to borrow from my testimony and my paper that was distributed to the FDA committee, which made the recommendations (Breggin, 2003/2004).

DOES IT TAKE WEEKS FOR THE DRUG TO WORK?

Although it may take time for a psychiatric drug to have its sought-after effect, the most severe adverse effects frequently occur shortly after starting a drug or changing the dose up or down. For example, I was a medical expert in a case in which a man drowned himself and his two children in a tub after developing akathisia during 3 days on Paxil 10 mg/day. I was empowered by the court to examine original documents in the manufacturer's archives, where I found that many severe adverse psychiatric reactions developed during the first few days of exposure to the drug (Breggin, 2006a, 2006b, 2006c). Too often, prescribers think that the patient needs an increase in dose, worsening the adverse reaction, when the patient really needs to stop taking the drug (Breggin, 2008a).

LISTENING TO FAMILY CONCERNS

Families and significant others are often the first to notice when a patient is suffering from an adverse drug effect, especially if the effects are mental or behavioral. In the case of antidepressants and stimulants, for example, the individual may develop insomnia and seems "hyper." In the case of benzodiazepines there may be the typical signs of "drunkenness." In poly-drug cases, there is often a mixed picture. Because of medication spell-binding (see Chapter 9), patients are often the last to realize that they are being overmedicated. Family and friends are often the first to notice signs of overmedication and may contact the prescriber or therapist.

Prescribers and therapists may be misled into believing that the patient is taking "too small" of a dose to cause signs of intoxication or other problems. However, prescribers can rarely be certain that the patient is taking the drug as prescribed rather than in larger intermittent doses. In addition, patients respond differently across a broad spectrum to the same "small" doses of medication. I have seen patients who have felt "zonked" by as little as 10–20 mg of amitriptyline (Elavil) given to treat headache or 2.5 mg of diazepam (Valium) given for anxiety.

Always take seriously the concerns of family and friends; they can be the prescriber and the patient's best ally during psychiatric medication treatment and withdrawal.

THE IMPORTANCE OF VARIED SOURCES OF INFORMATION

No one source is sufficient to cover the full range of psychiatric adverse drug effects, not even annual compendia like the *Physicians' Desk Reference* (PDR, 2012), which reprints most of the FDA-approved drug labels and *Drug Facts and Comparisons* (2012), which organizes very simi-lar material in a more usable format and includes drugs like Xanax and Ritalin that have been left out of the *PDR* in recent years. There are many good handbooks that are also updated annually, including the *Nurse's Drug Handbook* (2012).

Blogs, chat rooms, and online patient peer support groups focused on specific drugs often provide alerts and information about adverse drug reactions long before healthcare providers become aware of them and before they appear in scientific sources. Of course, professionals and laypersons should take a cautious perspective toward information made available on the Internet, but—as this chapter has documented—caution must also be exercised in relying solely on standard sources, including scientific articles and the FDA.

When psychiatric drugs are prescribed, clinicians as well as the patient and family should be aware of our limits of knowledge about the potentially harmful effects of psychiatric drugs on the human brain and mind, as well as the reminder of the body. Awareness of the brain's vulnerability to known as well as undiscovered adverse effects should caution clinicians, patients, and their families about the psychiatric medication effects, especially on a long-term basis.

KEY POINTS

▪ Controlled clinical trials used for FDA approval of drugs are too small to guarantee detecting all serious adverse drug effects, including those that appear in the first few weeks.

▪ Controlled clinical trials used for FDA approval of drugs are much too short-term to detect longer term risks associated with these drugs.

▪ When serious adverse drug reactions do surface in drug company clinical trials, they sometimes go unrecognized and unreported, and sometimes information about them is suppressed.

▪ The scientific literature concerning adverse drug effects is inadequate and frequently manipulated by advocates of the drugs.

▪ The patient's family and friends are often the first to notice adverse drug effects, including overmedication, and the prescriber and clinicians should pay close attention to their concerns and observations.

▪ Because knowledge of adverse drug effects is limited and often unreliable, clinicians should be cautious about prescribing psychiatric drugs, especially long-term, and should attempt to withdraw patients from medication as soon as feasible.

CHAPTER 3

Chronic Brain Impairment: A Reason to Withdraw Patients From Long-Term Exposure to Psychiatric Medications

Prescribers, therapists, patients, and their families need to understand the hazards associated with long-term exposure to psychiatric drugs, but too little emphasis is given to long-term risks in the scientific literature and clinical practice. The syndrome of chronic brain impairment (CBI) can be caused by any trauma to the brain, including months or years of exposure to one or more psychiatric medications. Better knowledge and awareness of CBI can enable early identification of long-term adverse effects by the patient and by everyone involved in the patient's care. CBI is probably the major contributor to the current epidemic of "mental illness" and escalating psychiatric disability.

By learning to recognize drug-induced CBI, clinicians can enhance their ability to identify patients who need to be withdrawn from long-term psychiatric drug treatment. CBI symptoms are the main reason why patients and their families seek professional help in withdrawing from psychiatric medications.

Most patients begin to recover from CBI early in the withdrawal process. Many patients, especially children and teenagers, will experience a robust recovery. Others may recover over a period of years. Even when recovery is limited or psychiatric relapses occur off the medication, most patients remain grateful for their improved CBI and wish to remain on reduced medication or none at all.

Every type of psychiatric medication initially produces effects that are specific to a particular drug's unique impact on neurotransmitters and other aspects of brain function. For example, the selective serotonin reuptake inhibitor (SSRI) antidepressants block the removal of the neurotransmitter serotonin from the synapses; the antipsychotic drugs suppress and block dopamine neurotransmission; and the benzodiazepines amplify gamma-aminobutyric acid (GABA) neurotransmission, which in turn suppresses overall brain function.

Although all psychiatric drugs have specific initial biochemical effects, over time other neurotransmitter systems then *react* to the initial drug effects and, as a result, broader changes begin to take place in the brain and in mental functioning.

Studies of all classes of psychiatric drugs have yielded similar findings of mental dysfunction and atrophy of the brain in humans after long-term exposure, abnormal proliferations of cells, and persistent biochemical dysfunction in animals (reviewed in Breggin, 2008a; for benzodiazepines see Barker, Greenwood, Jackson, & Crowe, 2004; Tata, Rollings, Collins, Pickering, & Jacobson, 1994; Lagnaoui et al., 2002; for lithium see Grignon & Bruguerolle, 1996; for antidepressants see El-Mallakh, Gao, & Jeannie Roberts, 2011; Gilbert et al., 2000; Malberg, Eisch, Nestler, & Duman, 2000; Wegerer et al., 1999; Zhou, Huang, Kecojevic, Welsh, & Koliatsos, 2006). Unfortunately, because of the dominating influence of the pharmaceutical industry and the efforts by drug advocates to control information within the health professions, the subject is so taboo that critical studies are rarely followed up (Breggin, 1991, 2008a). Chapters 4–8 will include data confirming CBI for each class of psychiatric drug.

The clinical effect of chronic exposure to psychoactive substances, including psychiatric drugs, produces effects very similar to those of closed head or traumatic brain injury (TBI; Fisher, 1989) or the postconcussive syndrome (McClelland, Fenton, & Rutherford, 1994). Generalized or global harm to the brain from *any* cause, produces very similar mental effects after a period of months or years. The brain and mind respond in a very similar fashion to injuries from causes as diverse as electroshock treatment, closed head injury from repeated sports-induced concussions, TBI in wartime, chronic abuse of alcohol and street drugs, long-term exposure to psychiatric polydrug treatment, and long-term exposure to most or all psychiatric drugs.

Global or generalized brain impairments—those that involve the whole brain—look so much alike in their mental symptoms because the injured brain and mind have only a limited repertoire of reactions. The healthy brain and mind seem almost infinite in their capacity to create, so that the mental life of individuals with normal brains is very complex, rich, varied, and always unique. The wounded brain and its associated mental malfunctions are much more limited, uninspired, and predictable. Any remaining richness and complexity depends on the existence of sufficient remaining brain function to allow for unique self-expression.

Based on these observations I have introduced the syndrome and diagnosis of CBI (Breggin, 2011c).[1] The specific cause of the CBI is added as a prefix, as in alprazolam CBI, antipsychotic drug CBI, or poly psychiatric drug CBI.[2] Other examples are electroconvulsive therapy (ECT) CBI, polydrug abuse CBI, and concussive CBI.

BASIC DEFINITIONS

For the purpose of this book, *brain dysfunction* refers to drug-induced changes in biochemical processes, often including changes in the function of neurotransmitter systems, sometimes detected on positron emission tomography (PET) scans in human subjects and more commonly found in a variety of animal studies. *Brain damage* refers to drug-induced changes in brain morphology (form or structure), often detected on magnetic resonance imaging (MRI) or computerized axial tomography (CAT) scans in living humans and animals or on gross and microscopic examination of autopsy material. Drug-induced *atrophy* of the brain (a form of brain damage) is synonymous with shrinkage or loss of volume. Atrophy can be caused by neuronal cell death or shrinkage, glial cell death or shrinkage, and increased packing density of brain cells.

Symptoms of CBI are associated with either brain dysfunction or brain damage.

SYMPTOMS AND CHARACTERISTICS OF
CHRONIC BRAIN IMPAIRMENT

Knowledge about CBI can help the clinician to identify the effects of long-term exposure to psychiatric drugs and aid the clinician in determining the need to reduce or terminate drug treatment. CBI is the most frequent reason families express a desire to take a family member off psychiatric drugs. They notice that the patient has become lethargic or apathetic, suffers from memory lapses, or does not "seem like himself" anymore. CBI also leads patients to seek psychiatric help for themselves, but often they do not attribute their worsening condition to drug effects. Instead,

---

[1]The phrase "chronic brain impairment" appears in various places in the literature on psychoactive drugs, but it has not been used as an overarching concept for a generic brain condition caused by multiple stressors, including long-term exposure to psychiatric drugs.
[2]Psychiatric drug CBI and ECT-induced CBI are aspects of my work concerning the brain-disabling principle of biopsychiatric treatment (Breggin, 1979, 1980, 1981a, 1981b, 1991, 1997a, 2006d, 2008a, pp. 233–234). For a recent analysis of the brain-disabling principle, see Moncrieff 2007a, 2007b).

they attribute it to their psychiatric condition. Parents and clinicians may mistake these symptoms for a worsening of their children's psychiatric disorders. In older adults, family and clinicians may mistake these symptoms for dementia.

Concern about symptoms of CBI is the most common reason why patients and their families seek help in withdrawing from long-term treatment with psychiatric drugs.

Psychiatric drug CBI, like all CBI, is associated with generalized brain dysfunction and/or damage, and therefore manifests itself in an overall compromise of mental function. To help in identifying these deficits in clinical practice, the CBI syndrome can be divided into four symptom complexes.

1. *Cognitive dysfunction*: Manifested in the early stages as short-term memory dysfunction and impaired new learning, inattention, and difficulty concentrating, which can progress to the whole array of symptoms of mental dysfunction, including loss of executive functions, abstract reasoning, judgment, and insight. The patient may describe "foggy thinking" or mental sluggishness. When severe and persisting, these deficits can lead to dementia. However, the symptoms can at times be reversed, if the medications are stopped in time.

2. *Apathy and indifference*: This includes a "not caring attitude" and often loss of energy and vitality, and increased fatigue. The individual commonly loses interest in spiritual and artistic activities, as well as other endeavors requiring higher mental processes, sensitivity to others, and spontaneity.

3. *Emotional worsening* (affective dysregulation): This is characterized by emotional worsening with decreased empathy and increased impatience, impulsivity, irritability, and anger, or frequent mood changes with depression and anxiety. Mild manic-like symptoms are frequent, and judgment may be impaired. This deterioration usually has a gradual onset over months or years, so that it seems "normal" or becomes attributed to "stress," "mental illness," or "getting old."

4. *Anosognosia*: Patients commonly lack awareness of their symptoms of CBI. Whether it involves TBI, Alzheimer's disease, drug-induced tardive dyskinesia, or psychiatric drug CBI—patients commonly fail to identify their mental and physical symptoms of brain dysfunction (Fisher, 1989). Often, someone other than the patient is the first to notice or to take seriously the symptoms of CBI. Anosognosia can develop into what I have described as intoxication anosognosia with medication spellbinding in which the individual not only fails to recognize extreme symptoms of drug intoxication but may even feel improved and on

occasion will take uncharacteristic dangerous actions (see Chapter 4; also Breggin 2006d, 2008b).

As a result of these CBI deficits, there is an associated reduction in the quality of life. Regarding CBI, psychiatrist Doug Smith, a clinician with considerable experience in clinics treating a broad spectrum of patients, made these observations on CBI and the quality of life.

> I am very interested in the long-term adverse mental effects of medication— what we can now call CBI. I find that people on antidepressants are often somewhat out of touch with their emotional life even before they take medicines, which is part of what makes them very susceptible to the medical model and the idea of a chemical imbalance. But it becomes worse after they take medicines. They become out of touch with their emotional life except at a rudimentary level. For example, they feel outrage and boredom and not much else. They are very much unable to "mentalize" their experiences—to bring their experiences into emotional and intellectual awareness and to evaluate them. But deeper than that, at the heart of it is impaired empathy—empathy being the most human part of us that allows us to step outside of ourselves and our pain and to see things from another perspective, someone else's perspective, a relational perspective. Doing psychotherapy with someone on antidepressants is very difficult because they seem forever stuck in a solipsistic world of boredom and outrage, with no movement and little connection.

> People brave enough to come off their antidepressants come alive and experience intense pain, remorse, gratitude, grief and mourning, concern for others, empathy, love, and growth (personal communication, 2012).

Confounding Factors

When a patient has been exposed to years of psychiatric medication, other factors can cause or exacerbate psychiatric drug-induced CBI. The long-term impact of the individual's original psychological and emotional problems can induce apathy and emotional instability and some degree of psychological denial that could be easily confused with anosognosia. However, there is no convincing evidence that primary psychiatric disorders, such as bipolar disorder or schizophrenia, can cause cognitive disorders or generalized brain dysfunction. In addition, CBI usually develops specifically in relationship to the persistent use of psychiatric drugs and can often be seen to worsen as doses are increased. Furthermore, CBI will usually begin to improve when the psychiatric drug dose is reduced. In contrast, pathology caused by a primary psychiatric disorder would be expected to worsen as the medication is reduced. After a syndrome consistent with CBI is identified, improvement with drug withdrawal is probably the most useful diagnostic criterion in distinguishing psychiatric drug-induced CBI from other disorders. The symptoms are partially or entirely relieved, and the quality of life improves.

Another potential confounding factor is exposure to other psychoactive substances. Many individuals who are exposed to long-term psychiatric medication will also be taking other prescribed medications that have psychoactive potential, including antihypertensive agents, pain medications, and anticonvulsants. Others will be exposed to psychoactive herbal remedies, alcohol, or illegal drugs. A detailed clinical history is required to disentangle these drug effects. Improvement during psychiatric drug withdrawal confirms that the symptoms were at least in part caused by the medications.

Many people in long-term psychiatric treatment, especially combat veterans, will also suffer from closed head injury. Also, any accompanying post-traumatic stress disorder (PTSD) could become confused with CBI because the symptoms overlap. Except for improvement over time during withdrawal from the psychiatric medications, CBI can be difficult to distinguish from closed head injury, with or without accompanying PTSD.

Comparison to Dementia and Organic Brain Syndrome

The cognitive criteria for CBI are less severe than those for dementia as defined in the *Diagnostic and Statistical Manual of Mental Disorders* (4th ed., text rev.; American Psychiatric Association [APA], 2000, p. 168). Only the most severe patients with CBI will develop dementia symptoms, such as apraxia (inability to generate skilled or purposeful movements), aphasia (inability to generate or comprehend communication), and agnosia (inability to interpret sensory input). Any disturbances of executive functioning would likely be subtle. From a clinical standpoint, patients suffering from CBI are rarely diagnosed with dementia even if they meet the criteria because clinicians miss the subtle signs. Also, clinicians tend to think of dementia as a very severe and disabling disorder. In addition, clinicians are reluctant to diagnose dementia when it is caused by psychiatric drug treatment.

Also in contrast to the diagnosis of dementia, the clinical criteria for CBI are more consistent with the actual clinical phenomenon associated with more subtle aspects of generalized or global brain dysfunction, including subtle cognitive deficits, apathy, emotional worsening, and anosognosia. If a case of CBI becomes very severe, it would qualify as dementia.

The concept of CBI also resembles the concept of organic brain syndrome (OBS). However, OBS is no longer used in the diagnostic system or in clinical practice (APA, 2000). When used in the past (APA, 1980), it was not defined as a specific syndrome or a specific diagnosis with defined criteria. OBS was used to subsume a class of disorders that included specific diagnoses, such as dementia or organic personality disorder. It did not have the nuance and broad spectrum of effects associated with CBI. It was not viewed as a unitary syndrome resulting from any global physical harm to the brain.

> The syndrome of CBI consists of the following four symptoms clusters:
> - Cognitive dysfunction
> - Apathy and loss of interest
> - Emotional worsening (affective dysregulation) with loss of empathy, emotional lability, and increased irritability
> - Anosognosia—the failure to recognize symptoms of brain dysfunction in oneself
>
> Most commonly, all four are present at the same time, and there is a reduction in the quality of life.

Many patients desire to come off psychiatric drugs because they have some awareness of their deteriorating mental function. However, they almost never fully grasp how impaired they have become. This lack of self-awareness of impaired brain function stems from two sources—psychological denial and neurologically induced anosognosia. Psychological denial means that the individual has enough intact brain function to recognize symptoms of brain dysfunction, but psychologically rejects this awareness and goes into denial. Anosognosia is a physical phenomenon in which brain injury impairs the capacity for this aspect of self-awareness. Obviously, the two different phenomena can be difficult to separate.

Short-term memory loss is probably the problem that patients most often report. Because it is so frustrating, disruptive of daily life, and sometimes frightening to forget recent communications and events, short-term memory losses seem to more readily break through the tendency toward denial and anosognosia.

Frequently, patients will not report CBI symptoms to the healthcare provider, even though they may complain about them to family or friends. For example, the clinician may ask a patient, "Has your memory been affected over the years?" and, while awaiting an answer, the spouse may chime in, "You bet it has! She forgot we had this appointment today and driving here she lost her way. That's why we were late."

Similarly, the clinician may ask the patient, "Have you been noticing any loss of interest or enjoyment in your life?" The patient may shrug until his wife reminds him, "You were saying yesterday that you haven't felt that excited about summer coming. You don't even want to make plans to go on vacation. Yesterday, you told the boys you didn't feel like taking them fishing."

The patient's inability to report adverse psychiatric drug effects is one more reason to involve significant others into the therapy process, especially when starting medication, changing the doses up or down, or initiating withdrawal.

ILLUSTRATION: HE WAS AFRAID THAT HE HAD ALZHEIMER'S

Jim, a 50-year-old high school English teacher, was brought reluctantly to his initial psychiatric evaluation by his wife Janice. She explained to me that her husband had been taking alprazolam (Xanax) for anxiety for 10 years with the dose leveling at 1 mg four times/day in the last few years. The drug was prescribed by their family doctor.

Janice further explained that her husband was having trouble remembering the simplest things. In the past, he was always enthusiastic about calls from their grown children and would gladly relate the details of the conversations to her. Now, he completely forgot to tell her about the calls. Even when he made up his mind to take notes on the pad by the phone, he forgot to do that as well. As another example, she had asked him several times in the past week to pick up some items at the grocery store on the way home from work, but he had forgotten each time.

Jim perked up angrily and responded, "You know I've got other things on my mind." She reminded him, "Jim, you never complained before. You used to ask me in the morning and even call me on your way home to check to see if I needed anything." "There's nothing wrong with me," Jim bristled. "No one has complained at school."

More hesitantly, Janet explained, "Jim's not really like this, getting so annoyed with me. Something's changed about him. He doesn't even have his same old enthusiasm for teaching." I had the sense she wanted to add, ". . . or for me."

Jim shrugged and said, "Maybe I'm just getting old."

His wife went on to explain that she thought her husband's anxiety had been helped years ago by the alprazolam but that now it seemed to be worse than ever. In the morning, he would frequently wake up in a state of panic until he took his first dose on an empty stomach and quickly felt better. At night, his insomnia was getting worse.

"It's the only thing that keeps me going," Jim said in defense of taking the medication.

When the necessary background information had been obtained, I explained to Jim and his wife that he was suffering from chronic brain impairment (CBI) in the form of (a) impaired short-term memory, (b) loss of engagement in his life, (c) irritability with mood swings, and (d) the inability to recognize how seriously he was impaired (anosognosia).

I told Jim that the "panic attacks" in the morning were caused by withdrawal from the sedative drug, which was metabolized during the night while he slept. He was physiologically dependent on the drug and woke up feeling desperately anxious and in need of it. This is called *interdose rebound* (see Chapter 7).

The increased difficulty sleeping was in all likelihood also caused by increased tolerance to the drug, so that it was no longer having a sedative effect on him.

After I finished explaining these points, as well as answering a few questions, Jim began to cry. They were tears of relief. "It's just the drug effect? I thought I had Alzheimer's." He confessed that while he hadn't been criticized about his work at school, he was sticking to the same old curriculum each year and limiting his interactions with students in the classroom, in effect relying on old props and deeply embedded memories to continue teaching.

I reassured Jim and his wife that his symptoms were almost certainly caused by alprazolam and that they would improve a great deal as we tapered off the drug. I could not guarantee a complete recovery, but both Jim and his wife were glad for the considerable hope that I was able to offer.

Jim's case is very typical of long-term exposure to sedative drugs used to treat anxiety and insomnia. Alprazolam, because of its potency, produces especially virulent CBI after years of exposure, but all psychoactive substances, including all psychiatric drugs, can produce these effects. In Jim's case the four categories or criteria were relatively easy to identify. He had cognitive problems, including memory loss, which is often the first to be noticed. He had developed apathy toward most or all of his life activities. His emotional instability manifested itself by increased irritability with angry outbursts. Finally, his anosognosia was partial because he had sufficient awareness of his symptoms to fear that he had Alzheimer's. In addition, he also had effects that were specific to alprazolam in the form of rebound anxiety in the morning and tolerance to the sedative effects at night.

HOW TO DIAGNOSE AND ASSESS CHRONIC BRAIN IMPAIRMENT

Although minimal cases will sometimes be difficult to detect or diagnose, it is not usually difficult to identify CBI in the clinical setting. Clinical evaluations are much more subtle and sensitive than neuropsychological testing or brain scans and will typically detect CBI before more "objective" techniques can identify the disorder. If the patient has been exposed to psychiatric medications for months or years, the following evaluation can be made with relative ease:

1. *Cognitive dysfunction*: Ask the patient and at least one significant other if the patient began to display signs of memory difficulties, inattention, difficulty focusing, slowed thinking, "spacing out," "fuzzy" thinking, or other subtle symptoms of cognitive dysfunction after starting psychiatric medication. Because of anosognosia, family or friends will often be more aware of these changes than the patient.

2. *Apathy or indifference*: Ask the patient and significant others about the patient's loss of interest in daily activities, hobbies, recreational endeavors, creative outlets, and socializing with family and friends. Ask about fatigue and lack of energy. Inquire about creative activities requiring higher mental function, sensitivity to others, and spontaneity—such as art work, writing, music, close friendships, and lovemaking. Individuals exposed long-term to psychiatric drugs will commonly report a loss of interest, intensity, or satisfying engagement in these activities. Because of anosognosia, they frequently deny the degree of their losses, which are nonetheless confirmed by asking specific questions or by the observations of family members and loved ones.

3. *Emotional worsening (affective dysregulation)*: This aspect of CBI is often reflected in the patient's past history and medical record. Before long-term exposure to medication, the patient may have been diagnosed with attention deficit hyperactive disorder (ADHD) or an anxiety disorder, which soon became dysthymia, depression, or bipolar disorder under the influence of prescribed psychoactive medications. Ask the patient and the family about changes in emotional responses since exposure to the prescription drugs, including dissatisfaction with life, irritability, impatience, emotional outbursts, emotional "ups and downs," worsened "blues," and unexplained mood changes. Subtle manic-like symptoms may be present at the time, or periodically in the past, including poor judgment, disinhibition, impulsivity, racing thoughts, or insomnia. Affective and related behavior changes are the only aspects of CBI that are routinely identified by most clinicians because they are mistakenly considered signals for increased medication.

4. *Anosognosia*: Although seldom looked for by clinicians, it is relatively easy and very important to identify anosognosia. Ask patients to describe the severity of their symptoms of cognitive dysfunction, apathy and indifference, and emotional worsening. Typically, self-reporting will not reflect the degree of symptomatology and disability that can be seen firsthand in the office, heard from relatives, or found in the

records. Often, gentle questioning will reveal greater degrees of impairment than originally described, especially when patients are questioned about specific symptoms and behavioral changes and about the evolution of their symptoms from before they began taking medications until the present time. Anosognosia is so common that patients frequently deny that they have gotten worse on medication when their history, the medical record, and family members will confirm a striking deterioration over the years.

Based on these assessments, help the patient and the family assess the patient's overall quality of life before and after the start of psychiatric medication and over the subsequent years to the present.

OTHER PSYCHOACTIVE SUBSTANCES

Probably, any psychoactive substance with prolonged or intense enough exposure can cause CBI. Drugs used in psychiatry and medicine for their psychoactive effects are probably always sufficiently potent to cause CBI alone and especially in combination.

A confusing array of psychoactive substances is commonly prescribed both in psychiatry and in general practice. Antipsychotic drugs, such as olanzapine and quetiapine, are too often prescribed as sleep aids. Antidepressants are given for pain, including premenstrual discomfort and menopausal symptoms. Drugs originally used for the control of seizures, especially gabapentin (Neurontin), have been highly promoted for off-label use and end up being given for an endless variety of emotional problems. Drugs originated for the control of pain, especially pregabalin (Lyrica) can be profoundly suppressive of central nervous system (CNS) function and bring about neuroleptic-like apathy and indifference.

The clinician, patient, and family involved in any area of medical practice must be aware that all psychoactive substances—prescribed or not—carry the risk of causing psychiatric adverse drug reactions, including CBI.

In addition, the treatment team must remain aware that many patients—including those receiving prescribed psychoactive substances— are also likely to be taking nonprescription psychoactive drugs. Sometimes they will be using these nonprescription drugs recreationally, sometimes as a result of addiction, sometimes in an attempt to self-medicate the same problems that they have brought to the clinician, and sometimes to self-medicate the adverse effects of the prescribed medications. Even when confronted, patients and sometimes their families may deny the patient's use or abuse of illegal drugs, herbal and other alternative substances, and/ or alcohol. These drugs can contribute to CBI.

FREQUENCY OF PSYCHIATRIC DRUG CHRONIC BRAIN IMPAIRMENT

Prescribed medication-induced CBI was relatively rare in the early decades of my career in psychiatry when far fewer children and teens were treated with psychiatric drugs, when polydrug treatment was looked on much more critically, when doctors rarely encouraged patients to stay on psychiatric drugs for the remainder of their lives, and when potent antipsychotic drugs were not given out so freely to patients with no signs whatsoever of psychosis. Undoubtedly, the widespread use of alcohol and illegal drugs, often taken in combination with prescription drugs, has helped turn CBI into an epidemic.

There is insufficient research to determine what percentage of patients will develop CBI after years of exposure to various psychiatric drugs. In my clinical experience, nearly all patients who remain on these chemical agents for many years will develop some symptoms of CBI. CBI is probably the most important cause of the current escalating epidemic of psychiatric disability.

In the 1960s, when I was in psychiatric training, in psychiatric hospitals we might see one or two obvious cases of mania a year and a few others diagnosed with a history of manic-depressive disorder (now bipolar disorder). Nowadays, it is routine for half or more of patients to have a diagnosis of bipolar disorder in both private offices and hospital settings. This is due in part to an overexpansion of the diagnosis, but in my clinical experience it is mostly because of manic-like and also psychotic episodes induced early in the patient's treatment by the newer antidepressants and the stimulants. In children, nearly all the cases of manic-like episodes have been induced by psychiatric drugs.

By definition, starting with Emil Kraepelin in the 1890s, bipolar disorder was intended to describe cycles of mania and depression without any overall or long-term deterioration. Characteristically, these patients lived highly productive lives in between episodes and did not get worse with time. Not so anymore. Patients with a diagnosis of bipolar disorder are routinely continued on antipsychotic drugs and mood stabilizers—often in combination with antidepressants, stimulants, and/or benzodiazepines—for years and decades at a time. Inevitably, most get worse over time and some become "rapid cyclers" with extreme mood variations and instability. After years of exposure to polydrug therapy, they develop CBI with cognitive deficits, apathy, emotional lability (misdiagnosed as bipolar disorder), and anosognosia.

In my practice, I routinely see young men and women in their 20s who have been on psychiatric drugs, starting with stimulants and antidepressants, since childhood. At age 25, many have already spent more than half of their lives on psychiatric drugs. Among their diagnoses, they are almost always labeled bipolar. Almost inevitably, they were exposed to either stimulants or antidepressants as children or youth when the first manic-like symptoms developed and almost inevitably, they were misdiagnosed with bipolar disorder instead of a substance-induced mood disorder with manic features (292.84). In nearly every case, they were then exposed long-term to mood stabilizer and antipsychotic drugs in a polydrug cocktail.

Years ago, we were accustomed in private practice and in hospitals to seeing patients recover from episodes of psychosis (schizophrenia and mania). Although they might have recurrences, they rarely got worse and worse over the years. Nowadays, it is so commonplace for patients to deteriorate that prescribers routinely assume that "mental illness" is a chronic disorder and must be treated with ever-increasing doses and numbers of drugs over the individual's lifetime. This constitutes a dramatic and tragic decline in the treatment of people with psychiatric diagnoses.

Journalist Robert Whitaker (2010) recently confirmed these clinical observations with his analysis of epidemiological studies and reported data on psychiatric disability. Whitaker observed that

> The Food and Drug Administration approved Prozac in 1987, and over the next 2 decades, the number of disabled mentally ill on the SSI and SSDI rolls soared to 3.97 million. In 2007, the disability rate was 1 in every 76 Americans. That's more than double the rate in 1987, and six times the rate in 1955. (p. 7)

Children did not escape this epidemic of "mental illness." Again according to Whitaker (2010),

> In the short span of twenty years, the number of disabled mentally ill children rose *35* fold. Mental illness is now the leading cause of disability in children, with the mentally ill group compromising 50% of the total number of children on the SSI rolls in 2007. (p. 8)

Although the studies have yet to be done, in all likelihood many, if not most, of the "mentally ill" currently on disability in fact suffer from psychiatric medication CBI. This has grave implications for clinical practice and for public health.

BIOCHEMICAL IMBALANCE OR GENUINE MEDICAL DISORDER

Even before Prozac was approved by the FDA, the manufacturer Eli Lilly was promoting the drug as unique in its ability to "correct biochemical imbalances." In that regard, psychiatrist Ronald Pies, Editor-in-Chief of *Psychiatric Times*, recently ridiculed the concept of "biochemical imbalances," declaring, "In the past 30 years, I don't believe I have ever heard a knowledgeable, well-trained psychiatrist make such a preposterous claim, except perhaps to mock" (Pies, 2011). Although the biochemical imbalance theory has no scientific basis, it has in fact become one of the most successful public relation campaigns in history, at the start turning Prozac into the largest selling drug in the world. Millions of Americans—and then innumerable people around the world—have become convinced that they suffer from biochemical imbalances correctable by psychiatric drugs when there is no scientific evidence for this claim (Lacasse & Leo, 2011). It is commonplace for advocates of psychiatric drugs to define all emotional disorders, including anxiety and depression, as physical in origin, leading to outlandish claims, such as 40% of Europe's population suffer from "brain disorders" (Wittchen et al., 2011).

Medical Disorders Masquerading as Psychological Disorders
Depression: underactive thyroid, low vitamin D or B_{12} or folate, diabetes, hormonal changes, heart disease, Lyme disease, lupus, head trauma, sleep disorders, fatigue and exhaustion, some cancers, and cancer drugs
Anxiety: overactive thyroid, respiratory problems, abnormal blood pressure, low blood sugar, and concussion
Irritability: brain injury, Alzheimer's disease and early stage dementia, parasitic infection, and hormonal changes
Hallucinations: brain tumor, fever, and substance abuse
Cognitive changes: brain injury or infection, Alzheimer's disease, Parkinson's disease, liver failure, mercury or lead poisoning
Psychosis: encephalitis, brain tumors and cysts, stroke, steroids, and substance abuse
Modified from Beck (2011) based on Schildkrout (2011).

Ironically, there are many genuine biological or medical disorders that do cause psychiatric symptoms, including thyroid disorder, sleep apnea, Lyme disease, diabetes, encephalitis, and head injury, but in their mistaken emphasis on mythical biochemical imbalances, some clinicians are likely to miss these real physical disorders (Beck, 2011; Schildkrout, 2011). All clinicians in the mental health field should become aware that many physical disorders first manifest themselves with psychological symptoms. When any suspicion arises, an appropriate medical referral should be made with emphasis on the need to examine for an underlying medical disorder. Schildkrout points out that more than 100 medical disorders can cause or contribute to psychological symptoms.

WHAT CAUSES CHRONIC BRAIN IMPAIRMENT—MENTAL DISORDER OR MEDICATION?

It is important to reemphasize that there are no known physiological or biochemical imbalances in the brains of people suffering from psychiatric disorders. That is why there are no laboratory tests for psychiatric disorders, such as anxiety, depression, bipolar disorder, or schizophrenia; there are no known abnormalities to detect. Instead of correcting biochemical imbalances, the drugs cause biochemical imbalances. In the process, every psychoactive medication disrupts the normal homeostasis of the brain, causing additional biochemical distortions within the brain as the organ attempts to overcome or to compensate for the drug-induced disruption of normal function (Andrews, Kornstein, Halberstadt, Gardner, & Neale, 2011; Breggin, 1991, 2008a; Breggin & Breggin, 2004; Science Daily, 2011a). The deterioration seen in so many contemporary patients is not caused by any inherent disease process within the brain but rather by toxic exposures to psychiatric medications. The FDA-approved label for all antidepressants warns about the potential "worsening of the patient's condition" (see Chapter 1; for Paxil warning of patients taking antidepressants see *Physicians' Desk Reference*, 2011, p. 1496). Similarly, the FDA-approved label medication guide for stimulants warns about the following, as illustrated in the Metadate label (*Physicians' Desk Reference*, 2011, p. 3263):

- new or worse behavior and thought problems
- new or worse bipolar illness
- new or worse aggressive behavior or hostility

The medication guide also warns about "new psychotic symptoms" in children.

A careful examination of most drug labels will disclose that some if not many patients are actually getting worse on the drug. But the focus is always on emotional instability (affective dysregulation) with little or no attention given to the other characteristics of CBI: cognitive dysfunction, apathy, and anosognosia.

The FDA does not require neuropsychological assessments of potential drug-induced cognitive deficits as a part of the drug approval process. The agency and the drug companies have in general ignored reports of cognitive dysfunction and other signs of CBI associated with psychiatric drugs.

Study of the mechanisms of brain injury is still in its infancy even regarding gross trauma, such as found in TBI. Regarding iatrogenic or treatment-inflicted brain injury, such as lobotomy, ECT, and long-term psychiatric drug treatment—the field is even less developed. My own research and publications concerning the mechanisms of damage caused by lobotomy, ECT, and drugs remain the most extensive available (e.g., Breggin, 1979, 1980, 1981a, 1981b, 1983, 2008a).

As the most complex and subtle biochemical system ever found, the human brain is very sensitive to biochemical disruptions. To impact on this organ, psychiatric drugs are specifically tailored to cross the blood-brain barrier that protects it. It should not be surprising that all psychiatric drugs that have been studied have toxic effects on neurons. They are neurotoxic. Chapters 4–8 will look at the adverse effects of the individual drugs and drug categories, as well as the particular cytotoxic and neurotoxic qualities of each class of psychiatric drugs.

TREATMENTS FOR CHRONIC BRAIN IMPAIRMENT

The only effective treatment for CBI is a carefully conducted withdrawal from all psychiatric drugs, as well as all other psychoactive substances. Those afflicted with CBI need to give their brains a chance to recover from toxic exposures. During the withdrawal process, it is important to establish healthy living practices regarding good nutrition (no special diets), moderate exercise, and sufficient rest and sleep.

Supportive psychotherapy can always be helpful in overcoming the effects of brain dysfunction by offering encouragement and guidance in the mastery of oneself and life. Couples or family therapy is potentially the most effective. It can help the uninjured partner understand the struggle to triumph over brain dysfunction and strengthen the relationship in supportive ways for both partners (see Chapter 13). Cognitive-behavioral therapy can be useful in promoting better ways to think of responsibility and self-determination, but nothing is more important than supportive relationships when brain function is impaired.

Programs for cognitive rehabilitation can be found on the Internet, but I'm not convinced that they are as good as engaging in useful, pleasurable, and stimulating physical and mental activities (Science Daily, 2006; Small, et al., 2006). Encourage individuals with CBI to rediscover activities that they once loved. Frequently, they have given them up under the influence of psychiatric drugs.

Many people feel that meditation, massage therapy, acupuncture, and other alternative medical approaches can enhance their physical and mental well-being, and if delivered by ethical practitioners, they are at least unlikely to be harmful. Art therapy and recreational therapy, as well as play therapy for children, can inspire people to make the most of their brain function, whether or not it is impaired.

Many patients with CBI continue to want a quick fix, but instead of seeking out additional psychoactive substances—including Chinese medicine and herbal or natural remedies—the

> People with CBI should avoid seeking shortcuts to improved health through psychoactive substances, including herbal and natural remedies. Instead they should abstain from all psychoactive substances for the indefinite future and focus on healthy living.

individual should abstain as much as possible from all psychoactive substances for the indefinite future.

RECOVERY FROM CBI

Recovery from CBI depends on medication withdrawal. However, it is not always possible to withdraw patients completely from psychiatric medications, especially if they have been exposed to multiple medications for much of their lifetime. Withdrawal may be prohibitively hazardous if the patient is isolated and has no social support network. It is also extremely difficult if not impossible to withdraw a patient who remains dependent on parents or caregivers who will not fully and enthusiastically cooperate with the healthcare provider and the withdrawal process (see Chapter 13). Ultimately, if the patient is unwilling to take responsibility for managing his or her own life, then successful drug withdrawal is greatly hampered, especially in an outpatient setting where close supervision is difficult or impossible. Under these circumstances, the first task of psychotherapy is to encourage the individual's sense of personal responsibility. Medication withdrawal can also be stymied by the patient's continued covert use of alcohol, street drugs, or nonprescription drugs, including large doses of herbal remedies.

Recovery from CBI almost always begins early in the process of drug withdrawal. As the number of drugs and their dosages are reduced, patients and their social network almost always report significant improvements in memory, engagement in activities, and mood stability. Because of anosognosia, the patient may not recognize the improvements as quickly or thoroughly as the treatment team and support network, but it would be unusual if the patient fails to notice or acknowledge any positive changes early in the drug withdrawal process.

If the patient does not begin displaying significant improvement in CBI symptoms during the drug withdrawal process, the clinician should suspect the presence of another underlying physical disorder and take appropriate steps to ensure adequate medical evaluation. Psychiatric drug CBI can be confused with or worsened by an almost infinite number of other causes of brain dysfunction, such as Lyme disease, thyroid disorders, Cushing's disease, and systemic lupus erythematosus, as well as a variety of neurological disorders that cause cognitive dysfunction and dementia.

In the meanwhile, the medication withdrawal should be continued, if possible, to clarify the clinical diagnosis and provide optimum conditions for healing

> Recovery from CBI usually begins early in the process of drug withdrawal. If improvement is delayed, other potential causes of brain impairment should be evaluated while the medication withdrawal continues.

any underlying physical disorder. Many underlying disorders, including neurological problems that impair brain function, are apt to be significantly worsened by continued exposure to psychoactive substances, including psychiatric drugs.

Patients with CBI that are removed from psychiatric drugs almost always have significant improvement in their overall mental functioning. They often experience some improvement shortly after getting started in the withdrawal process.

Of course, there is also a risk of psychiatric relapse. However, even if this occurs, improvement in the patient's CBI may be worth it to the patient and the family. In addition, these "relapses" are often caused by delayed withdrawal reactions manifested, for example, as the return of depression a few weeks after antidepressant withdrawal or the return of manic symptoms within weeks after withdrawal from lithium. Instead of reinstituting a starting dose of medication, it may be sufficient to provide drug-free psychotherapy or to extend the withdrawal somewhat longer with small doses of the medication.

Young children and teenagers often seem to experience full recovery from CBI despite years of exposure. It is imperative to prevent the long-term exposure of children and youth to psychiatric medications, all of which can impede learning and emotional development and injure the brain (Breggin, 2008a), but the good news is that children and youth are especially resilient after removal from the offending agents.

Adult patients are more likely to experience continued subtle CBI difficulties with memory, attention, or concentration after withdrawal from years of exposure to psychiatric medication, but even in the presence of residual symptoms, they can lead fulfilling lives filled with gratitude for their improvement.

Persistent multidrug exposure, high drug doses, length of exposure, and older age can contribute to the risk and severity of CBI. In my experience, length of exposure is the most significant factor in causing severe CBI and in impeding recovery. The best way to prevent CBI is to keep patients off psychiatric medications or to limit their exposure to the shortest possible length of time. Unfortunately, there are few if any clinical studies of recovery from mental dysfunction following the withdrawal of psychiatric medication. Clinical experience among practitioners who commonly withdraw patients is generally positive. The additional good news is that recovery from CBI usually begins early in the withdrawal process and can continue to an extended time, even for years after stopping all psychiatric medication.

> Recovery from psychiatric drug CBI can continue for years after stopping all medication.

Any effective psychotherapeutic approach—including individual, couples, and family work—will be much more effective when the patient begins to recover from CBI. CBI limits the effectiveness of psychotherapy by impeding insight and understanding, judgment, motivation, emotional stability, and the ability to relate to the therapist. Psychiatric medication itself, even without CBI, can also impede therapy by making the patient feel dependent on medication rather than on personal responsibility. Psychiatric drugs can also dull or confound the emotional signals needed for mastery of one's own life. Severe psychiatric problems, as well as substance abuse or dependence, can also interfere with recovery. In my own experience, however, removing psychiatric drugs helps in recovery from psychiatric disorders, including depression and anxiety.

After medication withdrawal, patients often declare, "I've gotten my life back. I'm myself again!" Family members often feel that they have regained the husband, wife, or child that they used to know and love before the adverse medication effects set in. The work of psychiatric drug withdrawal, although sometimes difficult and hazardous, can be very gratifying to the clinician and extremely empowering to the patient and family.

> The work of psychiatric drug withdrawal, although sometimes difficult and hazardous, can be very gratifying to the clinician and extremely empowering to the patient and family.

KEY POINTS

- A variety of stressors and trauma can cause chronic brain impairment or CBI. Long-term exposure to psychiatric drugs frequently results in CBI.
- CBI consists of the following four symptom complexes:
  - cognitive dysfunction, including short-term memory loss
  - apathy and loss of enjoyment of life activities
  - emotional worsening with lability, loss of empathy, and increased impatience and irritability
  - anosognosia—impaired self-awareness of these symptoms
- CBI leads to an overall loss in quality of life.
- CBI symptoms are the most frequent reason that patients and their families seek help for psychiatric drug withdrawal.
- Recovery from CBI almost always begins early in the drug withdrawal process.
- Children and teenagers are most likely to experience complete clinical recovery from CBI after termination of medication.
- Adults usually have substantial recovery from CBI, but it is not always complete. However, improvement can continue for years after termination of the medications.

- Even without full recovery, and despite psychiatric relapses, most patients remain grateful for their improved CBI and associated quality of life and want to remain medication free.
- The current escalating epidemic of "mental illness" and psychiatric disability is probably caused in large part by undiagnosed CBI caused by psychiatric medications.

CHAPTER 4

Antipsychotic (Neuroleptic) Drugs: Reasons for Withdrawal

Both the older antipsychotic drugs and the newer "atypicals" cause a wide range of serious and potentially life-threatening adverse effects, including tardive dyskinesia; neuroleptic malignant syndrome; and a metabolic syndrome with obesity, elevated blood lipids, elevated blood sugar, and diabetes. Combined with other adverse effects, including cardiac function impairment, they increase the risk of death. In addition, studies are showing that patients who take these drugs have a considerably reduced life span.

Antipsychotic drugs work by producing indifference and apathy without any specific effect on psychotic symptoms. There is considerable evidence that the short-term use of these drugs is not usually necessary and that the long-term use does more harm than good. Some therapists and clinics treat acutely psychotic patients with little or no resort to these drugs.

Given the current shortage of therapists or clinics to treat individuals labeled psychotic with individual and family therapy, the prescriber faces challenges with these patients. The prescriber and other clinicians should, when possible, avoid the use of these drugs or withdraw them as soon as feasible. When available, individual and family therapy in combination provides the best approach in both the short-term and the long-term and should always be used with or without accompanying medication.

The antipsychotic drugs include older ones such as chlorpromazine (Thorazine), haloperidol (Haldol), and perphenazine (Trilafon), as well as the "atypicals" or "novel" antipsychotic drugs such as olanzapine (Zyprexa), risperidone (Risperdal), aripiprazole (Abilify), ziprasidone (Geodon), and quetiapine (Seroquel).

Four newer atypical antipsychotics are paliperidone (Invega), iloperidone (Fanapt), lurasidone (Latuda), and asenapine (Saphris). All four are potent D_2 blockers (*Drug Facts and Comparisons*, 2012, p. 1627). For example, the FDA-approved label for Latuda (2010, p. 21) describes it as possessing "high affinity" for "dopamine D_2." As a result, they will pose the same risks as the older antipsychotic drugs for causing disorders related to dopamine blockade such as Parkinson's, akathisia, dystonia, tardive dyskinesia, neuroleptic malignant syndrome, gynecomastia, and an apathy or lobotomy syndrome. In addition, like the other atypicals, they also impact on numerous other neurotransmitter systems; and therefore, like the other atypicals, these newer ones will be at risk for causing a metabolic syndrome with diabetes, elevated blood sugar, elevated cholesterol, obesity, and cardiac problems (see the following discussion).

Neuroleptic drugs (dopamine blockers) used for nonpsychiatric purposes can cause the same adverse effects. Prochlorperazine (Compazine) and metoclopramide (Reglan) are used to control nausea during pregnancy or the flu, and both present serious risks including tardive dyskinesia.

A more complete list of antipsychotic drugs can be found in the Appendix.

Starting with chlorpromazine in 1953–1954, these drugs were originally called "neuroleptics" to designate their capacity to "grab the neuron" or cause toxicity. The term can be applied to all drugs that block dopamine neurotransmission. More recently, the term "antipsychotic" has been used to describe those neuroleptics specifically prescribed to treat psychosis.

As of April 2011, three atypical antipsychotic drugs were in the top 20 of all U.S. pharmaceutical products in regard to their total revenues: Abilify (5th), Seroquel (6th), and Zyprexa (17th) (IMS, 2011a). Globally, the order was Seroquel (4th), Zyprexa (10th), and Abilify (13th). No other type of psychiatric drug, even the antidepressant class, was close in generating revenues, mostly because the antipsychotic drugs are so much more expensive. This enormous revenue flow from antipsychotic drugs creates a mighty financial incentive for drug companies to push them for off-label purposes. Knowledge of the frequent and severe adverse effects associated with these drugs should encourage withdrawal from them as soon as feasible.

The antipsychotic drugs have many short-term adverse effects that may lead the clinician, patient, or family to consider medication reduction or withdrawal, including Parkinsonism, dystonias, akathisia (psychomotor agitation), sedation, and apathy. They also have many longer-term effects, including tardive dyskinesia, a general deterioration in the quality of life, metabolic syndrome, atrophy of the brain, and shortened life span, all of which indicate the need to limit the length of exposure to these drugs.

CHRONIC BRAIN IMPAIRMENT

Many longer-term patients develop neuroleptic-induced deficit syndrome (NIDS) with cognitive and affective losses (Barnes & McPhillips, 1995), leading to a misdiagnosis of chronic schizophrenia. One of the few studies to address the neuropsychiatric condition of a large group of individuals exposed to antipsychotic drugs found generalized cognitive dysfunction (Grant et al., 1978).

Cellular Changes

On a cellular level, the neurotoxicity of antipsychotic drugs has been studied and demonstrated for decades. Clinical doses of haloperidol and olanzapine over 17–27 months duration in macaque monkeys have been shown to cause 8%–11% loss of tissue weight throughout the brain (Dorph-Petersen et al., 2005). The toxicity of the antipsychotic drugs on a cellular level includes the inhibition of most enzyme systems in the mitochondria (Inuwa, Horobin, & Williams, 1994; Teller & Denber, 1970). Kim et al. (2006) observed that chronic blockage of dopamine neurotransmission by antipsychotic drugs "results in persistently enhanced release of glutamate, which kills striatal neurons."

The "cytotoxic properties" of the older antipsychotics are acknowledged as "well known" by researchers (Dwyer, Lu, & Bradley, 2003). A study of the atypical antipsychotic drugs found them to be cytotoxic but less so than the older drugs (Dwyer et al., 2003). In defense of olanzapine, these researchers stated that olanzapine "actually stimulated proliferation of neuronal cells," implying that this should be considered beneficial. Instead, it should be viewed as a spectacular and ominous sign of toxicity. Neurons rarely proliferate—until recently, it was thought that they never did—and are known to do so only in response to injury. That many psychiatric drugs have now been shown to cause cell proliferation is a very serious warning sign. In addition, many studies of drug-induced neurogenesis have found cells that look grossly abnormal under the microscope (reviewed in Breggin, 2008a).

Structural Brain Changes

In 2009, Navari and Dazzan reviewed and analyzed the literature, asking, "Do antipsychotic drugs affect brain structure?" They answered, "Yes." Regarding the animal literature, they found that "conventional antipsychotics may be neurotoxic and induce neuronal loss and gliosis in the striatum, hypothalamus, brainstem, limbic system and cortex" (p. 1763). In nonhuman primates, they found that both the typical antipsychotic haloperidol and the atypical olanzapine are "associated with reductions in both grey and white matter" (p. 1763). Their analysis of 33 studies showed that both the older and the newer antipsychotic drugs cause gross changes in brain volume in selected portions of the brain but that the older drugs produced larger effects. They were able to show the reversible early development of these effects in short-term treatment and the irreversible development with longer drug exposure.

A commentary on the Navari and Dazzan study observed "these results, if confirmed, raise ethical questions on antipsychotic use" (Borgwardt, Smieskova, Fusar-Poli, Bendfeldt, & Reicher-Rossler, 2009, p. 1782). In fact, more recent studies have confirmed atrophy of the brain attributable to the antipsychotic drugs in long-term treatment of patients diagnosed as schizophrenic (Ho, Andreasen, Ziebell, Pierson, & Magnotta, 2011; Levin, 2011; van Haren et al., 2011).

One explanation attributes the atrophy to shrinkage of dendrites and dendritic spines causing shrinkage in the synaptic connections in the cortex, reducing the brain's capacity for the full expression of cognitive and intellectual processes (Levin, 2011). Another explanation involves substantially reduced cell numbers (glial) and reduced volume induced by antipsychotic drugs (haloperidol and olanzapine) in monkeys (Konopaske et al., 2007; Konopaske et al., 2008). Whatever the specifics of causation, there is no doubt that antipsychotic drugs caused significant brain damage in human and animal studies, including loss of cells and atrophy.

In a study of intravenous haloperidol in normal volunteers, multi-modal pharmaco-neuroimaging found that "acute D_2 receptor blockade induced reversible striatal volume changes and structural–functional decoupling in motor circuits within hours; these alterations predicted acute extrapyramidal motor symptoms with high precision" (Tost et al., 2010, p. 920). These very dramatic acute effects indicate how more prolonged exposure could lead to irreversible atrophy of the brain as well as to persistent extrapyramidal symptoms in the form of tardive dyskinesia.

Studies showing brain damage from antipsychotic drugs are sufficiently convincing at this time that patients and their families should be warned in advance, and prescribers should exercise extreme caution in starting or continuing patients on these highly toxic drugs.

Tardive Psychosis and Tardive Dementia

Tardive dyskinesia is a very common neuroleptic-induced movement disorder with a prevalence of 40% or more in outpatient clinics and 50% or more in long-term facilities (see later in this chapter). As Gualtieri and Barnhill (1988) have stated, "In virtually every clinical survey that has addressed the question, it is found that TD patients, compared to non-TD patients, have more in the way of dementia" (p. 149). All neuro-psychiatric studies of patients with tardive dyskinesia have revealed an associated impairment of cognitive and affective functioning (reviewed in Breggin, 2008a; Myslobodsky, 1986, 1993). Several studies have described this euphemistically as "tardive dysmentia" (Goldberg, 1985; Myslobodsky, 1986, 1993).

A persistent withdrawal tardive psychosis has also been identi-fied, again confirming long-term chronic impairments in brain function (Breggin, 2008a; Chouinard & Jones, 1980; Moncrieff, 2006). I agree with Moncrieff's proposal concerning the mechanism as a "pharmacodynamic adaptation" or compensatory mechanism that is common to many drugs.

> Long-term use of drugs that suppress certain neurotransmitters is thought to cause a compensatory increase in the number and/or sensitivity of the relevant receptors (the concept of supersensitiv-ity). When these receptors are no longer opposed by drugs there is an over-activity of the neurotransmitter system or systems involved. This may result in the characteristic discontinuation syn-dromes, may cause rapid onset psychosis and may act as a source of "pharmacodynamic stress" which increases vulnerability to relapse (p. 521).

Children manifest tardive psychosis as a worsening of their behavior prob-lems far beyond their pre-treatment intensity (Gualtieri & Barnhill, 1988).

Taking into account only the harmful effects on the brain, prescrib-ing antipsychotic drugs long-term should be avoided; and a timetable for eventual withdrawal should be considered at the onset of treatment and periodically thereafter.

ACUTE ADVERSE NEUROLOGICAL REACTIONS

The antipsychotic drugs begin impacting on the central nervous system with the first dose. Depending on the dose size and individual reactivity, early within treatment the antipsychotic drugs frequently produce a slow-ing of all physical movements (akinesia) and Parkinsonism, which includes akinesia, rigidity, tremor, drooling, and other symptoms. The first doses commonly produce a depressed and apathetic feeling that increases with time and dose increases. Other neurological symptoms involve acute dys-tonias such as painful neck spasms, and acute akathisia manifested by torturous inner agitation with a compulsion to move.

Symptoms that specifically involve disorders of movement such as Parkinsonism, dystonia, and akathisia are called *extrapyramidal symp-toms* (EPS). Some of these can become persistent in the form of tardive dyskinesia.

TARDIVE DYSKINESIA, TARDIVE DYSTONIA, AND TARDIVE AKATHISIA

Tardive dyskinesia—often called TD—is a movement disorder caused by antipsychotic drugs that can impair any muscle functions that are partially or wholly under voluntary control, such as the face, eyes, tongue, neck, back, abdomen, extremities, diaphragm and respiration, swallowing reflex, and vocal cords and voice control.

TD afflicts the whole life span from infancy to old age. *Classic TD* involves either rapid, jerky movements (choreiform) or slower, serpentine movements (athetoid). In the extreme, a patient may look like he or she is playing a guitar in a wild rock band, be unable to sit or stand straight, or be unable to control constant head bobbing. A second form of TD, *tardive dystonia*, involves painful muscle contractions or spasms, often involving the neck; and a third form, *tardive akathisia*, involves psychomotor agitation. The various tardive disorders can exist separately or in combination. Unless they are identified at an early stage and the offending drugs are stopped, these disorders tend to become permanent.

> Early signs of TD are probably the most common signal that a patient on antipsychotic drugs needs to be withdrawn from the medication as quickly as possible.

Table 4-1 Symptoms of TD describes the basic symptoms that clinicians, patients, and families must be able to recognize to identify potential TD and to take appropriate action. *Table 4-2 General Characteristics of TD* summarizes information that should be known by the whole treatment team to understand, recognize, and evaluate the disorder.

From dozens of controlled clinical trials and epidemiological studies, we know that the rates for tardive dyskinesia are astronomical (reviewed in Breggin, 2008a, pp. 57–58; Chouinard, Annable, Mercier, & Ross-Chouinard, 1986; Glazer, Morgenstern, & Doucette, 1993; Smith, Kuchorski, Oswald, & Waterman, 1979). In physically healthy younger adults, regardless of any psychiatric diagnosis, exposure to these drugs produces tardive dyskinesia at the cumulative rate of 5%–8% per year. The American Psychiatric Association (APA) *Diagnostic and Statistical Manual of Mental Disorders, Fourth Edition, Text Revision (DSM-IV-TR)* (2000, p. 803) sets the rate at 3%–5% per year for young adults and 25%–30% per year for older patients. The rates are cumulative so that using the more conservative *DSM-IV-TR* estimates—after three years of exposure, a young adult has a 9%–15% risk of developing TD, and an older person has a 75%–90% risk of developing the disorder.

The rates and the prevalence for TD are very high; but unfortunately, clinicians too often fail to identify the disorder (Brown & Funk, 1986; Weiden, Mann, Haas, Manson, & Frances, 1987). It is important for the

Table 4-1 Symptoms of Tardive Dyskinesia

Tardive Dyskinesia (Classic)

Rapid, irregular (choreiform), or slow and serpentine (athetoid) movements; often bizarre looking; involving any voluntary muscle, including:

Face, eyelids and eye muscles, jaw (chewing movements, tongue biting), mouth, lips, or tongue (protruding, trembling, curling, cupping)

Head (nodding), neck (twisting, turning), shoulders (shrugging), back, torso (rocking movements), or abdomen

Arms and legs (may move slowly or jerk out of control)

Ankles, feet, and toes; wrists, hands, and fingers (sometimes producing flexion, extension, or rotation)

Breathing (diaphragm and ribs; grunting), swallowing (choking), and speaking (dysphonia)

Balance, posture, and gait (sometimes worse when slow; often spastic)

Tardive Dystonia

Often painful sustained contractions (spasms) of any voluntary muscle group; potentially causing muscular hypertrophy, arthritis, and fixed joints; frequently involving the following:

Neck (torticollis, retrocollis) and shoulders

Face (sustained grimacing and tongue protrusion)

Mouth and jaw (sustained opening or clamping shut)

Arms and hands; legs and feet (spastic flexion or extension)

Torso (twisting and thrusting movements; flexion of spine)

Eyelids (blepharospasm)

Gait (spastic, mincing)

Tardive Akathisia

Potentially agonizing inner agitation or tension, usually (but not always) compelling the patient to move, commonly manifested as the following:

Restless leg movements (when awake)

Foot stamping

Marching in place, pacing

Jitteriness

Clasping hands or arms

Inability to sit still

Table 4-2 General characteristics of Tardive Dyskinesia (TD)

1. No two TD cases look alike. Suspect any unusual movement.
2. TD can begin with any muscle that's partially under voluntary control and can occur in one muscle group or several, with varying muscles afflicted at different times.
3. TD waxes and wanes, and varies, from moment to moment and day to day.
4. TD can often be partially self-controlled; touching the patient can calm TD.
5. TD worsens with physical illness, anxiety, stress, and fatigue, and can improve with rest and relaxation.
6. TD disappears during sleep.
7. TD can be mistaken for "nerves" or "mental illness," and patients wrongly blamed for "exaggerating" and "dramatizing."
8. TD can rarely occur with one dose but most commonly after three months exposure.
9. TD can develop very slowly with subtle initial signs.
10. TD can cause a general worsening of the patient's mental condition.
11. TD often or always causes cognitive dysfunction and can lead to Chronic Brain Impairment (CBI).
12. TD can become physically and mentally incapacitating.
13. Early TD symptoms are masked (suppressed) by antipsychotic drugs while the underlying disorder develops and worsens.
14. Existing TD symptoms can be temporarily masked by increased doses.
15. Dramatic TD flare-ups accompanied by severe emotional distress can be caused by dose reductions or abrupt withdrawal.
16. Any suspicion of an early TD symptom requires immediate attention with a complete TD examination (including the tongue) and potentially a dose reduction or withdrawal to properly diagnose the disorder and to minimize severity and irreversibility.

clinician to inform and educate the patient and family about the disorder; to monitor for any signs of TD, including an examination of the tongue; and to withdraw the patient if at all possible at the earliest sign of abnormal movements. After the development of symptoms, continued exposure to these drugs tends to lead to more severe and lasting cases (APA, 1990). If the medication is stopped as early as possible, some cases will resolve.

Tardive dyskinesia is a cumulative drug effect. In a case in my

Tardive dyskinesia is so common and potentially devastating that the entire treatment team—prescriber, therapist, patient, and family—must understand and be able to recognize the disorder. The only effective treatment for TD is to remove patients from the drug as swiftly as possible after the first sign of abnormal movements.

clinical experience, an individual was treated with an antipsychotic drug for 2 months several years earlier and then developed TD within a month of exposure on a second occasion. Rarely, TD can develop after only one or two doses. I have seen this occur during treatment with prochlorperazine (Compazine) for nausea. I have also seen a mild case of TD become severe after reexposure to one dose several years after the last dose.

Tardive akathisia is a particularly virulent form of TD in which individuals are driven by a torture-like inner agitation that compels them into physical motion. Patients will move their hands or feet nervously or pace frantically about in an effort to relieve the distress. I have evaluated cases in which the inner agitation has not been accompanied by movements, or the movements could be contained by the patient clasping his hands together or sitting rigidly still. Tardive akathisia can drive a patient into despair, psychosis, suicide, or violence.

Anxiety, stress, and fatigue can worsen tardive dyskinesia, leading healthcare professionals or family into the mistaken belief that the patient's movement disorder is psychologically based. Frequently the patient can control some or all of the movement, usually with enormous, exhausting effort; again misleading professionals or family into believing it is psychological in origin. TD symptoms can temporarily improve while the patient is relaxing or resting.

In almost all cases, TD symptoms disappear after the patient falls asleep. However, TD symptoms can make it very difficult to fall asleep, leading some patients to mistakenly report that the movements do not go away in sleep. A family member is usually needed to confirm whether or not the symptoms disappear during sleep.

Claims have been made that the newer atypical antipsychotics have a lesser tendency to produce TD than the older ones; but this has not been proven, and the FDA continues to require the same or similar TD warning on the labels for all antipsychotic drugs. When given at dose equivalents, there is no significant difference in the frequency of extrapyramidal effects when comparing the older antipsychotic drugs to the newer ones (Lieberman, et al., 2005; Rosebush & Mazurek, 1999). Drawing on the Clinical Antipsychotic Trials of Intervention Effectiveness (CATIE) study, Nasrallah (2007) wrote about the comparison between the older antipsychotic drug perphenazine and the newer atypicals, "There were no statistically significant differences between the rates of extrapyramidal side effects, movement disorders, or akathisia" (p. 9). Similarly, Miller et al. (2009) concluded from CATIE, "The incidence of treatment-emergent EPS and change in EPS ratings indicated that there are no significant differences between second-generation antipsychotics and perphenazine or between second-generation antipsychotics in people with schizophrenia" (p. 279).

The CATIE researchers selected perphenazine as their comparison drug because of its "lower potency and moderate side-effect profile"

(Lieberman et al., 2005, p. 1215)—meaning that they hoped to skew the study in favor of the newer drugs by choosing an older drug that was less potent (less effective) and less likely to cause side effects.

In a recent study of 352 patients who were initially free of TD, Woods et al. (2010) found little difference in TD rates (approximately 5% per year) between the atypical and classic neuroleptics and concluded that clinicians must remain vigilant for the disorder.

> *Conclusions*: The incidence of tardive dyskinesia with recent exposure to atypical antipsychotics alone was more similar to that for conventional antipsychotics than in most previous studies. Despite high penetration of atypical antipsychotics into clinical practice, the incidence and prevalence of tardive dyskinesia appeared relatively unchanged since the 1980s. Clinicians should continue to monitor for tardive dyskinesia, and researchers should continue to pursue efforts to treat or prevent it (p. 463).

Even if the newer antipsychotic drugs produced 50% less risk of TD—for which there is no evidence—they would still be causing TD at an alarming and tragic rate of 2.5%–4% per year cumulative in healthy young adults and 10% or more per year cumulative in the elderly. Prescribers and clinicians must view TD as a serious risk with any antipsychotic drug.

An earlier section in this chapter, "Tardive Psychosis and Dementia," described the brain abnormalities and mental dysfunction associated with tardive dyskinesia.

LESS FAMILIAR MANIFESTATIONS OF TD

In addition to the familiar manifestations of TD—classic TD (choreoathetoid movements), tardive dystonia, and tardive akathisia—there are several less familiar expressions of this drug-induced movement disorder (Bhidayasiri & Boonyawairoj, 2010).

Tardive stereotypy involves seemingly purposeful and coordinated movements that are nonetheless involuntary.

Tardive tics or *tardive Tourette's* are "brief, repetitive, temporarily suppressible movements or sounds. There are usually premonitory sensations preceding motor or vocal tics. . . . Besides older age of onset and history of neuroleptic exposure, they are clinically indistinguishable from Tourette's syndrome" (Bhidayasiri & Boonyawairoj, 2010, p. 135).

Tardive myoclonus is relatively frequent, commonly involves posture and upper extremities, and is usually found in association with other TD symptoms. Myoclonus is characterized by abrupt-onset, quickly jerking movements.

Tardive tremor manifests as a high-amplitude, moderate frequency tremor that can occur at rest. It is similar to the tremor of Parkinsonism.

Tardive Parkinsonism, except for the similar tremor, remains a controversial syndrome.

CHILDREN AND TD

In 1983, in *Psychiatric Drugs: Hazards to the Brain,* I wrote perhaps the first detailed review demonstrating that tardive dyskinesia is a major threat to children. Fortunately, the issue is no longer in doubt—children are highly susceptible to developing tardive dyskinesia (reviewed in Breggin, 2008a; also see Mejia & Jankovic, 2010).

Although there are few reports in the literature on childhood TD in association with the newer antipsychotics, in my clinical and forensic work I have evaluated dozens of cases of childhood TD from atypicals, including risperidone, olanzapine, ziprasidone, aripiprazole, and quetiapine. Probably because of increased frequency of exposure to risperidone and olanzapine, as well as their potent D_2 blocking capacity, most of the cases have involved these two drugs.

Children are frequently given metoclopramide (Reglan) for nausea and gastroesophageal reflux. I am in agreement with Mejia and Jankovic (2010) that this drug is inducing many more cases of TD in children than is suggested by the literature. They report the case of a 12-month-old girl who developed orofaciolingual TD at 2 months of age after 2 weeks of treatment with metoclopramide for gastroesophageal reflux disease. It persisted for at least 9 months after the medication was discontinued (Mejia & Jankovic, 2005).

In my forensic work, I have evaluated several cases of infants who developed abnormal movements in reaction to metoclopramide. In these cases, the abnormal movements were accompanied by flaccidity and failure to thrive. Recovery over many years was incomplete.

NEUROLEPTIC MALIGNANT SYNDROME

Antipsychotic drugs, including the newer ones, can cause neuroleptic malignant syndrome (NMS), which can be fatal in 20% of untreated cases (reviewed in Breggin, 2008a, pp. 75–78). Any dopamine blocking agent used for other purposes, such as metoclopramide and prochlorperazine for nausea, can also cause NMS. The disease strongly resembles a viral disorder, lethargic encephalitis, which occurred in epidemic form during and shortly after World War I (Breggin, 1993; Brill, 1959; Deniker, 1970; Matheson Commission, 1939). Both strike the basal ganglia especially hard, causing a similar impact.

NMS typically includes impaired consciousness and mental deterioration, elevated temperature, autonomic nervous system instability (increased respiratory rate, blood pressure, heart rate, or sweating), and neurological impairments in the form of extrapyramidal signs (EPS) (see Table 4-1). NMS can present in varied and confusing ways and with varying intensity.

In my forensic experience, even severe and life-threatening cases are sometimes misdiagnosed as "schizophrenia" or "catatonia." The clinician must be alert for any symptoms that resemble NMS. Any report of fever should raise a suspicion. Early recognition with immediate termination of the causative agent and supportive measures in a hospital setting can be lifesaving.

Some diagnostic analyses describe "rigidity" as the main neurological sign associated with NMS, and I have seen cases misdiagnosed because rigidity was not apparent. In my clinical and research experience, rigidity may be transient or missing; and an array of EPS may occur, including Parkinson's symptoms with akinesia and any TD-like symptom. Indeed, TD can become a lasting sequela of nonfatal NMS (Zarrouf & Bhanot, 2007).

Usually described as "rare" in the literature, NMS is common— occurring in as many as 2.4% of patients in a retrospective chart review (Addonizio, Susman, & Roth, 1986). I suspect that many mild cases go unnoticed.

During and after an episode of NMS, all antipsychotic drugs should be stopped and not restarted.

Signs of Neuroleptic Malignant Syndrome

1. Recent exposure to any antipsychotic drug or dopamine blocker
2. Fever
3. Any irregularities in autonomic nervous system function, including respirations, heart rate, blood pressure, or perspiration; or the presence of nausea, incontinence, or difficulty swallowing
4. Decline in cognitive function and overall mental condition; in the extreme, severe confusion, delirium, and coma
5. Neurological signs similar to Parkinsonism and tardive dyskinesia
6. Elevated white blood cell count and CPK

METABOLIC SYNDROME

All antipsychotic drugs, and especially the newer atypical drugs, can cause a collection of adverse effects called the "metabolic syndrome," which includes weight gain and obesity, elevated blood sugar and diabetes, elevated blood lipids, and high blood pressure. Combined with the additional risk of cardiac arrhythmia, antipsychotic drugs produce both short-term and long-term cardiovascular risk. Potentially lethal pancreatitis is another related risk. The syndrome itself and its individual components are potentially lethal.

The CATIE study confirmed the high risk of developing metabolic syndrome. It measured weight change, proportion of patients gaining weight, average weight change per month, blood glucose increases, hemoglobin A_{1c} change (a diabetes test), cholesterol change, and triglyceride change (Lieberman et al., 2005). They did not measure another variable—blood pressure. In a cohort of 689 patients where the best data were available, the prevalence of metabolic syndrome was a shocking 40.9%–42.7%, depending on the criteria. More than 50% of the females developed metabolic syndrome. Olanzapine was the worst offender.

Given that the atypicals cause all of the disorders associated with the older antipsychotic drugs and that they more frequently cause an additional serious array of potential lethal reactions, they cannot be considered safer than the older drugs. Long-term exposure to any antipsychotic drug carries severe risks, and a plan for eventual withdrawal should always be part of the treatment.

CHILDREN AND THE METABOLIC SYNDROME

A recent study found that up to one third of children and adolescents given antipsychotic drugs were at risk of developing metabolic syndrome (see Goeb et al., 2010; Splete, 2011). Meanwhile, antipsychotic drugs are being increasingly prescribed to children and youth.

According to Moreno et al. (2007), "The estimated annual number of youth office-based visits with a diagnosis of bipolar disorder increased from 25 (1994–1995) to 1,003 (2002–2003) visits per 100,000 population" (p. 1032). That's more than a 40-fold increase. Most of these children (90.6%) received psychiatric drugs and nearly half (47.7%) received antipsychotic drugs.[1]

The dramatic increase in diagnosing bipolar disorder in children and rampant use of psychiatric medication, including antipsychotic drugs, have been driven by a prestigious team of Harvard child psychiatrists who promote the diagnosis of bipolar disorder in children and the use of potent adult psychiatric drugs. This team of Joseph Biederman, Thomas Spencer, and Timothy Wilens has recently been criticized for illegally and unethically accepting undeclared or under-the-table funds from the pharmaceutical industry and for working directly to promote their products (Sarchet, 2011; Yu, 2011).

As a result of these and other drug-company inspired promotional campaigns, the children's market for psychiatric drugs has enormously

---

[1]There was a much smaller but substantial increase in bipolar office visits for adults. Compared to adults diagnosed with bipolar disorder, a higher percentage of children were treated with psychiatric drugs, including antipsychotic medication.

expanded. The problem of overmedicating children has drawn some attention (e.g., Littrell & Lyons, 2010a, 2010b); but there's no evidence that this trend has abated.

STROKE AND DEATH IN THE ELDERLY

People older than 55 or 60 years and especially those with dementia are at higher risk of death when prescribed with these drugs. Given that approximately 50% will also develop TD after a mere 2-year exposure, these drugs should not be given to the elderly. A physician less critical of these drugs has nonetheless recommended in regard to the elderly, "Once a patient is clinically stable with an antipsychotic for a reasonable duration, a trial taper off the medication should be initiated" (Meeks, 2010).

INCREASED MORTALITY AND SHORTENED LIFE SPAN

For years, data have accumulated showing that antipsychotic drugs shorten the life span. A recent study found that this was not related to the lifestyle of patients diagnosed with schizophrenia and that the risk increased with polydrug treatment (see Gill et al., 2007; Joukamaa et al., 2006). The rates of mortality in the groups exposed to neuroleptics increased dramatically as two or three neuroleptics were added. This is another caution for the prescriber to reduce the number of drugs given to any one patient.

Studies also show that patients diagnosed with serious mental illnesses have a dramatically shortened life span—as much as 13.8 years in VA patients and 25 years in state mental health systems (Kilbourne, Ignacio, Kim, & Blow, 2009; Parks et al., 2006). Almost all patients diagnosed as seriously mentally ill in the VA and state systems are exposed to years of neuroleptics, no doubt contributing heavily to their much-shortened life spans. Young adults age 20–34 years taking antidepressants had increased mortality when taking antipsychotic drugs or mood stabilizers, excluding lithium (Sundell, Gissler, Petzold, & Waern, 2011).

Foley and Morley reviewed the literature concerning cardiac and metabolic outcome studies of first episode psychoses treated with neuroleptics. They believe that "the increased mortality associated with schizophrenia is largely due to cardiovascular disease" and tested the hypothesis that this is caused by antipsychotic drugs. They found (a) that there is no difference in risk factors between untreated first episode individuals with psychosis and normal controls, and (b) there is increased cardiovascular risk after the initial exposure to any antipsychotic drug.

No biochemical or physiological cause has been found for schizophrenia. When physical disorders are found in patients diagnosed with schizophrenia, it has always turned out to be caused by something other than the schizophrenia. Dementia, as we have seen, is associated with the medications rather than with schizophrenia. The increased rate of diabetes found in patients diagnosed with schizophrenia is caused by the frequency with which the antipsychotic drugs are administered to them (discussed in Parks et al., 2006).

In addition to increased heart attacks and other drug-induced disorders, it seems extremely likely that the indifference and anosognosia caused by these drugs is a major contributor to premature death. As a result, patients taking these drugs longer term lack the mental acuity, motivation, and concern with their personal well-being to identify when they are sick and to seek medical attention.

EFFICACY OF ANTIPSYCHOTIC MEDICATIONS

There is no sound evidence that the neuroleptics specifically target psychosis or its symptoms. Instead, these drugs produce a chemical suppression of the frontal lobes and reticular activating system, thereby producing relative degrees of apathy or indifference and docility (Breggin, 2008a). These effects occur in humans regardless of their psychiatric diagnosis or mental condition, accounting for their widespread use in foster homes and institutions for children, nursing homes, and prisons. Because the identical effect occurs in animals, the "antipsychotic" drugs are also used in veterinary medicine for "restraint" and produce "indifference" as they do in human beings (Read, 2002). The antipsychotic drugs, often with the first dose, create this condition of apathy, indifference, and docility (restraint), which is the primary clinical effect in humans and animals (reviewed in detail in Breggin 2008a, pp. 21–41).

The concept of "neuroleptic threshold"—that the therapeutic effect begins with the onset of adverse neurological effects—has continued to surface within the psychiatric literature (e.g., Miller, 2009) and confirms the brain-disabling principle of drug effect (discussed in Breggin, 2008a, and in Moncrieff, 2007a, 2007b).

Meanwhile, the best efforts of the National Institute of Mental Health (NIMH) and numerous pharmaceutical companies have continued to fail to demonstrate that these medications have any effectiveness beyond their initial subduing impact. A large study (CATIE) published in the *New England Journal of Medicine* (Lieberman et al., 2005) gave a bleak picture. This negative result was found despite multiple-source drug-company funding and the lead author having more than a dozen sources of income from drug companies (listed under potential conflicts of interest). The study found, "In summary, patients with chronic schizophrenia in this study discontinued their antipsychotic study medications at a high rate, indicating substantial limitations in the effectiveness of the drugs" (p. 1218).

In a commentary, the two lead authors of the CATIE study under-scored the limitations of the drugs: "By revealing the truth about the emperor's new clothes, CATIE has helped to refocus efforts on the need for truly innovative treatments and strategies that can make significant advances for persons with schizophrenia and related psychoses" (Lieberman & Stroup, 2011, p. 774). The two authors lament that "prescribing patterns have not markedly changed" as a result of the CATIE study (p. 773).

The CATIE results should not have been so surprising. From early in the history of antipsychotic drug studies, evidence began accumulat-ing that patients on continued antipsychotic drugs do more poorly than patients removed from their drugs (for a review, see Whitaker, 2010, pp. 99–104). An NIMH 6-week trial found that "patients who received placebo treatment were less likely to be rehospitalized than those who received any of the three active phenothiazines" (Schooler, 1967). Another NIMH study found that relapse was significantly correlated with increasing doses of antipsychotic drugs (Prien, Levine, & Switalski, 1971). Another study found that patients treated without medication were more quickly discharged and were grateful to have gone through the experi-ence without being numbed (Carpenter, 1977). Yet another looked at rehospitalization rates of patients treated with placebo and antipsychotic drugs and found that placebo far outperformed antipsychotic medication (Rappaport, 1978). A recent study indicated that the off-label use of risperidone as an adjunct to antidepressants in the treatment of military-related post-traumatic stress disorder (PTSD) "did not reduce PTSD symptoms" (Krystal et al., 2011, p. 493).

Accumulating evidence that long-term exposure to antipsychotic drugs does far more harm than good should encourage practitioners, patients, and family to consider medication withdrawal in order to avert long-term exposure.

EFFICACY OF PSYCHOTHERAPY ALTERNATIVES

Even in a traditional hospital setting, patients diagnosed with schizo-phrenia can be helped by intensive psychotherapy (Karon, 2005). When I was an undergraduate student at Harvard College (1954–1958), I ran a volunteer program in a state mental hospital that proved that untrained students with weekly group supervision by a clinical social worker could help nearly all of our assigned chronic back-ward patients leave the hos-pital for home or improved surroundings (Breggin, 1962; Breggin, 1991, pp. 3–9, 380–381).

A number of programs using limited or no antipsychotic drug treat-ment have demonstrated more successful outcomes than medication-based treatment approaches (reviewed in Bola, Lehtinen, Cullberg, & Ciompi,

2009). Loren Mosher, who was the head of schizophrenia research at NIMH, conducted a series of studies in his Soteria project involving drug-free treatment in a residential setting for first-episode patients diagnosed with schizophrenia and found that nearly all could be treated without medication with excellent recovery on follow-up (Mosher & Bola, 2004; Mosher and Burti, 1989). A Soteria-like approach in Berne, Switzerland, produced a similar good result (Ciompi, 1992).

Innovative treatment programs around the world continue to demonstrate that most acutely psychotic patients do best when treated with little or no medication and especially without antipsychotic drugs. A community-oriented and home-based treatment program that has lasted successfully for decades in Lapland, Finland, has rarely used antipsychotic medication, and those who do get medication do best when it is short-term (Lehtinen, 2000; Seikkula, 2006). Even that highly successful, well-published program has received little attention; and in the remainder of Finland, biopsychiatric theory and practice continue to dominate the landscape.

A series of studies by the World Health Organization (WHO) with follow-ups at 2 and 5 years demonstrated that modern psychiatric treatment in "developed" industrialized nations produced poorer results in the course and outcome of schizophrenia compared to "developing" nations such as India, Taipei, Columbia, and Nigeria (de Girolamo, 1996). In developing nations, more patients were in "full remission" (38% vs. 22%), while far fewer remained on antipsychotic drugs (16% vs. 61%). In addition, in the developing nations, 55% had never been hospitalized compared to 8% in the developed nations. In another startling finding, only 15% of the patients in developing nations "had impaired social functions through the follow-up time," whereas 42% of patients in the developed nations were in this impaired condition. Probably two factors play a role in these contrasting outcomes: Both the *presence* of extended traditional families and the *absence* of modern psychiatric treatments favor a good outcome in patients diagnosed with schizophrenia.

In actual practice, what can a prescriber, clinician, patient, or family expect when antipsychotic medications are not given or when they are stopped at various intervals after the initial episode? A prospective 15-year study of psychotic patients (both schizophrenic and nonschizophrenic) in Chicago, Illinois, demonstrated that at all intervals, patients not taking antipsychotic medication showed more symptom recovery and better global functioning (Harrow & Jobe, 2007). It appears that in many if not most cases, very little or no antipsychotic drug treatment provides better outcomes, *even in the absence of alternative treatments*. A recent study demonstrated that cognitive therapy improved the outcome of patients diagnosed with negative symptoms of schizophrenia (Grant et al., 2011).

The most successful interventions with psychotic patients involve working with both the individual and the family (e.g., see Leff & Berkowitz, 1996; Seikkula, 2006). Many therapists work with psychotic patients without the use of medications; and like the projects described in this section, individual clinicians report success in treating patients diagnosed with schizophrenia without resort to psychiatric medication (Breggin, 1991; Breggin & Stern, 1996; Karon 2005).

Ideally, the prescriber of antipsychotic medication will also provide individual and family therapy or work in close cooperative with a therapist who provides these services. Unfortunately, given limitations in current training and practice, not many prescribers and therapists are likely to try working with deeply disturbed patients without antipsychotic medication. My hope is that this brief summary will encourage an increased willingness to try supportive outpatient, family-oriented psychotherapy for psychosis, a more limited use of antipsychotic medication in the first few weeks, and an even greater reluctance to continue these medications longer-term.

KEY POINTS

- Antipsychotic drugs are highly toxic and produce many potentially severe and even lethal adverse effects, such as chronic brain impairment (CBI); atrophy of the brain; tardive dyskinesia (TD) including tardive psychosis and persistent cognitive impairment; neuroleptic malignant syndrome (NMS); and metabolic syndrome including obesity, elevated cholesterol, elevated blood sugar, and potentially lethal diabetes.
- Patients on antipsychotic drugs should be regularly evaluated and physically examined for symptoms of TD. They should also be regularly evaluated for metabolic syndrome and other adverse effects. Their families or others in their support network should be educated about these adverse effects and asked to report any potential symptoms.
- If used to treat psychosis, antipsychotic drugs should be given for as short a time as possible. It is a mistake to assume that individuals require many months or years of antipsychotic medication following a psychotic episode.
- Individual and family therapy can be used to treat acute psychotic episodes without resort to medication. The prescriber who decides to medicate should also provide these therapeutic services or work closely with therapists who can provide them.

CHAPTER 5

Antidepressant Drugs: Reasons for Withdrawal

Although antidepressants are the most widely prescribed category of psychiatric drugs, there is scant evidence for their effectiveness and considerable evidence for their hazards. Especially when starting the medication or at times of dose changes up or down, serious mental and behavioral abnormalities can occur, including suicide, violence, and mania. With prolonged use, there is a grave risk of a general worsening of the patient's condition, which remains resistant to any intervention.

When a patient has been on antidepressants for many months or years, consideration should be given to the strong probability that they are causing more harm than good. Often, patients have tried to withdraw from the drugs, only to experience distressing withdrawal reactions, which they confuse with a mental disorder and the need for continued medication.

In the last few decades, the older antidepressants, such as amitriptyline (Elavil) and clomipramine (Anafranil), have largely been replaced by newer ones. The use of antidepressants continues to escalate in society. In 2010, antidepressants were the second most frequently prescribed medications in the United States, way behind the number one lipid regulators and just above the number three narcotic analgesics (IMS Health Incorporated, 2011b). Medco (2011) found that an astonishing 21% of women ages 20 and older were on antidepressants in 2010. This is consistent with another estimate that between 2005 and 2008, 22.8% of women aged 40–59 were taking these drugs (Pratt et al., 2011), and it suggests that an even higher number in this older age group are taking antidepressants now. Between 2001 and 2010, there was a 40% increase in usage among women 65 and older (Medco, 2011). The elderly are a population that is especially vulnerable to adverse drug effects and especially in need of human services, such as companionship and social activities.

The most widely used are the selective serotonin reuptake inhibitors (SSRIs) with sertraline (Zoloft) and citalopram (Celexa) leading the pack in 2010 (IMS Health Incorporated, 2011c). Other SSRIs include escitalopram (Lexapro), fluvoxamine (Luvox), paroxetine (Paxil), and fluoxetine (Prozac or Sarafem). When combined with a neuroleptic, such as fluoxetine and olanzapine (Symbyax), the adverse effects of both classes of drug must be taken into consideration. Other commonly used non-SSRI antidepressants include duloxetine (Cymbalta), venlafaxine (Effexor), desvenlafaxine (Pristiq), mirtazapine (Remeron), and bupropion (Wellbutrin and Zyban). A list of antidepressants can be found in the Appendix.

Antidepressants are sometimes given in combinations with each other. One review stated the problem in its title, "Antidepressant Combinations: Widely Used, but Far From Empirically Validated" (Thase, 2011). There are many reasons to reduce or withdraw antidepressant medications at almost any time during treatment, but especially during longer-term treatment.

CHRONIC BRAIN IMPAIRMENT

Apathy and Indifference

The third criteria for chronic brain impairment (CBI)—emotional instability or affective dysregulation, including worsening of apathy and depression—is very common and potentially disabling during antidepressant treatment. Shortly after Prozac became the best-selling drug in the world, I cited considerable evidence that the drug would worsen depression and cause severe behavioral abnormalities. I attributed much of the problem to "compensatory changes" in neurotransmitters as the brain resists the drug effect (Breggin & Breggin, 2004). Since then, in a series of books and articles, I've documented antidepressant-induced clinical worsening and some of its underlying physical causes (Breggin, 2008a). Now the idea has gained ground in the broader research community and has recently been named "tardive dysphoria" by El-Mallakh, Gao, & Jeannie Roberts (2011).

"I have noticed that I am devoid of emotions most of the time. One of my dearest friends is dying from metastatic breast cancer, and I am finding that I am not able to cry or experience any emotions about it. I know that I want to cry, but I can't. I want to be able to express my anger at the unfairness of what is happening to her, but all I feel is numbness. I would describe myself as a robot who is going through the motions, but I have no feelings." Quote from a patient (Sansone & Sansone, 2010).

It has been apparent for many years that chronic exposure to SSRI antidepressants frequently makes people feel apathetic or less engaged in their lives and ultimately more depressed. In my clinical experience, this is a frequent reason that family members encourage patients to seek help in reducing or stopping their medication. SSRI-induced apathy occurs in adults and includes cognitive and frontal lobe function losses (Barnhart, Makela, & Latocha, 2004; Deakin, Rahman, Nestor, Hodges, & Sahakian, 2004; Hoehn-Saric, Lipsey, & McLeod, 1990). It has also been identified in children (Reinblatt & Riddle, 2006). Adults with dementia are particularly susceptible to antidepressant-induced apathy (Wongpakaran, van Reekum, Wongpakara, & Clarke, 2007).

Antidepressant-Induced Clinical Worsening

The 2011 study by El-Mallakh and his colleagues reviewed the antidepressant literature and concluded that any initial improvements are often followed by treatment resistance and worsening depression. They compare this problem to tardive dyskinesia caused by antipsychotic drugs and call it tardive dysphoria, "an active process in which a depressive picture is caused by continued administration of the antidepressant." Based on rat studies, they hypothesize that "dendrite arborization" caused by chronic antidepressant exposure may be the cause.

In a meta-analysis of 46 studies, Andrews, Kornstein, Halberstadt, Gardner, & Neale (2011) found the relapse rate for antidepressant-treated patients (44.6%) was much higher than for placebo treated patients (24.7%). Andrews et al. also found that the more potent antidepressants caused an increased risk of relapse on drug discontinuation. A 2010 Minnesota evaluation of patient care in the state found that only 4.5% of more than 20,000 patients were in remission at 12 months, indicating that they had become chronically

Clinical Worsening and Suicide Risk: Patients, their families, and their caregivers should be encouraged to be alert to the emergence of anxiety, agitation, panic attacks, insomnia, irritability, hostility, aggressiveness, impulsivity, akathisia (psychomotor restlessness), hypomania, mania, other unusual changes in behavior, worsening of depression, and suicidal ideation, especially early during antidepressant treatment and when the dose is adjusted up or down. Families and caregivers of patients should be advised to look for the emergence of such symptoms on a day-to-day basis, since changes may be abrupt. Such symptoms should be reported to the patient's prescriber or health professional, especially if they are severe, abrupt in onset, or were not part of the patient's presenting symptoms. Symptoms such as these may be associated with an increased risk for suicidal thinking and behavior and indicate a need for very close monitoring and possibly changes in the medication. (*Physicians' Desk Reference*, 2011, p. 1496) afflicted with depression during and probably as a result of their treatment (Minnesota Community Measurement, 2010).

The Food and Drug Administration (FDA) mandated a WARNINGS section in all antidepressant labels, and as exemplified for Paxil (see box on p. 59). This information is repeated throughout the label.

The prescriber should heed the admonition contained in these warnings from the FDA-approved antidepressant labels: "Families and caregivers of patients should be advised to look for the emergence of such symptoms on a day-to-day basis, since changes may be abrupt."

Antidepressant-Induced Brain Dysfunction and Cellular Abnormalities

SSRI antidepressants block the removal of serotonin from the synapses between neurons, in effect trying to flood these synapses with serotonin. Many studies confirm that the brain attempts to compensate for the impact of the SSRIs by reducing the brain's capacity to respond to serotonin. This leads to a loss of serotonin receptors that can reach 60% (Wamsley et al., 1987). Blockade of serotonin reuptake also causes a potentially harmful adaptive response in the form of a persistent hypertrophy of the reuptake mechanism (Wegerer et al., 1999). Additional studies show persistent biochemical changes in the brain following exposure to SSRI antidepressants (de Montigny, Chaput, & Blier, 1990). Research continues to show that the impact of antidepressants on the serotonin system is complex, with poorly understood clinical implications (Zhao, Zhang, Bootzin, Millan, & O'Donnell, 2009).

In addition, direct toxic effects on the brain can account for the emotional deterioration of these patients. Prolonged SSRI antidepressant use can produce abnormal cell growth (neurogenesis; Malberg, Eisch, Nestler, & Duman, 2000) and decreased thalamic volumes in children (tissue shrinkage from cell death; Gilbert et al., 2000). Research on brain neurogenesis indicates that the older antidepressants can cause the growth of new astrocytes in the brain (Zhou, Huang, Kecejovic, Welsh, & Koliatsos, 2006).

In describing his recent studies on antidepressant-induced neurogenesis, researcher Jason Huang does not view this as an abnormality leading to caution about exposing the human brain to these drugs. Instead, in a report from the University of Rochester Medical Center (2011), he is cited as describing "neurogenesis" as enhancing brain function.

It is dangerous to suggest that abnormal cell growth caused by antidepressants is somehow good for the brain and therefore the person. In the University of Rochester report, Huang is said to recognize that "brain injury itself also seems to prompt the brain to create more brain cells, perhaps as a way to compensate for injury." Neurogenesis in response to psychiatric drugs is a result of drug-induced brain injury. Drug-induced changes in brain cell structure and number, when found as a result of taking illegal drugs, are always publicized as evidence of brain damage and a reason not to take these substances.

OVERSTIMULATION AND MANIA

Especially when starting an antidepressant, or changing the doses up or down, all of the antidepressants can produce a stimulant or activation syndrome (Breggin, 2003, 2005, 2006d, 2006e, 2008a, 2010; Breggin & Breggin, 1994; also see the FDA-approved label for any antidepressant). Although some antidepressants have a lesser capacity to do so (e.g., trazodone), all antidepressants have the potential to produce overstimulation and mania, as well as behavioral reactions such as violence and suicide. Drugs that specifically suppress the removal of serotonin from the synapse, including all the SSRIs and venlafaxine, have a particular capacity to produce these life-ruining and life-threatening reactions.

In the first few decades of my training and psychiatric practice, cases of mania were rare, and bipolar disorder was an unusual diagnosis. Now, most patients in a typical practice seem to be diagnosed bipolar. There are two reasons for this: (a) overdiagnosis of mania and bipolar disorder and (b) manic-like reactions to antidepressants and sometimes to stimulants.

With very rare exceptions, all of the children and teens that I have seen diagnosed with mania or bipolar disorder have either been improperly diagnosed, or their disorder was caused by an antidepressant or stimulant drug. In adults I have evaluated, most mania or bipolar disorder cases have resulted from exposure to antidepressants.

The literature confirms that rates for antidepressant-induced mania are very high, and the resultant disability and distress are considerable. Howland (1996) found that 6% of admissions to a university clinic and hospital were because of mania and psychosis caused by a variety of SSRI antidepressants. Morishita and Arita (2003) conducted a retrospective review of 79 unipolar depressed patients treated with paroxetine and found that seven (8.6%) developed mania. Ebert et al. (1997) followed 200 inpatients treated with the SSRI fluvoxamine (Luvox) and found that 17% became hypomanic and that 1.5% developed insomnia, agitation, confusion, and incoherent thoughts while becoming potentially violent. These are very high rates for a high-risk adverse event and should discourage the cavalier prescription of antidepressants to depressed individuals.

If an individual has a prior history of a tendency toward mania or bipolar disorder, then the rates of antidepressant-induced additional attacks of mania become astronomical. For example, Goldberg and

Truman (2003) found that one-quarter to one-third of patients diagnosed with bipolar disorder will develop mania in response to antidepressant treatment. Henry, Sorbara, Lacoste, Gindre, & Leboyer (2001) found manic switches in 24% of bipolar patients treated with antidepressants.

Ghaemi et al. (2010), after an elaborate attempt to demonstrate antidepressant efficacy in the long-term treatment of bipolar patients, basically concluded that the drugs were of little or no help.

> *Conclusions:* This first randomized discontinuation study with modern antidepressants showed no statistically significant symptomatic benefit with those agents in the long-term treatment of bipolar disorder along with neither robust depressive episode prevention benefit nor enhanced remission rates. Trends toward mild benefits, however, were found in subjects who continued antidepressants. This study also found, similar to studies of tricyclic antidepressants, that rapid-cycling patients had worsened outcomes with modern antidepressant continuation. (p. 372)

Based on Ghaemi et al. (2010) and the growing number of studies demonstrating both the risk of mania and the lack of efficacy of antidepressants in bipolar disorder patients, Sparhawk (2011) recently concluded, "Beyond 10 weeks, the antidepressants appear to do more harm than good" (p. 871).

Antidepressants should not be given to patients with a history of bipolar disorder and when possible, patients with a history of manic-like behavior should be withdrawn from these drugs.

ANTIDEPRESSANT-INDUCED SUICIDE

Starting in 2004–2005, the FDA has required all antidepressants to display a black box warning about the risk of suicidality in children, teenagers, and young adults up to age 24. This parsing of an adverse drug effect by age groups—in which one or another age group is not susceptible—is rare if not unheard of in the scientific literature. Based on short-term (weeks, not months) trials that were not tailored to detecting suicidality, it is remarkable that a statistically significant correlation could be found and even more remarkable that a doubling of the rate of suicidality was found (Hammad, Laughren, & Racoosin, 2006; Newman, 2004).

Because of the age-related FDA-mandated warnings in antidepressant drug labels and because of selling points used by drug company representatives, many prescribers and clinicians believe that the risk of antidepressant-induced suicidality risk literally stops at age 24. It is not unusual for children and youth to be more vulnerable to an adverse effect, as is probably true regarding antidepressant-induced suicidality.

But children and youth are simply more sensitive to these effects which occur at all ages.

The manufacturer of Paxil (GlaxoSmithKline, 2006) issued a Dear Healthcare Professional letter, in which it warned that adults who are depressed and exposed to the medication also have an increased risk of suicidality: "Further, in the analysis of adults with MDD (all ages), the frequency of suicidal behavior was higher in patients treated with paroxetine compared with placebo (11/3455 [0.32%] vs. 1/1978 [0.05%])."

Although the numbers cited in the letter are relatively small, the importance is great. Depressed patients of all ages suffering from major depressive disorder (MDD) have a more than six times increase in suicidality on Paxil compared to a sugar pill.

Other studies have confirmed that the antidepressant suicide risk occurs in all age groups. Regarding paroxetine (Paxil), for example, a review of all available controlled clinical trials (not merely those sent to the FDA) revealed an increased risk of suicide attempts in double-blind, placebo-controlled trials (Aursnes, Tvete, Gaasemyr, & Natvig, 2005). A study of 1,255 suicides in 2006 in Sweden (95% of all suicides in the country) reported that 32% of Scandinavian men and 52% of Scandinavian women filled a prescription for antidepressants in the 180 days prior to suicide (Ljung, Björkenstam, & Björkenstam, 2008). A retrospective study examined the suicide rates among 887,859 by the VA patients treated for depression and found that "completed suicide rates were approximately twice the base rate following antidepressant starts in VA clinical settings" (Valenstein et al., 2009). Juurlink, Mamdami, Kopp, & Redelmier (2006) reviewed more than 1,000 cases of actual suicides in the *elderly* and found that during the first month of treatment, the SSRI antidepressants were associated with nearly a five-fold higher risk compared to other antidepressants. These and other studies (reviewed in Breggin, 2010, and Breggin, 2008a, pp. 141–151) should dispel the myth that the risk of antidepressant-induced suicidality is arbitrarily limited to children, teens, and young adults.

ANTIDEPRESSANT-INDUCED VIOLENCE

Compared to antidepressant-induced suicide, antidepressant-induced violence is probably relatively uncommon. However, a recent review of all adverse drug reactions reported to the FDA for a large number of psychiatric drugs found a definite pattern of increased reports for certain types of drugs (Moore, Glenmullen, & Furberg, 2011). The study authors identified all drugs with 200 or more severe adverse events reports from 2004 to September 2009. Then, they collected violence-related reports, identified as "any case report indicating homicide, homicidal ideation, physical assault, physical abuse, or violence related symptoms." They then located drugs with disproportional patterns of reporting these adverse events.

They summarized their results:

We identified 1,527 cases of violence disproportionally reported for 31 drugs. Primary suspect drugs included varenicline (an aid to smoking cessation), 11 antidepressants, six sedative/hypnotics, and three drugs for attention deficit hyperactivity disorder. The evidence of an association was weaker and mixed for antipsychotic drugs and absent for all but one anticonvulsant/mood stabilizer. Two or fewer violence cases were reported for 435/484 (84.7%) of all evaluable drugs suggesting that an association with this adverse event is unlikely for these drugs. (p. 1)

In their conclusion, they stated:

Acts of violence toward others are a genuine and serious adverse drug event associated with a relatively small group of drugs. Varenicline (Chantix), which increases the availability of dopamine and antidepressants with serotonergic effects were the most strongly and consistently implicated drugs. (p. 1)

Another recent study has found a strong relationship between SSRI exposure and violence, especially in patients with lacking or compromised liver enzymes (cytochrome P450 [CYP450] genotypes). These enzymes are required for metabolizing these drugs, and thereby reducing their concentration in the blood (Lucire & Crotty, 2011). When they are diminished or missing, drug toxicity and overdose is more likely to occur.

Using very strict clinical criteria, including no past history of violence, lack of sufficient provocation or motivation, and a recent change in antidepressant dose, I have evaluated many cases of antidepressant-induced violence (Breggin, 2008b).

Hypomania and mania are commonly associated with violence.

The *Diagnostic and Statistical Manual of Mental Disorders* (4th ed., text rev.; *DSM-IV-TR*) noted that "akathisia may be associated with dysphoria, irritability, aggression, or suicide attempts" as well as "worsening of psychotic symptoms or behavioral dyscontrol. . ." (American Psychiatric Association [APA], 2000, p. 801). It also observed that SSRI antidepressants can "produce akathisia

Based on my testimony and report, a Canadian judge in September 2011 found that a 16-year-old knifed a friend to death as a result of Prozac-induced adverse effects (Heinrichs, 2011; McIntyre, 2011). Although judges have found sufficient scientific evidence for antidepressant-induced violence and murder to allow me and other experts to take this position in criminal, malpractice, and product liability suits, this is the first time in North America that a judge has actually determined for himself that Prozac induced a murder.

that appears to be identical in phenomenology and treatment response to neuroleptic-induced acute akathisia (APA, 2000, p. 801).

Prescribers, clinicians, patients, and their families need to be especially aware of lesser degrees of hypomania, irritability, hostility, and aggressiveness that are very common and can disrupt and even ruin an individual's participation in the workplace and home. The new FDA class label for antidepressants repeatedly describes an activation syndrome that includes a virtual prescription for irritability, aggression, and violence. For example, the WARNING section of the label for "PAXIL" (2011) states:

> The following symptoms, anxiety, agitation, panic attacks, insomnia, irritability, hostility, aggressiveness, impulsivity, akathisia (psychomotor restlessness), hypomania, and mania have been reported in adult and pediatric patients being treated with antidepressants for major depressive disorder as well as for other indications, both psychiatric and nonpsychiatric. (p. 12)

The FDA-mandated medication guide for Paxil and other antidepressants, which as of the summer of 2007 applies to children and adults, further warns patients and their families to be aware of the following newly developed reactions during treatment ("PAXIL," 2011, p. 43):

- attempts to commit suicide
- acting on dangerous impulses
- acting aggressive or violent
- thoughts about suicide or dying
- new or worse depression
- new or worse anxiety or panic attacks
- feeling agitated, restless, angry, or irritable
- trouble sleeping
- an increase in activity or talking more than what is normal for you
- other unusual changes in behavior or mood

These symptoms are the result of overstimulation or activation of the central nervous system (CNS) and indicate a need to reduce or stop antidepressant medication.

HEART DISEASE RISK FROM OLDER ANTIDEPRESSANTS

It has been known for decades that the older antidepressants can cause arrhythmias and impair heart function. Once again, it has taken decades for research to catch up with the clinical observations. An 8-year prospective study of nearly 15,000 people in Scotland has shown that the older antidepressants, such as imipramine (Tofranil) and amitriptyline (Elavil), are linked to a 35% increase in the risk of cardiovascular disease (Hamer, David Batty, Seldenrijk, & Kivimaki, 2011).

SEROTONIN SYNDROME

Serotonin syndrome is a well-documented and potentially lethal complex of symptoms that can be induced by any drug that blocks the reuptake of serotonin. It consists of varied signs of CNS overstimulation, including hyperactive reflexes and muscle spasms; fever; gastrointestinal upset, including diarrhea; and impaired mental function, including mania and delirium. The disorder closely resembles neuroleptic malignant syndrome (see Chapter 4) but with greater signs of overstimulation.

Serotonin syndrome is usually described as having an acute onset, but I have seen cases with gradual onset and muted symptoms without fever. Clinicians need to be aware of the possibility that patients taking serotonergic drugs may develop signs of CNS overstimulation without a grossly apparent serotonin syndrome. In one case, a 40-year-old woman with several years of exposure to venlafaxine gradually developed severe neurological signs of overstimulation, including marked emotional instability, muscle cramping, dystonia, and very exaggerated reflexes and clonus. She was hospitalized for rapid withdrawal of the venlafaxine, with some immediate relief. Over several months, she continued to show improvement with lingering abnormal reflexes.

SEXUAL DYSFUNCTION

Antidepressant-induced sexual dysfunction in men and women was originally minimized by the FDA and the pharmaceutical industry, but it is now recognized that many, if not most, male and female patients will suffer from loss of sexual functioning. Most obviously, individuals become impotent or lose the ability to become aroused and to find enjoyment. Although it is seldom discussed, I believe the impact is not only on the physical aspect of sexual function but also on desire—caring or interest in the partner. In recent years, clinicians have sounded an alarm that many patients may not recover their normal sexual function (Bahrick & Harris, 2008; Csoska & Shipko, 2006; Shipko, 2002). Psychiatrist Stuart Shipko confirmed that "All too often the issue of sexual dysfunction is not taken into consideration when a couple is in therapy together. That is, one or both of the clients may be referred for psychiatric medication without consideration that the drug may well alter the dynamics of the relationship through alteration of sexuality" (personal communication, 2011). This potentially tragic consequence of permanent loss of sexual functioning could have been anticipated and is one more reason to be cautious about starting antidepressants and to avoid their long-term use.

OBESITY

The SSRI antidepressants were heralded as drugs that would help women lose weight, but clinicians and patients alike have found that prolonged exposure can lead to pathological obesity, which then persists even after the drugs have been discontinued. Recent animal research has confirmed the problem. The authors conclude, "Antidepressant exposure may therefore be a covert, insidious, and enduring risk factor for obesity even after discontinuation of antidepressant treatment" (Mastronardi et al., 2011, p. 265).

PREGNANCY AND NURSING

Antidepressants, much as all other psychiatric drugs, pose risks to the fetus, newborn, and nursing infant (Gentile, 2000). The newborn can go through withdrawal. One case report described withdrawal at birth consisting of "irritability, increased tonus, jitteriness, and eating difficulties" that lasted 6 weeks (Alehan, Saygi, Tarcan, & Gurakan, 2008). Another described an infant whose mother had used fluoxetine 40 mg for 4 years (Kwon & Lefkowitz, 2008b). Approximately 12 hours after the delivery, the child's serum fluoxetine level was "within the adult therapeutic range," and the child was suffering from an array of withdrawal symptoms, including severe tremors, markedly hyperactive Moro reflex, increased muscle tone, a respiratory rate more than 60, and excessive sucking. Jitteriness was the most prominent of his symptoms, all of which disappeared by 2 weeks. Another case study by the same authors described a neonatal withdrawal syndrome from citalopram that included extrapyramidal movements (Kwon & Lefkowitz, 2008a). Citalopram and its metabolites are known to cross the placenta with infant concentration levels as high as 64% of maternal serum levels (Lattimore et al., 2005).

In 2010, Lattimore wrote a detailed review of the literature concerning PAES—prenatal antidepressant exposure syndrome. PAES includes a broad array of neurological symptoms, including jitteriness, lethargy, abnormal movements and seizures, as well as gastrointestinal problems with low birth weight, metabolic problems with low Apgar scores, respiratory problems, cardiac symptoms, and body temperature instability.

In 2011, another study found a two-fold increase in the rate of autism in the offspring of mothers exposed to SSRIs during pregnancy (Croen, Grether, Yoshida, Odouli, & Hendrick, 2011). The strongest effect was associated with first trimester exposure. There was no increased risk for mothers with a history of mental health treatment in the absence of prenatal SSRI exposure. In addition to direct effects on the fetus, I suspect that the apathy induced by these drugs in some of the mothers after the delivery of their children may have impaired their bonding with their children and contributed to causing autism.

Women should be withdrawn from antidepressants if they are likely to become pregnant, are pregnant, or are nursing.

THE ELDERLY

The elderly are more susceptible to adverse drug reactions that affect the brain and mind. There is increasing awareness that giving these drugs to the elderly is not a benign process. Sherrod, Collins, Wynn, & Gragg (2010) offer a nursing perspective with two boxed warnings that are worth reproducing (shown at right).

> The complexities of SSRI pharmacotherapy with older adults are numerous and include serotonin syndrome and serotonin discontinuation syndrome. (p. 20)

Prescribers and clinicians should be cautious about starting the elderly on antidepressants, and the elderly should be carefully withdrawn from them whenever

> Increased use of SSRIs has led to a great likelihood of adverse reactions. These adverse responses are potentially life altering for old patients, who have decreased physiologic reserves. (p. 41)

possible. The next section examines an increased death rate in the elderly, as well as younger adults, taking antidepressants.

Increased Death Rate

A recent Swedish study of men and women aged 24–30 years taking antidepressants found an increased rate of mortality in this group (Sundell, 2011). The rate was further increased when combined with other medications, including antipsychotic drugs.

Another recent study from Great Britain involving 60,746 patients aged 65–100 years diagnosed with first episode depression from January 1996 to December 31, 2007 found that 89% had been given antidepressants (54.7% SSRIs; 31.6% tricyclics; 0.2% for monoamine oxidase inhibitors; and 13.5% for other antidepressants, including trazodone, mirtazapine and venlafaxine; Coupland et al., 2011). The four drug classes were compared for "all cause mortality." The 1-year rates for all-cause mortality were lowest for patients not taking antidepressants (7.94%). The older tricyclics had the next lowest rate (8.12%), followed by SSRIs (10.61%), and other antidepressants (11.43%). Two important conclusions were drawn from the data: (1) antidepressants shorten the lifespan in patients older than 65 years, and (2) none of the newer antidepressants (SSRIs or non-SSRIs) showed a reduced risk in any risk category (e.g., suicide, falls, accidents, stroke, myocardial infarction) compared to the older tricyclics.

These two studies confirm that, like the neuroleptics, the antidepressants shorten the life span. These studies continue to undermine the commonly held belief that the SSRIs and other new antidepressants are safer than the older tricyclics (Smith, 2011).

CHILDREN

In 2004–2005, an FDA-mandated reexamination of antidepressant placebo-controlled clinical trials for children confirmed a greatly increased rate of suicidality, resulting in a black box warning about suicidality in children and youth (Hammad et al., 2006). The warning was later extended to young adults. These suicidality studies confirmed that children and youth are even more susceptible than adults to antidepressant-induced psychiatric adverse drug reactions.

This scientific literature since the early 1990s has indicated that the newer antidepressants have a devastating impact on the mental life and behavior of children (reviewed in Breggin, 2008a, pp. 165–172). A study of youngsters aged 8–16 years found that 50% developed two or more abnormal behavioral reactions to fluoxetine, including aggression, loss of impulse control, agitation, and manic-like symptoms (Riddle et al., 1991). The effects lasted until the drug was stopped. Another study found that six out of 42 children became aggressive or violent while taking fluoxetine (King et al., 1991). A controlled clinical trial found that fluoxetine caused a 6% rate of mania in depressed children and youngsters aged 7–17 years (Emslie et al., 2002).

Wilens et al. (2003) evaluated 82 charts of children, mean age 12.2 years, treated with SSRIs for depression or obsessive-compulsive disorder (OCD) over 26.9 months. The drugs included sertraline, paroxetine, fluoxetine, fluvoxamine, and citalopram. Psychiatric adverse events were found in 22%, "most commonly related to disturbances in mood." The onset was typically within 3 months and, remarkably, reexposure to an SSRI resulted in another psychiatric adverse event in 44% of the children. This made an especially strong case for causation.

Of the 82 children, 21% developed *mood disorders*, including 15% who became *irritable*, 10% who became *anxious*, 9% who became *depressed*, and 6% who became *manic*. In addition, 4% of the children became *aggressive. Sleep* disorders afflicted 35% of the children, including 23% feeling *drowsy*, and 17% experiencing *insomnia*. Incredibly, 10% became *psychotic*.

As noted earlier in the chapter, children, like adults, are also found to suffer apathy from SSRIs (Reinblatt & Riddle, 2006). They also experience withdrawal symptoms.

There is very little research support for giving antidepressants to children and an enormous amount of research indicating a high risk of severe adverse drug reactions, including suicidal and aggressive behavior and overstimulation with mania and psychosis.

Hosenbocus and Chahal (2011) were putting it mildly when they concluded, "In considering the use of an SSRI in children, physicians must seriously weigh the not so clear benefits against the risks of adverse reactions, including the discontinuation syndrome" (p. 60). Children should be withdrawn from psychiatric medications whenever possible. In a routine pediatric or psychiatric practice, most can easily be withdrawn (see Chapter 18).

EFFICACY

To demonstrate efficacy for FDA purposes, drug companies are permitted to cherry pick two studies from innumerable others. In the case of fluoxetine, the company could find only two very marginal studies demonstrating efficacy, whereas several did not. Meta-analyses of all antidepressant controlled clinical trials conducted for FDA approval fail to show efficacy compared to placebo (Kirsch, Moore, Scoboria, & Nicholls, 2002) or show only marginal efficacy for the most depressed group (Kirsch et al., 2008). This negative result occurs despite the best efforts of the drug companies to choose friendly principal investigators and to plan, monitor, and evaluate their studies with an eye to proving efficacy. In a new book, Irving Kirsch reviews the studies on antidepressant effectiveness and concludes that psychotherapy works best, especially in long-term follow-up while avoiding the potentially devastating adverse effects of the drugs (Kirsch, 2010).

The largest antidepressant study ever conducted, the Sequenced Treatment Alternatives to Relieve Depression (STAR*D), made claims to demonstrate some effectiveness for antidepressants. In reality, despite the built-in biases and the reporting biases, only 2.7% of patients (108 of 4,041) had an initial remission that lasted or could be followed up for 12 months (Pigott, 2011; also, Pigott, Leventhal, Alter, & Boren, 2011). For every class of psychiatric drugs, long-term studies (a few months or more) have continued to show no proof of effectiveness.

Another new study has shown that patients using antidepressants are more likely to relapse than those who use no medication (Andrews et al., 2011). Researcher Paul Andrews commented (Science Daily, 2011b):

We found that the more these drugs affect serotonin and other neurotransmitters in your brain—and that's what they're supposed to do—the greater your risk of relapse once you stop taking them. All these drugs do reduce symptoms, probably to some degree, in the short-term. The trick is what happens in the long term. Our results suggest that when you try to go off the drugs, depression will bounce back. This can leave people stuck in a cycle where they need to keep taking antidepressants to prevent a return of symptoms. (p. 1)

Andrews also suggested that depression may not be a "disorder" at all, but rather an adaptation that helps the individual cope with the traumatic events.

Many different therapeutic approaches can help people diagnosed with MDD from the passage of time to placebo. Remarkably, a study conducted by researchers with profound ties to the pharmaceutical industry nonetheless concluded, "Our findings suggest that the studied CAM [Complementary and Alternative Medicines] therapies may have similar efficacy and better tolerability than standard antidepressants" (Freeman et al., 2010, p. 687). They reviewed all available randomized placebo controlled trials for three alternatives: St. John's wort, omega-3 fatty acids, and S-Adenosyl-L-Methionine (SAMe). Patients more frequently stopped the antidepressant trials because of adverse drug effects.

A number of studies have also shown that exercise works well (e.g., Blumenthal et al., 2007).

Because depression is primarily a feeling of helplessness, hopelessness, and despair, any therapy that offers empowerment and hope is likely to work. Depressed patients need help in finding renewed strength and courage to engage in life.

Many studies indicate that counseling and psychotherapy based on varied approaches can be helpful. In my clinical experience, depression in children and adults can be especially well treated by couples or family therapy (Breggin, 1997b; also see Keitner, 2005). This includes psychotic levels of depression (Karon, 2005).

Depression in children is usually related to problems in the family and, even if the problem lies outside the family, the parents are in the best position to help the child overcome depression. Depression in adults may have many causes, past and present, including current family conflict. Regardless of the cause, therapy that involves family or significant others is often the most powerful source of healing (Breggin, 1997b; also see Keitner, 2005). For the patient undergoing antidepressant withdrawal, family therapy is likely to help with both the withdrawal process and any underlying depression.

Antidepressant medications should not be so freely dispensed and when prescribed, should be given for a very short period, preferably a month or two.

KEY POINTS

▪ Especially at times of starting the drugs, or at times of dose changes up or down, antidepressants can cause a wide spectrum of mental and behavioral abnormalities, many of them typical of a stimulant or activation reaction, including insomnia, anxiety, agitation, impulsivity, aggression and violence, depression and suicidality, and mania.

- When used for months or years, antidepressants frequently cause apathy and dysphoria, worsening the patient's overall condition and quality of life.
- Patients often stay on antidepressants because they confuse distressing withdrawal reactions with a mental illness, and therefore mistakenly believe that they need to continue the drug.
- Because evidence for their efficacy is not nearly as strong as evidence for their harmful effects in both the short-term and the long-term, antidepressants should be used much less frequently and rarely if ever for many months or years at a time.
- Children are especially vulnerable to adverse emotional and behavioral reactions to antidepressants, including very substantial rates of suicidality, aggression, and mania. Evidence for efficacy in children is very slim.
- Children and adults should be withdrawn as quickly as feasible from antidepressants and long-term treatment should be avoided.

CHAPTER 6

Stimulant Drugs: Reasons for Withdrawal

In the last 4 decades there has been an escalating prescription of stimulant drugs to children, youth, and young adults for the treatment of attention deficit hyperactivity disorder (ADHD). Yet, ADHD is not a valid medical syndrome but instead reflects a broad spectrum of possibilities from variations in normal child behavior to behavior caused by boring or undisciplined classrooms; inadequate educational preparation for the class level; poor disciplinary practices in the home; anxiety and depression caused by losses, conflicts, and other problems in the child's life; and genuine underlying physical problems, such as poor nutrition, head injury, or diabetes.

The diagnosis of ADHD leads the clinician and family to neglect the real issues in the child's life while the stimulant drugs temporarily suppress the targeted behaviors by suppressing the child's overall spontaneity and by inducing obsessive-compulsive behavior, including overfocusing.

Stimulants are subject to abuse and addiction, lead to increased cocaine abuse in young adulthood, suppress growth, threaten cardiovascular functions, discourage the child's sense of independence and personal mastery, and frequently cause depression, insomnia, and other mental and behavioral adverse effects. There are always better therapeutic and educational alternatives to diagnosing and drugging children with ADHD-like symptoms.

The attention deficit hyperactive disorder (ADHD) diagnosis has continued to grow in use with 12.3% of boys and 5.5% of girls aged 5–17 years diagnosed with the disorder in 2009, according to the Centers for Disease Control (CDC; Akinbami, Liu, Pastor, & Reuben, 2011; Wolfe, 2011). Because the rates are growing fastest in the older age groups, we are looking a rate considerably in excess of 12.3% for older boys diagnosed with ADHD. An estimated 2.8 million children were taking stimulants for ADHD in 2008 (Sinclair, 2011). However, increasing numbers of children are being put on potentially more toxic adult antipsychotic drugs, selective serotonin reuptake inhibitors (SSRIs) and mood stabilizers, usually on the grounds of treating "childhood bipolar disorder." It seems probable that nearly 20% of older boys in America are on psychiatric drugs.

During the same time period, psychiatric admissions for children nearly doubled (Zoler, 2011). From 1996 to 2007, admissions to psychiatric facilities for adolescents aged 14–19 years went up to 42%, whereas they rose only 8% for adults aged 24–60 years and dropped dramatically for the elderly. Given the inevitably vast increase in adverse drug effects among medicated children and the known connection between psychiatric admissions and adverse drug effects, the increased rate of hospitalization is almost certainly because of the increased psychiatric medicating of children.

Recently, the American Academy of Pediatrics, with no new scientific basis, issued guidelines that overrode FDA guidelines and recommended that children as young as 4 years could be diagnosed with ADHD and treated with methylphenidate (Ritalin; American Academy of Pediatrics, 2011; Subcommittee on Attention-Deficit/Hyperactivity Disorder, 2011). This will almost surely have the intended effect with increased numbers of younger children psychiatrically diagnosed and medicated.

Meanwhile, stimulant drugs were the entering wedge into the widespread drugging of America's children. Once the door was opened, nearly all the other psychiatric drugs came rushing in. Now, they will further spread to the youngest children.

THE MYTH OF ATTENTION DEFICIT HYPERACTIVE DISORDER

A great deal has been written about ADHD, and how it does not constitute a valid diagnostic category and fails to meet the criteria for a medical syndrome (Baughman & Hovey, 2006; Breggin, 2008a; Whitely, 2011). Divided into three categories of behaviors—hyperactivity, impulsivity, and inattention—the ADHD diagnosis is nothing more or less than a collection of behaviors that cause problems for teachers and require their increased attention in the classroom. They do not reflect an underlying syndrome or single cause. There are no criteria that relate to the child's mental status, mood, or feelings—it's exclusively about observed behaviors. At times, these behaviors are part of the normal childhood continuum, and other times, they are exaggerated by boring and poorly disciplined classrooms, inadequate teaching, lack of age-level educational skills, anxiety or depression generated from problems and conflicts at home or in school, abuse or neglect, hunger or poor nutrition, insomnia and fatigue, and a variety of chronic illnesses, including diabetes and head injury (e.g., sports concussions).

In short, the diagnosis has no validity in terms of representing an underlying disorder or meaningful syndrome. It is actually a list of behaviors with infinite potential causes from undisciplined classrooms and homes to physical illness to normal variation.

When behaviors seem out of control, undisciplined, impulsive, hyperactive, or inattentive, the child or teen needs a basic medical evaluation and a thorough psychosocial and educational evaluation to get at the root causes. In my practice, the causes usually turn out to be either an educational misfit or inadequate discipline at home or both. Commonly, the "behaviors" have been worsened by psychiatric drugs and/or nonprescription "recreational" drugs. Except in the case of drug abuse or prolonged exposure to psychiatric drugs, the problems are relatively easily resolved by school interventions and/or family counseling on how to provide the child the necessary mixture of unconditional love and firm, consistent discipline (Breggin, 2000b, 2001c, 2002b).

Prescribers who deal with children who could potentially be diagnosed with ADHD and treated with stimulants should instead refer the child and his or her family to a therapist who can assess and meet the child's real needs in the family and at school (see ahead, Chapter 18).

THE CLASS OF STIMULANT DRUGS

Adderall and Adderall XR are pure amphetamine and among the most commonly prescribed medications to children and adults diagnosed with ADHD. Several years ago, the Food and Drug Administration (FDA) required considerable updating of the official labels for these drugs, including a black box warning about addiction and heart attack, plus additional information in the label about addiction and abnormal behavior reactions including aggression, psychosis, and mania. Perhaps because the current label would discourage clinicians, patients, and families from using the drug, the label has become very difficult to find, virtually scrubbed from the Internet. The manufacturer, Shire, has removed all Adderall products from the *Physicians' Desk Reference (PDR)* starting in 2010, and the 2009 edition of the *PDR* carries an older 2007 label. It is also difficult to find anywhere on the Internet, although the FDA's website as of October 2011, carried an undated copy of the 2010 label. On October 11, 2011, I obtained the 2010 label at two pharmacies when I specifically requested it as a physician. The pharmacists pealed it from the boxes they receive from the manufacturer. It is dated November 2011; I have made this label available on the Internet ("Adderall XR," 2010). Because it is difficult for clinicians to locate, I will quote substantially from it in the following sections. Everything that I quote is backed up by considerable scientific information (Breggin, 2008a). For most purposes, there is little or no difference between the effects of amphetamine products, such as Dexedrine, Adderall and Adderall XR, and methylphenidate products, such as Ritalin, Metadate, and Focalin.

THE "NON-STIMULANT" STIMULANT

Atomoxetine (Strattera) has been advertised by manufacturer Eli Lilly & Company as a "nonstimulant" treatment for ADHD, but in fact is a highly stimulating drug. Henderson and Hartman (2004) examined data from 153 sequential patients at two clinics: "We have observed extreme irritability, aggression, mania, or hypomania induction in 51 cases (33%)." Much as any stimulant, it can cause seizures in overdose. However, unlike the classic stimulants, the Drug Enforcement Administration (DEA) has not categorized it as addictive. Originally tested as an antidepressant, atomoxetine carries a black box warning about suicidality, as well as additional concerns about suicide in the WARNINGS AND PRECAUTIONS section ("Strattera," 2011).

The Strattera drug label also warns (section 5.5):

Emergence of New Psychotic or Manic Symptoms
Treatment emergent psychotic or manic symptoms, e.g., hallucinations, delusional thinking, or mania in children and adolescents without a prior history of psychotic illness or mania can be caused by atomoxetine at usual doses.

The label also warns about the emergence or worsening of hostility and aggression. The problem was serious enough to surface in short-term clinical trials.

Strattera is not a "safe alternative" to classic stimulants.

ANTIHYPERTENSIVE DRUGS

Drugs that lower blood pressure are frequently sedating, and any sedating drug is likely to be used in psychiatry for various purposes. Intuniv is a long-acting (extended–release) form of the antihypertensive drug guanfacine and has been approved for the treatment of ADHD. Tenex is the regular preparation of the same drug and has not been approved for any psychiatric purpose. Guanfacine reduces sympathetic nerve impulses to the heart and blood vessels, reducing heart rate and blood pressure. Given to physically normal children, this risks an abnormally slow heart rate, other cardiac abnormalities including heart block, and abnormally low blood pressure. Fainting or more serious cardiac problems can develop. When given in combination with other drugs that impair heart function, including stimulants, antidepressants, and antipsychotic drugs, the risks will increase.

If guanfacine is withdrawn too quickly, there is a risk of a spike in blood pressure. The manufacturer of Intuniv recommends a reduction of 1 mg every 3-7 days.

Catapres (clonidine) is another antihypertensive drug frequently given to children for its sedative properties, but is not approved for any psychiatric use. It too poses cardiac risks and in combination with stimulants can cause fatal cardiac arrest. It too should be tapered before stopping in order to avoid spikes in blood pressure.

The long-term cardiovascular risks from exposing children to these antihypertensive drugs have not been adequately studied, but common sense would suggest grave caution in prescribing them to children.

DEPENDENCE (ADDICTION) AND ABUSE

The drugs most commonly used to treat children diagnosed with ADHD belong to the DEA's Schedule II, which is the highest level of risk of addiction and abuse. The list includes amphetamines and methylphenidate (see Appendix for complete list). Although in pharmacology texts these drugs are usually treated as basically the same, their FDA labels differ depending on the time the drugs were approved. Ritalin, approved in the 1950s, has a much weaker label regarding warnings than the more recently approved Adderall XR.

> **WARNING: POTENTIAL FOR ABUSE**
> Amphetamines have a high potential for abuse. Administration of amphetamines for prolonged periods of time may lead to drug dependence. Pay particular attention to the possibility of subjects obtaining amphetamines for nontherapeutic use or distribution to others, and the drugs should be prescribed or dispensed sparingly [see DRUG ABUSE AND DEPENDENCE (9)]. Misuse of amphetamines may cause sudden death and serious cardiovascular adverse reactions. (From the FDA-approved label for Adderall.)

The black box warning at the top of the Adderall XR label should apply to all the stimulants used in psychiatry, including methylphenidate, but it is the strongest in the amphetamine labels (see "Adderall XR," 2010).

Further on in the label, the risks of addiction are reemphasized (Label section 9.2):

DRUG ABUSE AND DEPENDENCE
Adderall XR® is a Schedule II controlled substance.

Amphetamines have been extensively abused. Tolerance, extreme psychological dependence, and severe social disability have occurred. There are reports of patients who have increased the dosage to levels many times higher than recommended. Abrupt cessation following prolonged high dosage administration results in extreme fatigue and mental depression; changes are also noted on the sleep EEG. Manifestations of chronic intoxication with amphetamines may include severe dermatoses, marked insomnia, irritability, hyperactivity, and personality changes. The most severe manifestation of chronic intoxication is psychosis, often clinically indistinguishable from schizophrenia.

Nadine Lambert (2005) conducted a 28-year prospective study of children diagnosed with ADHD comparing those who received methylphenidate and those who received no drug treatment, and she found that the children exposed to methylphenidate were much more likely to abuse cocaine in young adulthood. This should be no surprise because methylphenidate, amphetamine, methamphetamine, and cocaine have very similar effects on the brain and body, except that cocaine is shorter acting with more initial punch, making it even more dangerous than the others. Animals and addicts alike will cross-addict to all of these substances (Breggin, 2008a).

CHRONIC BRAIN IMPAIRMENT (CBI)

The highly addictive nature of these drugs not only speaks to the risks of dependence and abuse; their addictive potential also indicates that these drugs significantly disrupt normal brain function, producing long-lasting biochemical changes (reviewed and documented in detail in Breggin, 2008a; also see Breggin, 1999a, 1999b, 1999c, 2001a, 2002b).

For several decades, studies have shown that children diagnosed with ADHD and treated with stimulants suffer from atrophy of the brain. At the National Institutes of Health (NIH) Consensus Development Conference on ADHD, Swanson (Swanson & Castellanos, 1998) reviewed the available studies purporting to show biological bases of ADHD, including brain atrophy (e.g., Castellanos et al., 1998; Giedd et al., 1994).

My own presentation at the same conference concluded that the findings of atrophy in children diagnosed with ADHD and treated with stimulants "are almost certainly measuring pathology caused by psychostimulants (Breggin, 1998a, p. 109; for a more extensive review see Breggin, 1999b, 1999c). Further confirmation came in the unpublished public discussion following Swanson's presentation, when neurologist Frederick Baughman, Jr., asked Swanson if *any* of the studies in his review involved children without a history of drug treatment. Swanson could not name a single study based on untreated patients and offered the disingenuous explanation that untreated children diagnosed with ADHD are difficult to obtain in the United States.

A recent 33-year follow-up of children originally diagnosed with ADHD continues the trend of blaming drug-induced atrophy of the brain on ADHD rather than on extensive exposure to psychiatric medication. Proal et al. (2011) found widespread atrophy in the brain, including a reduction in mean global cortical thickness in grown adults (mean age 41).

The authors relate the finding of brain shrinkage to childhood ADHD, but in fact the grown adults had polydrug exposure to psychiatric drugs starting in childhood and continuing in adulthood when most of them were given additional psychiatric diagnoses and, no doubt, additional psychiatric drugs. They also had a lower IQ than the control group and their death rate far exceeded that of the control group (7.2% vs. 2.8%, Table 1, p. 1123, for this and the following data). The ADHD group also had a much higher rate of incarceration (2.9% vs. 0.16%). Many more were also extremely obese as indicated by the higher rate of being too large for the scanner (8.2% vs. 3.4%). Their obesity is consistent with antipsychotic drug exposure. This study confirms findings from others involving every category of psychiatric drug that long-term psychiatric drug exposure leads to atrophy of the brain and other serious hazards, including in some cases, higher mortality. Because there was no difference in lifetime substance abuse and dependence (p. 1124), the real causal factor—unexamined by the authors—is polydrug exposure to psychiatric medications over a lifetime starting in childhood, with stimulant drugs continuing into adulthood with other psychiatric drugs.

It should come as no surprise that stimulant drugs cause brain damage. Numerous studies of stimulants in animals indicate that stimulant drugs are neurotoxic, causing long-lasting changes in neurotransmitter systems (see Breggin, 2008a, pp. 307–317). For example, Carlezon and Konradi (2004) from Harvard's Department of Psychiatry summarized their own research:

> When we exposed rats to the prescription stimulant methylphenidate during early adolescence, we discovered long-lasting behavioral and molecular alterations that were consistent with dramatic changes in the function of the brain reward systems.

GROWTH SUPPRESSION, INCLUDING LOSS OF HEIGHT AND WEIGHT

A massive federally organized and funded multicenter study was supposed to prove the safety and efficacy of these drugs for once and for all time but was only able to prove one more time that the drugs do in fact significantly suppress growth (Swanson et al., 2007a, 2007b). Compared to the unmedicated group, the children on methylphenidate (Ritalin) showed a 2 cm (0.8 inch) loss in height and a 2.7 kg (5.9 lb) loss in weight in less than 2 years.

Wholly unnoticed, however, is the ominous reality that these stimulant-induced losses in growth are caused by a disruption in growth hormone (Aarskog, Fevang, Klove, Stoa, & Thorsen, 1977) that could also adversely affect other organs of the body, including the brain (see Breggin, 1991). Unfortunately, some stimulant drug advocates continue to claim that the growth suppression is caused by loss of appetite, rather than by a more ominous disruption of the growth hormone cycle and to argue that in reality there is no long-term growth suppression (Pittman, 2010).

Finally and fortunately, after at least 5 decades of largely avoiding the issue, the FDA mandated that the Multimodal Treatment of Attention Deficit Hyperactive Disorder (MTA) Study growth suppression data be included in the labels for stimulants (e.g., "Metadate CD," 2011, p. 3267; Metadate CD contains methylphenidate in a long-acting preparation.). Nonetheless, the all-important FDA-mandated stimulant medication guide for parents does not include anything about growth suppression in the black box that provides "the most important information" (e.g., "Metadate CD," 2011, p. 3263).

BEHAVIORAL ABNORMALITIES

Under Warnings and Precautions, the upgraded label for "Adderall XR" (2010) carries strong warnings about drug-induced severe psychiatric abnormalities (label section 5.2):

> **Psychiatric Adverse Events**
> *Preexisting Psychosis*
> Administration of stimulants may exacerbate symptoms of behavior disturbance and thought disorder in patients with preexisting psychotic disorder.
>
> *Bipolar Illness*
> Particular care should be taken in using stimulants to treat ADHD patients with comorbid bipolar disorder because of concern for possible induction of mixed/manic episode in such patients. Prior to initiating treatment with a stimulant, patients with comorbid depressive symptoms should be adequately screened to determine if they are at risk for bipolar disorder; such screening should include a detailed psychiatric history, including a family history of suicide, bipolar disorder, and depression.
>
> *Emergence of New Psychotic or Manic Symptoms*
> Treatment-emergent psychotic or manic symptoms, e.g., hallucinations, delusional thinking, or mania in children and adolescents without prior history of psychotic illness or mania can be caused by stimulants at usual doses. If such symptoms occur, consideration should be given to a possible causal role of the stimulant, and discontinuation of treatment may be appropriate.[1]

---

[1] Based on drug company data, the label estimates that these symptoms occur only 0.1% of patients. Actual studies show that the figure is nearer to 10% of patients—or 100 times more common than indicated in the label (Breggin 2008a, p. 297).

Aggression

Aggressive behavior or hostility is often observed in children and adolescents with ADHD and has been reported in clinical trials and the postmarketing experience of some medications indicated for the treatment of ADHD. Although there is no systematic evidence that stimulants cause aggressive behavior or hostility, patients beginning treatment for ADHD should be monitored for the appearance of or worsening of aggressive behavior or hostility.

The section in the FDA label concerning overdose makes a remarkable observation that every clinician, patient, and family should be aware of— that *individuals vary widely in their reactions to amphetamines and that toxic symptoms can occur "at low doses" in some cases.*

OVERDOSAGE

Individual patient response to amphetamines varies widely. Toxic symptoms may occur idiosyncratically at low doses.

Symptoms: Manifestations of acute overdosage with amphetamines include restlessness, tremor, hyperreflexia, rapid respiration, confusion, assaultiveness, hallucinations, panic states, hyperpyrexia, and rhabdomyolysis. Fatigue and depression usually follow the central nervous system stimulation. Cardiovascular effects include arrhythmias, hypertension or hypotension, and circulatory collapse. Gastrointestinal symptoms include nausea, vomiting, diarrhea, and abdominal cramps.

DEPRESSION AND APATHY INDUCED BY STIMULANTS

The production of depression and apathy should be considered as a primary effect rather than a side effect of stimulants. In a study of children aged 4–6 years, methylphenidate produced symptoms of depression ("sad/unhappy") in 69% of children; and symptoms of apathy ("uninterested in others") in 62% of children (Firestone, Musten, Pisterman. Mercer, & Benett, 1998; see Breggin, 2008a, Table 11.1, p. 286). In a study that included older children up to age 13, nearly 19% experienced lethargy ("tired, withdrawn, listless, depressed, dopey, dazed, subdued and inactive"; Mayes, Crites, Bixler, Humphrey, & Mattison, 1994; see Breggin, 2008a, Table 11.1, p. 286). These effects sometimes develop slowly. Because of medication spellbinding (see Chapter 9), the child rarely notices these effects and simply adapts to a lesser quality of life. Parents and teachers, who no longer have to deal with such a rambunctious, high-energy child, mistake the depression and apathy for improvement. Frequently, the child will mistakenly be given higher doses as an "energy boost" and eventually antidepressants will be prescribed. As adverse effects mount, the number of prescribed drugs may increase to include at least one member of every class of psychiatric drugs: stimulants, sedatives, antidepressants, neuroleptics, and mood stabilizers. At this point, these children become viewed as severely emotionally disturbed when they are in reality in a state of drug toxicity.

OBSESSIVE-COMPULSIVE SYMPTOMS AND TICS INDUCED BY STIMULANTS

When a National Institute of Mental Health (NIMH) study focused on stimulant-induced symptoms of obsessive-compulsive disorder (OCD), it found that 51% of methylphenidate-treated children were afflicted (Borcherding, Keysor, Rapoport, Elia, & Amass, 1990). Much like the symptoms of depression and apathy, OCD symptoms are usually viewed as an improvement. Instead of requiring attention and discipline, the child obsessively watches TV or plays on the computer. In class, the child may compulsively copy everything down from the board as instructed, without actually learning anything.

The NIMH researchers also found a very high rate of 58% for methylphenidate-induced abnormal movements. They postulate that the OCD symptoms and the tics are functionally related in the brain. They probably stem in part from dysfunction caused in the basal ganglia. Permanent tics are a known consequence of stimulant drugs and are often incorrectly diagnosed as Tourette's syndrome.

HOW STIMULANTS WORK

It should not be a mystery about how stimulant drugs seem, initially at least, to improve behavior. We have seen that the drugs produce apathy and OCD-like symptoms. In addition to the studies of children, studies of animals, including chimpanzees, have repeatedly documented that stimulants reduce all spontaneous behavior and produce obsessive behavior (many studies reviewed in Breggin, 2008a, pp. 303–307).

These drug-induced brain dysfunctions appear beneficial to teachers and parents who are struggling to handle difficult, active, bored, or upset children, especially children who lack discipline or act rebelliously. The drugs seem especially effective in the classroom, where the child has been previously disruptive and bored. Now apathetic and compulsive, the child requires little or no attention and appears improved because of the suppression of behavior.

DISCOURAGING THE DEVELOPMENT OF SELF-CONTROL AND SELF-DETERMINATION

Millions of children are being told that they have a disorder called ADHD and the need of medications to control themselves. This undermines their normal child development, which primarily consists of progressively learning to take charge of one's own attitudes and behavior. As the drug effects amplify over the years, sometimes becoming a cocktail of drugs, brain dysfunction adds to the child's feeling that he can never exert control over his own mind and behavior.

The diagnosis of ADHD and the use of prescription medications in treating children have little scientific justification. School and family interventions provide more rational and direct approaches to the problems of children who lack self-discipline or are unable to engage productively with their parents and teachers.

EFFECTIVENESS

Advocates for the use of stimulant drugs have tried for several decades to demonstrate that the medications are useful for treating children diagnosed with ADHD. Despite massive funding of studies by drug companies and federal agencies, stimulants have never been demonstrated to accomplish anything other than the temporary suppression of all behaviors over a few week period before the brain begins to compensate and hence to complicate and often worsen the clinical picture (Breggin, 2008a). No long-term benefit of any kind has ever been demonstrated—no improved behavior, no improved socialization skills, no improved academic skills, and no improvement in learning. Rather than repeat my lengthy analysis in *Brain-Disabling Treatments in Psychiatry* (2nd ed.; Breggin, 2008a), it is more efficient to point to the relatively recent multicenter study by staunch advocates with NIMH funding, called the MTA (for a discussion of underlying flaws, see Breggin 2000a & 2001b).

At 36 months in the MTA study, stimulant medication approaches were no better than any other behavioral and educational approaches, including a brief stay at a summer camp (Swanson, Hinshaw, et al., 2007). Overall, it seemed that the children would have done at least as well if they had simply been left alone, and the authors were reduced to arguing that the ADHD simply got better regardless of the intervention over the 36 months. They neglected to add that the child who remained drug free escaped exposure to multiple adverse drug risks. The study did confirm the stunting of growth as measured by height and weight (Swanson, Elliot, et al., 2007).

Millions of children are taking stimulant drugs for ADHD, but healthcare providers and families should cast a skeptical eye on using these drugs and make every effort to remove patients from these ineffective but dangerous chemical agents.

KEY POINTS

▪ The ADHD diagnosis is not a valid syndrome. Its three diagnostic features—hyperactivity, impulsivity, and inattention—can be caused by innumerable factors, including a boring or undisciplined classroom; scholastic unpreparedness for grade level; anxiety about school or testing; lack of proper discipline at home; distressing stressors at school or at home, such as bullying or abuse, and conflict between parents; poor nutrition, insomnia, and fatigue; and multiple physical problems, such as concussive head injury, diabetes, and intestinal parasites. In a routine clinical practice, nearly all "ADHD" children will be entirely normal children who are in conflict with their teachers or parents and in need of more informed and/or dedicated attention from their teachers and parents.

- Making an ADHD diagnosis almost invariably means that a full evaluation will never be made concerning the child's real needs for improved education and parenting, and causative problems in the classroom or home will never be addressed. The children are encouraged to believe that they suffer from a "disorder" that renders them less able to take responsibility and to master their lives.

- Stimulant medications subdue spontaneous behavior in general and cause obsessive-compulsive behaviors, all of which can be mistaken for an improvement in behavior by busy teachers or overwhelmed parents.

- Stimulant medications suppress growth by disrupting growth hormone cycles and cause potentially irreversible tics, insomnia, depression and suicidality, OCD, apathy, overstimulated behavior, cardiovascular risks, and mania and psychosis.

- In long-term use, these drugs cause chronic brain impairment (CBI), with lasting biochemical imbalances and atrophy of the brain. Long-term use of stimulants should be discouraged in any age group.

- Stimulant drugs are Schedule II narcotics, indicating the highest potential for abuse and addiction and can cause serious withdrawal reactions. Prescribing stimulants to children with ADHD predisposes them to an increased rate of cocaine abuse in young adulthood.

- Despite decades of research and hundreds of studies, there is no evidence that stimulants have a lasting positive effect on behavior. There is no evidence that they improve academic performance or any measure of psychological and social functioning.

- There are always better approaches to helping children than suppressing their spontaneity by bathing their growing brains in highly toxic substances, such as stimulants.

CHAPTER 7

Benzodiazepines, Other Sedatives, and Opiates: Reasons for Withdrawal

Although very freely prescribed by a wide range of practitioners, all drugs that are effective for the short-term control of anxiety and insomnia carry very high risks including tolerance, abuse, and addiction; behavioral abnormalities including disinhibition with violence and suicide; and cognitive deficits, most obviously memory impairment. The long-term use of benzodiazepines causes severe cognitive and neurological impairments, atrophy of the brain, and dementia, and the newer sleep aids should be considered a potential but unproven risk in this regard. In long-term use, all of these drugs lose their effectiveness and probably do much more harm than good. Even in the short-term, the use of drugs that suppress anxiety and induce sleep can interfere with recovery and lead to chronic anxiety and sleep disorders. A new study of prescription sleep medications demonstrates a marked increase in mortality rates, even with relatively short-term use. The most commonly prescribed benzodiazepine, alprazolam (Xanax), is also the most dangerous drug used to control anxiety. Fortunately, there are many good psychotherapeutic approaches to anxiety and sleep problems.

The opiates (morphine) and opioids (oxycodone, hydrocodone) used to treat pain also have sedative properties and they also cause withdrawal reactions. Except in very severe cases, withdrawal from these drugs is easier and leaves fewer lasting effects than withdrawal from the benzodiazepines and other psychiatric drugs including stimulants and antidepressants.

The benzodiazepines include tranquilizers and sleep aids like alprazolam (Xanax), triazolam (Halcion), lorazepam (Ativan), clonazepam (Klonopin), temazepam (Restoril), and diazepam (Valium). They are used to reduce anxiety or as sleep aids and, in the *DSM-IV-TR* (2000), are categorized as "sedatives, hypnotics, and anxiolytics." Other drugs used as sleep aids have similar effects including zolpidem (Ambien), eszopiclone (Lunesta), and zaleplon (Sonata). Ambien was the 15th most prescribed drug in the United States in 2010 (IMS, 2011c). A complete list can be found in the Appendix.

IMS (2011b) lists "Tranquilizers" as the 11th top therapeutic class of drugs by prescriptions and "Hypnotics & Sedatives" as the 20th. However, if the two are added together, the combined group ranks 5th, lower than Beta Blockers and just higher than Ace Inhibitors. Xanax is the top drug in the group, ranking number 11. This should be of concern because Xanax is one of the most dangerous drugs used in psychiatry and medicine, causing serious behavioral abnormalities, severe abuse and addiction, a vicious withdrawal reaction, and long-term mental and neurological disability.

CHRONIC BRAIN IMPAIRMENT (CBI) AND DEMENTIA

Some of the most severe cases of chronic brain impairment (CBI) occur after years of exposure to benzodiazepines. Alprazolam is one of the worst offenders, probably because of its short action and high potency. Many individuals feel that their memory functions have been severely impaired and may not fully recover.

The literature confirms that long-term exposure causes atrophy of the brain and cognitive decline (Barker et al., 2004; Lagnaoui et al., 2002; Schmauss & Krieg, 1987; Tata et al., 1994; Uhde & Kellner, 1987; Wu et al., 2009). Bergman et al. (1989) conducted repeat neuropsychological assessments of 30 patients who had abused sedative drugs 4–6 years earlier, and despite some slight improvement "the prevalence of intellectual impairment was still increased and about as high as before" along with "increased prevalence of dilatation of the ventricular system" (p. 547).

Birzele et al. (1992), in a controlled study of 10 patients, tested for "the amnestic effects of benzodiazepines after long-term medication and during withdrawal." They summarized, "Results indicate that nonverbal visual memory tests, concentration, and subjective mood are significantly impaired by the drug. During withdrawal, most deficits showed a reversal; however, concentration and mood are still impaired" (p. 277). Golombok et al. (1988) found that long-term use of benzodiazepines produced dangerous levels of memory malfunctioning. Consistent with the anosognosia component of CBI, and of great importance to prescribers, the *patients were not aware of the degree of their losses until withdrawn from the drugs*.

As observed by Uzun et al. (2010), patients taking prescribed benzodiazepines are "more likely to have high scores on measures of overall symptoms and affective symptoms (anxiety and depression) and low rating for general quality of life . . ." (p. 91, citing Verbanck, 2009).

The American Psychiatric Association's *DSM-IV-TR* confirmed these risks by recognizing the official diagnoses of "Persisting Amnestic Disorder" (292.83) and "Persisting Dementia" (292.82) caused by sedative, hypnotic, or anxiolytic drugs (American Psychiatric Association, 2000, p. 285).

Benzodiazepines enhance the actions of the inhibitory neurotransmitter gamma-aminobutyric acid (GABA), producing a general suppression of brain function. This is accompanied by reduced metabolism in the cortex (Buchsbaum, 1987) and reduced blood flow throughout the brain (Mathew & Wilson, 1991)—mechanisms that can cause harm to the brain from chronic exposure.

For a more extensive review of benzodiazepine-induced brain damage, see Breggin 2008a (Chapter 12, pp. 319–345).

After the 2006 edition of the *Physicians' Desk Reference*, Xanax no longer appears in this most common source of information. Perhaps the manufacturer, Upjohn, prefers prescribers to remember only the earlier editions with their much weaker warnings. To rectify the problem, this section will quote extensively from the March 2011 version found on the UpJohn website ("Xanax XR," 2011).

From the *DSM-IV-TR*
Substance-Induced Persistent Dementia
This disorder is termed "persisting" because the dementia persists long after the individual has experienced the effects of Substance Intoxication or Substance Withdrawal. . . . This disorder usually has an insidious onset and slow progression, typically during a period when the person qualifies for a Substance Dependence diagnosis. The deficits are usually permanent and may worsen even if the substance use stops, although some cases do show improvement. (American Psychiatric Association, 2000, p. 169).

SHORTENED LIFE SPAN

A new study has examined the risk of increased mortality associated with benzodiazepines and closely-related sleep aids when given in relatively small doses for short periods of time in the treatment of insomnia (Kripke, Langer, & Line, 2012). The epidemiological study reviewed more than 10,000 U.S. patients taking sleeping aids and compared them to a larger number of controls. The two drugs most commonly prescribed were the benzodiazepine temazepam (trade name, Restoril) and the closely-related sleeping aid zolpidem (Ambien). However, their study included all of the regularly-used prescription sleep aids, including eszopiclone (Lunesta), zaleplon (Sonata), other benzos, barbiturates, and sedative antihistamines.

The study found that patients receiving any of these drugs for sleep compared to non-users suffered substantially elevated hazards of dying compared to those who took no hypnotics. "Even patients prescribed fewer than 18 hypnotic doses per year experienced increased mortality, with greater mortality associated with greater dosage prescribed" (p. 1). Overall, patients prescribed hypnotics had 4.6 times the hazard of dying over an average observation period of 2.5 years as compared to non-users. Patients prescribed 18 or fewer doses had 3.6 times greater mortality rate.

In addition to the increased death rate, there was an overall cancer increase of 35% among those prescribed high doses. However, this finding did not contribute substantially to the death rate, and the authors drew no firm conclusions about how the medications cause increased mortality.

Although not mentioned in the review, I suspect that the impairment of judgment caused by all sedating drugs may play a role in regard to taking proper care of oneself, including healthy living and avoiding accidents. Because of impaired judgment, these drugs often lead to unintentional overdose. This impaired judgment is an aspect of medication spellbinding.

Antianxiety and sedative medication can also cause depression, which can lead to poor self-care and other problems. All of these drugs are central nervous system (CNS) depressants, so they will reduce and impair respirations, gag and cough reflexes and other functions during sleep. They also can cause or worsen sleep apnea, which is associated with many health problems, including cardiovascular disease and accidents. Hypnotic drugs produce abnormal sleep cycles, which may reduce alertness while awake and produce other known and unknown health hazards. The newer sleep aids like Ambien and Sonata are noteworthy for causing sleep walking, sleep eating, and even sleep driving and sleep climbing out of windows. The authors of the study point out that in controlled clinical trials individuals taking hypnotics have "more adverse medical events overall" than placebo controls. All of these drugs can be psychologically habit-forming, and all of them except the antihistamines can be easily abused and lead to addiction.

When used to treat anxiety, benzodiazepines are typical given in much larger daily doses than for the treatment of insomnia. This should alert clinicians to the probability that the routine use of benzodiazepines to treat anxiety poses a considerable threat to the life span.

DEPENDENCE (ADDICTION) AND ABUSE

All of the benzodiazepines and the more common prescribed sleep aids are addictive. Patients taking these drugs continuously for several weeks will begin to experience tolerance and withdrawal reactions. In the case of the short-acting alprazolam, and to some extent with the others, withdrawal can occur in between doses (interdose withdrawal). The "sleeping pill" that helps the patient fall asleep can easily produce a withdrawal reaction with anxiety and agitation in the morning.

A recent report in the *New York Times* focused on alprazolam abuse and addiction (Goodnough, 2011). Last year, alprazolam became the eighth most prescribed drug in the United States. The Centers for Disease Control and Prevention (CDC) has reported an 89% increase in emergency room visits nationwide related to nonmedical benzodiazepine use. In Kentucky, where the report focused, "the combination of opiate painkillers and benzodiazepines, especially Xanax, is common in fatal overdoses, according to the state medical examiner. The fact that alprazolam is so widely prescribed—and yet so dangerous—indicates the need for prescribers, clinicians, and patients to be more wary of the drug.

Too many clinicians mistakenly believe that only high-dose, long-term treatment carries the risk of dependence and abuse. FDA-approved Xanax label contradicts this mistaken notion ("Xanax XR," 2011):

> While the severity and incidence of withdrawal phenomena appear to be related to dose and duration of treatment, withdrawal symptoms, including seizures, have been reported after only brief therapy with alprazolam at doses within the recommended range for the treatment of anxiety (e.g., 0.75–4 mg/day) (pp. 18–19).

In 8-week studies of alprazolam used for FDA approval, the patients were worse off at 8 weeks than they were before being started on the drug (Marks et al., 1989; reviewed in Breggin, 2008a, pp. 341–344).

Severe rebound anxiety and panic make it impossible for many to withdraw from alprazolam after only 6–8 weeks exposure. In the short trials used for FDA-approval, the number unable to withdraw from the brief drug exposure varied from a low of 7% to a high of 29% ("Xanax XR," 2011, p. 6). In the case of short-acting benzodiazepines, especially alprazolam, withdrawal or rebound (a worsening of the original anxiety condition) can occur between individual doses of the drug ("Xanax XR," 2011):

> *Interdose Symptoms*: Early morning anxiety and emergence of anxiety symptoms between doses of Xanax Tablets have been reported in patients with panic disorder taking prescribed maintenance doses. These symptoms may reflect the development of tolerance or a time interval between doses, which is longer than the duration of clinical action of the administered dose. In either case, it is presumed that the prescribed dose is not sufficient to maintain plasma levels higher than those needed to prevent relapse, rebound, or withdrawal symptoms over the entire course of the interdosing interval (p. 7).

In this vein, the Xanax label also warns, "Experience in randomized placebo-controlled discontinuation studies of patients with panic disorder who received Xanax Tablets showed a high rate of rebound and withdrawal symptoms compared to placebo treated patients" ("Xanax XR," 2011, p. 6).

Patients frequently abuse these drugs by taking large amounts at one time. Often they are mixed with alcohol, which can cause coma and death. Increasingly, they are mixed with opiates.

The FDA-mandated Medication Guide at the end of the label contains further warnings about addiction ("Xanax XR," 2011):

> Some patients may find it very difficult to discontinue treatment with XANAX XR due to severe emotional and physical dependence. Discontinuation symptoms, including possible seizures, may occur following discontinuation from any dose, but the risk may be increased with extended use at doses greater than 4 mg/day, especially if discontinuation is too abrupt. It is important that you seek advice from your physician to discontinue treatment in a careful and safe manner. Proper discontinuation will help to decrease the possibility of withdrawal reactions that can range from mild reactions to severe reactions, such as seizure (p. 10).

Benzodiazepines should rarely be administered for more than a few days at a time, with frequent periods of non-use; and it is sometimes safer to use long acting ones such as diazepam (Valium).

ABNORMAL MENTAL AND BEHAVIORAL REACTIONS

For decades, it has been documented that benzodiazepine and other sedative drugs can produce abnormal behavioral reactions. Much as a few drinks of alcohol can lead to disinhibition, in my forensic experience even one or two doses of a benzodiazepine can lead to violence that is wholly out of character for the individual. Longer term, these reactions are most likely to occur during dose changes, either up or down.

The Xanax label mentions but somewhat minimizes the risks of abnormal behavioral reactions ("Xanax XR," 2011):

> As with all benzodiazepines, paradoxical reactions such as stimulation, increased muscle spasticity, sleep disturbances, hallucinations, and other adverse behavioral effects such as agitation, rage, irritability, and aggressive or hostile behavior have been reported rarely. In many of the spontaneous case reports of adverse behavioral effects, patients were receiving other CNS drugs concomitantly and/or were described as having underlying psychiatric conditions. Should any of the above events occur, alprazolam should be discontinued (pp. 17–18).

Under adverse reactions, the Xanax label again provides an ominous list of frequent (more than 1/100) and infrequent (1/100–1/1,000) events:

> **Psychiatric system disorders:** *Frequent:* irritability, insomnia, nervousness, derealization, libido increased, restlessness, agitation, depersonalization, nightmare; *Infrequent:* abnormal dreams, apathy, aggression, anger, bradyphrenia, euphoric mood, logorrhea, mood swings, dysphonia, hallucination, homicidal ideation, mania, hypomania, impulse control, psychomotor retardation, suicidal ideation (p. 10).

In my forensic experience, described in *Medication Madness* (2008b), the combination of Xanax in particular with selective serotonin reuptake inhibitor (SSRI) antidepressants turns up as a frequent combination in cases of mania, suicide, and violence. Like any benzodiazepine or sedative, Xanax causes "agitation, rage, irritability, and aggressive or hostile behavior," but on top of that, Xanax is the only benzodiazepine with a label warning concerning its capacity to cause mania. In the Precautions section, the label has a subhead for "Mania" ("Xanax XR," 2011):

> **Mania**
> Episodes of hypomania and mania have been reported in association with the use of XANAX Tablets in patients with depression (p. 9).

INTOXICATION

Patients vary enormously in the dose of benzodiazepine required to produce obvious intoxication similar to alcohol such as slurred speech, incoordination, unsteady gait, nystagmus, impairment in attention or memory, and, in the extreme, stupor or coma (American Psychiatric Association, 2000, p. 287). Much more commonly, lesser degrees of intoxication go unnoticed by the patient because of medication spellbinding (Chapter 9). Usually, family or friends are the first to notice. The prescriber often has no idea that the patient in everyday life is showing signs of intoxication, and consultations with family are useful in that regard. Warning calls from family that the patient is "over-medicated" should be taken very seriously in regard to this group of drugs, as well as in regard to all psychiatric drugs.

Obviously, signs of intoxication require dose reduction if not complete withdrawal because even minimal intoxication can be physically dangerous, encourages disinhibition, and usually indicates growing tolerance, abuse, and dependence.

PREGNANCY AND NURSING

Pregnant or nursing mothers, if at all possible, should not take psychiatric drugs. This is confirmed by the Xanax label (p. 12):

> *Pregnancy*: . . . It should be considered that the child born of a mother who is receiving benzodiazepines may be at some risk for withdrawal symptoms from the drug during the postnatal period. Also, neonatal flaccidity and respiratory problems have been reported in children born of mothers who have been receiving benzodiazepines (p. 12).

The label for Xanax makes clear that the risk continues after the child is born and during nursing:

> *Nursing Mothers*: It should be considered that the child born of a mother who is receiving benzodiazepines may be at some risk for withdrawal symptoms from the drug during the postnatal period. Also, neonatal flaccidity and respiratory problems have been reported in children born of mothers who have been receiving benzodiazepines (p. 12).

ILLUSTRATION: A CASE OF LONG-TERM EXPOSURE TO ALPRAZOLAM (XANAX)

Jacob, a practicing physician and associate professor of medicine, was placed on benzodiazepines for anxiety at age 30 and remained on them for 20 years. Most of the time, he was prescribed alprazolam 1.0–1.5 mg per day. In a failed attempt to withdraw him from alprazolam in the final several years, he was continued on diazepam (Valium) 10–20 mg per day. His anxiety was never fully controlled and gradually grew worse between doses and after awakening in the morning. He tried to stop the medications on his own on several occasions but was wracked by anxiety and insomnia. His psychiatrist reassured him it was safe to stay on the medication "for the rest of your life."

After a few years on alprazolam, Jacob began to complain of memory and "thinking" problems. A neurological consult for memory dysfunction attributed the problem to "depression" and failed to consider the diagnosis of alprazolam-induced amnestic syndrome or dementia.

In the last 10 years, Jacob became depressed as well as anxious and had mild manic responses to both the older tricyclic antidepressants and the newer SSRIs. He was incorrectly diagnosed with bipolar disorder instead of antidepressant-induced mood disorder with manic features.

At age 50 years, Jacob became unable to practice or to teach and went on disability. Following a difficult withdrawal from alprazolam with marked anxiety, his cognitive status stabilized with moderate dementia that fully disabled his work and family life.

When Jacob was medication free, clinical examination revealed signs of moderate dementia with short-term memory loss, the inability to learn new materials, and long-term memory loss in forgetting educational materials and friends he had known for years. His emotions were labile and his relationships were shallow. He was depressed in response to his loss of cognitive function and his disability. Neuropsychological testing confirmed generalized loss of cognitive function consistent with dementia. A magnetic resonance imaging (MRI) of the brain revealed mild atrophy in excess of that expected for his age.

As Jacob's story confirms, cognitive problems caused by benzodiazepines should not be overlooked or minimized. In themselves they impair the individual's quality of life as well as that of the family. After prolonged exposure, they can lead to dementia. Some cases of CBI will reveal at least mild generalized cognitive dysfunction on neuropsychological testing; but until they progress to dementia, there may be no findings on an MRI.

The progression of Jacob's decline follows that described by the *DSM-IV-TR* in the box on *Substance-Induced Persistent Dementia*. He first became dependent on the medication, insidiously developed cognitive disabilities, and then was disabled by dementia.

As commonly occurs in contemporary practice, Jacob also experienced manic-like episodes in response to treatment with antidepressants, but these were mistakenly diagnosed as bipolar disorder. Alprazolam can also cause mania, but these episodes were specifically associated with the antidepressants. The alprazolam-induced brain injury and dysfunction could have made Jacob more susceptible to developing a medication-induced manic-like reaction, but these are also frequent in patients with normal brain function.

There is no evidence that benzodiazepines provide relief for anxiety beyond a few weeks, and strong evidence that interdose withdrawal and rebound worsen the patient's condition by 6 weeks or less of exposure to alprazolam. At that point, many patients cannot withdraw because of the severity of withdrawal anxiety.

The failure of the neurologist in Jacob's case to attribute Jacob's cognitive decline to alprazolam is not unusual. Neurologists depend upon psychiatrists for referrals and frequently fail to diagnose iatrogenic disorders. Prescribers and clinicians need to evaluate their own patients as thoroughly as possible and to remain alert for adverse drug effects that may be overlooked or rejected by consultants and specialists who should know better. Again in Jacob's case, the prescriber's pattern of failing to properly diagnose adverse drug reactions, including cognitive deficits and manic-like reactions, is also unfortunately common. The patient's family is usually the first to notice these negative drug effects.

NON-BENZODIAZEPINE TRANQUILIZERS AND SLEEP AIDS

Non-benzodiazepine sleep aids such as *zolpidem* (Ambien), Lunesta (*eszopiclone*), and Sonata (*zaleplon*) are less effective than the benzodiazepines in producing sleep but are probably equally dangerous, producing the same patterns of memory loss and cognitive deficits. Like the benzodiazepines, they build tolerance and can lead to abuse and addiction (Griffiths & Johnson, 2005). They can cause a broad spectrum of abnormal behaviors from dangerous sleepwalking and sleep-driving to aggression and psychosis. They are particularly toxic to the older adult to whom they are frequently prescribed; but there are far safer and more effective methods of helping older people (as well as younger people) to sleep (Sivertsen et al., 2006).

The potential for abuse and addiction with *phenobarbital* and related compounds are well-known, and they are now seldom prescribed for sleep. None of the commonly used, effective sleep aids are much safer than phenobarbital or benzodiazepines, and none remain effective if used continuously.

> Use of benzodiazepines and most of the recently developed alternatives should be limited to a few weeks at a time or less for the control of insomnia or anxiety. Even during these brief periods, use should be intermittent in order to limit tolerance, abuse, and dependence.

OPIOIDS

The term *opioid* is used to designate all of the drugs derived directly from the opium poppy as well as the numerous synthetic versions. The opioids include morphine and codeine, which are derived directly from the opium poppy, and the synthetic opioids, including fentanyl, meperidine, codeine, oxycodone, hydromorphone, hydrocodone, and methadone. Hydromorphone is marketed as Dilaudid, oxycodone as Percocet, and hydrocodone as Vicodin, the latter two in combination with acetaminophen. Oxycodone is also marketed as OxyContin in a long-acting preparation.

When these medications are used by prescription, they have much less tendency to produce severe adverse effects on the central nervous system than most or all psychiatric drugs.

> The opioids do not commonly produce CBI in long-term routine use. Any finding of brain impairment is more likely caused by the associated use of alcohol, street drugs, and/or psychiatric drugs.

It usually takes 2–3 weeks of exposure for clinically significant withdrawal symptoms to develop. Regarding any drug, the more ingested for the longer period, the more likely a severe withdrawal reaction will probably occur; but this is variable from patient to patient. Significant withdrawal without associated physical signs can occur (Polydorou & Kleber, 2008; also see Gallanter and Kleber, 2008). Early to moderate withdrawal symptoms include anorexia, anxiety, cravings, dysphoria, fatigue, headache, increased respiratory rate, irritability, lacrimation (tears), mydriasis (widened pupils), perspiration, piloerection (gooseflesh), restlessness, rhinorrhea (running nose), and yawning. In more severe cases, withdrawal symptoms include a worsening of those previously listed as well as abdominal cramps, disturbed sleep, hot and cold flashes, increased blood pressure, increased pulse, low-grade fever, muscle spasm (hence the term "kicking the habit"), and nausea and vomiting (from Polydorou & Kleber, 2008, p. 268).

Depending on the medication, most withdrawal reactions begin within 3–12 hours and peak in less than 3 days. Severe symptoms are usually over in less than 3 days, and most symptoms are over in 4–10 days. Methadone is an exception in that the appearance of withdrawal symptoms may be delayed up to 72 hours, the peak withdrawal may occur up to 144 hours, and most symptoms may last up to 21 days (for details, see Polydorou & Kleber, 2008, Table 19-2, p. 269). The chronic use of larger doses of opioids can result in withdrawal reactions that may not completely subside for 6 months or more after discontinuation (Tetrault & O'Connor, 2009).

> Contrary to popular opinion, the withdrawal reactions associated with prescription opioids such as morphine, oxycodone, and hydrocodone are not usually as serious or dangerous as those associated with most prescription psychiatric drugs, including benzodiazepines, stimulants, antidepressants, antipsychotic drugs, and lithium.

Comparing the opioids to the sedatives and hypnotics (which include benzodiazepines), Tetrault and O'Connor (2009) observed, "Although some opioid withdrawal symptoms overlap withdrawal from sedative-hypnotics, opioid withdrawal generally is considered less likely to produce severe morbidity or mortality" (p. 593).

Consistent with the general principle that withdrawal effects tend to be the opposite of the drug effect, opiate and opioid withdrawal can produce rebound pain. It can also produce rebound hyperactivity of the central nervous system.

Opiate and opioid withdrawal tends to be more predictable than psychiatric drug withdrawal. If a patient has been using opiates or opioids, the ability to withdraw them in an outpatient setting depends, in most cases, on associated factors such as polydrug abuse, the severity of psychiatric issues, and the use of psychiatric drugs. Echoing a major theme in the person-centered collaborative approach, it also depends on "the availability of social supports such as family members to provide monitoring and transportation" (Tetrault and O'Connor, 2009, p. 593).

Although the use of prescription opioids is not as dangerous as the use of most psychiatric drugs in regard to producing adverse effects including CBI and withdrawal, clinicians increasingly recognize that the long-term use of opioids does not substantially relieve pain and may increase it (e.g., Halpern, 2011). *As a result, long-term use of these drugs should be avoided and patients chronically exposed to them will often improve with careful withdrawal from the drugs.*

There has been a growing trend to treat pain with non-opioid drugs such as mood stabilizers (Chapter 8), pregabalin (Lyrica) (Chapter 8), and antidepressants (Chapter 5). These drugs are not specific for pain, lack effectiveness, suppress emotional responsiveness, and cause considerable brain dysfunction, including CBI. The major set of 21 studies used to justify the use of Lyrica for pain management has been discredited (Gardiner, 2009; see Chapter 8 of this book). *Withdrawal reactions from these non-opioids can be considerably worse and more dangerous, with more lasting adverse effects, than from the opioids.* For short-term pain relief, the opioids are usually preferable.

Like the abuse of stimulants and benzodiazepines, abuse of opiates and opioids can result in unlawful acts. Special health problems such as HIV occur with intravenous abuse. Most drug abusers use more than one drug, commonly including alcohol and marijuana, greatly complicating the assessment, treatment, and withdrawal. This section has addressed prescribed, legally used opioids, involving mild-to-moderate abuse or dependence as found in patients who can often be safely withdrawn in an outpatient setting.

KEY POINTS

- All drugs that are effective in calming anxiety and inducing sleep work by causing an overall suppression of brain function, and are not specific for treating anxiety or insomnia.
- All drugs that are effective in calming anxiety and reducing insomnia have a short-lived effect, and after weeks and months they cause or worsen insomnia and anxiety, including panic disorder symptoms.
- All drugs that are effective in calming anxiety and reducing insomnia pose a serious risk for tolerance, interdose rebound, severe withdrawal reactions, abuse, and addiction. They should not be given to individuals with a history of drug and alcohol abuse.
- All drugs that are effective in calming anxiety and reducing insomnia pose the risk of behavioral abnormalities, especially disinhibition, and, in the case of some sleep aids, dangerous sleepwalking. The most commonly prescribed benzodiazepine, alprazolam (Xanax),

is especially short-acting and potent, and produces the most severe adverse effects including disinhibition and mania. Triazolam (Halcion), approved in the United States for insomnia, is even more short-acting and potent. It has been banned in some countries.

▪ In long-term use, benzodiazepines cause CBI with severe and potentially disabling cognitive deficits and neurologic abnormalities including paresthesias, atrophy of the brain, and dementia. Many people do not fully recover many months or years after withdrawal from benzodiazepines.

▪ Although benzodiazepines can reduce short-term anxiety and insomnia, their short-term use may distract from and interfere with recovery and lead to chronicity. There are many effective psychotherapeutic approaches to anxiety and insomnia that are more likely to lead to genuine recovery.

▪ Recent research shows that even the relatively short-term use of prescription sleep aids causes a several-fold or more increase in the mortality rate.

▪ The long-term prescription of all the effective drugs used to treat anxiety and insomnia will do more harm than good and should be avoided. All patients already on these drugs for a few months or more should be evaluated for possible withdrawal.

CHAPTER 8

Lithium and Other Mood Stabilizers: Reasons for Withdrawal

Almost any drug that slows down or blunts brain function, and hence emotional responsiveness, has been used as a mood stabilizer. Antiepileptic medications tend to reduce the electrical activity of the brain; many of them have been used off label and even approved for mood stabilization. Benzodiazepines suppress overall brain function and have also been used as mood stabilizers, especially clonazepam. Similarly, the neuroleptics, all of which suppress frontal lobe function and emotional responsiveness, are commonly used essentially as mood levelers. "Mood stabilization" is a euphemism for suppression of overall emotional responsiveness. Patients become less in touch with themselves, less able to express their feelings, and partially dulled. All of the drugs in this category have considerable and varied adverse effects.

The antipsychotics and benzodiazepine tranquilizers have been discussed in previous chapters. This chapter will examine lithium and other drugs used for mood stabilization.

LITHIUM

Effectiveness

In 2006, the largest study of the treatment of bipolar was published (Perlis et al., 2006). Called the Systematic Treatment Enhancement Program for Bipolar Disorder (STEP-BD), it took the "best treatment available approach," which included the whole array of lithium, antiepileptic drugs (mood stabilizers), antipsychotic drugs, and benzodiazepines. Fifteen hundred patients were followed for 2 years, and the results were very disappointing. Only 58.4% initially recovered, and 48% of those experienced relapse, leaving a recovery rate of approximately one quarter of patients. Consistent with receiving drugs that suppress the central nervous system, twice as many relapses involved depression rather than mania. The authors conclude, "Recurrence was frequent and associated with the presence of residual mood symptoms at initial recovery" (p. 217).

The Perlis study confirms many earlier ones that have cast doubt on the effectiveness of long-term drug treatment of bipolar disorder, including studies cited earlier in this book that the use of antidepressants vastly increases the risk of recurrent mania (reviewed in Breggin, 2008a, pp. 210–211). Gitlin, Swendsen, Heller, and Hammen (1995) conducted a prospective study of lithium for bipolar disorder and found that 73% of patients treated with lithium experienced relapse within 5 years. Of those who experienced relapse, two-thirds suffered multiple episodes, indicating that lithium increases rapid cycling. The authors concluded, "Even aggressive pharmacological maintenance treatment does not prevent relatively poor outcome in a significant number of bipolar patients" (p. 1635). As already noted, Perlis et al. (2006) found no better results from using the whole array of drugs commonly prescribed for bipolar disorder.

Chronic Brain Impairment

Lithium directly interferes with neurotransmission, causing it to slow down. Once touted as a "magic bullet" for mania, it is instead a very toxic drug that blunts the emotional responsiveness of any individual exposed to it, including animals, normal volunteers, and patients. Neonates and nursing infants of mothers taking lithium develop neurological impairments, including flaccidity, hypotonia, and lethargy (reviewed in Breggin, 2008a, pp. 194–203). Patients on lithium will inevitably become more apathetic and emotionally subdued. Especially in combination with neuroleptics, lithium can cause disabling encephalopathy and dementia from which recovery is incomplete. However, because of the drug's capacity to produce medication spellbinding, the afflicted individual may not notice the onset and progression of the neurotoxicity until it becomes lethal. Because lithium is so medication spellbinding, routine testing of lithium serum levels is required to prevent the individual from being severely neurotoxic without realizing or reporting it.

Exposure to lithium for many months and years is common and leads to cognitive deficits as well as a generalized deterioration of central nervous system function. Individuals exposed for years will find their quality of life deteriorating, sometimes into chronic depression. By 1990, Goodwin and Jamison, among the staunchest advocates of lithium, had to conclude "lithium can cause cognitive impairments of varying types and degrees." They warn the practitioner, "[I]t is important to bear in mind that impairment of intellectual functioning caused by lithium is not uncommon . . ." (p. 706). In fact, in exposure to lithium for short periods of time, a "therapeutic" dose produces biochemical abnormalities that are thought to impair cognitive function (Al Banchaabouchi, Peña de Ortíz, Menéndez, Ren, & Maldonado-Vlaar, 2004).

Adityanjee (1987, 2005) has identified a "syndrome of irreversible lithium-effectuated neurotoxicity" (SILENT), which is chronic and includes ataxia; dysarthria; impairments of memory, attention, and executive functions; and, in the extreme, dementia (also see Brumm, van Gorp, & Wirshing, 1998).

As the results of clinical reports and studies suggest, lithium is highly toxic to nerve cells (reviewed in Breggin, 2008a, pp. 203–210). For example, they cause neuronal growth and proliferation in the experimental lab. This has euphemistically been called "neurogenesis," when in fact the new cells are abnormal in size and shape (Lagace & Eisch, 2005).

The judicious prescriber will regularly evaluate the medicated patient for diminished quality of life and subtle signs of neurological impairment and will avoid maintaining individuals on psychiatric drugs, including lithium, for years at a time.

ILLUSTRATION: LOSS OF QUALITY OF LIFE ON LITHIUM

Under stress at work, Jane developed a brief psychotic reaction with paranoid fears. She recovered within 2–3 days in the hospital and shortly after discharge was removed from antipsychotic drugs and maintained on lithium. During the next several years, she became progressively depressed, stopped work, and was compelled to live at her mother's home. She became socially withdrawn. After 8 years on lithium, she developed severe lithium-induced kidney dysfunction, and the medication was stopped. Although faced with a potentially life-threatening disorder, she found her mood improving and especially her ability to take charge of her life. She now realized that the lithium had been clouding her mind, causing fatigue, and making her feel helpless. She refused the offer of alternative mood stabilizers and began treatment with me, which involved psychotherapy without medication. She was able to rebuild her life and after several months returned to work for the first time in many years.

Five years later, Jane again reacted to stress at work by developing a brief psychosis. With brief psychotherapy, twice a week for 3 weeks, she quickly recovered from the acute psychosis. She returned to work within less than a week—more quickly than I advised—and did well. Medication was limited to one dose of diazepam, 10 mg, to help her sleep on the day she began the therapy.

It is now known that withdrawal from lithium can cause manic episodes as well as depression, giving the misleading impression that lithium has been helping the individual when it has instead been priming the brain for further manic episodes (see Chapter 10; also, Cavanagh, Smyth, & Goodwin, 2004).

Lithium causes or worsens tardive dyskinesia (reviewed in Breggin, 2008a, pp. 206–207) and can cause thyroid disorder, parathyroid disorder (with abnormal behavior), kidney disease, cardiac arrhythmias, weight gain, skin diseases, hair loss, tremor, gastrointestinal problems, and a wide variety of other adverse effects that are discussed in standard sources.

> In my clinical experience reaching back to the 1960s, there were almost no clinical reports of "rapid cycling," and it was common to see bipolar patients live long lives with few or no recurrences. The new impression that bipolar disorder often takes a chronic downhill course is due to exposure to multiple neurotoxic psychiatric drugs.

Patients should not be kept long term on lithium and should be withdrawn whenever possible, but with great caution in the withdrawal process.

Several antiepileptic drugs have been approved for mood stabilization and for the prevention of recurring episodes of mania (see later in this chapter). The length of this growing list of attempts to substitute for lithium suggests, once again, that lithium has not been proven to be a "magic bullet" for mania or bipolar disorder.

In clinical practice, the newer "mood stabilizers" seem to have an unjustified reputation for being relatively safe, perhaps because of the comparison to the more well-known neurotoxicity of lithium.

> In light of the poor therapeutic outcomes and severe adverse reactions associated with bipolar treatment drugs, practitioners are well advised to limit long-term medication treatment for bipolar disorder.

OTHER MOOD STABILIZERS

Almost any drug that causes sedation and/or suppression of central nervous system activity has been used in psychiatry as "mood stabilizer." All of these drugs, in fact, flatten emotional responsiveness.

As noted in Chapter 5, young adults aged 20–34 taking antidepressants had increased mortality when taking antipsychotic drugs or mood stabilizers, excluding lithium (Sundell, Gissler, Petzold, & Waern, 2011). The mood stabilizers include carbamazepine, lamotrigine, and valproic acid.

These drugs suppress global mental function and can cause chronic brain impairment (CBI).

Antiepileptic Drugs

In addition, and probably little known to many clinicians, the FDA now requires the inclusion of a Medication Guide in the complete prescribing information for all antiepileptic (anticonvulsant) drugs and, hence, most mood stabilizers. The Medication Guide can be found at the end of the complete prescribing information in the *Physicians' Desk Reference*. The Medication Guide for antiepileptic drugs, including those used as mood stabilizers, contains the following admonition and warning:

All antiepileptic drugs, which include most mood stabilizers, now carry a warning about the increased risk of "suicidal thoughts or behavior in patients taking these drugs for any indication." So many psychiatric drugs now carry these or similar warnings that all psychoactive substances should be suspect in regard to causing or exacerbating suicidality. When a medicated patient becomes suicidal, clinicians should reexamine the medication regimen, including recently started medications and recent dose changes, either up or down.

Call a healthcare provider right away if you have any of these symptoms, especially if they are new, worse, or worry you:

- Thoughts about suicide or dying
- Attempts to commit suicide
- New or worse depression
- New or worse anxiety
- Feeling agitated or restless
- Panic attacks
- Trouble sleeping (insomnia)
- New or worse irritability
- Acting aggressive, being angry, or violent
- Acting on dangerous impulses
- An extreme increase in activity and talking (mania)
- Other unusual changes in behavior or mood

If this list looks familiar, it is identical—word for word—with the Medication Guide that the FDA has mandated for all antidepressants.

According to the FDA (2009):

The approved AEDs [anti-epilepsy drugs] affected by these safety label changes are Carbatrol, Celontin, Depakene, Depakote ER, Depakote sprinkles, Depakote tablets, Dilantin, Equetro, Felbatol, Gabitril, Keppra, Keppra XR, Klonopin, Lamictal, Lyrica, Mysoline, Neurontin, Peganone, Stavzor, Tegretol, Tegretol XR, Topamax, Tranxene, Tridione, Trileptal, Zarontin, Zonegran, and generics.

Valproic acid (Depakene), *sodium valproate* (Depakene syrup), and *divalproex sodium* (Depakote, an enteric-coated combination of the other two) are related chemicals that have been approved for the treatment of bipolar disorder. They commonly cause sedation, tremor, and ataxia. They have potentially strong psychoactive effects, including changes in mood and behavior, such as behavioral automatisms and confusion as well as somnolence or delirium, especially when combined with other sedatives (Silver, Yudofsky, & Hurowitz, 1994). They can cause liver damage, especially in children. There may be "mild impairment of cognitive function with chronic use" (Hyman, Arana, & Rosenbaum, 1995, p. 127). Like lithium, valproic acid causes delirium in a significant percentage of older patients (Shulman et al., 2005). It also causes a variety of endocrine disorders and metabolic changes (Verrotti, Greco, Latini, & Chiarelli, 2005).

Valproic acid and carbamazepine cause a small increase in the rate of major congenital malformations in infants (Wide, Winbladh, & Källén, 2004). Acute and potentially fatal pancreatitis has been reported with valproic acid (e.g., Grauso-Eby, Goldfarb, Feldman-Winter, & McAbee, 2003), as well as liver failure. Valproic acid is known to cause hyperammonemia with encephalopathy (e.g., McCall & Bourgeois, 2004).

All of the currently used mood stabilizers can cause serious and potentially lethal skin disorders. *Carbamazepine* (Tegretol) and extended-release carbamazepine (Equetro) are chemical cousins to the tricyclic antidepressants, and were originally used for partial complex seizures and in the management of tic douloureux—a facial pain syndrome. In the long-acting form, Equetro has been approved for the treatment of bipolar disorder.

Carbamazepine can cause potentially lethal suppression of the bone marrow with potentially lethal agranulocytosis or aplastic anemia. The practitioner, patient, and family should be alert for the onset of fever, sore throat, and other signs of infection.

Carbamazepine can also cause hyponatremia (low serum sodium), leading to a syndrome that includes lethargy, confusion or hostility, and stupor. As with most psychoactive substances, cognitive disturbances are more common with concomitant use of neuroleptics, with preexisting brain damage, and with aging (Hyman et al., 1995). Neurological intoxication can occur, including sedating, tremor, confusion, depression, and psychosis. Liver and cardiac function can also be affected. Sedation and fatigue are common.

Gabapentin (Neurontin) has been approved for epilepsy and posthepatic neuralgia, but due to heavy off-label pushing of the drug by the manufacturer, it became very commonly prescribed for a wide variety of psychiatric disorders in children and adults. These negligent acts in regard to Neurontin, as well as other drugs including Lyrica, resulted in the largest healthcare fraud settlement in the history of the U.S. Department of Justice, including a $1.3 billion *criminal* case settlement (U.S. Department of Health and Human Services, 2009). This drug has little or no legitimate use in psychiatry. Prescribers should avoid the use of Neurontin.

Lamotrigine (Lamictal)

Approved for maintenance therapy for bipolar disorder, this drug carries a black box warning for life-threatening skin reactions including Stevens–Johnson syndrome, drug rash with eosinophilia and systemic symptoms (DRESS) syndrome, and toxic epidermal necrolysis, as well as aseptic meningitis. These are heavy prices to pay for questionable efficacy. It can also cause cognitive dysfunction, including memory impairment.

Clonazepam (Klonopin)

Clonazepam (Klonopin) is a widely used benzodiazepine tranquilizer that is also used to treat acute mania and as prophylaxis for mania. It has all the many, sometimes severe, problems associated with the other benzodiazepines, including sedation, rebound and withdrawal syndromes, addiction, and behavioral abnormalities (see Chapter 7).

Especially in people prone to seizures, all antiepileptic medications can cause seizures during withdrawal, and none should be abruptly stopped.

With the increasing and unfounded diagnosis of bipolar disorder in children, many children are being prescribed these drugs. Given their toxicity, more concern should be shown about their impact on developing brain and mind of children (Loring, 2005).

Remember, all of these antiepileptic drugs that are used as mood stabilizers carry a suicide risk warning and Medication Guide alert for worsening condition, including suicidality, aggression, and manic-like behaviors.

Other Drugs Sometimes Prescribed Off Label as Mood Stabilizers

Verapamil (Calan and others) is a calcium channel blocker used for the treatment of cardiac disorders. Because of its sedative effects, it is sometimes prescribed for psychiatric purposes. It can produce a variety of cardiovascular problems. Because it can adversely affect cardiac function and blood pressure, as well as liver function, patients should be evaluated before beginning treatment and periodically during treatment.

Clonidine, an antihypertensive drug, also has sedative effects. Unfortunately, it is sometimes mistakenly prescribed to children as a sleep aid and calming agent, especially to counteract the activating effects of stimulants. When mistakenly prescribed with stimulants, it causes an elevated risk of cardiac arrhythmia and cardiac arrest. Sudden withdrawal can produce a rebound hypertensive crisis. It can produce many psychiatric symptoms, including sedation, vivid dreams or nightmares, insomnia, restlessness, anxiety, and depression. More rarely, it can cause hallucinations.

Children often develop illnesses involving nausea and vomiting that lead to missed drug doses, putting them at risk of inadvertently going into withdrawal. Clonidine can cause or contribute to depression, and it is unfortunately used at times in a cocktail of stimulants, selective serotonin reuptake inhibitors (SSRIs), and clonidine—three drugs that worsen or bring about depression, and risk cardiovascular crises.

PREGABALIN (LYRICA)

Pregabalin (Lyrica) is an antiepileptic and pain medication, which has become so widely used that the clinician is likely to find it being prescribed to psychiatric patients. Like Neurontin, it was falsely promoted by Pfizer (see earlier). In addition, in one of the largest cases of academic fraud in history, researcher Scott Reuben "concocted data for 21 studies" related to the use of pregabalin for pain management, as reported in the *New York Times* (Gardiner, 2009).

Pregabalin causes sedation, dizziness, and ataxia. It carries the same suicide warnings and Medication Guide warnings about overall mental deterioration that are required of all antiepileptic medications and antidepressants.

In my clinical experience, pregabalin can have crushing psychoactive effects similar to antipsychotic drugs, including a very heavy clouding of consciousness, apathy, and depression. For the patient suffering from physical pain, these effects can be confusing and medication spellbinding. Without realizing it, the patient progressively lapses into an overall emotional numbness without achieving any specific pain relief. Like Neurontin, it should have no place in psychiatric treatment.

VARENICLINE (CHANTIX)

Varenicline (Chantix) is an aid for quitting smoking. A recent study found a 73% increase of cardiac problems in individuals using varenicline for smoking cessation (Singh, Loke, Spangler, & Furberg, 2011). Lead author Sonal Singh of Johns Hopkins said people "don't need Chantix to quit and this is another reason to consider avoiding Chantix altogether" (Burton, 2011, p. B3). Curt D. Furberg, coauthor of the study, affirmed, "The sum of all serious adverse effects of Chantix clearly outweigh the most positive effect of the drug." Similarly, Moore, Furberg, Glenmullen, Maltsberger, and Singh (2011) concluded,

> Varenicline shows a substantial, statistically significant increased risk of reported depression and suicidal/self-injurious behavior.

Bupropion for smoking cessation had smaller increased risks. The findings for varenicline, combined with other problems with its safety profile, render it unsuitable for first-line use in smoking cessation.

As I have found in regard to other psychiatric drug manufacturers (Breggin, 2008a), Pfizer reportedly failed to inform the FDA about "150 cases of completed suicides, some dated back to 2007" (Institute for Safe Medication Practices, 2011, p. 2). The company had delayed reporting by classifying suicide deaths as "expected adverse events" rather than as serious, unexpected events (p. 14).

Suicide and violence are closely related risks. Chantix has the most disproportionally large number of reports for violence-related adverse events in the FDA data system (Moore et al., 2011).

KEY POINTS

- Mood stabilizers vary in their adverse effects depending on their pharmacological class, but none of them are especially effective or safe. Despite years of claims for the safety and efficacy of lithium, the treatment turns out to lack efficacy, to induce withdrawal mania, and to cause many severe and life-threatening adverse effects including acute and chronic central nervous system toxicity, hypothyroidism, kidney failure, and cognitive decline and dementia.
- Mood stabilizers cannot target "excessive" emotions and instead act by suppressing overall emotional responsiveness. Individuals become less able to feel and less able to identify and express their feelings. This reduces the quality of life and the capacity to recovery from emotional stress and trauma.
- The mood stabilizers, when prescribed for months and years, can cause chronic brain impairment (CBI), with a marked decline in the quality of life.
- Large studies regarding the effectiveness of lithium and other mood stabilizers do not provide evidence for substantial long-term success. Outcomes with drug therapy seem much worse than those achieved in early years before lifetime treatment was recommended.
- Mood stabilizers are frequently used off label. Prescribers should be very cautious regarding this practice.

CHAPTER 9

Medication Spellbinding (Intoxication Anosognosia)

Medication spellbinding (intoxication anosognosia) is caused by all psychoactive substances. It can render the individual unable to recognize or judge the adverse mental and behavioral effects of drugs. Medication spellbinding can lead to dangerous behaviors that are highly uncharacteristic of the individual. With longer term exposure to the medication, chronic brain impairment (CBI) with a loss of quality of life can insidiously occur without the individual recognizing or appreciating it. Clinicians and support networks need to understand that medicated patients often mistakenly believe that they are doing well or even better than ever when in reality, their lives are significantly and sometimes severely drug impaired. Medication spellbinding is frequent during drug withdrawal, causing patients to fail to recognize or appreciate dangerous withdrawal reactions.

Lack of awareness of cognitive and emotional deficits is well recognized in the field of traumatic brain injury. A recent review observes, "Deficits that are clearly evident to family or therapists are often not 'seen' by the individual, are judged to be inconsequential, or are discounted" (Flashman, Amador, & McAllister, 2011, p. 307). Individuals who are head injured are likely to be "less reliable in their assessment of their capacity for sound judgment, cognitive skills, interpersonal skills, and other aspects of social behavior."

This effect has been identified in most generalized disorders of brain function, such as Alzheimer's. It is also well known that individuals using recreational or illegal drugs, such as marijuana or alcohol, often and even characteristically lack judgment or insight into their cognitive and emotional impairments. But this lack of awareness or judgment about mental deficits or dysfunction has not hitherto been seen as an adverse effect of *all* psychoactive substances, *including psychiatric drugs*, even though there is considerable evidence for it in clinical experience and the scientific literature (Breggin, 2006d, 2008a, 2008b, 2011c). I have described this clinical phenomenon as medication spellbinding or intoxication anosognosia (not recognizing intoxication in oneself).

MEDICATION SPELLBINDING

Even in routine use at relatively low doses, people often fail to recognize the psychosocial impairment that they are experiencing from using psychoactive substances. Those who become disinhibited after drinking alcohol at a dinner party may feel certain that they are the life of the party. If they sense that something is going wrong—for example, when they start feeling embarrassed—they are likely to blame it on other people and not on the effects of alcohol on their behavior. If a friend suggests that they are too impaired to drive home, they may become resentful. If they decide to drive, they may endanger their own lives and the lives of others in ways they would never do when sober. Identical clinical phenomena are also found as effects of any sedative drug, including the benzodiazepines used in surgery for anesthesia and in psychiatry to treat anxiety and insomnia.

Medication spellbinding occurs when an individual who is taking or recovering from a psychoactive substance fails to appreciate the negative impact of the drug on his or her mental status or behavior. If individuals do perceive that they are impaired, they will blame it on something other than the drug, such as their "mental disorder" or stressors and provocations in the environment. In extreme cases, individuals may act in an irrational, out of character, and dangerous manner without perceiving that they are impaired or acting badly. They will be unable to evaluate their actions in a rational manner until they have recovered from the medication spellbinding.

Medication spellbinding is very common and probably occurs to some degree in most psychiatric drug treatments. Patients often fail to recognize drug-induced apathy. Individuals taking antipsychotic drugs, stimulants, mood stabilizers, or antidepressants tend to gradually lose their interest or zest for work, hobbies, lovemaking, and eventually the people in their lives. They may experience some relief of suffering from the apathy, but they will have little or no idea that they are impaired and increasingly disengaged from their lives.

Children frequently become less spontaneous and mildly depressed while taking a stimulant drug for attention deficit hyperactive disorder (ADHD), and yet be pleased that they are "better behaved" and gaining approval from parents at home and teachers at school. The children will not realize that they are less engaged with everything in their lives, including socializing and playing with their friends.

Anger is another common expression of medication spellbinding. An individual taking an antidepressant, or going through withdrawal, becomes very irritable and has a violent outburst of anger at family members without any significant provocation. Although he or she has been warned that the medication can cause an impulsive anger, medication spellbinding renders him or her unable to connect the warning with the behavior.

A family member may remind the spellbound individual that the doctor warned about antidepressant withdrawal causing irrational anger. Although it is generally a good idea to reassure the person that he or she is undergoing a drug effect, the spellbound individual may feel invalidated and further angered, believing that it "had nothing to do with the drug."

Anxiety can be caused by many psychiatric drugs and is frequently masked by medication spellbinding. The individual is likely to attribute the anxiety to his or her emotional problems or to current life stressors without considering that the drug might be driving the emotion.

After longer term exposure to any psychiatric drug, the individual is likely to develop cognitive problems, such as short-term memory dysfunction and difficulty maintaining attention or focus. He or she will blame it on getting old, being tired, being bored, having too much work to do, or resenting the boss—without giving consideration to the effect of the prescribed medication.

This failure to appreciate medication-induced mental and emotional impairment is especially insidious in long-term psychiatric drug treatment during which patients commonly fail to detect the gradual onset of apathy, along with the erosion of mental faculties that too often occurs. An obvious chronic brain impairment (CBI) may evolve toward dementia without the individual ever grasping the degree of his or her disability or its development in association with the medication. In these cases, the prescriber must be alert for mental deterioration and responsive to any reports from the therapist, family or support network.

EXTREME AND DANGEROUS REACTIONS

In *Medication Madness*, I reviewed more than 50 cases from my clinical and forensic practice of dangerous abnormal behavior produced by exposure to psychiatric drugs, including violence, suicide, and crime (Breggin, 2008b). In nearly every case I had complete access to medical and police records, occupational and educational records, and interviews with the individual or survivors. In very few of the cases did the individual have any inkling that the drug was worsening his or her behavior. In some cases, individuals felt the drug was helping—even as their mental condition deteriorated and their behavior became more dangerous. Among patients who left suicide notes, only in one case was there a hint that the medication was a problem.

A patient's professional knowledge about medication effects does not necessarily prevent medication spellbinding. In several cases that I describe in *Medication Madness*, the victims were physicians, including one sophisticated psychiatrist who assaulted a female colleague and made a bizarre suicide attempt while taking fluvoxamine (Luvox). He was convicted of assault, sent to jail, and remained on the antidepressant in prison. He did not realize that the drug might have been involved in his behavior until he was removed from it several months later. By the time he asked me to consult with him in jail, it was too late to change the legal outcome, and his sentence would soon be over. However, he was vastly relieved to learn that many others had also become unaccountably violent while taking the newer antidepressants.

As described in Chapter 5, a recent analysis of all adverse drug reactions reported to the Food and Drug Administration (FDA) found that three drug classes have the most reports per prescription for "homicide, homicidal ideation, physical assault, physical abuse, or violence-related symptoms" (Moore, Furberg, Glenmullen, Maltsberger, & Singh, 2011). Although all classes of prescription drug were examined, these three classes of psychiatric drugs were at the top in the following order: antidepressants, sedatives and antianxiety drugs, and stimulants. These findings correspond exactly with my clinical and forensic experience. By far, the most inquiries and cases I have received and evaluated concerning drug-induced violence involve the newer antidepressants, followed by the benzodiazepines, and then the stimulants.

> Extremely dangerous and destructive antidepressant adverse drug reactions are not very common, but they provide a window into drug-induced phenomena that affect most, if not all, individuals who receive sufficient psychoactive medication to modify their mental condition.

The following case history is based on the patient's complete medical and police records and extensive interviews with the individual, family members, and other sources:

ILLUSTRATION: MURDER CAUSED BY PROZAC

At age 16 years, Jack felt he was becoming depressed. He was passing in school, had friends, and had no history of criminal activity, suicidality, or violence. Although his feelings of depression were subtle enough that no one else recognized it, at Jack's request his mother nonetheless agreed to take him to their primary care doctor, who started Jack on fluoxetine 20 mg/day. Nine days later Jack attempted suicide for the first time by ingesting his grandfather's oxycodone.

After the suicide attempt, the primary care doctor and Jack's parents became concerned that the antidepressant could be making him worse, and Jack was referred to a psychiatric clinic. Unfortunately, the clinic psychiatrist seemed to respond positively to Jack's belief that the medication was actually helping him, and he continued the dose. Over the next 2 months, during a relatively stress-free summer vacation at home, Jack's condition markedly worsened. He initiated very angry confrontations with his parents, briefly ran away from home, cut himself for the first time, frequently seemed anxious and agitated, took unaccustomed risks, and on occasion asked his family bizarre questions with violent implications, such as "would you kill someone for a million dollars?"

After 6 weeks of worsening behavior with increasing anxiety, agitation, and irritability, Jack's mother was able to obtain a follow-up appointment at the clinic, where she explained that Jack was not acting "like my son" anymore. She feared that the fluoxetine was making him worse. Jack, however, told the psychiatrist the medication was actually helping him and denied having any serious problems. The psychiatrist decided to raise Jack's fluoxetine dose to 30 mg/day.

Seventeen days later, with only the most minor provocation, Jack abruptly killed a good friend with a single stab to the chest with a kitchen knife. He had no explanation for why he committed the assault and denied wanting to kill his friend.

In jail, Jack decided that the medication wasn't good for him, and he was allowed to taper off. Staff in the jail noticed a marked change in Jack when he was medication free. He became a normal teenager— someone wholly unlike the rest of the inmates. His counselor said that in 20 years he'd never seen an incarcerated youngster so wholly lacking in the characteristics associated with youthful perpetrators of violence and crime.

The defense hired me as a medical expert. Jack reported having no recollection of the assault itself and only a vague recollection of the two prior months under the influence of fluoxetine. He had no awareness that his behavior had deteriorated on the drug and did not promote the view that the drug had caused his violence. Although he had now learned about the adverse effects of fluoxetine, he admitted he could not recall any harmful effects while he was taking it. He continued to have no explanation for his violent attack on his friend.

Jack's case was heard before a judge who confirmed my testimony and my written report that a fluoxetine-induced mood disorder with manic features (292.84) had caused the 16–year-old to become violent. The judge also agreed that Jack was no longer a danger to himself or others, now that he was free of fluoxetine (Heinrichs, 2011). The judge sentenced Jack as a youth offender and ordered him released within 10 months.

Jack's case exemplifies the need to reduce or stop antidepressant medication; at the first appearance of potentially serious adverse psychiatric effects, in this case, the typical stimulation or activation spectrum of antidepressant-induced adverse effects. It also illustrates medication spellbinding—that the individual suffering from the adverse mental and behavior effects may not recognize them, may falsely believe that the medication is helping, and may even feel like he is doing fine—until taking a dangerous, harmful, out of character action. This case also confirms the importance of the practitioner listening to family concerns about adverse drug reactions.

Medication spellbinding often affects patients during medication withdrawal. With the newer antidepressants, hostility or aggressive feelings are relatively common during withdrawal. On a few occasions, I have educated individuals thoroughly at each weekly session about the risks of irritability and aggression during withdrawal, only to have them lose their tempers with loved ones in an unexpected fashion without giving a thought to drug effects.

Educating the family in a therapy session about withdrawal reactions has proven very useful in these cases. Their knowledge about irritability as a common withdrawal reaction has helped family members to remain calm, to reassure the patient, and to make sure the patient communicates with me.

When patients have been withdrawn from psychiatric drugs and medication spellbinding starts to abate, it often feels to them as if a veil is being lifted. They realize for the first time that they have been acutely or chronically impaired in their mental life and that they have been unable to accurately evaluate themselves. Individuals frequently find that they are returning to the level of mental and emotional functioning that they were at prior to the medication. For the first time, they are able to benefit from counseling or psychotherapy to help with their underlying problems, as well as the more recent problems created by medication spellbinding.

> Because of medication spellbinding, prescribers and clinicians cannot take patient reports at face value when they say they are doing well on medication.

It is necessary to thoroughly evaluate patients at each visit to determine their emotional and cognitive status and to assess as much as possible their actual behavior outside the clinician's office. In several of my forensic evaluations, within a week or two of starting an antidepressant, patients have told their doctors in effect, "I've never felt better in my entire life." The prescribers took this as a sign that the medication was helping, when it was in fact the start of drug-induced manic-like episodes that ultimately led to violence.

Reports from family and significant others can be critical regarding assessing the patient's well-being during treatment and drug withdrawal.

Special attention should be given to the possibility of *acute* adverse reactions when starting a medication or during dose changes up or down. Special attention should also be given to *chronic* changes developing after months of treatment, including aspects of CBI, such as apathy, emotional instability, cognitive decline, and reduced quality of life.

KEY POINTS

▧ Medication spellbinding (intoxication anosognosia) is the tendency of any psychiatric drug (or psychoactive substance) to render individuals unable to perceive or to fully appreciate the drug's harmful effects on their mental life and behavior. Individuals may even feel that they are doing better than ever while undergoing significant clinical deterioration.

▧ Because of medication spellbinding, individuals often do not recognize adverse mental and behavioral effects during drug treatment or withdrawal. If they do recognize that they are experiencing emotional distress, they tend to blame it on themselves (their "mental illness") or on other people or on stressors. They may become uncharacteristically and inexplicably suicidal or violent.

▧ Medication spellbinding is an aspect of chronic brain impairment (CBI). Individuals undergoing longer term treatment can become apathetic, emotionally unstable, and cognitively impaired (aspects of CBI), without realizing that their quality of life is growing worse and worse.

▧ Clinicians should be aware of medication spellbinding and carefully evaluate the patient's reactions to drugs, even if the patient feels he or she is doing "better than ever." The patient's support network can provide invaluable information about how the patient is really doing.

▧ After withdrawal from medication has been partially or fully completed, previously medication-spellbound individuals often realize for the first time that they were significantly impaired and that they are now recovering and returning to themselves. They become much more able to benefit from counseling or psychotherapy and to enjoy life.

PART II

The Drug Withdrawal Process

CHAPTER 10

Withdrawal Reactions From Specific Drugs and Drug Categories

Every psychiatric drug can produce withdrawal reactions. This is in part because the brain accommodates to the psychiatric drug, leaving the brain in an abnormal compensated state when the drug is reduced or stopped. In addition, brain dysfunction caused by the drug may become more apparent when the individual's perceptions and judgment are no longer clouded or otherwise impaired by the drug. This, too, will be experienced as a withdrawal reaction, although it is a direct toxic effect on the brain that the individual is more able to recognize after the dose reduction or stoppage. Patients exposed long-term to psychiatric drugs are likely to experience intense emotional reactions that may at times be frightening and even dangerous.

Withdrawal reactions can often be distinguished from the individual's preexisting psychiatric disorder and from newly developing psychiatric problems during the taper. They usually develop shortly after a drug reduction and disappear after a return to the previous dose.

Each class of psychiatric drug, as well as individual drugs, tends to have its own characteristic withdrawal reaction. However, variation is great from patient to patient, and knowledge of the interactions between drugs, brain, and mind is scanty at best. Clinicians, patients, and their families should be prepared for the unexpected during drug withdrawal.

DISTINGUISHING WITHDRAWAL SYMPTOMS FROM PSYCHIATRIC OR PSYCHOLOGICAL REACTIONS

It can sometimes be very difficult, and even impossible, to distinguish a withdrawal reaction involving anxiety, depression, mania, or other psychiatric symptoms from the patient's original psychiatric problem. It can be especially difficult to distinguish withdrawal symptoms from newly developed psychiatric symptoms when stressors arise during or shortly after the taper, such as conflicts at home or work or any other loss or stressor.

Despite the occasional difficulties, withdrawal symptoms can general be distinguished from previous psychiatric problems by the following:

1. The symptoms—such as anxiety, depression, suicidality, hostility, mania, or psychosis—emerge within days or weeks of reducing or stopping the drug. Only occassionally, they may emerge after longer periods.

2. The emotional symptoms are often associated with the development or worsening of known *physical* withdrawal symptoms from the drug, such as abnormal movements, dizziness, headache, paresthesias, flu-like symptoms, hyperactive reflexes, muscle cramps, gastrointestinal problems, and the broad array of physical symptoms described later in this chapter.

3. The symptoms are sometimes experienced by the patient as "physical" in nature or as alien, unusual, and unrelated to previous psychiatric symptoms. Sometimes the symptoms feel unnerving or frightening in a way that the patient's familiar psychiatric symptoms are not. This criterion is useful as a positive indicator of a withdrawal reaction.

4. The symptoms are greatly relieved or disappear shortly after resuming the previous dose of the drug, often within an hour on an empty stomach, and almost always within a few hours. In my clinical experience, the effect of resuming the medication is usually so rapid and positive that patients are surprised and convinced by the experience that they suffered a withdrawal reaction. This is such a consistent and predictable response that, when it does not occur, the clinician should suspect something unexpected, such as the development of an unrelated physical disorder, the covert use of nonprescription drugs, or a psychological stressor that the patient has not reported.

PRESUME IT'S A WITHDRAWAL REACTION

Too often, clinicians assume that any psychiatric symptom is related to an inherent disorder within the patient rather than related to a direct drug effect or a withdrawal effect. Drug doses are reflexively increased or additional drugs are added. This leads to patients being treated with too large doses of medication and too many different medications at the same time. These will always lead to a worsening of the patient's condition.

Whenever symptoms emerge or worsen during dose changes, *either up or down*, the clinician should evaluate the probability that the symptoms are related to medication. For example, if a patient develops manic-like symptoms during an antidepressant dose adjustment up or down, the clinician should assume it is drug induced until proven otherwise. If the manic-like symptoms appear during steady or increased dosage, then the drug dose should be reduced or stopped. If, instead, the manic-like symptoms appear during dose reduction and are intolerable or dangerous, then the previous dose should be resumed and close monitoring should be instituted.

Of course, clinical practice can be complicated, but in general the clinician will best serve the patient by being acutely aware of the possibility that a psychoactive medication is causing any emerging or worsening symptom, especially during dose increases or decreases or during long-term treatment.

ANTIDEPRESSANTS

Newer Antidepressants

Similar withdrawal reactions are produced by the selective serotonin reuptake inhibitor (SSRI) antidepressants and other commonly used non-SSRI antidepressants, including duloxetine (Cymbalta), venlafaxine (Effexor), desvenlafaxine (Pristiq), mirtazapine (Remeron), and bupropion (Wellbutrin and Zyban). A list of antidepressants can be found in the Appendix.

It is now recognized that withdrawal reactions from the newer and often more stimulating antidepressants present serious hazards. Clinicians and researchers have developed symptom lists for antidepressant withdrawal (Baldessarini et al., 2010; Breggin, 2008a; Haddad, Anderson, & Rosenbaum, 2004; Shipko, 2002). Combining these and other sources and drawing on my clinical experience, the following is an updated overview of antidepressant withdrawal symptoms from the newer antidepressants:

1. **Depression**, *a frequent and very serious risk requiring careful monitoring during withdrawal*, often episodic and sudden in onset with "crashing," easy crying, despair, and suicidality. This can be unexpected and feel overwhelming.
2. **Activation or stimulation**, *a less frequent but very serious risk requiring careful monitoring*, with euphoria, shallow emotions, giddiness, irritability, poor judgment, mania, agitation, anxiety, paranoid feelings, and impulsive outbursts of rage and violence. These symptoms, such as depressive feelings, can be unexpected and feel overwhelming.
3. **Cognitive dysfunction** with "fuzzy" or slowed thinking, poor concentration, memory problems, and in some cases, confusion and disorientation.
4. **Sensory symptoms**, including paresthesias, such as numbness and tingling; electric shock-like sensations (zaps), most commonly in head, neck, and shoulders; rushing noise in the head; ringing in the ears; and

palinopsia (visual trails). Abnormal sensations are very frequent and potentially very distressing and troublesome to the patient.

5. **Disequilibrium**, including dizziness or lightheadedness, vertigo, and ataxia, including a need to hold rigidly still.
6. **General somatic symptoms**, including flu-like symptoms, aching muscles, lethargy, headache, tremor, sweating or flushing, and heat intolerance.
7. **Movement disorders**, including hyperactive reflexes, akathisia, restless legs, tremors, difficulty coordinating speech and chewing movements, uneven gait, and bradykinesia (slowing of movements).
8. **Sleep disturbance**, including insomnia, nightmares, and excessive and vivid dreaming.
9. **Gastrointestinal symptoms**, including anorexia, nausea, vomiting, and diarrhea.

All of these symptoms can be abrupt in onset. The psychiatric aspects, such as despair, anxiety, and rage, are often amenable to the calming influence of an empathic intervention. When they subside, patients can be left with feelings of dismay and discouragement, followed by a relatively complete recovery as they accept that the episode was indeed neurological rather than psychological in origin.

I have seen withdrawal giddiness go on for several days, requiring resumption of the previous dose of medication, followed by immediate relief. Feelings of helplessness are often pronounced and recovery of confidence can take several days or more in serious cases.

Tricyclic Antidepressants

The older tricyclic antidepressants include imipramine (Tofranil), desipramine (Norpramin), amitriptyline (Elavil), nortriptyline (Pamelor), clomipramine (Anafranil), doxepin (Sinequan), and others (see Appendix). These antidepressants can cause severe withdrawal reactions frequently in the form of cholinergic rebound (Breggin, 2008a; Howland, 2010b). Withdrawal symptoms include the following:

1. **Psychiatric symptoms** including restlessness, anxiety, depression, mania, and psychosis.
2. **Sleep disturbances** including insomnia, vivid dreams, and nightmares.
3. **Cognitive dysfunction** including memory problems and in more severe cases confusion and delirium.
4. **Flu-like symptoms** including anorexia, nausea, vomiting, and diarrhea; runny nose; headache; fatigue; muscle aches and cramps.
5. **Cardiovascular symptoms** including arrhythmias, hypertension or hypotension, and palpitations.

Although not usually as severe as withdrawal from the newer antidepressants, after years of exposure, some patients have found the tricyclic antidepressants extremely difficult to stop. Nausea can be especially difficult.

Monoamine Oxidase Inhibitors

The monoamine oxidase inhibitors (MAOIs) have been used less often in recent decades, and a specific withdrawal syndrome has not been well defined. Reports in the literature indicate that the withdrawal reactions can be very severe, including extreme depression, anxiety and agitation, disorientation, delirium, and psychosis. As in any withdrawal, be prepared for any kind of extreme emotional or neurological reaction. Because these drugs tend to produce hypertension, be prepared for a rebound hypotension.

ANTIPSYCHOTIC DRUGS

Too rapid withdrawal of antipsychotic drugs is associated with the more rapid onset of severe psychiatric reactions, including psychosis (Howland, 2010a).

As described in Chapter 4, antipsychotic drugs produce a variety of syndromes that can become especially severe during withdrawal, including all of the dyskinesias associated with tardive dyskinesia (TD), tardive psychosis, and tardive dementia.

I have evaluated many cases of abrupt antipsychotic drug withdrawal that have resulted in extraordinarily distressing outbreaks of severe abnormal movements, along with enormous anxiety and sometimes psychosis, which have required emergency room visits. Too often, the obvious withdrawal reaction has been misdiagnosed as a primary psychiatric problem, such as schizophrenia or panic attack, and the antipsychotic drug has been resumed, leading to very severe and persistent cases of TD.

After withdrawal, improvement is sometimes seen in TD over months and years, but at other times, it becomes irreversible and worsens.

Because dopaminergic drugs suppress the vomiting center in the brain, nausea and vomiting are common and very difficult to tolerate withdrawal symptoms. Uncommonly, neuroleptic malignant syndrome (NMS), Parkinsonian symptoms, and dystonias can occur during withdrawal (Howland, 2010a).

With the exception of clozapine (Clozaril), all antipsychotic drugs block the neurotransmitter D_2 and therefore can cause all of these withdrawal reactions. Despite its lack of impact on D_2, clozapine is one of the most potent causes of tardive psychosis (Moncrieff, 2006).

Before withdrawing a patient from an antipsychotic drug, it is important to review its pharmacological effects because they vary considerably from agent to agent.

If the antipsychotic drug has anticholinergic effects, then withdrawal can produce cholinergic rebound, including nausea (which is also produced by dopaminergic effects common to all widely used antipsychotic drugs) and a fatigue-like syndrome and other complications described above in regard to the older antidepressants.

If the drug has significant alpha-adrenergic effects, then rebound can result in "rebound anxiety, restlessness, sweating, tremors, abdominal pain, heart palpitations, headache, and hypertension" (Howland, 2010a, p. 13).

In my clinical experience, withdrawal from the newer "atypical" neuroleptics, especially olanzapine (Zyprexa), can produce extreme feelings of despair, depression, and fatigue.

The patient who attempts to withdraw from antipsychotic drugs after years of exposure faces many roadblocks and hardships. The patient with the relatively drug-free brain and mind will also become more painfully aware of lingering and possibly irreversible adverse drug effects. As in withdrawal from all psychoactive substances, the brain becomes "more alive" when drug free. Cognition improves as chronic brain impairment (CBI) improves, and emotions become more powerful. With greater awareness and increased feeling, the patient may also have to deal with drug-induced effects on the central nervous system, including TD, tardive psychosis, and tardive dementia, as well as obesity, diabetes, and other disorders characteristic of the newer antipsychotic drugs. Individuals coming off antipsychotic drugs after years of exposure can expect a roller-coaster ride of emotions that requires considerable support from clinicians and the patient's support network.

Antipsychotic withdrawal reactions can include the following:

1. **Psychosis** may persist as tardive psychosis, which becomes irreversible. This is sometimes misdiagnosed as schizophrenia. It is often more severe and disabling than the original problem that led to treatment.
2. **Emotional lability or instability**, which can include anxiety, paranoid reactions, depression, irritability, violence, and mania. The depressive symptoms are commonly severe. These withdrawal reactions may be misdiagnosed as bipolar disorder. The symptoms are often more severe and disabling than the original problem that led to treatment.

3. **Abnormal movements**, sometimes very severe and frequently associated with extreme agitation and anxiety, often leading to emergency treatment. The abnormal movements may persist as TD, tardive dystonia, or tardive akathisia. These withdrawal reactions may be mistaken for anxiety, bipolar disorder, and even "hysteria" or some other psychological disorder.
4. **Cognitive dysfunction**, sometimes very severe, which may persist as tardive dysmentia (tardive dementia).
5. **Gastrointestinal problems**, including anorexia, nausea, vomiting, and diarrhea.
6. **Physical rebound** problems that may be characteristic of the particular drug, such as *cholinergic rebound*, with extreme gastrointestinal problems, including nausea and a flu-like syndrome or *alpha-adrenergic* rebound with anxiety, restlessness, sweating, tremors, abdominal pain, heart palpitations, headache, and hypertension.

After years of exposure, antipsychotic drug withdrawal can be very difficult and requires a strong support network or hospitalization.

BENZODIAZEPINES AND OTHER SEDATIVE DRUGS

Benzodiazepines increase the activity of the neurotransmitter gamma-aminobutyric acid, which is the major inhibitory system in the brain. Because the benzodiazepines have an overall suppressive impact on brain function, rebound involves central nervous system activation similar to the delirium tremens (DTs) from alcohol, with potentially more severe and longer lasting withdrawal effects. Shorter acting benzodiazepines, including alprazolam (Xanax), lorazepam (Ativan), and oxazepam (Serax), can have more serious withdrawal effects; but any benzodiazepine can produce serious withdrawal problems. I have seen clonazepam (Klonopin), which is commonly used as a sleep aid or tranquilizer, produce very difficult withdrawals.

As made clear in the "XANAX XR CIV" (2011) label, even in relatively small doses, benzodiazepines can produce tolerance, dependence, and withdrawal reactions.

Benzodiazepine withdrawal effects include the following:

1. **Anxiety and agitation**, often extreme, may be similar to symptoms for which the drug was originally prescribed but often much more distressing and disabling.
2. **Sleep disturbances**, including potentially severe insomnia and also vivid nightmares and dreams.
3. **Irritability and nervousness** progressing to episodes of anger, rage, and violence.

4. **Central nervous system abnormalities**, a wide variety that can become severe, including memory and attention problems, confusional states, depression, hallucinations, delirium, and psychosis.
5. **Gastrointestinal problems**, including nausea, vomiting, abdominal cramps, and weight loss.
6. **Hyperarousal** with hypersensitivity to environmental stimuli (sounds, light, touch).
7. **Neurological and muscular disorders**, such as trembling, tremor, twitching, muscle cramps, and paresthesias in my experience, including disabling pain in the feet, which may persist.
8. **Weakness and fatigue**
9. **Seizures**

The severity of the CBI may be unmasked by the withdrawal, so that individuals become painfully aware of the deficits in cognition, including memory and attention.

Withdrawal from benzodiazepines can be very painful and dangerous, and when slow tapering is not feasible, hospitalization may be required. A rapid withdrawal as a hospital inpatient in a detoxification program can be preferable to a protracted withdrawal, especially in the absence of a support network. Inpatient programs for withdrawal from benzodiazepines are relatively available compared to programs for withdrawing from other psychiatric drugs.

Especially with the short-acting benzodiazepines, such as alprazolam, withdrawal can occur between doses during the day or on awakening in the morning.

The aftermath of benzodiazepine withdrawal can be very protracted with many symptoms persisting for months or years. These effects reflect drug-induced damage to the central nervous system, and sometimes dementia, rather than withdrawal effects (see Chapter 7; also, Breggin, 2008a).

Nonbenzodiazepine sleep aids, including zolpidem (Ambien), zaleplon (Sonata), and eszopiclone (Lunesta), have similar but less severe withdrawal reactions unless they have been abused.

STIMULANTS

Stimulant drugs, such as methylphenidate (Ritalin, Metadate, Focalin) and amphetamine (Dexedrine, Adderall), can cause rebound after only one dose, and they can cause serious withdrawal problems after protracted use at higher doses. However, these withdrawal reactions vary greatly among children and adults who have been prescribed these drugs within recommended limits.

Some children and youth are routinely taken off these medications on weekends, holidays, and summers. They may display no noticeable withdrawal effects or become lethargic and eat more for a brief time without any serious adverse effects. Paradoxically, they may become more anxious and agitated, again without any significant impairment. Teachers and parents often notice a negative change in a child's behavior after missing a stimulant dose and mistakenly attribute the change to the child's need to take the drug rather than to a withdrawal reaction.

When some children and adults abruptly stop stimulants, especially after prolonged exposure and especially at higher doses, they will suffer from a classic stimulant withdrawal syndrome, including "crashing" with hunger, fatigue, exhaustion, apathy, excessive sleep, depression, and suicidality. Social withdrawal and irritability with aggression may also result.

If the individual has been covertly abusing the drug, then withdrawal may be unexpectedly severe. The risks associated with stimulant use regarding abuse and dependence have been unfortunately played down by some authorities, but the Drug Enforcement Administration (DEA) has made clear the enormity of this risk (Sannerud & Feussner, 2000; also see Breggin, 2008a, pp. 300–303).

Stimulant withdrawal symptoms include the following:

1. **Inattention, hyperactivity, worsening behavior**, or any of the other problems for which the child was being treated.
2. **"Crashing"** with depression, social withdrawal, fatigue, excessive need for sleep and food, and suicidality.
3. **Irritability and anxiety** with agitation, anger, and aggressiveness.

LITHIUM AND OTHER MOOD STABILIZERS

Lithium

For some time, it has been well established that lithium withdrawal causes withdrawal mania and, to a lesser extent, depression (reviewed in Breggin, 2008a; Howland, 2010a). The increased rate of manic episodes occurs within the first 1–2 months after stopping the drug (Suppes et al., 1991). A 7-year follow-up found that lithium withdrawal caused both mania and depression and that stopping the medication did not worsen long-term outcome (Cavanagh, Smyth, & Goodwin, 2004). Many clinicians seem to believe that medication is an absolute necessity for warding off future manic episodes in patients diagnosed with bipolar disorder. However, I have not found this to be true, and the 7-year follow-up confirmed that withdrawing from and then doing without lithium does not worsen long-term outcome.

It is thought that gradual withdrawal may reduce the risk of withdrawal mania (Howland, 2010a). When withdrawing a patient from lithium, clinicians, patients, and their support network must be prepared for a period of emotional instability and possible mania or depression.

Other Mood Stabilizers

Many drugs prescribed for mood stabilization were initially developed as anticonvulsive medication, including *gabapentin* (Neurontin), *carbamazepine* (Tegretol), and extended-release carbamazepine (Equetro); and finally, *valproic acid* (Depakene), *sodium valproate* (Depakene syrup), and *divalproex sodium* (Depakote, an enteric-coated combination of the other two). Withdrawing from them presents the hazard of rebound seizures. This is not commonly a problem unless the individual is being treated for seizures, has a history of seizures, or is taking very large doses. Nonetheless, even when used in routine doses as a mood stabilizer, a gradual withdrawal is advised to protect against withdrawal seizures.

In addition to potential withdrawal seizures, carbamazepine is chemically similar to the older tricyclic antidepressants and can lead to the withdrawal reactions described earlier regarding those drugs.

Clonazepam is also prescribed as a mood stabilizer. As a benzodiazepine, it has all of the manifold and serious withdrawal reactions described earlier that are associated with that group of drugs.

Clonidine, an antihypertension drug, is sometimes prescribed as a mood stabilizer because of its sedative effects. It can produce dangerous rebound hypertension with rapid withdrawal.

During withdrawal from psychiatric drugs, the best rule is to expect the unexpected. Any adverse effect on the body, brain, and mind that occurs during withdrawal from a psychiatric drug should immediately be suspected as originating from the withdrawal. If a return to the previous dose of the drug ends the reaction, it was probably a case of medication withdrawal. Of course, any serious or life-threatening reaction should require a general medical consultation and evaluation in the process of determining its cause. During withdrawal, I instruct patients and their social networks to notify me regarding any unexpected, rapid onset medical or psychiatric problems.

In general, the shorter the exposure to a psychiatric drug, the more likely that the withdrawal will be easier and that recovery will be complete. This is one more cogent reason that clinicians should use caution in prescribing psychiatric drugs, especially for durations of months or years.

DRUG WITHDRAWAL IN CHILDREN AND THE ELDERLY

In my clinical experience, drug withdrawal is easier and smoother with children at least through the high school years. I have taken children and youth off combinations of psychiatric drugs with relative ease over a period of a few months. However, there is a huge caveat. In every successful case, I have been able to work with a responsible parent and sometimes with concerned teachers. The success of drug withdrawal with a dependent child is determined not only by the resilience and self-determination of the child but also by the maturity and responsibility of the adults on whom the child relies. Withdrawing children from drugs allows them to grow in self-determination without the burden of a drug-compromised brain.

The elderly are often overmedicated with too large doses, too many drugs, unnecessary drugs, and drug combinations that produce dangerous interactions. Medication withdrawal in the elderly can vastly improve their quality of life, as well as their longevity.

Drugs can cause adverse effects in the elderly in infinite ways. Cognitive dysfunction is especially susceptible to drug-induced harm, and anyone who has worked with the elderly will attest to the fact that many brighten up and return to a much higher level of mental and emotional functioning when psychoactive medication is reduced. Many elderly suffer from polydrug-induced CBI. Multiple medications are also associated with falls and therefore with increased disability and mortality.

Fortunately, drug dose reduction and withdrawal can often be accomplished in the elderly. A review of the literature found, "In conclusion, there is some clinical trial evidence for the short-term effectiveness and/or lack of significant harm when medication withdrawal is undertaken for antihypertensive, benzodiazepine, and psychotropic agents in older people" (p. 1021). The evidence for safe withdrawal of psychotropic medications was particularly strong. The patients in all studies involving psychotropics were "weaned over several weeks" and no "withdrawal syndromes" were reported (p. 1029). Although this finding of no withdrawal syndromes is probably somewhat unrealistic, it is encouraging in regard to psychiatric drug withdrawal in the elderly.

KEY POINTS

- All psychiatric drugs can produce withdrawal reactions.
- Clinicians should presume that any new or worsening symptom may be the result of a psychiatric medication, especially during dose changes up or down, lengthy treatment periods, or drug withdrawal.
- Withdrawal reactions can usually be distinguished from preexisting psychiatric problems or from new psychiatric difficulties by the proximity of the withdrawal reaction to a lowering of the dose and especially by relief of the withdrawal reaction within hours of resuming the previous dose. Another criterion for distinguishing a withdrawal reaction from psychiatric symptoms is the emergence or worsening of new physical symptoms known to be associated with withdrawal from the drug, such as abnormal movements, dizziness, paresthesias, and flu-like symptoms.

- Patients taking any psychiatric drug for years at a time should be prepared for an emotionally stressful withdrawal experience. Not only will they endure withdrawal reactions but also as they become drug-free they will become more painfully aware of any persistent drug-induced harm to their bodies, brains, and minds.
- *Antidepressants* produce many physically distressing withdrawal symptoms, as well as potentially dangerous psychiatric symptoms, including depression, suicidality, violence, and mania. Some neurological symptoms can persist for years.
- *Antipsychotic drugs* produce many physically distressing withdrawal symptoms, including abnormal movements, as well as many disabling psychiatric symptoms, such as psychosis and dementia. Symptoms can become persistent in the form of TD, tardive psychosis, and tardive dementia.
- *Benzodiazepines*, when given in moderate doses, can nonetheless produce tolerance and dependence and very severe withdrawal reactions usually involving symptoms of activation or stimulation, including anxiety, insomnia, and seizures, as well as behavioral abnormalities.
- *Stimulants* can produce withdrawal reactions usually characterized by "crashing" with fatigue, social withdrawal, depression, and the potential for suicide.
- *Lithium* withdrawal produces withdrawal mania and also depression. Other *mood stabilizers* vary in their effects, but none are free of them.
- Either caused by direct toxic effects or by withdrawal reactions, patients taking almost any psychiatric drug can develop persisting and potentially permanent drug-induced adverse reactions. However, the shorter the time of drug exposure, the more likely it is that the patient will fully recover. This is a strong reason for caution in starting any psychiatric drug and for even more extreme caution regarding prolonged exposure over months and years.
- Children and the elderly are especially susceptible to adverse drug reactions and often in need of drug reduction and withdrawal. Fortunately, drug withdrawal can commonly be safely accomplished in these vulnerable groups.

CHAPTER 11

The Initial Evaluation: Creating a Medication History While Building Trust and Hope

The initial medication history is created on basis of an active collaboration between the client and the clinician, and should be used to begin building a relationship of trust and hope for the future. Both the prescriber and the therapist have the duty within their knowledge base to monitor the patient and to provide information on adverse drug effects and the potential need for drug reduction or withdrawal.

It is no longer appropriate for therapists to limit their role to encouraging or enforcing medication compliance. Therapists are often in the best position to know and to monitor the patient, and to communicate to the prescriber, patient, and family about the patient's overall condition and the need for drug reduction or withdrawal. Prescribers and therapists alike, as well as patients and their families, should learn as much as possible about the effects of the medications that their patients are taking.

With at least 20% of the U.S. population taking psychiatric drugs in a year (Medco, 2011), the use of psychiatric drugs is so widespread today that most patients are already taking one or more drugs when the practitioner first meets them as a prescriber or a therapist. This chapter, in particular, addresses the initial evaluation of patients who have been on psychiatric drugs for months or years.

CHOOSING TO USE THE PERSON-CENTERED COLLABORATIVE APPROACH

A person-centered approach is at the heart of all good therapy, but when is a collaborative team approach required? This is one of the most important decisions the clinician must make in the initial evaluation in collaboration with the patient.

Many people who seek help from mental health professionals can be treated as autonomous individuals without the necessity of communicating with other professionals or family members. Children can never be successfully treated in isolation and should always be treated with the collaboration of parents and/or other adults in their lives. Adults who are dependent on others, such as their parents or state authorities, will almost always need the collaboration of others to make progress. The same is true with any adults who are seriously disabled emotionally or cognitively. Patients receiving routine psychiatric medication are also likely to suffer from medication spellbinding and/or chronic brain impairment (CBI) and should often be treated in a collaborative fashion. Many elderly patients will require a collaborative approach, especially if they are impaired or institutionalized.

This book focuses on potentially difficult medication withdrawals, but the same principles of the person-centered collaborative approach apply to all individuals who may be compromised in their judgment or ability to take care of themselves, from children to older adults, from patients with brain injury to patients who are emotionally disabled.

THE IMPORTANCE OF THE PSYCHIATRIC DRUG HISTORY

Before deciding with the patient how to proceed, the clinician should take a careful history of how the patient's current medication regimen evolved. If a patient is seeking or hoping for psychiatric drug reduction or withdrawal, two aspects are central to the first session: establishing trust and taking a thorough medication history. The two are often closely related because a patient will develop a sense of trust if the clinician takes a sincere interest in the patient's viewpoint of his or her medication history and if the clinician offers observations that are empathic, scientifically based, and informative.

THE DIFFERENCE BETWEEN RELAPSE AND WITHDRAWAL REACTION

Early in the process of taking a medication history, patients find it very helpful to discuss their previous experiences with relapses and drug withdrawal. In almost every longer-term case, the patient will have attempted to reduce or stop some or all psychiatric medications, usually without professional help, and often with painful results that discouraged further attempts.

It often turns out that what the patient and prescriber considered to be a relapse requiring more medication was in reality a withdrawal reaction requiring patience, understanding, and perhaps a temporary resumption of a previous dose.

Because many patients will experience similar withdrawal symptoms the second or third time around, it is also useful for both the patient and the prescriber or therapist to be aware of these symptoms in advance in order to readily identify and respond to them.

However, patients almost always have difficulty distinguishing between a withdrawal reaction, a relapse, or a spontaneous worsening of their emotional problems. What caused the unusually severe episode of anxiety that erupted 1 or 2 days after briefly stopping alprazolam (Xanax) last year? What caused the abrupt worsening of depression and irritability that took place a week or 10 days after stopping fluoxetine (Prozac)?

These confusing and distressing past experiences with drug withdrawal typically leave patients fearful and in doubt about trying again to reduce or to stop taking psychiatric drugs. It is important to educate and to reassure patients that the abrupt onset of severe emotional disturbances within days, and sometimes weeks, after stopping a psychiatric medication, often indicates a withdrawal reaction. It does not mean that the patient has a biochemical imbalance that requires drug treatment for its correction. It does not mean that the patient has to stay on the drug for the rest of his or her life.

These difficult and at times distressing issues should be discussed with the patient in a forthright manner by the professional evaluating the patient, including both the informed prescriber and the informed therapist. For the sake of honesty, informed consent, and building trust—the clinician should not shirk from explaining how the medications may have adversely affected the patient over the months or years. At the same time, the clinician should communicate hope, including the potential to reduce or taper off medication, and to make a new beginning in counseling and life.

CREATING A MEDICATION HISTORY

Because patients can find it difficult to recall their past medications and even to identify their current ones, I try to speak to the patient and/or the family on the phone in advance on the first session. If psychiatric medications are involved, I ask the patient to bring a written history of medication treatment to the first session, along with a one- or two-page chronology of significant life events, such as schooling, employment, anniversaries, children, hospitalizations, and changes in prescribers and therapists.

Depending on the complexity of the medication history, I will also suggest that new patients stop by their pharmacy to obtain a printout of their prescription history as far back as available. This can usually be accomplished with relative ease at the pharmacy. If a few medications are being taken, I ask the patient to bring in the current bottles. If psychiatric hospitalizations are involved, I ask them to bring any available records. Especially if they have been seeing a prescriber for the past few months or years, I may ask them to obtain a summary note to bring with them.

As described in Chapter 2, drug companies have encouraged patients, doctors, and even the FDA to designate psychiatric drugs by their therapeutic aim rather than by their chemical structures. For example, instead of being told that they are being prescribed an antipsychotic or neuroleptic drug, patients are told that the aripiprazole (Abilify) is a "bipolar drug" or that quetiapine (Seroquel) is a sleeping pill. Even if told the actual name of the drug, the patient is more likely to recall being told she is taking a bipolar drug or a sleeping pill. This makes it nearly impossible for the patient to Google or read about the drug independently and it can confuse the professional who is taking the patient's history.

The medication history and the brief chronology prepared by the patient and/or family can be very helpful in the initial session, first in establishing the patient's viewpoint on his or her psychiatric and life experiences, and second in limiting the need for the clinician to focus on detailed note-taking rather than on building rapport. The clinician should think of "creating" rather than "taking" a medical history. It is a collaborative effort.

> In the first session, patients often express a combination of relief and gratitude when the clinician takes the time to unravel the medication history, shows interest in listening to their concerns and viewpoint on their medication experiences, and offers objective scientific information and new insights into medication experiences.

If patients have been on several medications or had several hospitalizations, the prescriber or therapist may want to spend more than one session tracing the patient's progress or lack of progress parallel with the medication history. Often, it will turn out that the patient has deteriorated over the years in every area of life. Frequently, it will be possible to correlate the decline with the start of specific medications or increases in doses.

In many cases, a careful history will disclose that one medication after another has been tried, and doses have been increased for years at a time, while the patient got worse. Commonly, episodes of euphoria or worsening depression will be associated with the start of an antidepressant, and apathy and withdrawal will be correlated with the start of an antipsychotic or mood stabilizing drug. Often, anxiety and insomnia will have worsened with increasing doses of benzodiazepines over months or years.

Very likely, previous prescribers at no point suggested a lengthy drug holiday, along with regular therapy, to see how the patient would have done with a drug-free mind. This history can become a learning process for the prescriber, therapist, and patient in which the failure of the medications to help and their harmful effects become apparent.

For patients who do not have a desire to limit or stop their medications, the history remains important. Based on the clinician's understanding of the hazards of the patient's particular drug regimen—including polydrug therapy or long-term drug exposure—the medication history should always examine the possibilities of drug reduction and withdrawal.

> In reconstructing a medication chronology with the patient, be sure the patient does not end up feeling that the task has wasted a significant portion of the first session. The first session should deal with issues that are foremost on the patient's mind. Also, reassure the patient that no one can remember these past details very well.

FOUR COMMON SCENARIOS INVOLVING LONG-TERM MEDICATION

Many of the most difficult clinical scenarios involving polypharmacy and/ or long-term treatment fit one of the following four examples of typical medication histories, all of which are complicated by unrecognized adverse drugs that have been mistakenly treated with new or increased medication, rather than by drug reduction or withdrawal. Often, one of the four following illustrative models will emerge from the medication history taken in the first session or two.

First Scenario: Children on Multiple Drugs Starting With Stimulants

The child was first seen in elementary school or perhaps later on for problems that were diagnosed as attention deficit hyperactive disorder (ADHD). After taking stimulants for a while, the child developed difficulty sleeping and was placed on a sedative drug, often the antihypertensive agent clonidine. This became the first step in a downhill course of adding one medication on another to handle emerging drug-induced adverse effects.

After a few months, the child became agitated, anxious, and irritable, and may have developed aggressive reactions never before seen at home or at school. Instead of recognizing these negative changes as probable adverse drug effects, the dose of stimulant was increased or changed to something deemed to be more potent.

Over the next few months, the child began to show signs of crying easily, fatigue, disinterest, or frank depression. No recognition was given to the fact that stimulants and sedatives can cause these symptoms. Instead of reducing one or both drugs, or stopping them, an antidepressant was added to the regimen, creating polydrug therapy and making it more difficult to assess drug effects or to assign them to one specific drug.

The antidepressant soon caused increased overstimulation or activation, often in the form of one or more of the following: worsened insomnia, irritability, impulsivity, anger, and "mood swings." The child was now diagnosed with bipolar disorder and placed on a mood stabilizer or an antipsychotic drug.

This child now presents to you as a practitioner on four or five drugs covering the basic categories of stimulants, sedatives, antidepressants, mood stabilizers, and antipsychotic drugs.

The parents or the grown child will have little or no sense that the drugs were piled on in response to adverse drug reactions and instead will feel despairing about dealing with a presumably lifelong or chronic "illness." During the initial interview, they will be shocked to recall that, before being given the first drug years earlier, their child seemed entirely normal, except for some commonplace school issues.

At this point, you can begin to reassure the child and parents that the child does not suffer from a genetic or biochemical disorder—because none are known to be associated with emotional and behavioral problems—and that with family therapy in the person-centered collaborative approach, the child will almost certainly recover and find himself or herself again.

Second Scenario: Adults on Multiple Drugs Starting With Antidepressants

This patient's first drug exposure was to an antidepressant. The drug could have been prescribed for any number of symptoms from anxiety and depression to insomnia. The intensity of the symptoms could have been mild or severe. It may even have been given for fatigue or the need to lose weight or stop smoking.

Whatever the initial reason for the prescription, the antidepressant caused some degree of stimulation or activation, and the individual was eventually placed on sleep aids, often a benzodiazepine, as well as "as needed" doses of benzodiazepines for anxiety during the day. Over time, the individual's moods became unpredictable and distressing, and a mood stabilizer was added such as extended-released carbamazepine (Equetro) or divalproex (Depakote). If the patient's condition continued to deteriorate as a result of the load of psychiatric medications, an antipsychotic drug was probably added.

The adult who now seeks help from you as a mental health practitioner will talk about attempts to come off the medications, the subsequent worsening of his or her symptoms, and the regretted "need" for continuing medication. None of the previous practitioners will have tried to help the patient understand the downhill spiral of progressively more elaborate medicating as a response to adverse drug reactions rather than the patient's emotional problems. The adult will feel renewed hope and even a sense of liberation in learning from the history that he or she was in fact in much better shape before the medications began and that the increased emotional disability correlated with exposure to increasing numbers or types of medication.

In my clinical experience, even if this patient had been seriously depressed and suicidal when the antidepressant was first initiated, he or she is likely to do much better with good therapy and a careful withdrawal from the drug. It is now abundantly clear that antidepressants in the long-term make people more depressed and often disabled (see Chapter 5).

Third Scenario: Adults on Multiple Drugs Starting With Benzodiazepines

The patient told the original prescriber about some degree of stress, trauma, or anxiety, and sometimes even grief in response to a death, and was placed on a benzodiazepine. After several weeks, the anxiety worsened and the doses were increased, without the patient being informed that this is a commonplace course of events when benzodiazepines are taken for more than a few weeks or months. Eventually, a variety of drugs were introduced at various times to deal with the patient's worsening anxiety, including stimulants to jump start the over-sedated patient in the morning and increased doses of benzodiazepines at night for sleep. As cognitive deficits became apparent, a drug for Alzheimer's might have been introduced. Eventually, increasing mood instability and dysphoria led to a diagnosis of bipolar disorder and the prescription of mood stabilizers and antipsychotic drugs.

Often, these patients are taking stimulants not only to stay alert during the day but also to treat their "ADHD," which was actually benzodiazepine-induced cognitive dysfunction.

These patients have no idea that benzodiazepines commonly worsen anxiety and insomnia, and cause cognitive dysfunction—almost inevitably after several weeks or more of exposure. Instead, the patient recalls that the drugs provided considerable relief "in the beginning," which led over time to an increasingly frantic search for something to "relieve" the increasing anxiety as well as problems with memory and attention.

When you meet these patients as a new prescriber, therapist, or other practitioner, you will find an enormous amount of ambivalence and anxiety. During the medication history, they may readily grasp that they have been getting worse, but they have experienced such severe withdrawal after missing just one dose—and sometimes in between routine doses—that they will be terrified of even thinking about dose reduction, let alone drug withdrawal. The practitioner will need to display a combination of empathy, scientific knowledge, and willingness to give these patients reassurance and attention.

Fourth Scenario: Adults on Multiple Psychiatric Drugs Starting With Antipsychotics

Perhaps in the teens or young adulthood, this patient possibly had a psychotic break and was hospitalized. After discharge, the patient and family were told that antipsychotic medications would be required indefinitely. Taking the drugs turned out to be a very unpleasant and distressing experience that made the patient feel like a "zombie." However, after futile and emotionally agonizing efforts, the patient gave up trying to withdraw from these drugs, even though they seemed to "sap the life" out of him. On the newer antipsychotics, he experienced weight gain, increased cholesterol, and constant fatigue.

At some time, the antipsychotic drugs caused mood instability or depression leading to an additional diagnosis of schizoaffective or bipolar disorder, and more drugs were added. Some of these patients may be on five, six, or even more psychoactive substances. They are almost always on disability and living quiet lives of despair. They will tell you, "I've had every diagnosis and every drug in the book."

Too often, patients who fit these four model scenarios have been told by prescribers and therapists that they have biochemical imbalances and that they need to stay on their medications indefinitely or for the rest of their lives. All of them will harbor wishes and will have made attempts to cut back or withdraw with limited success followed by a worsening of their condition and a return to medication. Few of them will have any understanding of the long-term effects of psychiatric drugs or the distinction between withdrawal reactions and a relapse.

THE DEPENDENT PATIENT

When heavily medicated adult patients are on disability and living at home, or otherwise dependent on and involved with their parents, there may be insurmountable barriers to drug reduction and withdrawal on an outpatient basis. Withdrawal from antipsychotic medication is likely to cause the flaring up of a withdrawal psychosis (tardive psychosis) and the unmasking of the underlying drug-induced brain damage (tardive dementia). There is often considerable conflict between the patient and family, with the risk of angry encounters breaking out. The family may feel guilty about having encouraged the patient to take the drugs for years at a time and equally terrified of the patient having an acute breakdown with the need for further hospitalization. These are difficult situations requiring patience and family therapy.

It can be very difficult to withdraw dependent adults from psychiatric drugs. A strong sense of personal responsibility is the single most important indicator for successful medication withdrawal and this is typically missing in dependent individuals.

The initial therapeutic goals are several-fold: First, helping the individual to understand the meaning, importance, and practical application of taking personal responsibility. The dependent individual will naturally turn to the therapist for guidance and instruction while simultaneously rebelling against it. The therapist must actively encourage the individual to take an active part in the therapeutic decisions.

Second, the therapist must work with the dependent person's family. Sessions should involve all relevant family members, especially the parents.

Third, the therapist must work with the dependent person's school or residential home, dealing with both supervisors and the personnel who have the most contact with the individual.

Not only is this a complicated and time-consuming process, there is no guarantee of a positive outcome in trying to help dependent individuals reduce or withdraw from their medication.

Here's a sampling of what can go wrong.

As soon as dependent individuals begin to feel increasing emotional distress during the withdrawal process, they are likely to panic and imagine a catastrophic worsening. This will elicit overreactions in their family and caretakers. Instead of a natural bump in the process, everyone will see the withdrawal process as a failure and emotions will run high.

Dependent adults on multiple psychotic drugs always have long histories of ambivalent and highly conflicted relationships with their families and with institutions. Commonly, a parent will feel guilty and defensive about having started the son or daughter on psychiatric medications. There may be conflicts within the family about the withdrawal plan. A parent or significant relative may be dead set against risking any reduction in medication. The dependent adult may stir up fears in a parent or spouse who is already fearful about the process.

Dependent adults on polydrug therapy almost always have a history of acting in very disruptive and destructive fashions. Family members and caretakers understandably fear that drug withdrawal will lead to a resurgence of negative behavior, and indeed it may, especially in the short run. At the first sign of anything similar to past bad performances, those around the dependent patient may become very frightened. They may insist on permanently stopping any effort to decrease medication.

Within the current mental health system, the clinician practicing in an outpatient setting will have to recognize his or her limitations regarding helping severely disturbed and dependent patients reduce or withdraw from medications. In these cases, it may be best to set aside the issue of drug withdrawal for a lengthy period while the therapist helps the whole family work on issues such as resolving conflicts without emotional and physical violence, positive communication, and encouraging the autonomy and personal responsibility of the identified patient. When the family of a dependent and heavily medicated patient is unwilling or unable to engage in this kind of family therapy, there is little or no possibility of successfully reducing or stopping medication, especially on an outpatient basis.

ILLUSTRATION: AN INITIAL EVALUATION IN A RELATIVELY UNCOMPLICATED CASE

Tim was a 20-year-old college student in the final quarter of his junior year who had been taking the antidepressant fluoxetine (Prozac) since he was 15 years old. Tim first started taking fluoxetine after becoming depressed as a teenager. He was never suicidal and never hospitalized. The medication was started by his pediatrician and has been continued at the college medical clinic. The dose was raised from 20 to 40 mg/day when he began college in order to deal with the "stress" of starting school and being away from home. Although he had brief counseling in high school, this was his first visit to a psychiatrist.

Tim continued to have occasional anxiety, especially around exam time, but he hadn't felt seriously depressed since he began dating his girlfriend in his sophomore year. At that time, Tim became concerned that the drug was causing him to be impotent when trying to have sexual relations. Tim explained that his girlfriend, who had known him for more than 2 years, was concerned that he also seemed to be losing his ability to have fun and to enjoy himself. Tim therefore decided to stop the drug by himself and began by reducing the fluoxetine from 40 to 20 mg. After 1 week, he "crashed" into feelings of agitation and depression, and with the urging of his girlfriend, he returned to his former dose of 40 mg and felt better in a day or two.

Tim decided that he "needed" fluoxetine and that his clinic doctor was right that he needed to take it for the rest of his life. However, when the impotence continued, he read more about the drug on the Internet and realized that he might have had a withdrawal reaction. That was when he called my office.

Tim was not initially aware that he was not only losing his interest in sex; he was also losing his zest for life. However, during the initial evaluation, he began to think that his girlfriend was right. He no longer felt as alive as he used to and his interests, other than his girlfriend, had narrowed to obsessive studying. He explained, "It's kind of like a low grade depression but so much a part of every day, I didn't even recognize it or think about it until now."

Tim already knew that fluoxetine could cause impotence. He now asked me if antidepressants could also cause loss of interest and even a chronic low grade depression. I told him I'd seen many patients who developed apathy and depression on the selective serotonin reuptake inhibitors (SSRIs) and it was recognized in the scientific literature.

I explained that current research indicated that long-term exposure was emotionally blunting and disabling to most patients. This new information increased Tim's motivation to stop the medication.

I asked Tim if the relationship with his girlfriend itself might be causing or contributing to his impotence and to his "lackluster" feelings. He responded that he felt very much in love with her and that she loved him, too. He could find no reason in his life for impotence or for his persisting depressed feelings. He explained, "I know I can get anxious before exams or before trying to make love since my sexual problems started on the drug; but the depression is just there almost all the time for no reason at all."

Knowing that university students often abuse nonprescription drugs and alcohol, I explained to Tim that any kind of drug abuse could also contribute to or cause his current emotional problems. Tim admitted that he used to binge on weekends and smoke some marijuana in his freshman year, but his girlfriend's influence had put an end to anything but occasional social drinking.

When I asked Tim for more details of his sexual life, he explained that he was also impotent when he tried to masturbate while alone. Because the problem was not limited to being with his girlfriend, this increased the likelihood that it was physical and not emotional in origin.

Tim was also feeling some increased pressure and additional anxiety over finishing his junior year. His final grades were critical to the success of his job applications in the coming year. Both he and his girlfriend were remaining in town during the summer to work and so I suggested to him that it might be best to wait the few weeks until school was over before beginning the withdrawal in the summer. It can be easier to withdraw successfully when a person's life isn't overly stressed or pressured.

I explained to Tim that we might be able to finish the withdrawal process in the 3 and one-half months before the fall of his senior year. This was a very rough clinical estimate. Tim was an able young man without any incapacitating emotional problems, and he had strong support from his girlfriend and parents. If we are successful in withdrawing him before the start of school in the fall, I explained, I would like to follow up with him throughout the fall semester to make sure he

Nothing is more important than a positive, enthusiastic, and hopeful attitude on the part of the patients' healthcare providers, including prescribers and therapists. Patients are extremely sensitive to any nuance of discouragement coming from clinicians and can easily fall into fear and helplessness. On the other hand, an enthusiastic, positive approach can help the patient through the normal anxieties and the frequent setbacks that are often associated with psychiatric drug withdrawal.

did not have a delayed withdrawal reaction or relapse into depression over unresolved emotional problems. Tim looked visibly relieved at not having to begin withdrawal as exam week approached.

I emphasized that his medication withdrawal would be a collaborative process in which we start with a small dose reduction and then taper according to how he felt from week to week. I would cooperate with any decision that seemed reasonable. I gave him my office, home, and cell phone numbers.

Tim responded very positively to my "collaborative" approach, saying "this is the first time a doctor has treated me as an equal or given me any choice or any real information." This meant a great deal to Tim as it does to almost all patients. He also found my hopeful attitude very encouraging.

Toward the end of this first session, I explained to Tim that withdrawal from an antidepressant can result in almost any kind of emotional reaction from feeling depressed and suicidal to feeling euphoric (manic) and violent. I told him, "If you get any unexpected feeling, anything uncomfortable, anything that makes you feel reckless, anything that makes you feel suddenly better than ever, assume it's a withdrawal reaction and give me a call right away. If you can't reach me quickly, then simply return to your previous dose, and you should feel improvement within hours."

Although we would not be starting for several weeks, I wanted Tim to become familiar with what he may be facing. I planned to remind him about the risks associated with withdrawal each time we met, and to reemphasize them each time we made a reduction.

Although I did not anticipate a great deal of difficulty, I asked Tim if he would be comfortable telling his girlfriend about the withdrawal process and perhaps bringing her to one of his sessions in order to inform her about what to look for during his withdrawal.

Because he was still financially and somewhat emotionally dependent on his parents, and remained in regular phone contact with them, I also asked him how he would feel about informing them as well about the withdrawal process. Tim felt very good about involving his girlfriend. It also turned out that his parents had become concerned about Tim's long-term exposure to the antidepressant, and they were already supporting and paying for his treatment with me. This was a good sign because parental fear or resistance, especially regarding a relatively young patient like Tim, is one of the most difficult obstacles to overcome during withdrawal. Parental anxiety becomes communicated to the patient, and the withdrawal becomes much more frightening.

I emphasized to Tim that it could become nearly impossible for him, or anyone else, to recognize a withdrawal reaction when they were caught up in the unexpected emotions. The emotions can feel so "natural" that he would not attribute it to drug withdrawal. For that reason, I wanted Tim to permit and encourage his girlfriend and parents to contact me if they became concerned about him during withdrawal. Tim was agreeable to my suggestion and seemed even more reassured about undertaking the withdrawal process.

If Tim had not agreed to allow his girlfriend and/or parents to call me during an emergency, I would have discussed it with him further. If he had decided against allowing anyone to contact me, it is possible that I would not have agreed to withdraw him from medication.

As he departed at the end of his first session with me, Tim told me that he felt more optimistic about the future than he had in a long time.

INFORMATION PATIENTS WANT TO KNOW EARLY IN THE TREATMENT

Patients Want to Know at What Point in the Withdrawal They Are Likely to Experience Withdrawal Reactions

Although some prescribers believe that withdrawal reactions can only occur within a day or two after stopping a medication, in reality they can occur within weeks—and sometimes longer—of any decrease in dosage. On the other extreme, in some cases drug rebound or withdrawal can occur after a single dose of a drug. Startling results were documented in a placebo-controlled double blind study conducted at the National Institute of Mental Health (NIMH) involving normal children ages 6–12 years given a typical therapeutic dose of an amphetamine (e.g., Adderall, Dexedrine) (Rapoport et al., 1978):

> A marked behavioral rebound was observed by parents and teachers starting approximately 5 hours after medication had been given; this consisted of excitability, talkativeness, and, for three children, apparent euphoria. This behavioral overactive was reported (by diary) for 10 of the 14 subjects following amphetamine administration and for none of the group following placebo.

This study was unusual in its focus on withdrawal effects and confirmed that these problems are far more common than suggested by clinical experience and most drug studies that fail to systematically look for them. These effects can be very serious. In these 10 of 14 children with withdrawal effects, 3 suffered from "euphoria." It illustrates how children can grow worse on these drugs, leading to a mistaken diagnosis of bipolar disorder (euphoria) and additional medications.

With some drugs, patients and the entire treatment team need to know that withdrawal commonly occurs in between doses. Interdose withdrawal is especially frequent with short-acting medications known to produce dependency. Nicotine provides a familiar example. It is so short-acting that the smoker may go into withdrawal minutes after finishing his or her last cigarette, and experience uncomfortable degrees of nervousness and anxiety.

Interdose withdrawal can occur with all benzodiazepines, all effective sleeping medications, and all stimulant drugs. Alprazolam (12- to 15-hour half-life) and lorazepam (10- to 20-hour half-life) are both very commonly prescribed for anxiety. Because they are relatively short-acting, they are especially likely to cause patients to go into withdrawal in between doses during the day. Clonazepam is somewhat longer acting (18- to 50-hour half-life), but the variation is so large that the onset of the acute withdrawal effect in any given patient will be unpredictable.

Patients Will Want to Know How Large a Dose Reduction Is Required to Produce a Withdrawal Reaction

Some prescribers believe that it requires a large dose reduction to cause a withdrawal reaction. Although a large dose reduction is more likely to cause a more severe withdrawal reaction, even small dose reductions (less than 10%) can cause serious reactions.

Patients Will Want to Know How Severe Withdrawal Reactions Can Become

I have evaluated cases of severe suicidality and violence following the abrupt termination of antidepressants. The most severe cases have come to my attention through my forensic work, but even in my routine clinical practice, it is not unusual for a patient during antidepressant withdrawal to become *uncharacteristically* angry, threatening, and aggressive without provocation.

In summary, the opening session with a patient should include at least the start of a medication history along with building trust and a hopeful attitude to medication reduction or withdrawal. The clinician should offer an honest, scientifically based analysis of the hazards of medication and how they may have affected the patient negatively in the past. There is so little basis for maintaining long-term treatment with any psychiatric drug, and so much reason to fear long-term adverse effects, that the clinician should always lean toward withdrawing long-term patients from psychiatric medications whenever possible.

Prescribers and therapists alike should be aware of the kinds of withdrawal reactions described.

KEY POINTS

- In the initial evaluation, it is important to determine if the individual needs a person-centered *collaborative* approach. Regardless of whether or not medication withdrawal is anticipated, a collaborative approach is needed if the individual is a dependent child or adult or emotionally or cognitively impaired.
- Two major intertwined goals of the initial evaluation are to create a medication history based on an active collaboration between the patient and clinician while simultaneously building a relationship of trust and hope for the future.
- The clinician should offer an honest, science-based evaluation of the effects of the drugs on the patient's progress or lack of progress over the years. This is not only the responsibility of the informed prescriber but also the informed therapist. When adverse drug reactions or withdrawal reactions have been misidentified as "mental illness" by the patient or previous clinicians, the clinician must address this error in an honest fashion in order to fully inform and educate the patient.
- Patients are very sensitive to the attitudes of healthcare providers. A negative attitude toward drug withdrawal can be demoralizing, while a positive attitude can give the patient hope, courage, and determination.
- Both prescribers and therapists should be prepared to answer questions about medication adverse effects and the withdrawal process within the range of their knowledge. In the complex world of modern psychiatric drug treatment, therapists should no longer see their role as encouraging or enforcing compliance, but should instead actively participate in monitoring patients while providing information to the prescriber, patient, and family.

CHAPTER 12

Developing Team Collaboration

The era of patient compliance has been replaced by the era of patient choice. Patients are now recognized as autonomous, informed individuals whose decision making is critical to the success of therapy. Most prescribers no longer have the time to adequately monitor their patients, especially in difficult cases when it becomes necessary to actively engage the patient, family, and therapist in the withdrawal process. Therapists can no longer be expected to limit themselves to enforcing compliance. Instead, they must become responsible members of the treatment team who are most likely in the best position to monitor patients, to share information with the patient on the ongoing drug treatment, and to come to decisions with the patient about how to proceed. Patients and families are no longer passive recipients of treatment. Because they are focused on the limited list of medications prescribed to the patient, they can often learn more about adverse drug effects and withdrawal effects of the specific drugs than the professionals involved in the case. Prescribers and therapists have much to teach each other and the collaborative team, and they have a lot to learn from patients and their families.

After several weeks or more of use, most psychiatric drugs will have caused sufficient dislocations in brain function that withdrawal is likely to produce distressing symptoms. Potent benzodiazepines like alprazolam (Xanax) can cause serious withdrawal reactions after only a few weeks exposure. After many months of exposure, almost any psychiatric drug—or any psychoactive substance—is likely to produce potentially serious withdrawal problems.

Most attempts to reduce or to withdraw medication are initiated by the patient. In the past, prescribers, therapists, and other clinicians tended to insist that the patient remain on the current regimen or increase the dosage. Families used to feel that they should enforce the prescriber's

147

instructions to the patient. As a result, patients often decided to withdraw themselves, often cold turkey and in relative isolation—with sometimes dire results that entailed undo risk and suffering.

So much is now known about the therapeutic limits and the hazards of psychiatric drugs that everyone involved in the psychiatric treatment of patients must take a more cautious view of psychiatric medications and listen much more carefully to feedback from the patient and family about potential adverse effects. The patient's desire to consider drug reduction or withdrawal should always be taken seriously. The era of patience compliance has passed; the era of patient choice has begun.

THE PATIENT AS AN AUTONOMOUS INDIVIDUAL

In the patient-centered model, the patient is viewed and treated as an autonomous, independent person who has the right to participate fully in all treatment decisions and to veto any of them. This includes the patient's right to end the treatment at any time and, if desired, to seek help elsewhere. If the prescriber or therapist, in turn, decides that the patient is behaving irresponsibly, these clinicians also have the right to end the treatment relationship, provided that they do so without abandoning the patient under dire circumstances.

> The modern clinician–patient relationship is built on trust rather than authority, coercion, or fear; and the patient at all times makes the final treatment decisions. When a child is the primary focus, the child, too, is treated with respect and dignity, although ultimate decision making rests in the hands of the parents.

Nothing is more important than this: Modern healthcare requires the patient to take ultimate responsibility for all treatment decisions. As already noted, if the healthcare provider cannot accept the patient's freely made decision, then the healthcare provider can end the relationship, but the healthcare provider should not attempt to get the patient to accept treatment by withholding or manipulating information in a way calculated to lull the patient into false security about the risks of psychiatric medication. The modern healthcare provider encourages and welcomes a patient who is self-educated and well informed about any and all proposed treatments and expects the patient to have the final say on what treatments to accept or to reject.

THE RELATIONSHIP BETWEEN PRESCRIBERS AND THERAPISTS

Nurses, psychologists, social workers, counselors, and other nonprescribing clinicians have often been taught that their task is to push their patients to conform or comply with a prescribed medication regimen. This is based on an authoritarian model of medical practice in which the prescriber—originally, only the physician—stands atop the professional hierarchy and prescribes pills much as one would expect an all-knowing judge to dispense justice. In this outmoded model, the patient is supposed to depend solely on the prescriber as his or her source of information. The nonprescribing clinician is treated as a second class professional whose duty is to encourage patient compliance without making any independent evaluations, judgments, or communications about drugs, much like the patient in this model.

This authoritarian model is no longer feasible, no longer adequate, and no longer ethical from a number of perspectives.

First, in our information age, patients and their families are no longer limited to their prescribers for information about medication. A patient who logs onto a consumer website to research a particular psychiatric drug is likely to learn more about the specific hazards of the drug than a physician who talks with drug company salespersons, listens to lectures by drug company-sponsored experts, or relies largely on data from drug company-run clinical trials. In addition, the sheer availability of information, plus the initiative now taken by informed patients and their families, renders the old model obsolete.

The "doctor" is no longer the god-like conduit of medical and pharmacological truth—nor should he or she hope or wish to be. The modern prescriber knows that it is impossible for one person to keep up with all relevant up-to-date information about a drug, let alone the latest breaking information on drug hazards, and therefore welcomes input and feedback from every available source, including therapists, patients, and families.

The concept of compliance has been replaced with patient choice.

Second, in this information age, it makes no sense to hamstring therapists by asking them to act as if they have even less right than their patients to inform themselves and to communicate about the medications that their patients are taking. Modern psychotherapy requires an honest, open relationship between the patient and therapist and not a rigid predetermined relationship in which the therapist is constrained from openly discussing the patient's medications in every aspect according to the therapist's own knowledge base. It is no longer safe, effective, or ethical for therapists to be compelled to act as mere enforcers of the medical regimen.

Third, the modern prescriber seldom sees the patient for more than a few minutes and seldom sees the patient frequently. As a practical matter, the prescriber is not in as good a position as a therapist (or the patient and his or her family) to observe and evaluate the effects that psychiatric drugs are having on the patient. The modern prescriber should welcome the active participation of the entire treatment team in evaluating the patient's progress, including the impact of psychiatric medications on the patient—and including the need for dose reduction or stoppage.

A more egalitarian and respectful model of treatment is often more accepted in other areas of medicine, for example, in the treatment of diabetes compared to the treatment of psychiatric disorders. Patients with diabetes are much more likely to be encouraged to learn everything they can about their disorder, to involve their families in monitoring their treatment, and ultimately, to take responsibility for themselves, including their medication treatment and the healthy improvement of their lifestyles. In the best treatment settings, patients with cancer are given the same encouragement to take responsibility for their treatment. Unfortunately, in the mental health field, where the patient's self-determination is central to recovery and growth, there remains a lingering tendency to view the psychiatrist or physician as a figure of authority whose decision making is unilateral and unquestioned.

The Most Effective Prescriber–Therapist Relationship

A nurse practitioner, family doctor, or pediatrician is likely to find that a large percentage of patients present themselves with emotional problems. Too often, psychiatric medications are prescribed and the individual and the family are sent off to fare as well as they can on their own until seen again—sometimes not for weeks or longer. Even if the patient is given a referral to a therapist, too often, there will be little or no coordination between the prescriber and the therapist, and the therapist will be expected to avoid getting involved in issues surrounding medication treatment. In many cases, the patient does not see the purpose or benefit and simply neglects to follow-up by making an appointment for therapy. It is up to the prescriber to make sure the patient finds a compatible therapist as a part of the treatment regimen.

Given what we now know about the risk/benefit ratio of psychiatric medications, prescribers in every specialty will provide the best service by developing one or more relationships with therapists who can be trusted to make an initial psychiatric or psychological evaluation, to focus on the psychological and relationship issues that are at the root of most problems for which patients are given psychiatric drugs, and to help in monitoring any patients who take psychiatric medication. The prescriber would, of course, provide the initial medical evaluation while deferring the more time-consuming and specialized psychological evaluation to the therapist.

In one model, the prescriber can build a good relationship with one or two therapists and make sure they have similar ideas about each other's roles. They then remain in touch about the patient's progress and any medication issues. In another model, the therapist works in the same office or facility as the prescriber. Sometimes introductions can be made during the same visit.

In both models, medication monitoring would be joint and far more thorough than under typical conditions today. Many prescribers will find that the majority of their patients actually have emotional disorders and would benefit from a well coordinated prescriber–therapist relationship, providing much improved service to patients.

Medication Education for the Therapist

Everyone in the collaborative treatment team—prescribers, therapists, patients, and their support network—needs to understand the adverse effects of the drugs they are dealing with, as well as their withdrawal problems. As a consequence, Chapters 2–10 of this book present an introductory overview of adverse drug effects, including withdrawal reactions. The therapist who works with medicated patients can begin by studying the information in these chapters. Note, however, that no guide can provide all the information needed.

Keeping up with the latest information requires familiarity with several sources, including pharmacology and psychiatric textbooks, as well as the *Physicians' Desk Reference, Drug Facts and Comparisons,* and drug manuals for nurses, all of which are revised on a yearly basis. My book, *Brain-Disabling Treatments in Psychiatry* (2nd. ed.; Breggin, 2008a), can be used as a supplement to this book.

In building a good relationship with therapists, prescribers may wish to help facilitate their medication education by holding seminars for them, consulting with them, or directing them to specific sources of information. Therapists in turn may have more time or opportunity to keep up with the latest developments because of the smaller number of drugs they deal with, and therefore, may be able to provide useful current medication information to the prescriber.

A Special Role for the Therapist

Chapter 11 described the importance of a detailed medication history that correlates with the patient's progress or lack of progress over years or months. Prescribers often lack the time or opportunity to take a detailed medication history that examines the course of the patient's life against the drugs that were prescribed at various times. Family members, as noted, can be very helpful in creating this history. By contrast, the therapist can produce an outline of medications, hospitalizations, and other related events and correlate them with the patient's improving or worsening condition. As also noted in Chapter 11, it is often possible to correlate medication changes and dose increases with deterioration in a patient's condition over months or years at a time.

Therapists are frequently in a better position than prescribers to observe any negative impact of drugs on their shared patients. Prescribers too often see several patients an hour, limiting their ability to observe adverse effects or to judge the actual impact of the medication on the patient's mental life and behavior. These brief encounters may be limited in frequency to once a month or less. In the brief medication sessions, patients do not have the time to think through their own desires or to evaluate how they have been doing.

In light of current medical practice, it often falls to the therapist to notice adverse drug effects, such as increasing sedation, apathy, agitation, irritability, or subtle abnormal movements typical of tardive dyskinesia in the form of eye blinking or an occasional facial grimace.

Depending on the relationship between the therapist and the prescriber, the therapist may become an advocate for the patient who needs or wants a reduction or complete withdrawal from medication. The therapist's greater involvement in matters pertaining to medication should benefit both patients and prescribers, who are often too burdened to do the job they would like to do as far as taking histories and getting to know the patient.

If you are a prescriber who regularly practices by giving "med checks" to patients, I understand that you may find my observations unsettling. But consider what a higher quality of professional service you could provide by working with a therapist who knows about medications and who can collaborate with you, the patient, and the family in the interest of providing improved service. When you are no longer practicing in a therapeutic vacuum—when you are in direct contact with a knowledgeable therapist who works with both your patient and your patient's family—you will be able to provide much safer and more effective service. Whether you view psychiatric medications skeptically or enthusiastically, it makes good sense for prescribers and therapists to work as a team that involves, whenever necessary and possible, the patient's family as well.

Learning Drug Information From Patients and Their Families

Because they have to deal with so many medications, prescribers and therapists can benefit from drug information brought to them by patients and their families. Patients and families, with their more narrow focus on the specific medications prescribed for the patient, can easily learn more than the prescriber or therapist about the adverse effects and withdrawal effects of a specific drug or two.

In my clinical experience, it is not unusual for patients or their families to spend many hours and even days learning about the medications that are being prescribed. This is usually done in desperation when the patient and family feel they can no longer trust what they are hearing from the professionals. By the time they come to me as a last resort, they have often made themselves expert in the drugs they are taking. Instead of patients feeling forced to search for information out of desperation and often in opposition to their healthcare providers, healthcare providers should welcome all the information they can get from the patient and support network.

Patients and families are often able to learn more about the effects of a specific drug or two than the clinicians involved in the case who must keep track of innumerable psychiatric drugs and their effects. The entire collaborative team—prescriber, therapist, patient, and support network—should share information with and learn from each other regarding the specific drugs involved in the patient's treatment regimen.

THE SUPPORT NETWORK

Whether we are dealing with a child, adult, or elderly client, the individual's mental state is the single most important barometer of the progress of withdrawal. Only by paying close attention to how the client is thinking and feeling, and in particular to changes for the better or worse, can the withdrawal be conducted in the safest possible manner. This is true even if the patient is infirm because of age or dementia.

However, the patient sees the prescriber or therapist for only limited time. During office visits, because of medication spellbinding, the patient may not be able to report accurately on his or her mental state, especially regarding adverse drug episodes that are occurring episodically at home. During withdrawal, patients can easily run into serious and unexpected withdrawal reactions, including suicidal or violent impulses. At such times, the patient may be totally unaware of what is happening. They will feel despair or rage without attributing it to the medication and without contacting a health professional. This risk of medication spellbinding requires not only careful monitoring by healthcare professionals but also the involvement of collaborating friends or family.

The patient's family and friends know the patient best. They also spend the most time with the patient. Therefore, they are best able to observe and monitor the patient's condition at critical times, such as medication withdrawal.

Many therapists work without ever involving the family in the therapeutic process. Some therapists are theoretically or personally devoted to individual therapy. Some patients don't want their spouses, children, or parents involved in their therapy. There is room for an infinite variety of approaches to psychotherapy, couples therapy, and family therapy with adults and children.

This situation changes dramatically when an individual is going through drug withdrawal. If the individual has been on multiple medications or prolonged treatment lasting for years, a family member or significant other should, whenever possible, be involved. In some cases, it is not safe to proceed with drug withdrawal in the absence of a personal support network that has some involvement in the treatment.

Even in routine medication withdrawals, for example, removing a patient from a selective serotonin reuptake inhibitor (SSRI) antidepressant or a benzodiazepine after 3 or 4 months of exposure, it is best if the patient has a support network consisting of at least one close person who can help monitor the individual's condition. This cannot be overemphasized—a patient undergoing drug withdrawal may be the least likely person to recognize when they are becoming emotionally unstable, abruptly manic-like or depressed, or dangerously suicidal or violent.

As quoted in detail in Chapter 5, the antidepressant labels contain language specifically warning about "clinical worsening," including "the emergence of anxiety, agitation, panic attacks, insomnia, irritability, hostility, aggressiveness, impulsivity, akathisia (psychomotor restlessness), hypomania, mania, other unusual changes in behavior, worsening of depression, and suicidal ideation, especially early during antidepressant treatment and when the dose is adjusted up or down."

The aforementioned quote from the FDA-approved label for Paxil is specifically intended for antidepressants. However, the symptoms that are described cover such a broad range that they encompass, to one degree or another, withdrawal phenomena seen with many, if not most, other psychiatric drugs.

Even after patients have been fully warned that withdrawing from a drug may churn up unexpected painful emotions, they may not recognize that this is happening to them. For example, although a patient has been told on several occasions that withdrawal from an antidepressant may make him or her irritable or excessively touchy and angry, he or she can easily forget the warning when abruptly overreacting angrily to a friend, family member, or coworker. Instead, he or she will feel completely justified in venting anger on himself or herself or someone else.

At such times, before the patient becomes dangerously out of control, friends or family can help by reminding the patient, "You're not being yourself. You're having a drug withdrawal reaction. Let's call the doctor, nurse, or your therapist." Individuals undergoing drug withdrawal should be urged to inform at least one other person, preferably their closest friend or family member, that they are undergoing withdrawal and to look out for unexplained changes in behavior.

In more difficult cases—for example, if a patient has been prescribed several medications in combination for several years—the prescriber or collaborative therapist may want to *require* that the individual have personal support in place before withdrawing from the medication. In potentially difficult cases, the therapist should also *require* the patient's permission to allow members of his or her personal support network to contact the therapist directly, if necessary, during a crisis or emergency.

The person-centered collaborative approach involving the family is consistent with FDA recommendations in general for antidepressants. As stated earlier regarding Paxil: *"Families and caregivers of patients* should be advised to look for the emergence of such symptoms on a day-to-day basis because changes may be abrupt. Such symptoms should be reported to the patient's prescriber or health professional, especially if they are severe, abrupt in onset, or were not part of the patient's presenting symptoms" (emphasis added).

Whenever possible, patients should be encouraged to bring a friend, significant other, or family member into a session to discuss the problems associated with medication withdrawal. If the patient is emotionally stable and responsible, the clinician may be satisfied by a phone call with the patient's significant other or with reassurances from the patient that a support team has been created and informed about withdrawal problems. During withdrawal, it is best to make sure that at least one significant other in the patient's life has the clinician's complete contact information.

> Few things are more important in mental health treatment than paying close attention to what relatives have to say about a patient's adverse drug response or worsening condition.

LEGAL LIABILITIES

Therapists often worry that they will be sued for malpractice if they do not refer patients for medication treatment. If this were true, then therapists would have high insurance premiums, which they do not. The prescribers of psychiatric drugs have the high insurance premiums.

In the more than 40 years of my experience as a medical expert in psychiatric malpractice suits, I have heard about only two or three cases in which therapists have even been threatened with a suit for failing to refer a patient for medication evaluation. This unrealistic fear has been trumped up by unconscionable psychiatric drug advocates who wish to intimidate therapists into making referrals to them.

If a therapist is worried about a possible legal risk associated with not making a referral for medication evaluation, discuss with each patient the options for medication referral *from your clinical viewpoint* while making clear there are a variety of other viewpoints that frequently urge the use of medication. This should be done anyway in routine clinical practice and a brief note made in your patient record concerning the discussion and the patient's decision to seek or not to seek a medication referral.

Clinicians are understandably concerned about the risk of a patient committing suicide. But keep in mind that the class of drugs most often given to suicidal patients, the antidepressants, carry suicide *warnings*. Referring a suicidal patient for medication has no scientific or clinical justification. Many drugs are associated with increased suicide risk, and none are associated with reduced suicide risk. Put it another way, all antidepressants and many other psychiatric drugs carry FDA-mandated warnings about increased suicidality, and no drug is FDA-approved for reducing the risk of suicide.

Prescribers, and not therapists, face considerable risk in regard to the prescription of psychiatric medications. Therapists, however, rarely get sued for failing to refer for drugs. I've only had one such case that I can recall in my career. That was about 30 years ago, and the defendants were exonerated. Healthcare professionals from psychiatrists to nurse practitioners and pediatricians are infinitely more likely to get sued for the drugs they prescribe than for the drugs they do not prescribe.

In my forensic experience, many malpractice cases are brought by frustrated relatives who feel that their loved one would not have died from a drug reaction or committed suicide if the prescriber had paid attention to their frantic calls to the office and especially to their concerns about medication making their loved one worse. When the concerns of family members are ignored, minor problems can grow into life-threatening catastrophes. Responding to relatives is not only a good clinical practice; it is also a significant protection against malpractice suits.

The best protection against being sued is an empathic relationship with the patient and family. Time and again, I have seen healthcare providers forgiven and let off the hook by the injured patient or surviving family because the providers cared about their patients and their patients' families. Time and again, I have seen healthcare providers sued not so much for making a mistake, as for acting in a superior, authoritarian, and callous manner toward the patient and family.

Your best clinical practice and your best protection against malpractice lawsuits are one and the same—an empathic relationship with those who seek your help.

KEY POINTS

- In modern healthcare, the patient has the ultimate responsibility for making all treatment decisions and is free to leave treatment or to seek help elsewhere. In the case of children, the parents have the ultimate responsibility.
- Clinicians can choose not to work with a patient who disagrees with their treatment opinions but cannot abandon the patient under dire circumstances.

- Therapists—including nonprescribing nurses, psychologists, social workers, and counselors—have been taught in the past that their task is to encourage or enforce compliance with the existing medication regimen. In modern healthcare, patient compliance has been replaced by patient choice. The therapist frequently has more time and opportunity than the prescriber to monitor and to evaluate the progress of the patient's medication treatment. By working with an actively involved therapist who conducts independent medication evaluations with the patient, the prescriber provides maximum benefit to the patient.
- Prescribers and therapists should work closely with each other, especially during medication withdrawals. Many practitioners spend much of their time prescribing for psychiatric problems and should consider having a therapist in their office or facility for close communication.
- The therapist is the glue in the collaborative effort and the leader in creating an optimal healing environment for patients and the support network of family and significant others.
- Prescribers and therapists can often learn important information about adverse drug effects from patients and families who often have the time to thoroughly study the limited number of drugs in the patient's regimen. In this era of modern healthcare and in the information age, prescribers and therapists should welcome everything they can learn from their patients and their patients' families.
- Many malpractice suits are brought by the families of patients who have died from adverse drug reactions or suicide after the prescriber failed to respond to their concerns and warnings. Keeping in touch with and responding to relatives is not only good clinical practice, but it will also prevent many catastrophes, as well as lawsuits. An empathic relationship with the patient and family is the best clinical practice and the best protection against malpractice suits.

CHAPTER 13

Psychotherapy During Medication Withdrawal

In the person-centered approach, relationships built among the collaborators—prescribers, therapists, patients, and their support network—are central to a safe and effective medication withdrawal in difficult cases. Many prescribers lack the time, training, or inclination to offer psychotherapy. In coordination with the prescriber, a psychotherapist is needed to work with the patient, family, or significant others, especially in hazardous cases of medication withdrawal. Several psychotherapy principles are especially important in dealing with medication withdrawal, including healing presence, empathy, and the importance of working with couples or families.

Although not all prescribers are psychotherapists, all prescribers need some basic therapeutic skills. Prescribing psychiatrists, internists, pediatricians, and other physicians, as well as prescribing nurses and physician assistants, often work under conditions in which they cannot pay the close attention they might ideally want to pay to the feelings and needs of patients and their families.

Patients in turn are extremely sensitive to the moods and attitudes of anyone who prescribes them psychiatric medication. Patients often recall in minute detail any signs of discouragement, disinterest, or conflict that they have perceived emanating from their healthcare providers, especially around the subject of medication.

The psychotherapist can become the glue for the collaborative team and the healing presence that enables the patient and family to get through the withdrawal period, to leave behind reliance on psychiatric drugs, and to move toward greater independence and mutual respect.

In nearly all of my cases, I am both the prescriber and the therapist. In many ways, this is a great advantage because I don't have to coordinate my efforts with a prescriber or a therapist. However, there are other advantages to having at least two professionals involved in treatment, especially where the patient is a dependent member of a very conflicted family. These families can be draining and even distressing to deal with, and clinicians can benefit from mutual support.

EMPOWERING THE PATIENT AND THERAPIST

In times past, psychotherapists had the luxury of seeing unmedicated patients on a regular basis. The patient who was also receiving psychiatric drugs was occasional enough not to require knowledge of psychiatric drugs on the part of the therapist. Nowadays, many, if not most, or even all patients in a psychotherapy practice will also be taking psychiatric medications, which will profoundly affect the course of the individual's life, as well as the therapy.

> The role of the therapist is changing, requiring greater knowledge and activism regarding patient medications.

Modern psychotherapists need to develop expertise concerning psychiatric medication effects, especially adverse drug effects. Not only will the drugs impact what is happening to their patients, but also the therapist is often in a far better position than the prescriber to evaluate the ongoing effects of the drugs, especially their adverse effects, which can become subtle yet disabling over time, interfering with both the patient's life and the therapy. Chapters 2–10 of this book focus on adverse drug effects. These can become an important aspect of the therapist's educational process in understanding psychiatric drugs.

Since the focus of this chapter is more on psychotherapy, it may prove helpful for the reader to review Chapters 1, 11, and 12. Chapter 1 emphasized the person-centered collaborative approach, which empowers the patient to take charge of the progress of medication withdrawal in consultation with the prescriber and therapist. It addressed how previous experiences in psychiatric treatment very likely encouraged the patient to feel helpless and dependent and to lack the requisite knowledge to make his or her own informed decisions. For those patients, developing confidence and self-determination in the psychiatric setting is the first step in recovery. Patients need, above all else, to overcome their feelings of helplessness to live responsible, satisfying lives.

Chapter 11 described the creation of the patient's medication history as a collaboration between the patient and the clinician in which viewpoints and information are shared and trust and hope are kindled in the relationship between the patient and the healthcare provider.

Chapter 12 reemphasized the autonomy of the patient as the ultimate decision maker. It focused on the autonomy of therapists—their release from the constraint of merely enforcing "compliance" with the prescription regimen. Many prescribers have too little time to spend with their patients to fully monitor and evaluate the medication treatment. Increasing knowledge about the limits and adverse effects of psychiatric drugs makes it advantageous for every member of the collaboration to do his or her part to stay abreast of the latest scientific developments. An emphasis on compliance too often leads clinicians to push drugs on the reluctant patient and family, who often have very good reasons to ask for a change, reduction, or withdrawal of medications.

In this new information age, prescribers often need and can always benefit from an informed patient and an informed therapist, who actively participate in the planning and decision-making process. In modern treatment with psychiatric medication, nonprescribing nurses, psychologists, social workers, and counselors can no longer be told to restrict themselves from sharing knowledge about medications, including their adverse effects, and from discussing the entire medication program with the patient.

Chapter 9 described medication spellbinding—the capacity of psychoactive substances to impair the patients' awareness or understanding of their adverse effects on mind and behavior. Because psychiatric drugs commonly impair judgment regarding their effects—for example, by inducing apathy or less commonly euphoria—it is especially important to educate not only the patient but also the family and to involve the therapists actively in the patients' choice-making process. Prescribers who work within this collaborative model provide the best possible care to patients.

THE PATIENT'S PERSONAL RESPONSIBILITY

When a patient begins to consider the possibility of withdrawing from one or more psychiatric medications, it is important for the prescriber or therapist to assess the patient's sense of personal responsibility. If the patient acts frightened and confused about making his or her own decisions regarding treatment, the withdrawal regimen should be postponed while the therapy supports the individual's self-determination and decision making. Otherwise, the emotional instability that often arises during withdrawal will likely overwhelm the patient.

Many people feel understandably offended at the suggestion that they are not being "responsible." Others resent being asked to take "responsibility" on grounds that their parents used this idea to hammer them into submission. For this reason, it may be best to focus on concepts such as self-determination and independence. Many people will readily admit that they have difficulty making choices, asserting themselves, or managing their lives. The issues should be dealt with early in therapy and are critical to the patient successfully managing the withdrawal. Supportive therapy begins with describing and encouraging the principle of personal responsibility, otherwise known as autonomy, independence, or self-determination.

Helplessness is the opposite of personal responsibility. Otherwise independent individuals may lapse into helplessness when dealing with clinicians, and especially with prescribers who hold so much authority and power in our society. They look to the prescriber or the therapist to tell them what to do. Even otherwise competent professionals or businesspersons may give up personal responsibility when they enter the healthcare professional's office.

Insight-oriented or psychodynamic therapy encourages the individual to remain in touch with feelings while taking full responsibility for personal conduct. It is a simple formula that requires practice and hard work: Always welcome and identify your feelings, but never act on the negative ones like guilt, shame, anxiety, irritability and anger, or apathy. Instead, try at all times to act with a positive, loving, and optimistic attitude.

Everything the clinician says or does should meet this test question: *Does this statement or action enhance the patient's sense of control over his or her life, including control over the therapy itself?* Anything that the therapist does to undermine the patient's feelings of confidence and self-determination will also undermine the therapy and the withdrawal process.

Prescribers and therapists can have enormous positive influence on patients by advocating basic principles that support independence and personal responsibility and by treating their patients in a manner consistent with these principles.

THE THERAPIST'S HEALING PRESENCE

Healing presence is the overall capacity of the therapist to find within himself or herself an abiding sense of confidence in the effectiveness of therapy, combined with an abiding interest in the patient's feelings and well-being. Empathy—including the willingness to be with the patient in distress and to bring a calming, caring concern—is at the heart of the healing presence and good therapy. Healing presence welcomes the patient and all of the patient's feelings, however frightening or negative. Healing presence is the therapist's state of being that communicates or radiates confidence, safety, and the opportunity for healing. It's all about the quality of the relationship that the therapist inspires in being with the patient.

The Non-Emergency Principle of psychotherapy is an important aspect of healing presence. As a therapist, always remember that when the patient has a crisis or an emergency, you don't have to have one. The crisis is in the patient's mind—or in the family's mind—and should not overwhelm your mind or spiritual state. Your comfort in relating to people through any storm of feeling, as well as your hopefulness for the future, will have a calming effect. In these critical situations, resorting to medication—except as a response to a withdrawal reaction—is likely to undermine the patient's confidence in himself or herself and in the therapist.

> Your personal conviction that any emotional crisis can be handled psychotherapeutically rather than pharmacologically is the key to calming the person and restoring reason and hope.

The Non-Emergency Principle is so important to good therapy that Chapter 14 focuses on it.

COUPLES THERAPY AND DRUG WITHDRAWAL

When an individual seeking help for drug withdrawal has a spouse or significant other, I often end up conducting couples therapy during the drug withdrawal. My aim is not merely to support the withdrawal, but also to facilitate a more loving and happy family life. The best way to avoid psychiatric drugs is to forge ahead with creating a wonderful life, and of course, having a wonderful life is a goal in itself.

Couples therapy is a subtle, complex endeavor, but a few recurring principles are worth specific mention.

First, the therapist must have a welcoming and caring attitude toward both members of the couple. Although one may have entered the process first, both must become of equal concern and focus.

Second, the therapist must have a positive attitude toward intimacy and love and grasp the power of loving people to heal each other's lifelong wounds. Without this optimistic approach, the therapist will unwittingly encourage a humdrum existence from which patients tend to seek relief through more drugs.

Third, the therapist must discourage self-defeating and disruptive communications while encouraging rational and loving communications. I suggest to people, "Don't say a word unless those words will further the relationship and enhance the love." This requires learning to rephrase how they talk about what makes them angry and resentful. It requires learning to express feelings in ways that the other can listen to.

Fourth, decide whose problem is being addressed at any given time and focus on that person and that problem exclusively. For example, if Tim brings up that his wife doesn't pay enough attention to his needs, that's the focus. Jane's similar concern will be addressed later. The formula is "One person, one problem at a time." The attitude is welcoming and hopeful.

Fifth, if the couple wishes, individual insight-oriented therapy can easily be conducted with two people at once, including exploration of childhood stressors and trauma and adult self-defeating patterns, such as withdrawing from conflict, shrinking from love, manipulating through threats or violence, and living by low expectations for oneself and one's spouse. When couples experience individual therapy together, they are more able to understand and to help each other at that moment in the session and in the future, without further need for professional help.

Sixth, love is real and enduring. If you once loved each other and are willing to take responsibility for reawakening that love, it is always possible to rebuild a loving and even wonderful relationship that exceeds all past expectations. Therapy is not about sticking on a Band-aid, it's about breaking new and better emotional and spiritual ground for a better life.

Seventh, even severe emotional crises can be handled if one of the partners keeps his or her head and doesn't have a crisis of his or her own. This is the same principle—don't have an emergency when your patient is having an emergency—that I described near the beginning of the chapter.

My preference for couples therapy also extends to my practice in general. The quality of most people's lives depends heavily on the quality of their most important or primary relationships. Happiness, to a great extent, results from happy, loving, responsible relationships. Most people who come to me for individual psychotherapy end up finding that couples therapy is either an important supplement or a complete replacement for individual therapy. In couples therapy, individuals learn to turn to each other rather than to the therapist for their basic needs, including the help they need in building a better and stronger relationship over the years. Nothing is as "therapeutic" as a responsible and loving relationship built on shared values.

THE FAMILY IN CRISES

The Non-Emergency Principle also applies to family members who may become frightened, distraught, and overwhelmed when the patient goes through a difficult time during withdrawal. Calming, reassuring, and informing family members, as well as listening to and learning from their concerns and observations, are among the most important functions of the therapist during a difficult drug withdrawal.

The therapist should also aim at teaching the Non-Emergency Principle to families for their dealings with the patient. This can be demonstrated by the therapist's healing approach during family sessions and by direct instruction.

FAMILY THERAPY

Working with heavily medicated patients can be very difficult. Parents, siblings, and spouses may feel guilty about conflicts in the family. They may harbor guilt and shame about emotional, physical, or sexual abuses perpetrated against the patient—a common clinical finding with individuals who are severely disturbed. They may feel guilty about having pushed medications and/or hospitalizations on the patient years earlier. They may feel angry at the patient for causing horrendous family disruption and suffering, including mounting monetary expense. They will certainly have fear and anxiety about the potential turmoil surrounding medication reduction or withdrawal. They may have their own serious emotional problems and alcohol or drug abuse problems that make them feel vulnerable and threatened by family involvement in a therapeutic process that might cause those issues to surface. They may have scapegoated the patient as the "problem" in the family and be unwilling or unable to self-examine or to change the family dynamics.

> It is important to explain to families that you are not assigning blame to them for the patient's condition and that they are in the best position to support the patient's recovery.

Under these complicated circumstances, what is needed is a family intervention involving a variety of wraparound services, including family therapy, individual therapy, parenting classes or instruction, homemaker services to provide relief or respite to caretakers, and financial and other forms of help. On occasion, this kind of wraparound service is available for treating acute first-episode family crises, but is not available for helping long-term patients come off their medications. On the contrary, the community is more likely to force the long-term patient to take drugs through involuntary outpatient commitment.

In this newly developing field of psychiatric drug reduction and withdrawal, there are severe situations for which there are at present few, if any, adequate solutions. This is one more lesson in the necessity of avoiding long-term exposure to psychiatric drugs, which cause chronic brain impairment (CBI), dependency, and disability.

Fortunately, for most patients, the person-centered collaborative approach to drug reduction and withdrawal is very successful and gratifying to everyone involved in the process.

LIMITS ON THERAPY DURING MEDICATION WITHDRAWAL

During medication withdrawal, the patient's brain is undergoing significant changes precisely in those areas—the frontal lobes and limbic system—that impact the emotions and intellect. Although very little is known about these biochemical changes, or the rate of recovery, we can observe their effects manifested as mood instability and impaired judgment. Any aspect of higher human functioning can be compromised in varying degrees during changes in medication dose, including withdrawal. Therefore, psychodynamic or insight-oriented psychotherapy should at these times be approached cautiously. An individual cannot explore childhood or past traumatic events in a meaningful way when cognitive functions are impaired. An individual cannot reach solid insights into negative patterns of thought and behavior when those patterns are in part driven by drug intoxication or withdrawal and when current judgments are clouded as well.

One useful "insight" is the patient's realization that any psychotropic substance, including psychiatric drugs, can have spellbinding effects, impairing emotional awareness and control, and self-evaluation. The medication spellbinding is more acute or dramatic when starting the medication, or during drug dose changes up or down, but it is almost always present to some degree if the drugs are having a clinical effect.

> When conducting therapy with an individual whose brain is impaired by drug treatment or drug withdrawal, avoid stirring up strong negative emotions or feelings of helplessness. Therapy that touches on painful subjects should be avoided until the individual's judgment and impulse control have improved.

The gradual reduction of the medication almost always produces sufficient improvement so that individuals start to realize how much the psychoactive substances have been impacting them. For example, very commonly during the reduction of selective serotonin reuptake inhibitor (SSRI) antidepressants, the individual will cry for the first time in years. If the medication was prescribed at the time of a loss—for example, shortly after the death of a loved one—at the reduction of the medication the individual may cry about the loss for the very first time. If the individual was prescribed a mood stabilizer or a neuroleptic after a diagnosis of bipolar disorder, he or she may see how muted his or her emotions and zest for life have become without fully grasping it.

Psychodynamic therapy is only appropriate when the withdrawal is relatively benign, so that the individual has the emotional stability and autonomy to handle emotional distress.

Be especially watchful of your patient's response to therapy during withdrawal. Be open to any hints that the therapy is not helping or even doing more harm than good. Few things will improve your skills as a therapist more than asking your patients if they are benefitting from it, including what seems to help them and what doesn't.

> If the patient feels worse rather than better during or soon after a therapy session, the therapist may be expecting too much from the person during withdrawal.

REASSURANCE AND HOPE

If the medicated patient feels unable to handle intense emotions, the therapist should respect this and refrain from overstimulating the individual's emotions with psychodynamic therapy. Reassure the patient that medication reduction will enable him or her to better handle emotions.

If the medicated patient feels apathetic and indifferent, he or she should be reassured that this emotional fog will lift with the reduction in medication.

If the medicated patient feels that his or her emotions are up and down, unpredictable, and unstable, especially on stimulants or the newer antidepressants, provide reassurance that increased emotional stability will follow with decreased doses of medication.

If the patient cannot distinguish between feelings that seem generated by the withdrawal and feelings in response to real-time living, explain that this is normal and that the patient's "real" emotions will become more apparent with further dose reductions.

If the patient no longer feels "like I used to" or "like the same person I was" while taking psychiatric drugs, then early in dose reduction, provide reassurance that the sense of normalcy will return with dose reduction.

If patients feel mentally slowed down and easily fatigued, less able to concentrate, and less able to remember routine events, remind them that psychoactive substances cause these effects and that there will be improvement with dose reduction.

As patients becomes more drug free, symptoms of CBI may become more apparent and distressing. Reassure them that the brain can recover over months and years. The trajectory of this healing can be much slower than with nonbrain injury, but it can progress for a long time and reach full recovery in many cases.

EMPATHY IN THERAPY

Empathy is the key to therapy. Empathy involves a combination of understanding and caring. Empathy is the ability to understand the individual's feelings and attitudes while viewing them from a caring perspective.

Empathy is not sympathy; it doesn't accept or enable feelings of helplessness or self-pity. Instead, empathy shines a positive and encouraging light on the individual's subjective viewpoint, often adding light to the darkness and providing strength to bolster the individual's confidence. Empathy is an active, caring, and even loving approach to the other person.

Because therapy requires and imposes boundaries and restraints on the patient and the therapist, empathy is made more possible. The individuals can feel freer to appreciate each other because they know they will not act on those feelings in a romantic way or in any way outside the therapy.

THE IMPORTANCE OF RELATIONSHIP

It can be hard for some prescribers, and even for some therapists, to realize the importance of the quality of their relationship with their patients. Building relationship begins with the moment the patient walks into the waiting room and continues until the moment the patient and clinician say goodbye at the end of the session.

When the task ahead seems especially overwhelming—as it often feels to psychiatric and therapy patients—the quality of the relationship may spell the difference between success and failure. In any arena of life—sports, education, business, the military, and healthcare—the encouragement of a positive and caring individual can make the difference in an individual's success.

Patients seeking help from a prescriber or therapist should be encouraged to feel

- that they are personally welcome in the office
- that there is plenty of time to handle the day's task
- that they are the complete center of attention
- that their feelings—including fears, doubts, and concerns—are welcome and will be taken very seriously
- that their thoughts and observations are valued
- that they can ask as many questions as they want and recieve complete and honest answers
- that they are involved in a respectful collaboration that focuses on meeting their real needs

If the therapist adheres as closely as possible to these few principles, the therapy will prove helpful to the individual, who will, in turn, be grateful for the help.

Can it possibly be that simple? Yes, it can. Basically, the therapist is required to act in a manner that is honest, respectful, and caring—qualities that are universally valued. Bring out the best in yourself as a person and you will bring out the best in your clients and patients.

Especially during difficult drug withdrawals, where more sophisticated aspects of psychodynamic therapy are not appropriate, the creation of a supportive, caring setting for the patient provides most of what is needed. Beyond that, some experience and wisdom about the withdrawal process will be helpful—a need this book attempts to help fulfill.

GUIDELINES FOR EMPATHIC THERAPY

This is not an instructional manual for therapy, but these guidelines are basic therapeutic principles which are wholly consistent with any patient-centered approach and actually required to make the most of almost any form of psychotherapy.[1]

As empathic therapists,

1. We treasure those who seek our help, and we view therapy as a sacred and inviolable trust. With humility and gratitude, we honor the privilege of being therapists.

2. We rely on relationships built on trust, honesty, caring, genuine engagement, and mutual respect.

3. We bring out the best in ourselves to bring out the best in others.

4. We create a safe space for self-exploration and honest communication by holding ourselves to the highest ethical standards, including honesty, informed consent, confidentiality, professional boundaries, and respect for personal freedom, autonomy, and individuality.

5. We encourage overcoming psychological helplessness and taking responsibility for emotions, thoughts, and actions—and ultimately for living a self-determined life.

6. We offer empathic understanding and, when useful, we build on that understanding to offer new perspectives and guidance for further fulfillment of personal goals and freely chosen values.

7. When useful, we help to identify self-defeating patterns learned in childhood and adulthood to promote the development of more effective choice making and conduct.

8. We avoid using coercion, threats, manipulation, or authoritarianism.

9. We encourage people to understand and to embrace the depth, richness, and complexity of their unique emotional and intellectual lives.

---

[1] Modified from Guidelines for Empathic Therapy of the Center for the Study of Empathic Therapy (http://www.EmpathicTherapy.org). Copyright 2011 by Peter R. Breggin, MD. Reprinted with permission.

10. We focus on each person's capacity to take responsibility and to determine the course of his or her own life.

11. We recognize that a drug-free mind is best suited to personal growth and to facing critical life issues. Although sometimes providing short-term relief from suffering, psychiatric drugs can cloud the mind, impair judgment and insight, suppress emotions and spirituality, inhibit relationships and love, and reduce will power and autonomy. Long-term psychiatric drug exposure also causes brain dysfunction and damage.

12. We apply the guidelines for empathic therapy to all therapeutic relationships, including persons who suffer from brain injuries or from the most profound emotional disturbances. Individuals who are mentally, emotionally, and physically fragile are especially in need of the best we have to offer as empathic therapists.

13. Because children are among our most vulnerable and treasured citizens, we especially need to protect them from the hazards associated with psychiatric drugs. We need to offer them the family life, education, and moral and spiritual guidance that will help them to fulfill their potential as children and adults.

14. Because personal failure and suffering cannot be separated from the ethics and values that guide our conduct, we promote basic human values, including personal responsibility, freedom, gratitude, love, and the courage to honestly self-evaluate and to grow.

15. Because human beings thrive when living by their highest ideals, individuals may wish to explore their most important personal values, including spiritual beliefs or religious faith, and to integrate them into their therapy and their personal growth.

There is, of course, much more to psychology and psychotherapy than the observations and principles offered in this brief chapter, but they contain some of the essentials on which to base your approach to patients during medication withdrawal. I've written more extensively about psychotherapy in *The Heart of Being Helpful* (Breggin, 1997b).

KEY POINTS

▪ The nonprescribing therapist—registered nurse, clinical psychologist, social worker, marriage counselor, or family therapist—often sees the patient more often and for longer periods than the prescriber and is in an ideal position to monitor and evaluate medication effects.

▪ The role of the therapist now requires increased knowledge and a more active role regarding the patient's psychiatric medication, including providing critical information and helping the patient plan his or her medication regimen.

- To provide optimal care for the patient, the prescriber and therapist share responsibilities for patient education and monitoring and for developing and regularly reevaluating the treatment plan.
- The therapist's healing presence and empathy is an essential quality of good therapy and includes the Non-Emergency Principle of psychotherapy (see Chapter 14).
- Couples therapy and family therapy can be critical to the success of difficult medication withdrawals.
- Distressed, conflicted families can make it difficult or impossible to withdraw dependent, emotionally fragile family members in an outpatient setting.
- Especially when a patient is undergoing an emotionally distressing withdrawal, therapy should be supportive and not stir up highly emotional issues, such as childhood experiences and adult trauma or losses.
- The therapist should encourage the patient's sense of personal responsibility, self-determination, or autonomy.
- The patient should feel welcome and valued.
- The 15 Guidelines for Empathic Therapy provide the psychotherapeutic basis for helping patients through difficult medication withdrawals.

CHAPTER 14

Handling Emotional Crises

It is critical to distinguish between how to approach medical crises and how to approach emotional crises. Drug withdrawal can become a medical crisis that is often easily treated by returning to the previous dose of medication. By contrast, emotional crises during drug withdrawal are best handled with supportive psychotherapy or family therapy, without resorting to medication, so that the individual's opportunity for medication-free mastery and growth are maximized.

When a patient is struggling with symptoms of drug withdrawal, psychotherapy should be limited to reassurance and guidance. However, if the withdrawal process is conducted gradually at a comfortable pace for the patient, it is possible to conduct person-centered individual or family therapy that deals with emotionally charged issues. This can result not only in drug-free living but also in living with a considerably improved quality of life.

The Non-Emergency Principle is an important starting point for handling psychiatric or emotional crises: When the patient feels in the midst of an overwhelming emotional crisis, the therapist should welcome the opportunity to help the patient gain understanding and personal strength. Put simply, when the patient has an emotional crisis, the clinician should not go into emergency mode. By welcoming the patient's painful and seemingly overwhelming emotions and by dealing with them confidently, most emotional emergencies can be readily handled in the office without resorting to drugs or hospitalization.

INTERACTION BETWEEN MEDICAL AND PSYCHOLOGICAL CRISES

Medical crises and emotional crises can feed on each other. A medical crisis often stirs up an emotional crisis. Almost any medical emergency, from head injury to heart attack, or a difficult medical procedure, can be made worse or more hazardous if the patient becomes overwhelmed with fear and anxiety. Individuals can also feel guilty or ashamed about becoming physically ill, and that can worsen their condition and impede them from seeking medical help. Physical illness can stir up childhood trauma and feelings of abandonment resulting from injuries or painful treatments and medical hospitalizations. The disability associated with physical impairments can also become shameful, depressing, or anxiety-provoking. In addition, many physical illnesses can cause cognitive and emotional dysfunction by directly impairing brain function or by producing physical exhaustion.

Despite this overlap between physical illness and emotional issues, there are important distinctions between how to approach medical and emotional crises. For the practitioner, it is especially important to recognize that an *emotional crisis is best approached with psychotherapeutic interventions that can often turn the "emergency" into a life-changing learning experience.*

CHARACTERISTICS AND TREATMENT OF A MEDICAL EMERGENCY

If you are a mental health provider, and your diabetic patient shows up in your office in a state of confusion, breathing heavily and sweating profusely, and cannot recall the last time she took her insulin, you should not spend too much talking with her about her underlying feelings. You want to keep her as calm as possible, but your goal is to get her quickly to the hospital for emergency treatment. Similarly, if your patient shows up complaining of anxiety but now, for the first time, has severe chest pain and is out of breath from walking up the stairs, you should suspect a heart attack and speedily arrange for him to get to an emergency room as quickly as possible for evaluation.

But emotional crises should not be treated like medical crises, where talking about feelings is limited and the prescription of drugs often becomes the primary treatment. In the current mental health environment, clinicians are apt to respond to acute or extreme feelings, violent or suicidal impulses, or psychotic symptoms as if they constitute a medical emergency. They turn to medication as their first resort, or try their best to get the patient to an emergency room or hospital. Clinical judgment is required in these situations, but the basis of that judgment can begin by welcoming the feelings as important emotional signals that can provide an opportunity for growth.

But there are real differences between the medical and the "psychiatric" or psychological emergency, and how we should approach them. These are the characteristics of a *medical emergency*:

1. Although emotional stress may have contributed to the development of the diabetic condition or heart attack, the medical emergency has a

known biological basis such as elevated blood sugar or cardiac arrhythmia that must be addressed.

2. There are specific physical interventions to treat the biological dysfunction, for example, insulin or cardiac medication.
3. If the treatment succeeds, the patient will improve and very likely completely recover from the acute emergency in a relatively short period.
4. Unless inappropriately or improperly applied, the treatment is not likely to prolong the disorder or to harm the brain or mind.
5. The patient is almost certain to feel grateful for the help and to bear no resentment toward the healthcare providers.
6. A psychotherapeutic intervention in the clinician's office could not have resolved the acute situation, which would have gotten worse without medical intervention.
7. No opportunity for learning or personal growth will have been lost by relieving the medical emergency with a medical intervention.

CHARACTERISTICS AND TREATMENT OF AN EMOTIONAL CRISIS

Now consider the patient who arrives in your office feeling suicidal or violent. For each of the seven points, the approach is very different:

1. Unless the individual has an underlying diagnosable physical disorder—such as an adverse drug reaction, a drug withdrawal reaction, Alzheimer's, or hypothyroidism—there is no identifiable biological basis for the emotional crisis. Instead, an evaluation is likely to disclose stressors or conflicts that have caused or contributed to the acute emotional distress.
2. Even if there were a biological basis to the disorder, such as an as-yet-unidentified biochemical imbalance that causes or exacerbates suicidality or violence, there is at present no known medical intervention that can directly treat it.
3. If a psychiatric drug is given, the patient will become subdued and emotionally blunted but will not recover speedily. In fact, medication is likely to turn the acute episode into chronic emotional distress.
4. Medication is likely to cause harm to the brain and, if continued for weeks or months, will impair brain function and impose the risk of chronic disability and even brain damage.
5. Instead of being grateful for the pharmacological treatment, and readily accepting of continued treatment, the patient is likely to be resentful, ambivalent, or eager to stop the treatment. By contrast, the patient is likely to feel very unambivalent gratitude for an empowering psychotherapeutic experience.
6. A calm and confident intervention with psychotherapy can often resolve the crisis sufficiently within an hour to permit the patient to remain living at home. The patient will feel grateful for the clinician's

concern and genuine engagement and agree to stay in touch until the next session.

7. An opportunity for growth will occur with the resolution of the crisis through psychotherapeutic means, empowering the patient and family to manage their lives more effectively and to continue to improve the quality of their lives.

MEDICATION WITHDRAWAL CRISES CAN BECOME GENUINE MEDICAL EMERGENCIES

Medication withdrawal can become a medical emergency requiring a medical intervention, in which case it will respond very much like a diabetic crisis to insulin. Withdrawal can unexpectedly turn into a physical and psychological nightmare for the patient, and can usually be medically managed by resuming the previous dose of the withdrawal medication. Much like any medical crisis, it can be very helpful to reassure the patient, but a return to the previous dose level will effectively relieve the emergency without psychotherapy. However, much more commonly than in a medical crisis, the patient may find it unnecessary to readjust the medication and instead elect to get through the withdrawal-induced crisis through supportive therapy, including reliance on his or her support network.

MEETING THE PATIENT'S CRITICAL, IMMEDIATE NEEDS

If a withdrawal crisis is severe, then the clinician needs to enlist the patient's support network in meeting the patient's acute needs. Usually, the patient's most basic need is for intensified caring support and increased monitoring, all of which the clinician can seek to provide through therapeutic contacts and the patient's support network. As mentioned many times and illustrated in Chapter 16, almost any withdrawal reaction can be readily handled by increasing the dose of the drug to nearer its previous level.

Commonly, the individual in a withdrawal crisis has insomnia and is sleep deprived. This is one of the few times I will add a new psychiatric medication to the treatment regime, limiting it to a few days at a time, in order to help the patient break out of the cycle of sleeplessness. I address the use of sleep aids in the next section of this chapter when discussing mania.

On rare occasions, the individual's condition may be compromised by lack of food and fluids. Unless they suspect an abdominal disorder requiring emergency intervention, in which case the patient should be sent to an emergency room, clinicians need have no hesitation in supplying a snack or water to their patients. However, once a person-centered collaborative approach has been established, the patient should be in regular contact with his or her clinicians and social network so that serious nutritional problems do not develop.

Sometimes, individuals exhaust themselves by compulsively overworking in an attempt to distract themselves from their negative emotions. They need encouragement from their support network to slow down and to rest.

The therapist should calmly ask the patient questions along these lines: "What do you need? How can I help you? What's the biggest problem right now? Is there something that requires immediate attention?" Especially if the therapist can also ask similar questions of someone close to the patient, the patient's immediate needs are likely to be made clear. Often, these needs have more to do with unrealistic fears than with real problems and can be handled with encouragement and reassurance; but sometimes the patient needs more specific help from the therapist, family, or friends, such as obtaining and taking medications they have missed, getting some groceries, or making a list of things to do. Therapists should feel comfortable making simple suggestions and even working with patients in distress to decide priorities and to take the first steps in getting them done, such as taking a moment in the session to call a friend to pick them up when they are in no condition to drive.

DEALING WITH MANIA AND MANIC-LIKE SYMPTOMS AND BEHAVIORS

Nothing is more difficult to deal with than mania or manic-like symptoms. The euphoric individual who feels omnipotent and invulnerable is likely to reject even the most skilled and dedicated empathic approaches. Yet this same individual, far from being invulnerable, is extremely vulnerable to sexual abusers, con artists, and other predators. Less often, this person's extreme irritability and need for instant gratification can lead to aggression and even violence. These individuals become an enormous strain on family members whose help they reject when they need it the most.

If these individuals are brought to an emergency room, they are quickly subdued by antipsychotic drugs and are often certified for involuntary treatment. Although this is seen as "treatment" for the manic episode, it is better understood as chemical and physical restraint. The individual in a euphoric or manic state is an extreme challenge to clinicians who do not want to involuntarily hospitalize patients or to use drugs as chemical restraints.

In the era of Moral Therapy in the 18th and 19th century, these individuals were successfully treated without resort to drugs in genuine asylums that provided round-the-clock monitoring, caring social interactions, and moral support, often in the form of religious persuasion (Tuke, 1813; also see Bockoven, 1963; Breggin, 1991, 2008a).

Unfortunately, today's clinicians do not have access to genuine retreats that are willing to treat individuals in a manic condition without resort to medications. Depending on the clinician's professional role and philosophy, he or she may feel the need to encourage or to force the individual into a psychiatric facility. In my practice, I never force hospitalization or drug therapy on patients, and so I am limited to working with the social network, usually family and friends, to watch over and support the individual while I offer individual and family therapy and frequent telephone contact. Over many decades of treatment, only two or three of my patients in a manic state have ended up in psychiatric hospitals.

In contemporary mental health, most cases of hypomania and mania are medication-induced, usually by the antidepressants and sometimes by stimulants, and can be handled by a person-centered collaborative approach. In many cases in my practice I have been able to reduce medications and to calm the patient down with the help of the patient's support network. I have not needed to add additional medications, except for a few days of sleeping medication usually in the form of diazepam (Valium), which is longer-acting and less likely to overstimulate or disinhibit than the shorter-acting benzodiazepines.

Chapter 16 describes several patients who experienced medication-induced manic-like symptoms and who were helped without additional drugs by the empathic person-centered collaborative approach.

My therapeutic approach to the individual displaying manic symptoms, whether spontaneous or drug-induced, is accepting but firm. I acknowledge the person's euphoric feelings without affirming them. Instead, I encourage these individuals to recognize that they are, in reality, afraid of being overcome by anxiety and depression, and try to help them recognize these underlying feelings and to accept emotional support from me and from others in their lives. People who know they are anxious and depressed, and feeling helpless and impotent, can acknowledge vulnerability and more readily accept help.

Mania, when psychologically generated by the individual, is an escape from depressed and helpless feelings. It's a shortcut out of despair into euphoria. Like all shortcuts, it avoids the hard work of dealing with painful emotions and the responsibilities of life, and is doomed to failure. These insights can help individuals who suffer from non–drug-induced mania once they have let go of feeling manic in favor of feeling their underlying negative emotions.

However, in most manic reactions that are medication-induced, I do not find that the individual has had a predisposition to generate manic-like symptoms. Instead, the symptoms come out wholly in reaction to drug intoxication. It's a myth that medications merely unmask an underlying mania. In placebo-controlled clinical trials, individuals with no predisposition to mania can be driven into a manic state (Breggin 2008a; Breggin and Breggin, 1994).

Individuals can go through a period of manic symptoms when withdrawing from almost any psychiatric drug, but I have seen it most commonly during withdrawal from the newer antidepressants. I know of no cogent explanation why antidepressants would cause mania during dose increases, dose decreases, and withdrawal other than the general observation that in all these instances, they are jarring the biochemistry of the brain.

THERAPY DURING A WITHDRAWAL CRISIS

Withdrawal crises are not a time for insight-oriented psychotherapy. The patient is neurologically impaired by the withdrawal process and is probably in no condition to benefit from insight—other than from reassurance that it's a withdrawal reaction, followed by guidance concerning what to do next. Even if the individual decides to "tough it out" without resuming the previous dose of the drug, therapy should remain limited to providing reassurance and emotional support during the acute withdrawal reaction.

Because of medication spellbinding, it is often hard for individuals to believe that they are so on edge, so anxious, or so uncontrollably angry because they are suffering from medication withdrawal. They often need to be reminded that they will soon feel better if they take a dose of medication to bring it up to the previous level. The family or significant others may also need this reassurance.

Withdrawal crises can be precipitated by stressors, such as conflict in the family. This occurs because the withdrawal process has rendered the individual less able to exercise good judgment and emotional self-control. However, even at these times—when psychological stressors have contributed to the emotional upheaval—it is not usually safe or effective to explore feelings or to seek deeper insight into the conflicts and stressors. Highly emotional issues are much better addressed after the withdrawal crisis has been handled.

During a slow withdrawal managed comfortably by the patient over a period of time, it is often possible to do very good psychotherapeutic work. But as soon as the patient starts to experience significant emotional distress caused by the drug withdrawal, it's time to stop looking at any highly charged subjects such as childhood trauma or self-defeating patterns of life. That kind of therapeutic work will stir up feelings that the patient is likely to find overwhelming. Instead, it's time to focus on supportive measures, such as reassurance and guidance, until the patient recovers from the acute symptoms of withdrawal. It may be useful at such times to reassure everyone involved that personal and family conflicts should be set aside until the patient has recovered from the stress of the withdrawal.

When a withdrawal reaction is relatively mild—perhaps the patient feels inexplicably saddened, anxious, or angry—I will explain to a patient on the phone, "Don't worry now why your children made you so angry this morning" or "Put aside that conflict at work for now." If talking on the phone is insufficient to calm the patient, but an emergency trip to my office seems unwarranted, I will suggest the resumption of the previous dose of the drug and urge the patient to put off the psychological issues until recovered from the acute withdrawal symptoms. When the emotional turmoil subsides, we'll be able to talk more effectively about any persisting issues in the family or at work.

This model of treatment conforms to the medical model of treatment. Medication withdrawal is a specific, identifiable, and diagnosable physical reaction that can usually be treated very effectively by resuming the previous dose or, if the patient wishes and is able, by weathering the withdrawal reaction until it abates.

THE NON-EMERGENCY PRINCIPLE FOR HANDLING EMOTIONAL CRISES

The Non-Emergency Principle for handling emotional crises states, "When the patient is having an emotional crisis or an emergency, you as the clinician do not have one."

The non-emergency approach is similar to the practice of nonviolent communication, which emphasizes that the individual in a position of power or authority—whether a clinician or a police officer—must first take personal responsibility for his or her own emotions and actions (Sears, 2010). The Non-Emergency Principle or nonviolent communication requires the clinician to be self-confident and self-controlled, and react in an empathic manner, despite provocations or emotional turmoil emanating from the other person. *In terms of psychiatric "emergencies," this means that when the patient has a psychiatric emergency or crisis, the clinician does not.*

A feeling of emotional crisis or psychiatric emergency can become contagious and it can push the clinician to overreact. When a patient feels in the midst of an emotional crisis or emergency, the therapist should react with calmness and reassurance, and avoid taking steps that will undermine the patient's self-confidence and confidence in psychotherapy.

When a patient is experiencing overwhelming feelings of helplessness, guilt, anxiety, or anger, or even psychosis, the situation will tend to escalate if the therapist treats it as a crisis or an emergency. Fortunately, creating an environment of security and safety can overcome the underlying feelings of helplessness. If the therapist approaches the patient with a firm belief in his or her own ability to handle the situation, much of the patient's sense of emergency will usually abate within a short time. In psychiatry and psychotherapy, which are all about emotions, the emergency may literally disappear as soon as the clinician communicates a continuing sense of professional competence and confidence to help the individual handle the situation. It is therefore important and even critical to distinguish between handling an emotional crisis and handling a withdrawal crisis.

A patient undergoing a withdrawal reaction may feel emotionally tortured or overwhelmed and reassurance and guidance may help, but the root of the problem is biological. A patient undergoing an emotional crisis, however, can best be helped by a psychotherapeutic intervention. In both cases, the attitude of the therapist is important. The therapist must of course remain confident and hopeful in treating the medical crisis. But in a purely emotional crisis, the therapist's attitude is the fundamental therapeutic tool, and psychological skills, along with the patient's collaborative efforts, will determine the outcome.

Again, the handling of nonmedical emotional crises starts with and depends on one basic approach: *When the patient is having an emotional crisis or an emergency, you as the clinician do not have one.* The Non-Emergency Principle reminds you, "The emotional crisis exists in the mind of the patient and never in mine." Even if the patient needs prompt and serious attention, you as the clinician—or even as a family member—must approach the crisis with the conviction that you are not personally experiencing an emergency of your own.

The Non-Emergency Principle of psychotherapy is an aspect of Healing Presence (Chapter 13)— the therapist's state of being that communicates confidence, safety, and the opportunity for healing.

> The Non-Emergency Principle reminds the clinician that the emotional crisis exists in the mind of the patient and never in the mind of the prescriber or therapist. When the patient perceives that the prescriber or therapist is confident and able to handle the patient's feelings, however distressing and overwhelming, the patient will usually respond by calming down and regaining confidence in himself and the clinician.

When patients say that they are suicidal or homicidal, as the therapist you should not react as if they are about to harm themselves or someone else. For you and for the patient, you should distinguish between the patient's feelings and the patient's potentially harmful actions, and address the feelings rather than the fear surrounding the patient's possible actions. Find within yourself the ability to welcome your patients' painful emotions and encourage even more communication from them about their distress, including any impulses to harm themselves and others. Provide reassurance that airing these emotions in a safe place will help to better understand them and to bring them under control.

Reassure these patients that many, if not most people, have potentially destructive impulses or feelings at one time or another. Make clear that these suicidal, violent, or even psychotic feelings and thoughts—like any other feelings and thoughts—can be managed and understood, eventually overcome, and ultimately learned from. Settle down for a leisurely discussion about the immediate origins of these feelings. If you're a psychotherapist, you may end up with a very fruitful therapy session about the more remote origins of these feelings in earlier adult and childhood experiences, and their contribution to the patient's self-defeating tendencies.

Violent feelings usually occur as a reaction to feeling shamed or humiliated. Having been made to feel obliterated, powerless, and rejected, the individual wants to reclaim power and respect with a violent outburst against someone else. The therapist should help patients decide not to throw away their ethics and their life over someone else's misguided abuse of them. Validate their feelings, understand their feelings, and help them get past their feelings in their own best interest.

Suicidal feelings are usually reactions to feelings of guilt, although shame, anger and anxiety can play a role. Help the individual understand that suicidal feelings are always time-limited and can be overcome, but suicide is forever. Restrengthen your empathic relationship, which is central to preventing suicide. A miracle of therapy is that your genuine interest in the other person's suffering and sense of hopelessness and helplessness is usually sufficient to prevent suicide.

Overwhelmingly anxious feelings and panic take over when a patient lapses into abject helplessness in their own mind. The person in a panic attack literally gives up control over his or her own mental processes and emotions. The person's sense of self-mastery is lost, and the individual feels on the edge of death. It's an emotional death of abject helplessness and surrender. Acute, severe anxiety can almost always be quickly allayed by firm guidance aimed at having patients focus their attention on the physical space surrounding them, on you as a therapist who can be trusted, and on a few procedures such as thinking rationally about when the emotions started. Anxiety is a state of emotional know-nothingness in which the individual succumbs to helplessness. A calm coach can usually bring this person down to earth again. A teaching moment occurs when you show your patient that reason can in fact retake control of his or her anxious mind.

Hallucinations, delusions, and other psychotic experiences are reactions to feeling completely alienated from other human beings. The root emotion is almost always *abject humiliation* in which the individual feels utterly worthless and nearly nonexistent. Psychosis is driven by dreadful emotions associated with trauma and despair in relationship to other human beings. The wounded individual withdraws into a private nightmare. Fantasies replace real-life relationships.

Individuals immersed in psychosis can often experience relief within minutes of settling down with someone who takes them seriously and is skilled in creating honest, trusting relationships. The person's terror and humiliation must be taken seriously and not minimized, and feelings of danger must be seen as emotionally real.

As the therapist appears comfortable in the presence of the patient with psychotic symptoms and welcomes the most seemingly bizarre and outrageous communications, the patient will almost always become less frightened and more trusting, and the symptoms will tend to subside in front of the therapist's eyes. Of course, these symptoms very likely will recur, perhaps even during the session, but the patient will have begun to learn to overcome them through relating with you.

By our attitude and words with the acutely disturbed person we are communicating, *Hang in there with me. Just sit with me for a while. We'll be able to figure this out and get through it to a much better place.* The "much better place" goal is critical. Individuals who have become psychotic have left a reality they do not wish to return to. Help them see that they can seek and create a better way of life.

People who have episodes that get labeled "schizophrenic" almost always are struggling with spiritual crises (Breggin, 1991). If you encourage them to talk and to look for meaning in the hallucinations and delusions, you will find very sensitive self-aware souls struggling with what seems to them to be a spiritual black hole devoid of reason, love, caring, or justice. In fact, it is the strength of their imagination and their wounded creativity that makes them look "crazy" rather than simply depressed, anxious, or obsessive-compulsive. Psychosis is like broken poetry: a flagging soul's last metaphorical stand in isolation and humiliation. These individuals long for someone who will take them seriously and explore their sometimes labyrinthine thoughts and emotions without humiliating them with diagnoses and without telling them they cannot master their lives without psychiatric drugs.

MAKING THE MOST OF EMOTIONAL CRISES

Much of a therapist's best work and much of a patient's progress in therapy involves handling crises. Crises usually reflect the patient's greatest sources of helplessness— the patient's greatest vulnerability to becoming overwhelmed. In addition to helping the patient calm down, the experienced and

Crises, including psychotic breaks, are opportunities for individuals to learn to handle their worst fears and most frightening emotions. Crises are opportunities to go beyond what once seemed normal and to live in a better and more inspired fashion.

skilled therapist can turn a crisis into a lifetime learning experience for the patient.

In an emotional crisis, if the therapist begins to feel frightened or overwhelmed by the patient's feelings, and therefore feels the necessity of bringing up the need for medication—then the patient learns that his or her feelings are indeed beyond control and require management with drugs. He or she miss the opportunity to learn that a crisis can be handled and become the source of important learning. The patient will also conclude that even the therapist cannot handle such frightening feelings, at least in therapy, and probably not in his or her own life. The patient will be taught that pills and not people are the ultimate solutions in times of emotional trial. If the patient is then prescribed drugs for months or years on end, what once was an opportunity for growth can become lost for the remainder of the patient's life.

On the other hand, handling a crisis without resorting to medication teaches a patient that he or she can handle life with a drug-free mind. The patient may also discover that therapy actually works.

> Recommending medication in a crisis in effect says to the patient, "You and I cannot handle this. We need to do something to your brain." Instead of growing through the crisis, the person succumbs to the crisis. A great opportunity for learning and self-transformation is wasted.

A single dose of numerous drugs can initially blunt extreme emotions, but doing so confirms the patient's entrenched belief that he or she is incapable of learning how to manage feelings and that the therapist and therapy are relatively impotent in the face of serious problems. In contrast, handling the emotional crisis together psychotherapeutically in a person-centered collaboration confirms the patient's strength, the therapist's reliability, and the importance of the therapeutic relationship.

Crushing or muting emotions with drugs in time of crisis also shuts down the patient's emotional signal system and puts off any meaningful insight into what has caused the crisis. By learning to handle emotions, the patient overcomes learned helplessness and becomes more self-directed.

> Psychiatric medications can suppress or blunt emotional suffering in the short-term in emotional crises, but they suppress the patient's internal signal system, discourage a sense of personal mastery, and undermine confidence in the psychotherapeutic process.

Adding new medications or increasing medications to handle emotional crises during withdrawal is likely to be counterproductive for the patient. Not only does this complicate the withdrawal—either by adding new psychoactive substances into the patient's brain or by increasing the exposure to existing psychoactive substances in the brain—but it also undermines the patient's hope for achieving a drug-free life.

AN ACUTELY SUICIDAL WOMAN

Rhonda, a 22-year-old married woman with no children, had recently separated from her husband. She called me at home on Sunday afternoon. She had just gotten off the phone with her estranged husband who told her, "I never want to see or talk to you again. My lawyer will be contacting you." Then he hung up.

Rhonda sounded extremely gloomy. We had only been working together for two therapy sessions—and she was shy, emotionally guarded, and withdrawn. Rapport was still in the making, and I had explained to her in the last session that she seemed to be a woman who never really stood up for herself and had too little idea about building a wonderful life either on her own or with someone else. I wanted to empower her to find her ideals, to take control over her life, and to aim for the kind of life she really wanted. She understood me intellectually, she explained, but emotionally she couldn't begin to respond. Then came the trauma of her husband definitively ending the marriage.

Rhonda's tone on the phone was so dark that I asked her outright, almost as an assertion, "You're thinking of killing yourself, aren't you?"

"Well, yeah, I'm looking at a bottle of aspirin," she replied bitterly. "It's nearly full."

"Thanks for telling me," I said gratefully. "I'll leave for the office now and see you in 30 minutes. And please, bring the aspirin with you."

"No, I don't need to see you. I don't feel like talking. Your wife will be pissed if you got out on Sunday. I'll be fine."

"Rhonda, maybe you will be fine, but I won't be—not worrying about you. But I'm so grateful you called; it would have been horrible if you had harmed yourself. So, please, it's a 30-minute ride to my office. Meet me there."

"I'll be fine," she bristled.

"Would you consider going to the emergency room?" I asked and was not surprised or disappointed when she shot back, "You can't mean that. You know they will drug me up and even lock me up."

"Look, if you won't come to me, I'll pick you up and bring you to the office. Will you open the door when I knock?" To stave off any issues about my coming to her house alone, I added, "My wife Ginger will be coming along with me in the car to the office."

"You'd do that? You and your wife?"

"Yes, I'm on my way. Believe me; your life is worth it."

"Doc, you don't need to pick me up. I'll meet you at the office."

After she fully reassured me and I felt we had a good emotional connection, I agreed to let her drive by herself.

Rhonda arrived on time at the office. Within minutes she was crying and talking helplessly, even pitiably, about how she had nothing left to live for. She had thought about suicide as a teenager, but this was the only time she felt close to doing it. She couldn't or wouldn't turn to her family. Her only friends were on the West Coast. She'd only scare them if she called them, and it would be humiliating, so she wouldn't turn to them.

"Listen, Rhonda, I think we can get a lot done in an hour or two today. Then I'll see you or talk to you on the phone every day this coming week."

"I can barely pay you for once a week. My husband cleaned out our bank account."

"Rhonda, you're suicidal. I don't want to lose you. I'll see you for free all week if necessary. In the long run of life—yours and mine—the money means nothing. All you need to do is get through the week and, believe me, you'll find many good reasons and the will to live."

I was willing to see Rhonda daily, for free if necessary. It was a matter of life and death, and I'd rather see her for free than encourage her to go to a hospital. I also knew that most patients feel so reassured by the offer of free sessions during an emergency that they don't need many of them.

"We'll see," she said, but I could see her softening as she realized I intended to do whatever was necessary to help her through this emotional crisis.

I reminded Rhonda that suicidal impulses are short-lived. A woman who thinks she cannot live without her husband often finds out that life is actually better without him. She smiled just a little at that thought. And if she wants, I explained, a woman can usually find someone a lot more to her liking in a matter of months if she's willing to learn to make better choices and to risk reaching out with love.

When I mentioned the high probability of finding someone else, Rhonda burst out with a slew of curse words about her husband and all men. Now we were dealing with one of Rhonda's strongest underlying feelings—her husband's phone call had not so much activated feelings of genuine loss as much as feelings of rejection, humiliation, and outrage. She wanted to kill herself, yes, but she really wanted to kill her husband and her husband's girlfriend. Until that moment, Rhonda had been too ashamed to tell me that her husband had begun an affair during the marriage and was planning to move in with the other woman.

I talked with Rhonda about how humiliated she was feeling. I even shared with her something similar that I'd been through years earlier before my marriage to Ginger. Rhonda expected people to treat *her* badly, but she could hardly believe that anyone would treat *me* that badly. I explained to her that people don't treat us badly because we deserve to be abused; they treat us badly because they are abusers. We were able to talk briefly about how she repeatedly chose men who couldn't be trusted.

By the end of the session, Rhonda had decided—perhaps for the first time in her life—that she didn't want to throw her life away because of what "some guy" was doing to her. She wanted to stop living in that dreadful world where the actions of men determined how she was going to feel about herself. Yes, I explained, other people can always hurt us, but they don't have to control the outcome of our lives. We should be free to choose people who are better for us. It was a breakthrough moment for Rhonda. She glimpsed that she could strive to live by her own emotional and spiritual compass rather than being buffeted around by untrustworthy men for the rest of her life. Killing herself no longer seemed like the only option.

We spent a few minutes exploring the kinds of self-defeating choices she had made in her romantic life and their origins in her childhood experiences with her father and mother, as well as an abusive older brother. I spent only a few minutes on this in order to give her a taste of the kind of understanding she could look forward to in future sessions.

As we finished, almost as an afterthought, Rhonda said, "I will miss the bastard. Is that stupid?"

"Not stupid. I'm sure you're going to be lonely. Loneliness is almost always a problem for awhile during a separation, but it doesn't have to last long. But missing him and killing yourself over him are too different things."

"Never," she said, "Not over him or anyone else." Still a youngster at age 22 years, Rhonda was like a student proud to show me she had learned her lesson.

"Call me tonight around 9 pm," I reminded her.

"You're sure? I'm doing fine now. I'll sleep fine."

"Hearing you're okay will help *me* sleep," I laughed.

The warm look on her face showed that she valued my honesty and my caring.

When the session was over, Rhonda felt much more trusting of herself and me and of our therapeutic relationship. On the way out, she asked if she could thank my wife for taking Sunday to come to the office. She was very gracious with Ginger and looked transformed when she departed the office.

To prescribers and therapists used to responding to suicidality with drugs or hospitalization, my treatment of Rhonda may sound unusual or even dangerous. In reality, it's not an exceptional story in the lives of therapists who warmly engage their patients, feel confident that emotional crises are opportunities for growth, and who do not disempower themselves and their patients by prescribing or referring patients for medication. Always remember, emotional crises are in the mind of the patient or family members and should not become emotional crises in the mind of the prescriber or therapist.

AFTER THE CRISIS

After a crisis has begun to calm down during a session, it can be very helpful to talk about practical everyday actions that the individual can take over the next few hours and days—basic self-care like good grooming and pursuing fun or worthwhile activities; handling upcoming work schedules; going to school or doing homework; reaching out to family or friends; or addressing a pressing matter in a more confident manner. The focus should be on one or two activities that will encourage the individual to return to managing his or her life in a more optimistic fashion.

Because conflict within the family is often at the root of an emotional crisis, this can be a good time to ask the patient to bring in one or more family members to the next session.

It's also useful to remind the individual that you are always available to chat on the phone. I have found that making myself available to my patients results in very few emergency phone calls. I believe that I receive few emergency calls because my patients feel secure just knowing that they can easily get in touch with me.

Although I have a general practice of psychiatry dealing with individuals, couples, and families with children, almost all of the crisis calls that I get between sessions are about medication withdrawal reactions. Patients can become very anxious within the few most critical days after a dose reduction and I encourage them to call me at the slightest concern. Often, they want nothing more than a little reassurance that it won't last long and that they can get through it. Sometimes, we'll agree that it might be best to return to the previous dose. It depends almost entirely on whether or not the patient feels confident about handling the emotional or physical distress caused by the withdrawal. On rare occasions, we might decide that he or she needs to come see me before the next scheduled session.

In summary, it is important to distinguish between medical crises and emotional crises. Drug withdrawal can become a medical crisis that is easily treated by returning to the previous dose of medication. By contrast, emotional crises are best handled with psychotherapy or family therapy without resort to medication, so that the individual's opportunity for mastery and growth are maximized.

KEY POINTS

▪ The Non-Emergency Principle states that the emotional crisis exists in the mind of the patient and never in the mind of the therapist. When the patient feels emotionally overwhelmed by frightening feelings, the therapist should not go into emergency mode.

▪ Patients in withdrawal crises may have acute needs that must be addressed, such as the need for rest, sleep, and proper nutrition. The short-term use of sleeping medications for a few days may be useful, but caring human companionship and emotional support is the most basic and important need to be filled.

▪ A therapist who feels competent to handle any emotional crisis will have a calming effect without resorting to new psychiatric medications or to increasing medication dosage, except as a part of adjusting the medication during the withdrawal process or occasionally adding a sleeping aid for short-term use.

▪ The prescription of psychiatric medication during emotional crises can sometimes relieve emotional suffering in the short-term, but at the same time it will blunt the patient's emotional signal system and undermine the patient's confidence in handling extreme emotions, without resorting to medications.

▪ Withdrawal reactions can become genuine medical emergencies that can almost always be quickly resolved by returning the medication to its previous dose level. Although withdrawal reactions can sometimes be well handled by a purely psychotherapeutic intervention and by "toughing it out," it is not always feasible or necessary. If the patient wants to relieve emotional suffering or help in preventing negative behaviors, a simple increase in the dose to the previous level should bring a rapid beneficial result.

▪ Manic-like reactions are common during dose changes—up or down—including during withdrawal. They can usually be handled without hospitalization and without adding additional medications.

▪ Withdrawal reactions, with their associated brain impairment, are not the time for learning experiences. Little or nothing is lost by returning to the previous dose to provide expeditious relief.

▪ During acute withdrawal, psychotherapeutic interventions should usually be limited to reassurance and guidance. Patients undergoing emotional stress because of withdrawal reactions may not have the judgment and self-control to handle personal or family issues that stir up painful emotions.

▪ Effective person-centered psychotherapy can be conducted during drug withdrawal if the withdrawal is conducted at a gradual pace that is easily tolerated by the patient. Emotional crises—in the absence of distressing withdrawal reactions—are growth opportunities for patients that can transform their lives for the better.

CHAPTER 15

Techniques for Beginning Medication Withdrawal

Whenever possible, it is best to conduct psychiatric drug withdrawal at a pace that is comfortable for the patient. Even small dose reductions can sometimes become emotionally painful or even behaviorally dangerous and, because of medication spellbinding, patients may fail to recognize that they are undergoing a withdrawal reaction. Therefore, close monitoring is required by the entire collaborative team. There is no way to predict how long a withdrawal will take, but after a few dose reductions, a rough estimate can sometimes be made. When more than one drug is being withdrawn, a collaborative decision based on sound principles should be made concerning which drug to start with. The size of the initial reduction should be small and viewed as a "test dose" of the patient's tolerance for withdrawal. Making very small dose reductions can be difficult because of the relatively large dose size of the tablets or capsules, but there are ways around this problem, such as using fluid preparations (solutions) or by removing pellets from a capsule.

Rapid withdrawal from psychiatric medication is associated with more frequent and serious discontinuation symptoms as well as with an earlier and more severe return of the patient's original emotional problems. This has been found regarding antidepressants (return of depression and/or panic), antipsychotic drugs (return of psychosis), and lithium (return of mania; Baldessarini, Tondo, Ghiani, & Lepri, 2010).

USE OF PREDETERMINED REGIMENS FOR DOSE REDUCTION

Textbook strategies for drug withdrawal tend to be rote. For example, Hales, Yudofsky, and Gabbard's (2008) *The American Psychiatric Publishing Textbook of Psychiatry* recommends

> For patients who have been taking benzodiazepines for longer than 2–3 months, the benzodiazepine dose should be decreased by approximately 10% per week. Therefore, in the case of a patient receiving alprazolam 4 mg/day, the dose should be tapered by 0.5 mg/week for 8 weeks (p. 1079).

Although this 10% per week method may work some of the time for any psychiatric medication, including the benzodiazepines, it has drawbacks. If a patient has been on the medication for only 2 months, this method would double the exposure by adding another 8 weeks. On the other hand, for many patients who have been taking psychiatric medication for many months or years, including benzodiazepines in relatively high doses, 8 weeks is likely to be much too fast when done on an outpatient basis. In addition, there is great variation in patient response to the rate of drug withdrawal. This variation is probably because of a combination of biological, psychological, and circumstantial factors, including stressors and the strength of the individual's support network.

Beyond all of the variables above, many patients are taking combinations of several drugs, making any withdrawal strategy far more complicated. In addition, every class of psychiatric drugs can produce sufficiently severe adverse effects, such as serotonin syndrome or neuroleptic malignant syndrome, to require immediate withdrawal. In some cases, hospitalization may be required for drug withdrawal.

It is useful to observe that it is probably safe from a physiological perspective to go no faster than 10% per week while withdrawing patients who have been taking psychiatric medications for several months or more, but in many cases, that is either too fast for a comfortable and successful withdrawal or not fast enough to meet the patient's needs. Except in emergencies requiring rapid withdrawal, which may require hospitalization, the person-centered collaborative outpatient therapy is the least painful and the most likely to succeed.

Predetermined routines for withdrawing patients from medications work best in hospital settings, especially on wards dedicated to treating drug dependence. These facilities typically use protocols with fixed schedules for drug withdrawal, which are applied to most or all patients, depending on the type of drug. This more rigid, prescriber-centered approach is feasible in hospital settings where patients can be closely monitored, even one-to-one when necessary, allowing for quick responses and adjustments to the treatment plan while ensuring the individual's safety. These formal protocols for drug withdrawal are also consistent with the pressure to limit the cost and length of hospitalization. As one disadvantage, these hurried withdrawals are often associated with the prescription of other psychiatric drugs to replace those from which the patient is being withdrawn. A much more person-centered approach provides better service to individuals in outpatient settings.

Patients vary enormously in their feelings about withdrawing from medication. Some want to go very slowly. Others are understandably in a hurry. "I want to get my life back" is a frequent lament. Piet Westdijk, a child and adult psychiatrist and therapist in Basel, Switzerland, told me,

> I often observe an enormous urge to get rid of the medication because patients don't like the feelings of intoxication, such as slowed thinking and emotions. At this moment, they need a very empathic attitude from the doctor, who should inform them about the dangers of abruptly stopping the medication and about the improved results from withdrawing step by step (P. Westdijk, personal communication, 2012).

Westdijk's comment reemphasizes the importance of empathy at every stage of the withdrawal process, including encouraging patients to take the necessary steps in the process.

A SMALL DOSE REDUCTION CAUSES A DANGEROUS WITHDRAWAL REACTION

Mrs. Marx, a 38-year-old married woman wanted to taper off her psychiatric medication. She had been taking venlafaxine (Effexor) 75 mg for 3 years, and prior to that she had taken paroxetine (Paxil) for 7 years, giving her a 10-year exposure to antidepressants. She had been taking antidepressants ever since she became depressed following the birth of the third of her three children. Because both paroxetine and venlafaxine have similar side effects and withdrawal effects, I viewed her case as a 10-year exposure to antidepressants, indicating that a slow withdrawal would probably be required.

To facilitate a gradual taper, I changed the single 75 mg venlafaxine tablet to three 25 mg tablets to be taken in the morning as done previously. The taper was begun by the patient using a pill cutter to remove one-fourth of one of the tablets (approximately 6.25 mg or 8.3% of the total 75 mg).

Within 2 days after starting the slightly reduced dose, Mrs. Marx began to feel increasing fatigue, anxiety, and depression. Six days after the reduction, while making a routine afternoon drive to a friend's house, she became temporarily confused and lost. Her irritability flashed into rage, and she felt a frightening compulsion to drive her car into a post.

Mrs. Marx arrived at her friend's house and withdrew into a bedroom, explaining that she had a headache. She phoned her husband and told him that she had a severe headache. She was so overcome with anxiety and depression that she was afraid to try to drive home by herself. Before picking her up, her husband called me. I called and talked with my patient, and she agreed to take one-half of one 25 mg tablet immediately, then to call me within a few hours.[1] She had not eaten in several hours, so her stomach was empty. Within 2 hours she was markedly improved.

The following morning, she agreed to resume taking her original dose of 75 mg, and within 2 days, she was back to her baseline before the attempted withdrawal.

It is possible that the three 25 mg tablets were not equivalent to the 75 mg tablet, but they were manufactured by the same company, which makes significant variation less likely. Since she responded so quickly to having a small replacement dose, this confirmed that it was a withdrawal reaction.

Mrs. Marx was an intelligent health professional. As with all of my drug withdrawal patients, I encouraged her and her husband to call my cell phone the moment she felt any unusual or disconcerting changes in her emotions. Nonetheless, she did not call as the anger, dysphoria, and confusion grew—she failed to connect what was happening to the withdrawal and therefore did not call the doctor.

Mrs. Marx's husband, a busy professional, did not notice the initial changes in his wife during the drug withdrawal but immediately recognized the possibility of a withdrawal reaction when she phoned him in such distress, and so he took the necessary action of immediately calling me.

It cannot be overemphasized that individuals undergoing adverse psychiatric drug reactions often do not connect them to changes in medication, even if they have been fully informed, and that someone close to the patient needs to know about the hazards of withdrawal reactions and needs be enabled to contact the prescriber directly.

All the hazards associated with withdrawing from psychiatric medications are also associated with routine reductions and even small dose reductions. When a dose reduction is associated with a relatively rapid worsening of the patient's condition, a withdrawal reaction is the most likely cause and can usually be dealt with by a return to the previous dose.

---

[1] Usually, it is sufficient to resume the previous dose, which would have meant taking one-fourth of the tablet instead of one-half tablet. Because of the difficulty in breaking up the pill into quarter doses and because of the severity of the reaction, I chose to treat the reaction with one-half pill.

HOW LONG IT TAKES TO WITHDRAW FROM MEDICATIONS

"How long will it take?" is one of the most common questions asked about withdrawing from psychiatric drugs, but there are no easy rules to apply to the length of a psychiatric drug withdrawal. There are too many differences in each person's medication exposure, as well as in each person's sensitivity to withdrawal reactions. During the withdrawal process, life stressors vary greatly, and psychological responses will also vary greatly from person to person and from time to time. Crises in the individual's life frequently cause them to want to delay additional reductions for a time. Because of so many unpredictable variables, the person-centered method is best for obtaining a safe and relatively comfortable outcome. It emphasizes that the patient's response to each new reduction is the best barometer for how fast to proceed.

Although exact lengths of time cannot be predicted, if the patient has been on the drug for a lengthy period, perhaps a year or more, then a successful withdrawal will probably take considerably longer than most prescribers believe. Many prescribers, including highly trained psychiatrists, now believe that patients cannot do without lifelong medication, precisely because these prescribers have not taken sufficient time or care in withdrawing their patients from medication. The prescribers have become discouraged, and have stopped trying to help patients come off their medications; instead, they encourage their patients to remain on the drugs indefinitely. In the current practice of mental health, nearly all attempts at withdrawal or reduction come at the request of the patient rather than the prescriber.

Perhaps because many prescribers are uncomfortable with reducing doses or withdrawing patients from psychiatric medications, especially after months or years of exposure or because they are insufficiently experienced or knowledgeable regarding the withdrawal process, prescribers often go about withdrawal in an unsystematic fashion. Instead of titrating the withdrawal to the patient's needs and comfort, these prescribers tend to abruptly withdraw drugs in one, two, or three steps over a few days or weeks; a practice which can result in painful, if not dangerous, withdrawal reactions from almost any psychiatric drug. Similarly, many prescribers have come to believe that "mental illness" is a lifelong disorder, again because every abrupt attempt to stop medication leads to a withdrawal reaction, which is mistaken for a return of the patient's original disorder.

The Size of the Initial Dose Reduction

Instead of setting a schedule in advance, the person-centered approach starts with a small dose reduction that hopefully will be endured without much discomfort. This can be viewed as a "test reduction" aimed at finding the patient's comfort level.

The size of the first dose reduction, and subsequent ones, will vary from drug to drug, from person to person, and from time to time with the same person. However, it is often possible to talk with patients about their past experiences with lowered doses, and to arrive at what seems like a safe and comfortable dose reduction. In my experience, it is often in the range of 10%–15% of the most recent dose (see later in this chapter for the methodology for prescribing small doses).

If nothing untoward occurs after the first reduction, it is often a good idea to wait a few weeks and then reduce the dose again, depending on how the patient is feeling. Once the process has begun, in the absence of a grave necessity for stopping the drug as quickly as possible, the patient's response to each drug reduction ends up determining the length of the withdrawal.

One patient may take a single month to withdraw from a year's exposure to fluoxetine, and another patient may require a whole year. Yet another patient may end up staying on a small dose indefinitely because he or she cannot seem to endure the withdrawal reaction. An occasional patient, against my advice, may go "cold turkey" and survive the experience in reasonably good condition, but I never recommend this because of the potentially painful and even disastrous consequences.

There is no way to predict how long a person-centered withdrawal will take, but the patient sets the pace depending on his or her needs and comfort. However, after a few dose reductions have been accomplished, the patient and clinician may be able to make a rough, if tentative, estimate on the length of time.

Absent an emergency that requires rapid withdrawal, there are no formulae for how long it takes to withdraw safely, comfortably, and effectively from a psychiatric drug. In the person-centered approach, the patient's experience will determine the time it takes to complete the withdrawal. It all depends on how the patient responds from dose reduction to dose reduction. Therefore, it cannot be determined in advance how long a drug withdrawal will take.

Choosing the Order of Drug Withdrawal

Patients who seek medication reduction or withdrawal are often taking more than one drug. Here are some rough guidelines for selecting the order of drug withdrawal. As every other important decision, the final choice should be up to the patient. When possible, the therapist and the family should also be involved in the decision-making process. The following suggestions cannot substitute for the wisdom, experience, and scientific knowledge of the individual clinicians, along with input from the patient and support network.

First, it is generally best to withdraw one drug at a time each step of the way. Changing the dose of two or more drugs at once makes it very difficult to assess the cause of any untoward effects. As a result, the practitioner will have difficulty deciding which drug to return to its previous dose to calm the withdrawal reaction.

Second, it is often, but not always, advantageous to finish one drug reduction or withdrawal at a time. For example, if a patient who is nonpsychotic is taking an antipsychotic drug along with a mood stabilizer and an antidepressant, it is probably a good idea to withdraw the antipsychotic drug first, because it is the most dangerous, and to withdraw it entirely before deciding what to do about the mood stabilizer and the antidepressant.

Third, when two drugs tend to counteract each other's effects, such as a stimulant and a benzodiazepine, it can help to reduce them alternately over time. If the stimulant is reduced without reducing the benzodiazepine, the patient can become excessively sedated. If the benzodiazepine is reduced without reducing the stimulant, the patient can become overstimulated. Similarly, in the case of a patient who is nonpsychotic, when the antipsychotic drug is successfully withdrawn, then the mood stabilizer should probably be reduced together with the antidepressant to avoid an antidepressant-induced manic-like episode as the mood stabilizer is reduced. Once again, it is usually best to reduce one drug, then the other, and so on, so that no two drugs are reduced at the same dose change.

There is no specific formula for reducing two drugs over the same period. The idea is to reduce a small amount of one of the drugs and then to reduce a small amount of the other drug.

Fourth, it is often best to remove the class of medication that has been most recently started. If a patient has been taking mood stabilizers for several years and antidepressants for only several months, it's probably best to start by withdrawing the antidepressant. In estimating length of exposure to benzodiazepines, stimulants, antipsychotic drugs, and most of the newer antidepressants, drugs in the same class should be cumulative. Thus, a year on Haldol haloperidol (Haldol) and a second year on quetiapine (Seroquel) should be counted as 2 years of exposure to antipsychotic drugs. Similarly, a year on citalopram (Celexa) and a year on venlafaxine (Effexor) should count as 2 years on antidepressants. The same is true regarding stimulants, such as amphetamine (Adderall) and methylphenidate (Ritalin, Focalin), as well as benzodiazepines, such as alprazolam (Xanax) and clonazepam (Klonopin).

Antipsychotic drugs present a somewhat special problem when calculating length of exposure. Tardive dyskinesia is associated with cumulative drug exposure, even when the patient has taken the drugs at widely separated time periods with long intervals in between. For example, if a patient was prescribed an antipsychotic for a year as a 20-year-old and then again for a year as a 40-year-old, there is a risk that this constitutes a 2-year exposure. This is not as well established with other medications and other adverse effects: If a patient has been off a stimulant or benzodiazepine for many years, the effect of another year of exposure may not be cumulative. However, clinicians should err on the side of caution and consider that a patient with several years of exposure to any psychiatric drug, however long ago, should be spared as much as possible from further exposure.

Furthermore, when damage has already been detected in the brain, liver, kidney, or other organs, the clinician should be cautious and assume that the earlier damage will be cumulatively increased by renewed exposure to the drug.

Fifth, because antipsychotic drugs and lithium pose such a broad array of potentially severe acute and chronic adverse effects in patients who are nonpsychotic, it is usually best to make their reduction and withdrawal a priority. Obviously, if a patient is actively delusional or hallucinating, there are serious cautions about withdrawing the patient on an outpatient basis. I have successfully and actively withdrawn patients who are psychotic from all medication in the context of a strong support system, such as a devoted husband or wife, or devoted parents, willing to come to every outpatient session. I have only done so when the patient was cooperative and personally responsible, a combination of positive traits not often found along with symptoms of psychosis. At times, I have attempted a drug withdrawal under these conditions and eventually determined that it could not be done at that time with the particular patient and family.

Sixth, a nighttime sleep aid should usually be the last drug reduced or withdrawn. Insomnia is so demoralizing and anxiety provoking for many patients that the removal of sleep aids should usually be done last. If a patient is taking sedative drugs several times a day, such as alprazolam 1 mg three times a day and again at night, then the nighttime dose should usually be the last one reduced and stopped.

Finally, it is extremely useful to talk with the patient and family about the potential order of drug withdrawal, including which one to start with and which one to leave to last. The patient or the family may recall that it was particularly easy or difficult to withdraw from one of the drugs at an earlier time. That doesn't mean it will be the same with a new withdrawal attempt, but the information is useful and will also affect how the patient or the family anticipate the severity of withdrawal effects with that particular medication.

HOW TO MAKE SMALL DOSE REDUCTIONS

Although the underlying mechanism is yet to be explained, some patients have severe withdrawal symptoms when they reach the very end of the taper, causing them to want to take very small doses.

Some drugs are manufactured in a wide variety of doses, including relatively small doses and in a variety of formulations, such as tablets, capsules, and fluids or solutions. Other medications come in more limited forms.

Many patients are able to cut tablets into quarters with the aid of a pill cutter that can be bought at most drug stores. However, with the small doses required at the end of many tapers, this method becomes too inaccurate. The following alternatives can be useful in making small dose reductions during or at the end of the withdrawal process.

> **Safety Warning**
> Whenever there is uncertainty about the physical constitution of the tablet or the capsule, the prescriber should consult with a pharmacist on whether or not it is safe and feasible to break up the tablet into smaller pieces or to remove pellets from the capsule.

Using Pellets From Capsules

If the medication comes in capsules, such as fluoxetine (Prozac), small doses can be obtained by opening the capsule and removing a percentage of the pellets. These can be mixed into water, milk, or small amounts of food. If the prescriber needs more information about mixing the medication into a specific drink or food, the prescriber should consult a pharmacist.

If pellets are going to be removed from a capsule, the prescriber must be sure to prescribe either the brand name or the same generic manufacturer each time. For example, the number of pellets in a capsule can vary widely depending on the particular manufacturer of the generic. Pharmacies may purchase the same generic drug from more than one manufacturer, but the pharmacies can be selective if required by the prescriber to order the particular prescription from a particular manufacturer.

Even with these precautions, there may be some variation in the number of pellets from capsule to capsule, even from the same manufacturer. Therefore, I instruct patients to count the total number of pellets in every single capsule that they use and then to remove the proper percentage of the total number of pellets, for example, six of 60 for a 10% reduction.

In some instances, the standard doses of the drug may come only in tablet form and halving or quartering the smallest tablet may be too difficult or may not provide a small enough dose. However, the same drug may come in extended-release forms, such as venlafaxine XR (Effexor XR), which involves numerous coated pellets contained within a capsule. This can be very useful for withdrawing small portions at a time, for example, two or three pellets out of 65 or 70.

There is considerable flexibility in using the extended-release pellets. Again, using venlafaxine (Effexor) as an example, a patient who is prescribed a 25 mg tablet may not feel comfortable trying to taper by halving or quartering this smallest available tablet dose. Instead, this patient can be prescribed venlafaxine 37.5 mg in the extended release form. A test dose of approximately 25 mg can be taken in the form of 66% or approximately two thirds of the pellets in the 37.5 mg capsule. If the new pellet dose seems to produce an effect equivalent to the previous 25 mg tablet, then small dose reductions can be achieved by starting with the number of pellets in the 25 mg dose and then removing a few more pellets at a time from the 37.5 mg extended-release capsule.

This method of using the pellets from within an extended-release capsule has the great advantage of accommodating very small dose reductions when necessary, including the use of only one or two pellets toward the conclusion of the withdrawal when patients sometimes become very sensitive to the slightest drop in dose. Because they are longer acting, pellets from the extended-release capsules also have the advantage of reducing the risk of withdrawal reactions later in the same day or the next morning, when the patient is taking only one dose each day.

Using Fluid Formulations

Many psychiatric medications come in a fluid or solution formulation, and in every class of drug, it should be possible to obtain at least one represented as a solution. Small fluid doses of drugs are administered from a bottle with an eyedropper. In these cases, the prescriber must become familiar with the particular fluid preparation, and the best way to take it with food, so as to explain its use to the patient. To supplement my own instructions, I always enlist the help of a pharmacist in taking my patient through the process.

SWITCHING FROM SHORT-ACTING BENZODIAZEPINES TO DIAZEPAM

Psychiatrist Heather Ashton (2002) recommends switching to long-acting diazepam (Valium) when trying to withdraw from short acting benzodiazepines such as alprazolam (Xanax) and lorazepam (Ativan) in order to make the withdrawal smoother. Her informative booklet, "The Ashton Manual," is readily available on the Internet. It describes the withdrawal process and provides dose equivalents for making the switch, while warning that these equivalences are only approximate and vary from individual to individual. I usually attempt to withdraw the individual from the original drug before attempting to switch from a shorter-acting drug to Valium, but this is a matter of choice for the patient and treatment team.

SWITCHING FROM SHORT-ACTING ANTIDEPRESSANTS TO FLUOXETINE

Withdrawal from selective serotonin reuptake inhibitor (SSRI) antidepressants can be very difficult. Fluoxetine (Prozac) may be marginally easier to withdraw from because it is long acting, so that the blood level is reduced more gradually over more than a week. I am not convinced that switching from other SSRIs, such as paroxetine (Paxil) or sertraline (Zoloft), to fluoxetine (Prozac) provides much advantage regarding easing the withdrawal. Introducing a different antidepressant complicates the process by subjecting the brain to somewhat new and different toxic effects.

However, switching to fluoxetine (Prozac) may also be useful at times because it comes in a variety of doses and formulations that make tapering easier. Fluoxetine is available at 10 mg, 20 mg, and 40 mg *capsules*; 10 mg *scored tablets*; an *oral solution* of 20mg/5 ml; and *long-acting 90 mg capsules*.

The scored 10 mg tablet makes it easy to prescribe doses of 5 mg each.

The oral solution makes it possible to prescribe 4 mg doses with relative ease (see the next section).

The 90 mg extended-release weekly capsules may also provide flexibility, but I have no experience with the formulation, and little has been written about it.

When in doubt, prescribers and others in the treatment team can check for unexpected drug formulations that might facilitate tapering. When drugs become generic, the *Physicians' Desk Reference* may not list all the available formulations. However, complete information can usually be obtained with an Internet search, such as "Prozac preparations" or "Xanax preparations." Most pharmacists are happy to talk with prescribers and patients about all the drug formulations that are available and to make special orders.

WITHDRAWING FROM PROZAC

Fluoxetine (Prozac) has the longest half-life of any of the SSRIs, and withdrawal reactions may sometimes (but not always) be delayed for a week or more after the last dose. If a patient has reduced fluoxetine (Prozac) from 15 to 10 mg and a week later becomes agitated, anxious, and depressed, the first thing to do is to talk about anything in his or her life that may have been upsetting. If nothing else can be found to account for this abrupt onset of emotional distress, then it becomes a matter of deciding whether or not to ride it through, perhaps with the help of phone calls to me or an extra office visit, along with support from family or friends and perhaps a bit of stress reduction, such as staying home or doing something interesting for a day or two. If none of these sounds sufficient to the patient, then the patient can choose to resume the previous 15 mg dose. If taken on an empty stomach, this should reduce the distress very quickly, sometimes in less than an hour and definitely within a few hours.

At the next session, we would then decide how long to remain on the fluoxetine 10 mg dose before trying another reduction. Because the previous reduction to 5 mg was so stressful, we would discuss an intermediate step. Fluoxetine does not come in tablets smaller than 10 mg, and it can be difficult to break a tablet into quarters. We might decide to alternate days, 10 mg one day and 5 mg another. Because it is long acting it would be easier to do with fluoxetine than with the other SSRIs. To be even more cautious, we could use the 10 mg dose 4 or 5 days a week, and the 5 mg dose 2 or 3 days a week. Another possibility is to crush the 10 mg tablet (not the capsule) and then divide it into quarters.

If the individual was struggling with reducing fluoxetine to less than 5 mg, we could use the fluid with the eyedropper dispenser.

ADDITIONAL MEDICATION AND DIETARY SUPPLEMENTS

On rare occasions, if anxiety, agitation, or insomnia is a big part of the withdrawal reaction, I might prescribe diazepam (Valium) 5 mg, starting with one-half tablet, to see if it helps. I would limit this to two or three doses per day for no more than a day or two.

Much like alcohol, the benzodiazepines do reduce anxiety as an aspect of reducing overall alertness or higher mental functioning. Diazepam is longer acting and smoother in its impact and perhaps somewhat less likely to cause emotional instability than the shorter acting benzodiazepines, such as alprazolam (Xanax), clonazepam (Klonopin), or lorazepam (Ativan), none of which I would use. Even a small dose of diazepam can cause disinhibition and depression and can interfere with cognitive processes and driving, so I rarely resort to this alternative. Even a few doses can restimulate cravings in addiction-prone individuals.[2] It is always preferable to return to the previous dose of the drug from which the patient is withdrawing.

Some experts in drug withdrawal recommend the use of one or another herbal or "natural" remedies to ease the withdrawal. Unfortunately, if the new psychoactive agent works, it has added an additional complicating biochemical effect to the patient's already compromised brain function. If there are exceptions to this rule, I am not familiar with them. Again, I can imagine an experienced practitioner attempting to use alternative substances to ease the suffering of withdrawal, but it would be experimental.

There are a variety of practitioners and books available that suggest the use of dietary supplements as an aid during the withdrawal process. Charles Whitfield (2010), an addiction specialist and critic of psychiatric medications, finds that a variety of supplements can be helpful in the withdrawal process without compromising the function of the brain and mind (Whitfield, 2011). Provided that the substances are non-toxic and not psychoactive, I have no objection to their use, and supplements should remain among the choices available to clinicians and patients if they wish to utilize them.

---

[2]My emphasis here is on using the benzodiazepine for only a day or two, in which case it's not likely to stimulate craving in anyone who is not addiction prone. But when benzodiazepines are prescribed for weeks at a time, individuals with no past history of addiction and no known tendency toward addiction can become dependent on the drug.

Commonsense measures provide the best methods for easing the symptoms of withdrawal, including empathic counseling, a good support network, a wide variety of psychologically and spiritually uplifting activities, moderate exercise, reasonable limitations on caffeine and alcohol, and good nutrition. I will discuss this overall improvement in the quality of living in the final chapter.

KEY POINTS

- Predetermined withdrawal regimens, such as a 10% per week reduction, are most useful in a hospital or rehabilitation facility with round-the-clock medical care and support to facilitate the withdrawal. Typically, insurance coverage lasts for 30 days and so inpatient drug withdrawals, usually from addictive substances, are scheduled for completion in that allotted time.
- Except in emergencies, such as the development of tardive dyskinesia or a serotonin syndrome, outpatient psychiatric drug withdrawal is best conducted at a pace that is comfortable for the patient. This patient-directed approach is at the heart of the person-centered collaborative method of drug withdrawal.
- Even small dose reductions can at times cause severe emotional reactions and dangerous behaviors. At other times, unexpectedly large dose reductions may prove easy for the patient to sustain, but they are usually less safe.
- Because of medication spellbinding, patients commonly fail to realize that abrupt changes in their mental condition and behavior are related to the ongoing medication withdrawal, hence the need for close monitoring by the informed prescriber and/or therapist and the patient's support network.
- There is no way to predict in advance how long a withdrawal will take, but after the first few dose reductions, the patient and clinician may be able to develop a rough, tentative estimate.
- When more than one drug is involved, there are numerous considerations in choosing which drug to reduce first. Often, it is best to reduce the class of drug most recently started in the hope that it will be the easiest. Sometimes it is important to reduce the most dangerous drug first.
- The size of the initial dose reduction is determined by a small "test dose" to aid in determining the patient's tolerance to withdrawal from the drug.
- Making small dose reductions can be inconvenient when the available pills or capsules come in relative large dose sizes, but there are ways to get around this problem, including the use of fluid preparations (solutions) or pellets taken from a capsule.
- In general, it is best to avoid adding new psychoactive substances (drugs or natural remedies) to the withdrawal process.

CHAPTER 16

Cases of Antidepressant and Benzodiazepine Withdrawal in Adults

This chapter presents three cases of relatively uncomplicated drug withdrawal.

1. *Angie: Withdrawing a depressed patient from long-term paroxetine (Paxil) and alprazolam (Xanax).*
2. *Sam: Withdrawing an anxious patient from long-term sertraline (Zoloft) and lorazepam (Ativan).*
3. *George: Withdrawing a suicidal and delusional patient from short-term citalopram (Celexa) and olanzapine (Zyprexa).*

Chapter 17 presents two cases of withdrawal from multiple medications over a lengthy period.

COMMON ELEMENTS OF THE PERSON-CENTERED COLLABORATIVE APPROACH

By definition, the person-centered collaborative approach starts with "the person"—the individual who seeks help. Because human beings are unique and enormously varied in their infinite qualities, every therapy and every withdrawal process will be unique and varied.

Surprises will abound. Plans will be changed. Mistakes in judgment will be made. Some people will withdraw with remarkable ease and others with unexpected difficulty. Occasional withdrawals may become impossible to complete, at least in an outpatient practice setting. But some things should remain constant, such as:

- respect for the individual seeking help
- careful attention to the patient's feelings
- patient control over the pace at every step of the withdrawal
- open, honest discussions about adverse drug effects and withdrawal reactions
- commitment to a withdrawal that is as safe and comfortable as possible
- careful clinical monitoring
- rational clinical planning in regard to reducing multiple drugs
- psychotherapy tailored to the patient's wishes and circumstances
- in relatively difficult withdrawal cases, a person-centered collaborative approach involving the prescriber, therapist, and patient, as well as significant others to provide support and monitoring

The three cases in this chapter involve circumstances hazardous enough to need a collaborative approach. Many patients in private practice, especially emotionally stable patients who have taken one drug for only a few months, will be much easier to withdraw from medication. Some will be much more difficult and even impossible on an outpatient basis, especially patients taking multiple drugs for many years while becoming increasingly impaired and dependent on others. The cases in this and the following chapter are challenging but not impossible.

To describe the person-centered aspects of these cases, I offer some details about the interactions between myself, the patient, and the patient's significant others. However, I am not promoting my particular style of conducting therapy as a model. Instead, I encourage clinicians to bring out the best in themselves, so that they can bring out the best in their patients and clients. This is also the emphasis in my video, *Empathic Therapy: A Training Film* (Breggin, 2011a).

THREE ILLUSTRATIVE CASES OF PSYCHIATRIC MEDICATION WITHDRAWAL IN ADULTS

Angie: Medicated Through Her Divorce and the Death of Her Father

Selective serotonin reuptake inhibitor (SSRI) antidepressants are commonly prescribed in combination with benzodiazepines. This practice arose in part because SSRIs can be overstimulating, requiring sedatives to dampen drug-induced agitation, anxiety, and insomnia. Paroxetine (Paxil) is sometimes combined with alprazolam (Xanax), but among benzodiazepines, alprazolam is particularly likely to produce paradoxical overstimulation, causing the very same symptoms it is supposed to control, including depression, agitation, anxiety, and insomnia. In addition, paroxetine and alprazolam are the shortest acting and hardest hitting representatives of their classes, and hence among the most difficult to withdraw from. Prescribers should be cautious about combining these two drugs and also about using either one by itself.

Angie was a 44-year-old single mother of two teenage boys. She had been divorced for 6 years in what she described as an "amicable" fashion from her "generous" ex-husband. At that time, her family doctor had placed her on paroxetine (Paxil) 20 mg/day for several months. Angie felt that the antidepressant "helped me get through it."

Three years before coming for an evaluation, Angie's father died. Angie reported that she had never been "that close" to her dad, and so she was caught off guard when she became very despondent following his death.

The day after her father died, Angie's family doctor again placed her on paroxetine and added alprazolam to calm her agitation and to help with sleep. With gradual increments in dose, she was now taking alprazolam 1 mg four to five times a day and paroxetine 40 mg/day.

After 3 years, medication failed to lift her depression and even seemed to worsen it. Angie's family doctor suggested for the first time that she might need "therapy." She came to me seeking expertise in both medication and psychotherapy.

When I specifically asked about supplements and other drugs, Angie reported that she was also taking St. John's wort to help with her "bad moods." I explained to her that the herbal remedy had similar effects to the SSRI antidepressants. Because she was only taking it two or three times a week "as needed," we agreed she could simply stop using it before we began her medication withdrawal.

> Always ask patients if they are taking other psychoactive substances, such as alcohol, herbal remedies, and illegal drugs that can interfere with the withdrawal process.

From the start, I was struck by Angie's intelligence and her willingness to examine herself and her feelings. In the first session, I explained that my goal was not to mute or subdue her feelings, even her most frightening ones. My goal was to help her welcome her feelings, so that she could get to know them and to deal with them. She liked the idea.

I asked her if she had ever mourned the loss of her marriage, and she responded that she had "marched ahead" through the divorce. She had cried many times toward the end of the marriage but in talking with me, she realized for the first time that she had stopped crying over the marriage after her doctor started her on paroxetine.

"That's not right, is it?" she asked, and I agreed that it wasn't. She realized, "The same thing happened when my father died. I shed some tears when I first heard he was sick and also on the day he died, but by the next day, I was already on the drugs again." Angie hadn't cried since.

"But why would I feel so bad when Dad died? He was never loving, never close. He made me feel like I didn't matter."

I responded, "The hardest deaths for us to handle can be the ones where we never got what we needed or wanted. The death makes us face what we never got from the person. When you feel ready, we can look at your feelings about your father."

Angie decided she wanted to come off the medications as soon as possible and to work with me in therapy. I explained how medication spellbinding prevents individuals from recognizing that they are having a drug-induced emotional crisis when taking or withdrawing from psychiatric drugs, and so she would need someone to stay in touch with her on a daily basis, if possible. Angie chatted on the phone almost every day and often met for lunch with her friend Francine.

Angie's friend, Francine, came for half of the next session. Francine, like Angie, was a very bright and responsible woman. I explained the range of potential medication withdrawal effects from Paxil and Xanax and gave Francine my phone numbers. Francine promised to talk to Angie at least once every day on the phone, and more often if necessary, and promised to call me if Angie seemed in difficulty.

Angie felt highly motivated to cut back quickly, especially on the antidepressant paroxetine, which she thought was making it the hardest for her to have feelings. She also reminded me that she had stopped the same drug after several months following her divorce without any problems.

Somewhat reluctantly, I agreed to reduce her dose from 40 mg paroxetine to 30 mg, a 25% reduction. Two days later I received a call from Angie's friend Francine. Angie had phoned her in a "rage about men." Wholly unlike her usual self, Angie had involved her two teenage sons in her upset, and Francine had heard them in the background of the call begging their mother to calm down. I thanked Francine and then called Angie who by then was feeling very remorseful. She said she had been ashamed to call me because she knew on "some level" that she was "behaving badly."

We agreed to have a half-hour phone session, during which time I confirmed that she was going through paroxetine withdrawal. Although her anger was "real," her lack of self-control was the product of an abrupt 25% drop in her dose.

Angie didn't want to delay the withdrawal by returning to her original dose of 40 mg, but fortunately, I had prescribed some 10 mg tablets. These were scored, so that she could easily break them in half to take a 5 mg dose, which she did. Angie checked back with me 2 hours later to confirm that she was feeling much better after taking the additional

5 mg of paroxetine. We tentatively decided to make the taper from 40 mg to 35 mg, instead of the 30 mg as originally planned.

When I saw Angie a few days later for her weekly appointment, she told me how glad she was that I had involved Francine in her treatment. "I mean you told me about medication spellbinding—that I might not recognize an emotional overreaction during withdrawal. You even mentioned I might get irrationally angry—but I didn't really believe it could happen to me and when it did, I didn't see it coming or recognize it as withdrawal."

> In a person-centered collaborative approach, it is important to be flexible in planning the withdrawal, adjusting drug reductions according to the patient's responses and input from the collaborators.

"It can happen to anyone," I reassured her.

Angie wondered why she had had such a strong reaction to a partial reduction when she had stopped the same drug without difficulty after her divorce. "Overall, it's unpredictable," I explained, "But this time you were on higher doses for a longer period of time." I also explained that some patients have worse adverse reactions and withdrawal reactions to a drug the second time around.

I also took partial responsibility for her upsetting withdrawal reaction. "I may have started too quickly talking about your feelings about your father's death. Maybe for awhile we should avoid delving too deeply into your feelings. You're very good at getting insights, Angie. You're great at therapy, and I think you could have handled the divorce and your father's death very well with counseling. But during the withdrawal, we've got to be more cautious about stirring up too much feeling." Angie greeted my suggestion with a mixture of disappointment and relief.

Over the next 8 weeks, with three 5 mg dose reductions, we reduced Angie from 35 to 20 mg of paroxetine. She suffered only a few brief and mild episodes of irritability with her teenage boys.

I invited Angie to bring the boys in for one session during which I reassured them that their mother would not be so irritable forever. Both boys said, "It's worth it," because their mother seemed more caring and involved with them than ever before.

After her boys stepped out of the session, Angie cried for the first time in years. She was sad that the boys hadn't felt fully engaged with her while she was taking the paroxetine, and she was glad that they now felt her presence more strongly in their lives. She needed reassurance that she shouldn't blame herself. I reminded her how wonderfully her sons were doing and how much they loved and cared about her.

Now taking only 20 mg of the antidepressant, Angie began to more fully appreciate the effects she was having from the four to five daily doses of 1 mg of the sedating drug alprazolam (Xanax). She was getting anxious in between the doses (interdose withdrawal), and she was waking up in the morning feeling irritable and anxious (overnight withdrawal). She used to think she just needed more of the alprazolam; now, she realized she was taking too much of it and was going through withdrawal many times a day, most severely in the morning, which was 8 hours or more after her last dose.

We began to reduce alprazolam by changing from four to five doses per day to a regular four doses per day. After a few weeks, she felt comfortable without the occasional extra dose. Then, we reduced the benzodiazepine by 0.5 mg every 2–4 weeks, depending on what she felt, until we were down to 1 mg twice a day. She had numerous episodes of mild anxiety and some worsening insomnia during the withdrawal but wanted to keep forging ahead.

At one point during the alprazolam withdrawal, Angie called with feelings of irritability and anxiety, very similar to her earlier withdrawal reaction, but we hadn't changed her dose for a week or more. It turned out that it was the time in her menstrual cycle when she often became irritable and anxious.

> Women often find it difficult to distinguish between withdrawal reactions and changes in their menstrual cycle, probably because the menstrual cycle itself involves severe ups and downs in the intensity of exposure to potentially psychoactive hormones.

With her medication doses reduced to paroxetine 20 mg/day and alprazolam 2 mg/day, Angie began to feel much more alive. She realized that she had very little memory of the months after her father's death. It was "like his death almost never happened." She also had trouble remembering milestones in her children's lives over the past 3 years, including Christmases and birthdays. Memory gaps such as these are common in patients exposed to alprazolam or any benzodiazepine over a period of months or years.

Although she was becoming more aware of her memory difficulties, past and present, Angie's sons and her friend Francine told her that she was getting better at remembering what they said to her. Francine also observed that Angie was thinking more clearly. I had noted these improvements as well, but Angie doubted she was improving that much until her boys and her friend confirmed it. Medication spellbinding makes it difficult for patients to see their prior impairments, as well as their degree of improvement.

In addition to the more limited clinical phenomenon of medication spellbinding, Angie was suffering from chronic brain impairment (CBI), including (a) *cognitive dysfunction* in the form of slowed thinking, short-term memory dysfunction, and the loss of many important memories during the period of exposure to alprazolam; (b) *apathy* in the form of not being fully engaged with the people in her life; (c) *emotional instability* in the form of cycling through anxiety and irritability on a daily basis; and (d) *anosognosia* in the form of not recognizing how seriously she had been impaired by the medications. Medication spellbinding includes anosognosia but can also produce abnormal mental states and behaviors, such as her heightened irritability and anger.

Toward the end of the alprazolam withdrawal, Angie began to experience "prickly" feelings in her arms, hands, legs, and feet and then pain in the bottoms of her feet when she stood, and sometimes even when she sat. The alprazolam had caused nerve injury that was becoming more apparent now that she was less numbed by the previously larger doses of both drugs.

We proceeded toward completion of the withdrawal by reducing the paroxetine and the alprazolam by small amounts on alternative weeks. On occasion, we waited more than a week in between dose changes. When we neared the end, Angie was taking 5 mg of paroxetine by breaking the scored 10 mg dose in half and 0.5 mg of alprazolam at night to help with sleep.

At this point, we began reducing Angie's paroxetine dose by 5 mg every other day for 2 weeks and then we stopped it entirely. Angie became extremely fatigued and depressed a few days after the last dose. After discussing it, we resumed the antidepressant by prescribing the liquid suspension for oral administration, which contains 5 mL of orange-flavored liquid equivalent to paroxetine 10 mg. I explained to her—and asked the pharmacist to also go over it with her—that one drop from the eyedropper provided her 2 mg doses. Using this method, we successfully weaned her from paroxetine over several weeks.

When Angie was no longer taking paroxetine, we weaned her off the alprazolam by skipping a dose each week, then two doses each week, then three doses, and so forth, until she was done. During this time, I worked with her on developing comforting rituals for getting ready for bed, which for Angie included making sure she said goodnight to her sons and chatting with them for a few minutes, reading fiction and listening to music, having a hot chocolate, and then saying a prayer when she went to bed. If she had trouble falling asleep in bed, she used simple relaxation techniques or imaging of peaceful places.

It took 8 months to withdraw Angie from medications she had been taking for 3 years. As often occurs in my experience, my patient wished to go considerably slower than I might have preferred. At other times, patients want to go much faster than I do.

During the last several weeks of the withdrawal, Angie felt stable enough to talk about emotionally stimulating subjects, and we began to explore more about her relationships with men, her divorce, and the death of her father. She decided that her ex-husband, whom she previously saw as so generous, in reality was not providing as much child support as a judge would require in court, and she was able to demand an increase from him. The emotional blunting effect of the antidepressant had caused her to gloss over any conflict with him during the divorce.

Angie also came to understand that her despondency over her father's death centered on never getting what she needed from the men in her life. She saw that in the future it might be possible to seek what she really needed in a new romantic relationship. For the first time, she talked honestly with her mother by phone and then in person about what her father had been like. She felt a renewed bonding with her mother.

At the last session, about 2 years after we started, Angie brought her sons to "celebrate" how much closer she was with them, and how happy they were about the changes in her. By then, she was seeing a man who not only loved her but who also managed to have good relationships with her two sons—something previously beyond her expectations for a man in her life.

Angie did not feel completely recovered and experienced a persistent CBI. Typical of benzodiazepine withdrawal, the memory blanks for important events over the 3 years did not return. Her short-term memory function had greatly improved, but at times she still needed to make lists to keep track of things. She continued to feel "not quite right" in her legs and feet, and sometimes had pain in her feet when she stood for long periods. But she continued to improve and was determined not to let these persisting problems impede her progress in improving her quality of life.

> Although some patients do not feel completely recovered from adverse drug effects after withdrawal is completed, most feel much more willing and able to take control of their lives and to improve their quality of life.

Sam: Withdrawing a Patient Who Didn't Want Psychotherapy

Many patients ask to be put on psychiatric medication because they want a "quick fix" or because they are uncomfortable thinking psychologically about themselves. After taking the medications for months or years, they realize that the drugs may be harming them, but they remain unmotivated for psychotherapy. Clinicians must adjust their approach to the patient's particular values and wishes, providing of course that they do not violate professional ethics. In this case, Sam was leery of anything that sounded like "therapy," but he wanted to stop taking psychiatric medications.

Sam was a 30-year-old married man with three children who worked as a store clerk and was determined to improve his career and income by completing a demanding 2-year technical degree at the local community college. His spouse, Adrian, was very supportive and a dedicated full-time homemaker and wife, but despite her help, Sam often felt overwhelmed by the requirements of being a husband, father, employee, and student.

On a routine visit to his family doctor 2 years earlier, Sam described his feelings of fatigue, stress, and occasional episodes of severe anxiety. Sam was put on sertraline (Zoloft) 50 mg, which was eventually raised to sertraline 150 mg. He was also prescribed the benzodiazepine lorazepam (Ativan) 1 mg "as needed," which he took a few times a week during "panic attacks."

Sam had called his family doctor about increasing anxiety and was told to start taking the lorazepam three times a day on a regular basis, but Sam decided against it. He never did want to "take pills," but neither did he want to "talk to someone about my problems."

Sam's wife urged her husband to go to a local mental health clinic to get further evaluated. At the clinic, a clinical social worker told Sam that he was probably getting worse as a result of his medications. She pointed out multiple warnings in the *Physicians' Desk Reference* about a potentially "worsening condition" on sertraline and gave him a copy of the Food and Drug Administration (FDA)-mandated medication guide that she had copied out of the book. She told him that benzodiazepines, such as Xanax, could also worsen the anxiety they were supposed to help. She then told Sam there was no chance that the clinic psychiatrist would do anything but increase his drugs, and instead, she referred Sam to me. Although I didn't know the social worker, I did know it was an act of courage and honesty on her part to put her patient's interests first in the face of possible censure from the authorities at her clinic.

Sam told me that he was increasingly fatigued and felt "blah" much of the time. He used to have a satisfying sex life but no longer seemed to have much interest in it. His panic attacks were becoming more intense and frequent. He would suddenly feel frightened as if the world were coming to an end. His heart would pound like it was going to jump out of his chest, and he was afraid he might die. The panic attacks seemed to come unpredictably and "out of nowhere." They lasted many minutes, leaving him drained, discouraged, and frightened.

"I don't have 'problems,'" he explained to me. "I'm stressed out by having too many things to deal with at the same time." I told him I would have some useful ideas about how to handle the anxiety before we finished up the hour.

Because he felt ill at ease talking to a psychiatrist, we spent the first few minutes chatting somewhat informally about his life in general, the various stressors, and how his wife and children were doing. I reassured him that I did not think he was "mentally ill" and that I agreed with his assessment that he was stressed out by all of his duties and obligations.

Sam found the "panic attacks" particularly distressing. I explained that he could learn to understand and master them without having to take the lorazepam, which he said really didn't "kick in" anyway until the episode was over.

It made sense to Sam when I suggested that these anxiety attacks grew out of feeling overwhelmed and helpless, so that he no longer felt in control of himself, his life, or even his mind. He readily admitted that his life often seems out of control and then was able to see that, in a state of panic, he was losing control over his mental process and succumbing to overwhelming feelings of helplessness.

We were able to pinpoint the immediate stressor of his most recent panic episode as something he described as "really nothing." He had almost forgotten to do a school assignment and only remembered it at the last minute, so that he had to stay up late at night to finish. It was just "one more thing" making him feel lost and overwhelmed, like he "couldn't go on like this anymore."

Sam felt reassured about being able to identify one of the triggers for his episodes of anxiety. He also found it useful to connect the panic attacks to his broader feelings of being overwhelmed with too much to deal with. "It's like I just can't ever get on top of things."

In this initial session, I showed Sam how he could recognize his anxiety triggers, identify that he was lapsing into helplessness and emotional overwhelm, and instead put his mind to work on regaining his sense of power and control. He also liked the idea of focusing on something practical to do at the moment the anxiousness started, such as making a list of things needing to be done the coming day or putting his focus on a concrete task that he wanted to do, while also reminding himself he could take charge of his emotions. He liked the idea of standing up for himself, so I told him that the anxiety could not kill him and that he could, if he wished, tell it to try its best to hurt him, the way he might stand down a bully. At the end of the session, he said that I'd given him some good practical advice. A hardworking, logical man—he appreciated the concept of taking charge of his emotions. I suggested that next session we look at how his life had gotten so overwhelming, and what he could do about it.

On the second visit, Sam told me with pride that in the previous week he had actually sensed an anxiety attack coming on and then had "used my mind to stop that damn thing from getting out of control." Building on his growing sense of confidence in therapy, we went on to talk further about the psychiatric medications. He expressed gratitude that the social worker had warned him about the drugs and referred him to me.

I reassured Sam that there would be no withdrawal reaction from stopping the "as needed" occasional use of lorazepam, but there could be serious withdrawal problems from 2 years of exposure to sertraline.

Although the social worker had already done it, and I had started the discussion the previous week, I, once again, reviewed many of the adverse effects and the withdrawal effects of the two different drugs, and I also described medication spellbinding.

It is critical for healthcare professionals, prescribers, and nonprescribers alike to be familiar with the most common and most dangerous adverse drug effects and to remind patients about them. No matter how many other professionals have treated or evaluated the patient, a clinician should never take for granted that patients know or remember the hazards associated with their drugs. By simply asking patients to share their knowledge about the drugs they are taking, including patients on long-term treatment, clinicians can uncover their lack of knowledge and sometimes their lack of proper concern about potential harmful effects from drugs.

> Every knowledgeable and dedicated clinician—prescriber or therapist—should take responsibility for making sure that patients understand the risks associated with their medications. Clinicians should not assume that someone else has done the job. Beyond that, patients easily forget about adverse drug effects and assume their prescribed drugs are safe, and therefore, they need regular reminders about the risks and what hazards to look out for.

Sam was aware that his thinking was slowed and his emotions were more unstable. His wife felt that he was losing interest in her and the children. After 2 years on an SSRI antidepressant, with occasional use of a benzodiazepine, Sam had a mild case of CBI.

Sam decided he was not taking any more Ativan and that he wanted to "get off the Zoloft as fast as I can."

With about 15 minutes left in the second session, I asked Sam if his wife might be willing to come to the third session to discuss withdrawal reactions, so that she could help to identify them. He laughed, "With three kids? If Adrian gets away, she's going to get her hair done. We haven't been bowling in 3 years!" He was agreeable to me phoning her while he was with me in the office. He laughed again, "You'll get an idea about what life is like at home."

Adrian was very surprised to "hear from the doctor" and made an effort to "shush" the children in the background. I asked her how she felt about Sam coming off the antidepressant medication, Zoloft. She said she didn't know the names of the drugs he was taking, but something had "changed" him. Even the kids noticed, "He doesn't seem to pay us as much attention as he used to. I thought it was just him trying to do too much."

I went over the various withdrawal effects Adrian could expect and emphasized, "Look out for anything new that's at all worrisome, like getting angry easily or 'crashing,' such as feeling down and wanting to hurt himself or the opposite, getting 'high.' If Sam doesn't call me at times like that, I want you to call me."

I told Adrian that if I couldn't be reached, she should remind Sam about returning to his previous dose. I gave her my office, home, and cell phone numbers. As so often happens, she was "grateful beyond words" that I was taking such an interest in her husband, "even bothering to call me." She said she'd keep my phone numbers with her at all times.

I prescribed Sam 25 mg tablets of sertraline to facilitate the withdrawal and reduced his dose from 150 mg/day to 125 mg (five tablets per day). He liked the idea of using only 25 mg tablets because having several different pill sizes was confusing for him. Also, he would enjoy the satisfaction of reducing his dosage one pill at a time until there were no more pills. Because the pharmacy might question a prescription which specified taking five 25 mg tablets of a drug at one time, I wrote on the prescription, "Small pill size for tapering."

Because it was his first dose reduction, I asked Sam to give me a call the following day and for several days afterward. Because cost was an issue and we had good rapport, I agreed to his request to spread out the sessions to every 2 weeks—provided he made frequent no charge calls to check in with me. Sam called as scheduled and said he was doing fine.

At the next session, Sam was eager to continue the taper. We agreed on reducing him another 25 mg, to a total of 100 mg of sertraline. We continued to discuss how to handle anxiety without resort to medication.

Two days later, his wife called me in the late afternoon, and I called back after my last patient was finished at 6 pm. I could hear the background chaos of children. She apologized profusely for bothering me, but Sam was really acting "funky," like he had the flu or a fever, but he didn't have a temperature. Sam then got on the phone. He hadn't realized it, but Adrian was right—he felt "crappy all over," and he had "this thing" I'd warned him about, a weird sense of imbalance that made him want to sit quietly and to hold his head still. That sealed it for me—he was having a typical SSRI antidepressant withdrawal reaction.

"I don't want to go back up to 125 mg," he said. "It would feel like I'd been wasting time." I suggested taking half a pill or 12.5 mg. Because he hadn't eaten yet, I told him it might work in half an hour or less. He called me back in 40 minutes and said he was much better and thought he'd feel fine by bedtime. He promised to call me if he wasn't completely better by 10 pm.

At the next visit, I made sure that Sam felt comfortable at the pace we were going—reducing him 25 mg every 2 weeks. I also reminded him that the withdrawal reactions might become more serious because we'd be taking out bigger percentages of the drug each time. I explained, "When you take 25 mg from 100 mg, it's only a 25% drop. When you take 25 mg from 50 mg, it's a 50% drop. It's possible it could have a greater withdrawal effect."

The withdrawal went smoothly on schedule. Then the day after we reduced Sam's dose down to only 25 mg, his wife Adrian called me for a second time, saying that Sam was getting very irritable with her and their children. I conducted a 30-minute couple's counseling with the two of them huddled over Sam's cell phone set on speaker. There had been an obvious misunderstanding between them about how to respond to a problem with one of the children. When Sam was better able to explain himself to her, Adrian was no longer so distressed. They resolved the conflict on the phone without a change in Sam's medication.

I reminded Sam and his wife how hard it is to for parents to get on the same page about raising three children and took the opportunity to recommend that they take a local parenting course that was free. Neither of them showed any enthusiasm, and so I bookmarked it in my mind to bring up again at a later date. Next session, I also gave Sam a childrearing book, which he later said, "Helped me a little, but mostly my wife read it. She's a bit more relaxed now with the kids."

During the withdrawal, Sam remained surprisingly stable, and I took the opportunity early in the sessions to chat with him—trying not to make it look like "therapy"—about the stressors in his life. He decided that his wife and I were right—he was trying to do too much too fast— and he dropped one course the next semester at the community college. He also took my advice and made sure his wife arranged for a babysitter Saturday nights, so they could go bowling together. He had forgotten how much they loved it, especially getting away from the kids and being with old friends again.

Now that we had reduced the sertraline to 25 mg, Sam reported that he was becoming unusually fatigued. He also had a recurrence of the odd sensations of imbalance that wouldn't go away, as well as some "funny feelings," such as crawling sensations under his skin. I suggested he halve the pills, and he stayed on 12.5 mg for a month before he felt comfortable stopping. Within a few weeks after being drug free, Sam felt "normal" for the first time in years. All signs of CBI had abated.

Once again, I offered to see him and his wife in couple's counsel- ing to help with some of the stress at home or to work with him alone on the issues, but he said, "I got what I came for. I'm off these head pills, and the anxiety is nothing much anymore. Also, that other stuff is better," referring to his loss of interest in sex. Sam was pleased with the outcome.

A few months later, Sam sent me a Christmas card with a family photo signed by himself and his wife and his three children.

Sam's withdrawal from an SSRI antidepressant was relatively easy, probably as a result of a person-centered collaborative approach, where he controlled the pace of the drug reductions. Also, his wife lent her support to make sure that any withdrawal reactions did not get out of control before contacting me. Although I encourage people to work in therapy for a few months at least after stopping medication, Sam was eager to "be on my own," and he agreed to no more than two 30-minute follow-up visits before we concluded the treatment. I reminded him that he could return any time he wished, even if only for one or two visits. He was very pleased with the invitation, but I could see it was the last thing on his mind.

George: Withdrawing a Suicidal and Delusional Patient From Medication

George's case demonstrates the feasibility, at times, of removing an individual quickly from psychiatric medications, even after an episode initially diagnosed as severe major depressive disorder with suicidality and psychotic features.

George was a 45-year-old married man with two children, who lost his job and took a considerable pay cut, working less than full-time in his subsequent employment. This was a dramatic blow to his self-esteem, raised anxieties about his family's financial future, and resulted in him becoming depressed and withdrawn. Conflicts developed with his wife Miranda and her teenage daughter from a previous marriage. Miranda convinced him to see a psychiatrist.

The psychiatrist diagnosed George as suffering from major depressive disorder and started him on citalopram (Celexa), an SSRI antidepressant. He instructed George to take a 20 mg tablet each day for 1 week, followed by two 20 mg tablets the second week. Three days after his second dose of citalopram 40 mg/day, George drove his car into a telephone pole in a suicide attempt, but the airbag protected him from serious injury. In the emergency room he was involuntarily hospitalized, and on admission to the ward, his psychiatrist continued the citalopram 40 mg/day.

Within 3 days on the ward, George developed a paranoid delusion, suspecting that his wife, stepdaughter, and doctors were conspiring to kill him for his insurance money. Olanzapine (Zyprexa) 20 mg/day was added, and George was released 4 days later, having been a week in the hospital.

George was now diagnosed with major depressive disorder with psychotic features and taking citalopram 40 mg/day and olanzapine 20 mg/day, both at the maximum recommended dose. The hospital discharge summary noted that he had "psychomotor agitation" and "an agitated depression" but did not mention the possibility that George had drug-induced akathisia, which is easily confused with emotionally induced agitation.

George's wife, Miranda, began to search the Internet and found many cases of adults experiencing suicidal feelings and actions as a result of taking SSRI antidepressants. She asked the psychiatrist if George's unprecedented suicidal act and even his delusion could have been caused by the medication. The psychiatrist declared that antidepressants can only cause suicidal *feelings* and not actual suicides and that the problem was limited to children and adults much younger than George. He said that antidepressants can "unmask" psychosis but not cause it unless the individual is genetically susceptible. His observations, *although entirely incorrect*, were consistent with the prevailing pharmaceutical industry viewpoint.

Miranda decided to bring her husband to me for a second opinion.

George was barely able to sit still in the office. He wanted to pace, and when he sat down, his feet jiggled. He was wringing his hands. His speech was slow and lifeless. His face was expressionless and wooden. He was suffering from a combination of akathisia (drug-induced psychomotor agitation) and drug-induced Parkinsonism (psychomotor retardation), now superimposed on his original problems related to the loss of his job.

When I systematically questioned George, he was able to tell me that the akathisia started when he began taking the antidepressant sertraline, and that it might have gotten worse after the antipsychotic drug olanzapine was added. He said he had wanted to kill himself to get rid of "the horrible feelings inside my head." After listening, Miranda now recalled that George had seemed very "jumpy" and "jittery" the morning before he drove his car into a tree.

As described in earlier chapters, the newer antidepressants frequently cause a state of overstimulation, along with a worsening of depression. As a part of that overstimulation, the drugs can also cause akathisia—an unbearable need to move about in a futile attempt to control extreme inner turmoil and agitation. The experience is likened to being tortured from the inside out.

Both the SSRI antidepressants and the antipsychotic drugs can cause or worsen akathisia, and the antipsychotic drugs very commonly cause a flattening of emotions and slowed-down movements typical of drug-induced Parkinsonism.

Both medications can also cause paranoid delusions and psychosis, although those reactions are relatively uncommon compared to akathisia. As the *Diagnostic and Statistical Manual of Mental Disorders* confirms (4th ed., text rev.; *DSM-IV-TR*; American Psychiatric Association, 2000), akathisia can worsen an individual's overall condition and lead to depression and suicidal feelings, as well as a general worsening of the patient's condition and psychosis.

Miranda was eager for me to know what her husband was really like before the medications. She brought a video camera to show me home movies taken the weekend prior to his starting on citalopram. Although George's face showed a degree of stress, he was warm and loving toward his family and able to laugh at the antics of his teenage boys who were filming the family get-together. He was not the nervous, jittery, and anguished man sitting in my office. His facial expressions were not deadened.

Any attempt at guidance or counseling would have been largely futile with George in his current drug-intoxicated condition. I would have to work very closely with his wife. I explained to George and Miranda that his suicide attempt was probably caused by akathisia induced by the citalopram and possibly worsened by olanzapine. The suicide attempt occurred shortly after starting the antidepressant; it was associated with akathisia, it was unprecedented and out of character, and it displayed the extremely violent quality commonly associated with antidepressant-induced suicide attempts.

George also had a severe case of CBI, but after such short-term medication exposure, it would probably completely resolve when the medications were stopped.

The continued akathisia and drug exposure in the hospital, along with the stress and humiliation of being made into an involuntary psychiatric inpatient, had probably combined to cause the paranoid reaction.

I reviewed with George and Miranda many of the other adverse effects of the two drugs. I suggested that George probably would have done well if he and his wife had been directed toward couple's counseling to deal with the stress surrounding his job loss. He never needed the medication.

George and Miranda decided that it was best for him to come off the drugs as quickly as possible. Miranda reassured me that there were no guns in the house in case he became suicidal or violent and that she could remain with George at all times. "I'm such a light sleeper," she explained, "He couldn't get out of bed without me knowing it." She would also be willing to bring her husband with her for as many sessions a week as necessary for a couple of weeks, if that would make it possible to remove him speedily from the medications. She would do all the driving.

Because George had been taking citalopram for less than a month, I suggested that we taper him quickly in two steps. Instead of 40 mg of citalopram she would start the following day by giving him 20 mg per day. She would stay in touch with me every day. If all went well, we would then stop the drug after our next office visit, in 2 or 3 days.

By phone over the next 2 days, Miranda reported that her husband quickly improved on the lower dose of citalopram. He was much less jumpy, agitated, and anxious—confirming that the stimulation and akathisia were being caused mostly by the citalopram, although it could have been caused by the Zyprexa as well.

When Miranda brought George to the office for the second time that week, he was minimally agitated and overall much calmer. He was able to express gratitude for the efforts being made by me and by his wife. We all agreed to stop the citalopram completely and then to assess how he was responding.

I reminded them to call me if George seemed to be getting worse again. I doubted that he would have an olanzapine (Zyprexa) withdrawal reaction after such short exposure. I did mention, however, that I had seen patients become exhausted and despairing coming off the drug.

Miranda stayed in touch with me every evening, with George getting briefly on the phone as well. He continued to affirm that he had no suicidal, violent, or delusional thinking.

Without the stimulation caused by the antidepressant, it was even more obvious that George remained in a zombie-like state from the olanzapine. Because he had only been on the drug about 2 weeks, I suggested that we again attempt a rapid taper starting with a reduction from 20 mg to 10 mg, followed by a period of observation.

Within a week of the reduction to olanzapine 10 mg, George was a much improved man who was able to actively participate in a conversation and to offer opinions. He was feeling ashamed and remorseful about the suicide attempt, but I reassured him it was drug induced. He was enormously relieved to hear that antidepressants cause many patients to experience medication spellbinding and to undergo suicidal and violent thoughts and acts.

George winced when I mentioned "violent" thoughts and acts. He looked at his wife, hoping for forgiveness, and then confessed to her that he had briefly thought of harming his family, but it had so appalled him that he chose suicide instead. The session ended with a loving hug between husband and wife and a shared hopefulness about their future.

George—a man who suffered from loss of self-esteem and anxiety because of job loss—had almost been turned into a chronic mental patient by overzealous medicating and a distressing admission to a psychiatric unit. Worse yet, he had almost been turned into a suicide or a perpetrator of horrendous violence.

George and Miranda continued to work with me in couple's therapy. With a drug-free mind, George returned to his usually assertive mentality—at times, at the expense of a collaborative relationship with his wife. George's recent stresses were not only caused by his employment issues but also by his conflicts with his wife and stepdaughter over childrearing issues. George's setback at work had forced him to be at home more of the time and that had brought the family conflicts to the fore front.

Great progress was made regarding George's 12-year-old stepdaughter when she attended a few sessions with her mother and stepfather. Because she often treated George like he didn't belong in the family, he was shocked and deeply moved to hear from his stepdaughter's lips that she really liked him and wanted to spend more time with him.

With the extra time at home and his involvement in therapy, George became much better at relating to his family in a caring and collaborative manner. As a result, his self-esteem grew, and he was able after 6 months to find a job that was equally well paying and more satisfying than the job he had lost.

After a little less than 2 years in therapy, George and Miranda were living far better lives than they had ever imagined, and their daughter had asked George to formally adopt her. With his new interpersonal skills, George also improved his professional life beyond his expectations.

> Withdrawing patients from psychiatric medications often allows them to deal with their original problems in much more creative and satisfying ways, leading to a much improved quality of life for them and their families.

George's story is not uncommon in terms of his severe adverse reactions to psychiatric medications. I have given many other examples in more detailed clinical studies in my book, *Medication Madness: The Role of Psychiatric Drugs in Cases of Violence, Suicide and Crime*. A careful medication history will often disclose that an individual's worst emotional disturbances occurred *after* starting psychiatric medication and that those adverse drug reactions were never properly diagnosed. If this diagnostic mistake is quickly discovered and corrected, as in George's case, the drugs can be stopped relatively fast and proper therapy can begin. But if the medication exposure has lasted for months or years, the withdrawal process can become very complicated, and getting to the roots of the individual's underlying emotional problems can be difficult.

OBSERVATIONS ON THE CASES

In all three of these person-centered collaborative medication withdrawals, I worked with the patient and a family member to develop, maintain, and regularly readjust a plan for drug withdrawal. In Angie's case, I met with her best friend on one occasion and also talked with her on the phone, while she stayed in touch regularly with Angie. I also met Angie's two teenage boys for a session. In Sam's case, I was only able to work with his wife on the phone. In George's case, his wife Miranda worked very closely with me, came to all the sessions, and the treatment evolved into family therapy with his stepdaughter.

Each case involved some element of psychotherapy, tailored to the needs and desires of the participants. In Angie's case, we examined her difficulties relating to men that had caused her to become depressed as a young woman, as well as during her divorce, and after the death of her father. In Sam's case, psychotherapy was mostly limited to guidance in handling episodes of anxiety, as well as some guidance in childrearing, in relating to his wife, and in reducing the stressors, in particular, his heavy course schedule. In George's case, we conducted a lengthy family therapy.

Each of these three individuals developed some degree of medication spellbinding and each developed CBI, but only Angie was left with some residual signs of brain dysfunction.

Chapter 17 examines two longer-term and more complicated withdrawal cases from multiple drug treatment in adults and summarizes the key points for all five cases in Chapters 16 and 17. The following key points emphasize one aspect of psychiatric medication treatment and withdrawal: informing, educating, and monitoring patients regarding adverse drug effects during treatment and during withdrawal.

KEY POINTS

- Patients almost always assume their drugs are safer than they are. They trust their prescribers and do not believe their doctors would expose them to such potentially serious hazards as exist with all psychiatric medications.
- Even patients who have been treated by numerous prescribers and clinicians may never have been told about the most frequent and the most serious adverse effects associated with their drugs, even those that are potentially lethal. Long-term harmful effects common to most or all psychiatric medications—such as apathy, a general worsening of the patient's condition, and CBI—are rarely discussed with patients.
- Medication spellbinding tends to blind patients to adverse effects when they experience them, so that they minimize or ignore them, or attribute them to something else such as stressors at home or at work.
- Even when fully educated about adverse drug effects, there is a natural tendency for patients to stop thinking about them and eventually to forget or ignore them.
- Because of the aforementioned factors, the new prescriber or clinician can never assume that patients know or will recognize adverse drug effects during treatment or during withdrawal. Prescribers and other clinicians, including therapists, should periodically review adverse drug effects with each of their individual patients to help monitor them and also to make sure that their patients grasp and remember the effects and will be able to recognize them. This process will always require several discussions on separate days. In addition, whenever possible, at least one discussion should involve a family member or significant other in the monitoring process.

Cases of Multiple Drug Withdrawal in Adults

This chapter describes two cases of withdrawal from long-term exposure to multiple drugs:

1. *Janis: Withdrawing a patient over a lengthy period from multiple medications—fluoxetine (Prozac), clonazepam (Klonopin), quetiapine (Seroquel), and lamotrigine (Lamictal).*
2. *Husker: Withdrawing a hallucinating alcohol abuser from very long-term exposure to multiple antipsychotic drugs, including aripiprazole (Abilify).*

The chapter then addresses how to work with other therapists and the use of Twelve-Step programs. It comments on the importance of medication withdrawal in older adult patients and concludes with Key Points for all five adult drug withdrawal cases in Chapters 16 and 17.

JANIS: A SLOW WITHDRAWAL FROM MULTIPLE MEDICATIONS

Janis felt the need to withdraw cautiously.

Janis was a 35-year-old woman who came to me for the first time with her mother, who lived several hours away and was very concerned about the effect of psychiatric drugs on her daughter's mental condition. Janis had been married for 5 years; she and her husband were in the process of finalizing their divorce; and she was living alone in an apartment. She had no children.

For several years before starting on medication, Janis had been in conflict with her husband about her future ambitions and dreams. Against his wishes, she wanted to quit a lucrative job and use her savings

225

to go to graduate school while working part-time. She wanted to pursue becoming a writer and a teacher.

After becoming "stressed out because of conflicts in my marriage," about a year before seeing me, her family practitioner prescribed the selective serotonin reuptake inhibitor (SSRI) antidepressant paroxetine (Paxil). She became "high" on several occasions while taking paroxetine, and her husband discovered her having an affair with a casual acquaintance. He ended the already conflicted marriage.

Four months before my initial evaluation, Janis' general practitioner realized that paroxetine might be making her behave in a disinhibited and manic-like fashion, and he referred her to a psychiatrist. The psychiatrist diagnosed Janis as bipolar. He stopped the paroxetine and began Janis on fluoxetine (Prozac) 20 mg/day. At the same time, he started her on lamotrigine (Lamictal) 150 mg/day and clonazepam (Klonopin) 4 mg/day for "mood stabilization" as well as quetiapine (Seroquel) 25 mg in the evening for sleep. This kind of mistake is a potentially disastrous but common prescribing error. Instead of stopping all antidepressants at the first sign of a probably drug-induced manic-like episode, the prescriber continues the antidepressant or a similar one and adds other drugs to control the manic-like symptoms. This typically leads to very unstable emotions (sometimes called "rapid cycling") and chronic brain impairment (CBI).

After the separation, with the divorce in process, Janis quit her full-time job, took a part-time job, and enrolled in graduate school. At the time, she had no regrets about the breakup of the marriage. Besides, she explained, it would be futile to care about it because her husband had already moved in with another woman.

In the initial session, Janis' speech was somewhat pressured and slightly loud. She seemed immature compared to her age but very intelligent. She wept unexpectedly on several occasions and could not account for her feelings. She was in a medication-induced state of emotional instability with mild euphoria.

Janis was surprised that both her mother and I described her as "high" or euphoric. "Maybe a little," she laughed, almost with a giggle. "I told my psychiatrist, 'I've never been better,'" she laughed again. "I guess I'm bipolar like he said." She was suffering from medication spellbinding, which is always an aspect of drug-induced euphoria. As a result, Janis had only a vague idea that her emotional responses were superficial, at times giddy, and not in keeping with her level of maturity and her real-life situation.

As described in Chapter 14 of this book, manic symptoms are potentially dangerous and must be dealt with effectively. My approach usually involves empathic acceptance followed by firm guidance in pointing out the symptoms, the risks involved, and the need to manage them more rationally as quickly and safely as possible.

In a case of medication-induced symptoms like this, I do not psychologically examine underlying emotions of anxiety, depression, and helplessness. Medication-induced euphoria and mania often occur without any predisposition or underlying psychological vulnerability. Reducing or stopping the medication usually relieves these symptoms, often within days, but in severe cases it sometimes takes longer and can even require hospitalization for the patient's safety.

Janis, at first, denied that she was cognitively impaired, but in response to my questions her mother chimed in that Janis had become "forgetful" and complained of difficulty concentrating on her studies. Janis then admitted that her memory wasn't working as well as it used to, that it felt laborious when she tried to read, that focusing was unusually difficult, and that multi-tasking was nearly impossible. In the classroom, her mind would "go off in a million different directions."

Despite the great value she placed on her intellect and school performance, Janis didn't seem particularly upset about her cognitive problems. Although graduate school was proving harder than anticipated, she wasn't worried and figured "everything will turn out all right." She felt "happy" for the first time in years, she explained to me and her mother.

In addition to a drug-induced acute hypomanic state, Janis was suffering from all four features of CBI: (a) cognitive dysfunction, (b) indifference or apathy toward her divorce and potential school failure, (c) emotional worsening (euphoria and lability), and (d) anosognosia—lack of awareness or appreciation of medication-induced mental dysfunction. She also suffered medication spellbinding—feeling better than ever when she was in fact impaired.

After discussing Janis's condition with her and her mother, we reached agreement that she was in a hypomanic state started by the paroxetine and sustained by fluoxetine. The additional three sedative drugs were very likely suppressing a more severe underlying manic-like state induced by the antidepressants.

I explained frankly to Janis and her mother that the previous psychiatrist should have stopped her paroxetine without continuing her on fluoxetine, and then her manic symptoms probably would have abated without further medication intervention. I also told her that she did not fit the bipolar diagnosis because the euphoria had developed while taking antidepressant drugs known to frequently cause these symptoms. She had an antidepressant-induced mood disorder with manic features, I explained.

The more we talked in this initial session, the more confident Janis became in my honesty and genuine concern for her. She said that her previous psychiatrist had limited her visits to 10 minutes and had never gotten to know her.

Janis now acknowledged that she was feeling "weird" and "impulsive," and had gotten herself into a potentially dangerous situation a few nights earlier when she accepted an unfamiliar male student's invitation to go to his room. Fortunately, she had been able to resist his advances and leave. She was reminded several times by her mother that her personality had begun changing dramatically after she was started on antidepressants.

Because Janis was euphoric and prone to risk taking, the first task was to reduce the fluoxetine without reducing the sedative drugs that were suppressing her manic-like symptoms. As we progressed with drug withdrawal, Janis would be able to decide more rationally whether or not she wished to taper off all of her medications.

I explained to Janis that I would help her with medication withdrawal provided that she came for at least weekly therapy and was closely monitored. I proposed that her mother move in with her for a week or more, or that she move in with her mother, until she was no longer so euphoric. Janis's mother readily agreed to stay with her.

Her mother's decision had an obviously sobering effect on Janis, who was beginning to realize that her condition was serious. It also made her feel that her mother and I both cared about her well-being.

I also requested that her mother be allowed to contact me directly if she felt Janis was having more difficulty than she realized or could handle. Janis said that the plan reassured her and made her feel more comfortable about starting to taper off her medications.

I explained to both of them in detail the most serious side effects of her medications and what could be expected during withdrawal. I emphasized that *any* mental or behavioral change during a taper should be treated as a potential withdrawal effect and that both of them should feel free to contact me if at all concerned.

I further emphasized that Janis would be more in control of the rate of withdrawal when she was more emotionally stable, but right now I strongly suggested that we reduce the antidepressant as rapidly as her comfort level permitted. I wanted to avoid any harm coming to her while the euphoria impaired her judgment.

Because we easily developed a good rapport, and because her mother would be temporarily living with her, we decided to reduce the fluoxetine at the first visit. To facilitate reducing the dose, I changed her prescription from 20 mg fluoxetine *capsules* to 10 mg fluoxetine *tablets*. We agreed she would begin taking one full 10 mg tablet, plus three-quarters of another 10 mg tablet, for a 2.5 mg or 12.5% reduction in dose.

She said she had used a pill cutter in the past and would get one at the drug store. She said she would call me if she had any trouble cutting the 10 mg tablet of fluoxetine.

At the end of the session, I gave Janis and her mother my home and cell phone numbers, and once more reminded them to call me with any concerns.

This initial session took 90 minutes. Future sessions would be weekly and last an hour.

The next week Janis came in for the second time, again with her mother. She had experienced no obvious withdrawal reaction from taking one and three-quarter pills and her mother and I felt that she was much less euphoric—almost "back to herself," in her mother's words. We then reduced her dose to 15 mg of fluoxetine.

A few days after reducing the fluoxetine to 15 mg/day, Janis's husband began the final stages of the divorce, and Janis fell into despair. With a reminder from her mother, Janis telephoned me and explained that suicide had crossed her mind. She also said that she had faith in what we were doing, would never want to hurt her mother, or betray our trust by killing herself, and therefore would never harm herself. I asked her to come in the following morning, which she readily agreed to.

In the session the next day, Janis said she thought that the reduction in dose from 20 mg to 15 mg of fluoxetine was already making her "real feelings" more available to her. She was "experiencing the loss" of her husband and marriage. The euphoria was now gone. She was dealing with both the dose reduction and the news about her husband pressing on with the divorce. I brought up the possibility of returning to her initial dose, but both Janis and her mother said they wanted to continue the taper. Her mother said she would continue to stay with her.

Janis continued to feel very reassured with all the interest both her mother and I were taking in her welfare.

We left the fluoxetine dose at 15 mg for the next week and I arranged for Janis to phone me every evening at a set time. I was concerned Janis might again crash back into depression and have suicidal feelings. She reassured me that she was glad to have a doctor who really cared and really wanted her to succeed with medication reduction, and that she would never harm herself. "My mom's here," she explained, "How could I do that to her?"

At the end of 2 weeks on 15 mg of fluoxetine, Janis felt more emotionally stable but continued to display a mild euphoria. We agreed to reduce her antidepressant to one 10 mg tablet. This was a relatively rapid dose reduction, but her mother agreed to stay with her for at least another 2 weeks while both continued to see me regularly.

On fluoxetine 10 mg/day, Janis' mood continued to go up and down, although not to the point of either euphoria or marked depression. Our work together had firmed up her relationship with her mother and the two women felt closer than ever before. We all agreed that it would be safe for her mom to return to her own home, provided Janis was in touch with her every day.

Janis remained at the 10 mg dose for 2 months. She began to feel much more alive and in touch with her feelings. Her euphoric symptoms were gone, but she had sad feelings every day, which she attributed not only to the withdrawal but also to her mourning the loss of her husband and marriage.

I encouraged Janis to think of her feelings as "sadness" and "mourning" rather than "depression." It gave her considerable comfort and strength to view herself as going through a normal process of loss rather than a "clinical depression."

Janis was still fearful about further reducing the fluoxetine. Because the suppressive effect of quetiapine (Seroquel) could be contributing to her depressed feelings, I suggested to her that we taper and eliminate it before continuing with the reduction of the antidepressant. Because her exposure was relatively brief and her dose was small, we started reducing quetiapine by taking the 25 mg dose every other night for a week.

Meanwhile, Janis was continuing to take the 4 mg of the benzodiazepine clonazepam in a divided dose of 2 mg in the morning and 2 mg in the afternoon. With the reduction in quetiapine, I suggested she continue the same amount of clonazepam but switch the afternoon clonazepam dose to the evening. I explained that withdrawing from the quetiapine might produce rebound insomnia, and that she could probably alleviate the insomnia, at least temporarily, by taking the second dose of clonazepam nearer to bedtime. She readily agreed.

Because we were beginning a new taper, I arranged to have her call me a few times during the week and reminded her to stay in touch with her mother every day.

Janis took the quetiapine every other night for a week and then felt able to stop. She had no noticeable withdrawal effects, probably because she was taking the clonazepam later in the evening to prevent insomnia.

Because she continued to feel apprehensive about further reductions of the antidepressant, and because she was no longer euphoric, we next began to withdraw lamotrogine. Again we were dealing with relatively small doses taken for only a few months, and Janis was able to taper rapidly by reducing it from 150 mg to 100 mg the first week, and then to 50 mg for the second week, and then stopping. She felt a brief increase of euphoria for a day or two, and then became stable again. It was apparent that the fluoxetine in combination with clonazepam was most probably her major problem, producing instability with emotional ups and downs.

No longer under the influence of so many drugs, Janis now began to talk more about the issues in her life—the lackluster nature of her relationship with her husband, her low expectations for what a man could give her, and her marriage to a man with limited ambition who resented her quitting work and going to school. She felt extremely ashamed and guilty about her brief affair, but an examination of her otherwise faithful behavior in relationships indicated that fluoxetine-induced euphoria and disinhibition had almost certainly driven the affair that ended her marriage.

Having reduced fluoxetine to 10 mg and having stopped lamotrigine and quetiapine, Janis wanted to wait awhile before making any further reductions. She was dealing with the divorce and with school, and worried about adding withdrawal reactions to the stressors. Janis wanted a very cautious taper, even if it took as long to stop the medications as the time she had spent taking them.

One month after stopping the lamotrigine, Janis asked my opinion about continuing to reduce either the remaining fluoxetine 10 mg/day or the remaining clonazepam, which was unchanged from the beginning at 2 mg twice a day. With only fluoxetine and clonazepam remaining, I suggested that we might try alternate reductions of one drug and then the other. The antidepressant was stimulating her and the benzodiazepine was sedating her, so it made sense to keep a balance between the two drugs as we reduced them.

We decided to reduce the clonazepam because it was a large dose that was making her sleepy and interfering with school work, including her sharpness and memory. I suggested that she reduce the morning dose because it would improve her daytime performance without affecting her sleep. Because insomnia can be so distressing, we would delay reducing the evening dose and stop it only after she was off the antidepressant.

I prescribed 0.5 mg clonazepam tablets so that she could begin the taper by taking 3 tablets of clonazepam 0.5 mg in the morning for a total of 1.5 mg. She would continue to take 2 mg in the evening, for a grand total of 3.5 mg/day. That was a 12.5% reduction, which I felt she could probably handle based on how she was doing, her mother's monitoring, and our therapeutic relationship.

The next day at around 5 pm, Janis called to tell me that she was feeling anxious. We examined whether or not anything had happened that day to stimulate anxiety, but came up with nothing. I reminded her that anxiety, agitation, irritability, and other stimulant-like symptoms were inevitable in withdrawing from a benzodiazepine and that it was simply a matter of how much she felt she could tolerate and handle.

She decided to "tough it out" by staying on the 12.5% reduction and agreed to call me if she felt any worse. I also asked her to check in by phone the following day, which she did. She still felt some increased anxiety but wanted to stay on the reduced dose. There was no evidence of euphoria, which could have been unmasked by reducing the sedative drug. (Xanax has sedative qualities that can suppress overstimulation but, in some patients, can cause overstimulation and frank mania.)

From then on, depending on how Janis was doing with her emotional ups and downs, we cut her medication doses by small amounts every few weeks, alternating between reducing fluoxetine and reducing clonazepam.

After a few more months, Janis was down to taking one-half of a 10 mg fluoxetine (5 mg) and one-half of a 0.5 mg tablet of clonazepam (0.25 mg). The 0.5 mg clonazepam tablet is scored, making it easier to halve it.

Janis felt that the final reductions of fluoxetine were making her feel very fatigued and somewhat down. Nonetheless, she wanted to continue with the dose reductions. She continued to struggle with issues surrounding her divorce, and often felt better after the therapy session.

Because of her prior overstimulation on fluoxetine, I suggested to Janis that she try to finish by tapering all of fluoxetine while remaining on the half tablet of clonazepam 0.25 mg every evening.

We tapered the fluoxetine by eliminating one of her seven weekly 5 mg fluoxetine doses. When this worked well for a period of 1 week, we continued by removing a second daily dose for 1 week, and so on, until she had finished taking the antidepressant. The half-life of fluoxetine, which averages more than a week, would hopefully smooth out these reductions.

Janis came off the final dose of fluoxetine with little more than a slight bit of irritability and a mild headache on-and-off for another week.

Because Janis was comfortable with this method, we then reduced the clonazepam in the same way, by removing one daily dose each week until it was eliminated.

Janis struggled with insomnia for several weeks after stopping the sedative. I encouraged her to start a mild exercise program and so she began taking walks every other day. She started a yoga class, which also helped her relax. We worked on developing evening habits that would relax her before bed, such as finishing her studies at least 2 hours before bedtime and having a light snack. At the same time, we examined the "worries" that kept her up at night, which became important in terms of her overall work in therapy.

During this time, Janis continued to make a great deal of progress in her social life and began a relationship with a man who appreciated her strengths, ambitions, and ideals, and who loved her very much. She, in turn, found that being loved did indeed scare her.

Janis continued in therapy for 6 months after the completion of her drug withdrawal. She felt for the first time in her life that she was "real," understood her emotions most of the time, and felt confident she could handle the stresses of life while continuing to mature and to grow. She did well in school and become engaged.

When she first came to see me, Janis had been taking SSRI antidepressants for only a year, and lamotrigine, quetiapine, and clonazepam for 4 months. Nonetheless, she took more than a year to come off the medications. My preference would have been for her to move faster in order to avoid any lasting CBI, but Janis's comfortable pace was relatively slow, and it turned out very well. Fortunately, she developed no lasting CBI symptoms.

HUSKER: WITHDRAWING A HALLUCINATING, ALCOHOLIC PATIENT FROM ANTIPSYCHOTIC DRUGS AND ALCOHOL

Never underestimate a patient's ability to grow. Even someone who's preoccupied with hallucinations, works like a lumberjack, and drinks like a sailor may surprise you, as Husker surprised me, in his ability to be sensitive and understanding and to completely overcome his psychosis. As with many patients undergoing withdrawal, he also surprised me in other ways.

Husker and his wife Katrina came to see me at his wife's insistence. Husker was a 57-year-old retired laborer who had spent his youth on fishing trawlers in Alaska, then in oil fields in Texas, and finally on construction sites across America. He never developed a skilled trade and joked about always being employed as a "work horse, maybe even a dumb mule." He was a physically strong individual who spoke loudly and with determination. He proudly described himself as bullheaded.

Husker had a long history of using psychoactive drugs until he had stopped a decade earlier. He was also accustomed to "hard drinking to go along with hard work." He had become psychotic on several occasions, but was hospitalized only briefly on one occasion many years earlier. He had been treated with antipsychotic drugs for a cumulative period of more than 15 years, including several recent years on aripiprazole (Abilify) and never had counseling or therapy.

His wife Katrina was a contrast—educated, professionally trained, gentle, but self-assured with a no-nonsense streak that enabled her to handle Husker. She supported the family financially while he took care of the home and always prepared a "great meal" for her at lunch and dinner. At first glance, it was hard to understand how this couple got along so well and in fact seemed deeply committed and in love after being married for many years.

Katrina wanted Husker to get help because for the last 2–3 months, he was "spacing out" a great deal and was often irritable with her. In addition, for several years he had increasingly lost interest in activities that used to give him great pleasure, including playing jazz piano and gardening. When I pointed it out to her, she agreed that he seemed to talk very loudly, almost as if arguing with me, while not addressing her at all. She said this was "Husker," but it had gotten worse.

In this first session, Husker talked *at* me and *over* his wife. He showed me no deference and clearly distrusted all "shrinks." Living in the country as I do, Husker reminded me of several of my friends, although a bit more extreme.

A couple of times during the session, I noticed that Husker seemed to be listening to voices. When I asked, he admitted bluntly, "Yeah, I'm hearing the damn voices again." Perhaps because of his working class appearance and attitudes, none of his previous psychiatrists had seemingly taken the time to talk to him about hallucinations. He'd barely heard the word and didn't associate it with his experiences. The prior psychiatrists had never encouraged him to talk about the content of what he was hearing either. "Doc, they just drugged me up and that was fine with me."

Because of his embarrassment, getting him to talk about or describe these voices was difficult. It turned out that Husker's "voices" were coming from unknown persons outside his head and said "mean things" to him such as "you'll never get anything right," "you don't deserve anything," or simply repeated the word "jerk."

I explained to Husker that "voices" are our own thoughts and feelings that feel too painful for us to accept as our own—and so we imagine or push them outside our heads. I told him the psychological process is called "projection."

"That's it exactly!" he burst out in his blustery manner. "Why the hell hasn't anyone else told me that? Doc, you got it."

I thought maybe he was feigning this abrupt acceptance of insight, but time and again it would turn out that Husker always said what he meant, and that he was adept at psychological analysis. No one had ever encouraged this quality in him.

Husker also quickly recognized that the voices sounded a lot like somebody's mean parents, and although he couldn't remember his mother or father saying "stuff like that," he readily acknowledged coming from an alcoholic and "screwed up" family.

I suggested to Husker, "Since the voices are really your own, you can control them. You can tell them to shut up if you want. Tell them they can't get to you anymore and to shut up, go away, disappear."

Husker took to this idea "like a duck to water, Doc," and at my urging he practiced confronting them in the session. Before going home, he practiced one more time telling the voices, "Shut the hell up!" and then smiled proudly, "I got 'em that time. Bye, bye voices."

I also explained to both of them that "psychosis" (withdrawing and hearing voices) was the opposite of being in touch with other human beings. They easily grasped my analysis—that when people "withdraw from reality, they are really withdrawing in fear and hurt from other human beings. We lose our trust and our connections with others, and then we withdraw into craziness." I continued, "You two really love each other. Love is the opposite of craziness. When each of you get better at expressing your love for each other, then, Husker, you won't have to struggle with withdrawing and hearing voices anymore."

During this first session, I also checked Husker for signs of tardive dyskinesia (TD). He had a fine tremor but no signs of TD. I told him that he had a remarkable constitution and that most people with so many years of exposure to these drugs would show some symptoms of the movement disorder. As the therapy progressed, it would also become apparent that Husker had, in a nearly miraculous fashion, escaped any serious signs of CBI. His rigidity and initial stubbornness seemed more related to his lifelong personality, and—as it turned out—to his having secretly stopped his Abilify before ever seeing me.

One week later, Husker came in a second time with Katrina.

Husker said he wasn't "spacing out so much anymore" and that he was "telling off" the voices on a regular basis. They were losing their strength. Katrina happily confirmed that her husband was returning to being more loving with her, as he had been when they were younger. She was enthusiastic, but also fearful "it won't last." She made him promise not to stop therapy prematurely.

During this session, I asked at what times during the day the voices interrupted his thoughts. After some time exploring the question, it turned out that the voices often reared up when his wife wanted to be more emotionally intimate: for example, when she wanted to sit quietly with him, finishing one of his great meals.

Husker denied any fears of being loved or about loving, but when I asked him to sit quietly and look tenderly into his wife's eyes, he spaced out, and then resumed by talking with me as if she weren't there. A quick study, Husker got the point when I described his reactions.

Having established very good rapport with both of them, we discussed beginning to withdraw from the antipsychotic drug. At this point, Husker got extremely defensive and declared he had no need for therapy. *It turned out that he had stopped the aripiprazole "cold turkey" on his own 3 months earlier—exactly the time his wife saw him becoming more withdrawn and difficult.* Husker was in the third month of withdrawal from years of exposure to antipsychotic drugs, probably accounting for his, at times, obsessive loudness and argumentativeness, which can be signs of brain dysfunction.

That Husker would withhold such vital information hurt and angered Katrina. When offended, she was more than a match for his macho obstinacy, and she told him in no uncertain terms how unacceptable it was for him to lie to her. At the end of the session, Katrina said she wasn't sure she would return for another session, because her husband could no longer be trusted to tell the truth.

They did return for their next session. Husker wasn't exactly contrite, preferring to admire himself for how he had been able to stop the psychiatric drug on his own.

"Yeah, but look at the toll on your wife and the marriage," I replied. "She had no idea what was going on and now you've made her distrust you."

Husker conceded that he never wanted to hurt Katrina and he apologized. At that point we were able to discuss whether or not the hallucinations had worsened during the withdrawal. He was sure they had. I explained that it could be a withdrawal psychosis called tardive psychosis or it could be that the hallucinations grew stronger because his brain was more alive without the drug.

Husker agreed that he was thinking more clearly and having more feelings now that he was drug-free, and that maybe the voices got stronger as his overall "ability to experience life" got stronger. He added, "I mean, the voices have been part of my life for as long as I can remember, and they're coming back along with everything else." Once again, he was able to self-examine remarkably well.

Katrina now declared that she thought the problem wasn't limited to drug withdrawal—it was also Husker's heavy drinking. Too often, Husker was under the influence of alcohol when she got home.

"My drinking is my own damn business and I like it," he shot back, mostly looking at me.

I appreciated Husker's ability to be blunt with me and to accept bluntness in return. I said in a teasing tone, "So, Husker, why don't you look at your wife and tell her, 'Katrina, I love you, but not enough to talk about how my drinking upsets you.'"

That led to a more than lively if not heated exchange between me and Husker, but in the end, Husker admitted that at least once a week he would down a 12-pack of beer over a few hours in an afternoon. He also admitted, with prodding from his wife, that he drank at least another two 12-packs over the remainder of the week, usually in a short period. Husker was a severe binge drinker.

Husker and his wife decided that he had probably doubled his intake since coming off the antipsychotic drug 2 or 3 months earlier. "Self-medicating," Katrina observed.

Husker had been drinking heavily since the age of 16. But in the couple's therapy, he was able to listen to Katrina telling him, "Husker, honey, it's like you're not there when you drink so much. And then you get mad over nothing. And I think the voices get worse because you sure space out more. You may love to drink, but it's no fun for me, Husker."

Over the next several months, Husker listened to my concern that binge drinking was especially dangerous. Through discussions and negotiations with me and his wife, Husker agreed to give up binge drinking, to limit his drinking to one 12-pack a week, and to never drink more than two beers at a time. With minor deviations, he followed these limits for several months.

I strongly support Alcoholics Anonymous (AA) and recommended it to Husker, but he wasn't interested in "fellowship," and was determined to succeed without it. Besides, he knew AA required complete abstinence, and that wasn't his goal.

As his marriage and his life improved, Husker found himself drinking less and less, until he was down to no more than a six-pack a week without bingeing.

During this time, I continued to emphasize that relating

> The involvement of family members or friends in the withdrawal process can be especially useful in confronting the patient's abuse of alcohol, marijuana, or other drugs, which will require attention if the psychiatric drug withdrawal is likely to succeed and if the patient is to maximally recover and grow.

with Katrina was the opposite of withdrawing into voices, and Husker continued to work on "telling off" the voices while "staying in touch with Katrina."

Gradually, the voices disappeared, and Husker became more and more able to communicate with Katrina. We worked in every session on the quality of their lives together—spending more time in romantic and interesting ways, and in particular, being more open and tender with each other.

Over time, it became more obvious to me why Katrina loved this rough-hewn man. As Husker recovered from drug withdrawal and from alcohol abuse, his real nature came forth. He was a sensitive, intelligent man with a mind as strong as his body and his will.

Katrina bought her husband a new piano and he began practicing the self-taught skills originally learned in bars as a youngster. In a brave new step, he began to take formal piano lessons for the first time in his life. He also resumed gardening, sharing with me a mutual love for lifting up and moving heavy rocks around the landscape—albeit much larger rocks than I could handle.

Husker and Katrina continued to come back every month or 6 weeks for a "tune up," as he called it. The voices were gone, his drinking was limited to a six-pack a week with no bingeing, and their marriage and love life thrived. When Katrina got a better job out of state and they left town, I felt as if two dear friends were departing.

OBSERVATIONS ON THE CASES

As in the three earlier cases in Chapter 16, the involvement of family or a significant other was critical to success. In Janis's case, her mother came to the first office visit and then agreed to move in temporarily with her to monitor her manic-like state. Later, Janis attended by herself and worked on her problems in romantic relationships. In Husker's case, he and his wife were involved in couple's therapy from the start. Deepening their love relationship became a significant aspect as Husker gave up periods of emotional "spacing out" and auditory hallucinations, as well as alcohol bingeing.

In both cases in this chapter, the withdrawal process was continually modified along the way, depending on how the patient and I, or a family member, felt about the progress being made. Flexibility was the key. Even when it turned out that Husker had been misleading his wife and me, I tried not to take it personally, but continued working with the two of them with the goal of helping Husker through his protracted withdrawal and his alcohol abuse.

Each of the five cases suffered from medication spellbinding and each case suffered from CBI. Fortunately, only one of the cases, Angie (Chapter 16), developed persistent CBI. In my experience, Husker should have developed a severe case of persistent CBI after abuse of street drugs as a young man, lifelong alcohol abuse, and more than a decade of exposure to antipsychotic drugs. But the only signs I could see were his initial tendencies to speak loudly, to focus argumentatively on me, and to exclude his wife. These kinds of social insensitivity are often early signs of brain dysfunction, but no other signs of CBI were detectable. His good outcome in this regard is unusual. It is probable that the strength of his personality and his enormous willpower enabled him to function without showing overt signs of underlying cognitive problems, but other aspects of CBI were also absent, such as apathy and emotional instability, especially after he stopped his medication and cut back on alcohol.

In Janis's case, we eventually carried out depth psychotherapy regarding her relationship problems and their origins in childhood. In Husker's case, we talked very little about his childhood but carried on intense psychotherapeutic couples work in which he shed some of his "macho" defensiveness and allowed himself to become more openly tender and loving. I also dealt with his social withdrawal and hallucinations in a direct manner.

WORKING WITH OTHER THERAPISTS

Because I'm a psychiatrist who does psychotherapy, I rarely work with other therapists during the withdrawal process. On occasions that I have, I see the patient less often and stay in touch by phone with the primary therapist. I also try to meet with someone close to the patient at least once to educate them about the withdrawal process. I make myself available for calls from the therapist, patient, or family whenever it might be useful or necessary. I also make my own psychotherapeutic contributions to the process.

Therapists who are seeing the same patient should not feel competitive with each other. Several of my psychotherapy patients have seen and benefitted from other therapists while they were also seeing me. In a person-centered collaborative approach to therapy, it should be up to patients to pick and choose their therapists, including more than one at a time if they wish. Unless there are issues of compromised mental function as in drug intoxication or withdrawal, I do not ask to talk with or to be in touch with the other therapist. Adult patients can manage their own affairs regarding seeing more than one therapist.

Some therapists believe that patients must stick with one therapist at a time; otherwise the patients could become "confused" by different approaches or "use the therapists against each other." This viewpoint is a throwback to authoritarian psychotherapy in which the therapist is the master of the relationship. Person-centered therapists should be happy with all the freely chosen help their patients can get.

> Except with children, severely impaired patients, or patients undergoing a difficult drug withdrawal, there is no special need for two therapists seeing the same patient to communicate with each other. And while it's often ideal to involve a patient's family in the therapy, it should not be required unless the patient is a child, is severely impaired, or is undergoing a difficult drug adverse reaction or withdrawal.

TWELVE-STEP PROGRAMS

Whenever possible, I encourage my patients to attend AA, Narcotics Anonymous (NA), or another Twelve-Step Program. There are Twelve-Step Programs that address children of alcoholics, families of alcoholics, emotional problems, and other aspects of mental health. One of my patients established a Twelve-Step meeting that focuses on withdrawal from psychiatric drugs and I hope many more will sprout up around the country. These programs can be found through the Internet, telephone information services, and the phone book. Twelve-Step Programs provide sound ethical principles, practical steps to recovery, common sense wisdom, a spiritual connection, and fellowship.

THE ELDERLY

I have not provided any examples of withdrawing the older adult from drugs, but a review of the literature confirmed that drug withdrawal can be safe and lead to considerable improvement in quality of life (Iyer, Naganathan, McLachlan, and Le Couteur, 2008). It is important to recognize the overmedicating of our senior citizens, many of whom are being hurried along to their death in a stupefied state in nursing homes and other long-term care facilities. Many, if not most, older adults, especially those in institutions, are receiving too

Elderly patients are especially in need of drug reduction and withdrawal. Because these patients are usually living under relatively close supervision in facilities, they can be withdrawn with relative ease and safety, provided of course that the institution's monitoring is frequent, informed, and caring—and provided that the staff works closely with the family.

many prescriptions of all kinds. Not only are older adults more susceptible to most adverse drug effects, but psychoactive substances in particular are likely to reduce their fragile cognitive abilities and cause delirium and organ failure. They are also likely to cause falls, leading to fractures with suffering and death.

In particular, the current use of the so-called "atypical" antipsychotic drugs such as risperidone (Risperdal), quetiapine (Seroquel), olanzapine (Zyprexa), aripiprazole (Abilify), and ziprasidone (Geodon) in these patients has reached scandalous proportions. In my opinion, these drugs have no place in the treatment of the older adult because they cause a variety of devastating effects with increased intensity and frequency, including TD, cardiovascular disease, diabetes, and shortened lifespan. If the patient is not already grossly demented, these drugs will hurry along the dementing process by impairing and damaging the frontal lobes and basal ganglia. The patient, now emotionally numbed and physically restrained by the drugs, is less demanding and "troublesome" to caretakers, but has less to live for and will languish in a briefer life.

Given the lack of adequate staff in these facilities, limiting the prescription of psychiatric drugs will usually require increased attendance by family members, who may have to insist on frequently communicating with the staff and the prescriber. The older adults are entitled to treatment that enhances whatever quality of life remains to them, and that requires a mind free of intoxicating substances.

Many families find that their wishes for their elderly loved ones are ignored or thwarted by institutions. For these families, the first approach is to insist on as much direct contact with the staff and prescriber as possible. In some cases, the involvement of an attorney may be required to obtain and/or to assert guardianship rights. For prescribers, therapists, and staff, there can be immediate satisfaction in seeing older adults rapidly brighten up and start communicating when their psychiatric medications are reduced.

> Whatever the prescriber, therapist, or family can do to limit the exposure of the older adults to all psychiatric drugs, and especially the antipsychotic drugs, will improve the quality of their lives.

KEY POINTS

This chapter and the previous one illustrate many of the key points regarding medication withdrawal within a person-centered collaborate approach:

- The clinician must listen carefully and be thoughtful toward what the patient and family think and feel.
- The clinician must encourage the patient to become a partner with ultimate control over the medication withdrawal process.
- Every withdrawal is different and must be tailored to the patient's needs and wishes.
- A careful medication history will often indicate that many of the patient's "psychiatric problems" are in fact medication-induced.
- Successful medication withdrawals often take much more time than the patient, therapist, or prescriber initially anticipated.
- Emotional crises will often erupt during withdrawal. The clinician should not overreact by assuming they are emergencies or that the patient cannot live without psychiatric medications. Instead, the clinician should respond with reassurance, an analysis of the cause for the crises, and, if necessary, a temporary return to the previous dose.
- Medication spellbinding clouds the judgment of patients concerning the severity of their adverse drug effects during treatment and during withdrawal.
- Nearly all patients who have been taking psychiatric drugs for months or years will display symptoms of CBI, but because of anosognosia and medication spellbinding, they will not perceive their degree of impairment until after they have been partially or wholly removed from psychiatric medication.
- Some patients will "self-medicate" while taking psychiatric medications and during withdrawal. These psychoactive substances include over-the-counter drugs and herbal remedies, various supplements and megadoses of vitamins, alcohol, and illegal drugs such as marijuana and cocaine. It is important to question patients about their use of nonprescription substances and to recognize that the patient may not always be forthcoming, especially about the abuse of alcohol and illegal drugs. Involvement of a family member can be critical in discovering nonprescription drug use and abuse, and in encouraging the patient to stop.

- Some clinicians switch patients from drugs that are difficult to withdraw from to drugs that are perceived to be easier to withdraw from, for example, from alprazolam to diazepam or from paroxetine to fluoxetine. For several reasons, I rarely use this approach, but I have no objection to experienced clinicians using it in their practices.
- Use of additional or supplemental psychoactive substances to ease withdrawal can complicate the withdrawal. I limit the introduction of new drugs to the occasional prescription of sleep aids. I respect those other clinicians who believe that they know of supplements that help with withdrawal, provided that these substances do not impact the brain to complicate the withdrawal process.
- Difficult withdrawals conducted on an outpatient basis require the participation of a family or friend in the patient's support network to help monitor the withdrawal process. Medication spellbinding commonly prevents the individual from identifying or perceiving the intensity of a medication withdrawal reaction. In addition, CBI can cloud the individual's insight and judgment. The social network monitor should be permitted to make direct contact with the clinician. In addition to this monitoring, many patients will need and want individual, couples, or family therapy.
- Therapy that may uncover or stimulate painful and difficult emotions should usually be avoided until patients have recovered sufficiently from drug intoxication or withdrawal.
- Because they occur so frequently as toxic effects and as withdrawal effects, it is important to recognize that medication-induced manic-like symptoms can usually be handled effectively without hospitalization and without the addition of new drugs. A strong social support network will be needed at times to monitor and guide the patient.
- As described in detail in the Key Points of the previous chapter, new prescribers and clinicians must assume that their patients have not been fully informed and educated about potential adverse drug reactions during treatment and withdrawal, even life-threatening ones. Every prescriber and clinician, including therapists, should take the time on more than one occasion to make sure that both the common and the serious adverse reactions are understood and can be recognized by the patient. It is always best to involve a significant other in the educational and monitoring process as well.
- Medication withdrawal—especially accompanied by individual, couples, or family therapy—often leads to an enormous improvement in the patient's quality of life, enhancing the lives of everyone involved with the patient. This significant improvement in the patient's quality of life can also be a great source of satisfaction to prescribers and therapists.

CHAPTER 18

Cases of Drug Withdrawal in Children and Teens

Children and teens can usually be withdrawn from psychiatric drugs with relative ease and safety, provided that their parents or caregivers are responsible and cooperative. Children who meet the criteria for attention deficit hyperactivity disorder (ADHD) are particularly easy to withdraw from stimulants when their parents are willing to improve their child-rearing approaches and/or when the child's educational environment is improved or changed. Children and teens often suffer less than adults from chronic brain impairment (CBI) and recover more completely. This optimistic viewpoint should not encourage the psychiatric medicating of children, which can impair their physical growth, cause serious developmental delays, harm their brains, undermine their sense of self-control and autonomy, and steal their childhoods.

WHAT CHILDREN DIAGNOSED WITH ATTENTION DEFICIT HYPERACTIVITY DISORDER REALLY NEED

If a child is diagnosed with attention deficit hyperactivity disorder (ADHD) and is taking stimulants, *and no other psychiatric drugs*, medication withdrawal can usually be accomplished with relative ease—provided it is accompanied by family therapy and, when necessary, consultation with the child's teachers. Sometimes the child's behavioral problems disappear with placement in a better classroom or school.

ADHD is a list of behaviors that does not reflect a real syndrome or underlying "disorder." The three categories of ADHD behavior—hyperactivity, impulsivity, and inattention—have multiple unrelated causes from an undisciplined upbringing or a boring classroom to distress over conflicts in the school or home. It can also be caused by bullying or emotional, physical, and sexual abuse. Similar behaviors can be produced by underlying physical disorders, such as head injury or diabetes. Insomnia with fatigue will produce similar behaviors. As a result, it is misleading to give validity to the existence of a specific syndrome or diagnosis of ADHD (Baughman & Hovey, 2006; Breggin, 2001c, 2002b, 2008a).

In a routine clinical practice, behaviors labeled ADHD are commonly displayed by entirely normal children who lack discipline at home or who are bored and poorly managed at school. Sometimes the children's educational needs have been overlooked at school and they have fallen too far behind to retain their interest in learning. Frequently, well meaning or stressed parents have been unable to provide proper discipline at home.

By definition, children who meet the criteria for ADHD are not severely emotionally disturbed, or they would carry other diagnoses, such as generalized anxiety disorder, major depressive disorder, or schizophrenia. Because they are not usually very unstable, they can be relatively easily withdrawn from medications while working with the family. Also, because these youngsters are not very disturbed, they do not generally come from very disturbed families. The relatively higher degree of responsibility found in these families enables them to respond well to any therapy or program that helps them improve their child-rearing approaches.

Most children labeled ADHD can be treated as ordinary discipline problems. The child is out of control, impulsive, and distractible because the parents have not helped in developing a consistent and effective disciplinary program. In the initial evaluation, parents should be asked if the child's problem shows up mostly at school or at home. If the problem is mostly limited to the home, the therapy focuses on parental disciplinary practices. If instead the problem is mostly at school, the problem can often be resolved by an improved educational environment through working with the school, changing classrooms or school, or home schooling. If the child's problem is both at school and at home, the initial focus is on improving parental discipline, which often resolves the school problems as well.

> Children always respond to positive changes in their parents. Even if the parents didn't cause the child's problem, they are the ones most able to heal the child.

It's very easy to communicate in therapy with most children labeled ADHD. They pay close attention to explanations about the lack of validity in the diagnosis, the many reasons not to use the medications, and the new opportunities for the entire family to develop better ways of relating. The new opportunities begin with both the children and the parents treating each other with respect. For the parents, I emphasize their parental responsibility in helping their child mature into an effective, happy adult. For the children, I emphasize their personal responsibility for taking charge of their behavior in good ways that will improve their lives and propel them toward success as adults.

In some cases, the first session indicates that there is nothing to change about the child's behavior, which is fine at home. The youngster is simply bored to death in school. I've seen ADHD-like behavior from the classroom disappear with a switch to a more effective teacher or a new school.

Withdrawing Children From Stimulants

Many children diagnosed with ADHD are already medication free on weekends and during holidays and summertime, without experiencing noticeable withdrawal symptoms. Therefore, the drug can be stopped at any convenient time, sooner rather than later.

After hearing about the hazards associated with the drugs used to treat ADHD, parents and children usually decide to work together to teach the child self-discipline and self-determination, medication free. They often decide not to resume the drug on the coming Monday when they would normally take it for school. Instead, we work together on discipline problems and the resolution of family conflicts and school problems. I also may recommend parenting classes and books on parenting.

Many teachers who have been convinced by authorities that "children with ADHD" need stimulant drugs have largely given up seeking classroom solutions to the child's inattention, impulsivity, or hyperactivity. These teachers need encouragement to find new approaches to working with children diagnosed with ADHD.

Provided the child has a few days off to go through any mild withdrawal at home rather than at school, teachers usually do not notice any immediate change in the child. Over time, the teacher may be pleased to see that the child—now relieved of drug-induced apathy—has become more enthusiastically involved in school.

It can be more difficult to withdraw a child who has been taking stimulants in increasing doses for many months or years without any drug holidays. In these cases, it is sometimes best to withdraw the child during a lengthy winter break from school or during the summer. Or, if withdrawal is attempted, the teacher and other members of the school team may need to be involved because the child is likely to display withdrawal symptoms in school, and these will be mistaken for proof that the child needs the medication. In extreme withdrawal cases, "crashing" with suicidal behavior is the gravest risk. Family therapy to engage the children and parents in meaningful and caring communication is the best approach to preventing suicidality.

CHILDREN AND TEENS DIAGNOSED WITH BIPOLAR DISORDER

As a result of pharmaceutical industry efforts conducted hand in hand with paid psychiatric consults (see Chapter 6), great numbers of children are being diagnosed with bipolar disorder. Often, these children have suffered from nothing more than temper tantrums. When they display manic-like symptoms, this is almost always an adverse drug reaction to stimulants or antidepressants. In my clinical experience, nearly all children and teens diagnosed with bipolar disorder, including those with manic-like symptoms, quickly improve when removed from psychiatric drugs with supportive family therapy.

CHILDREN AND TEENS DIAGNOSED WITH AUTISM SPECTRUM DISORDERS

Children diagnosed with autism spectrum disorders suffer from difficulties relating to and communicating with other people. Those diagnosed with Asperger's are sometimes quirky kids who are unusually shy and sensitive. If they do have serious problems, they always involve relationships. Children who meet the diagnostic criteria for autism spectrum disorders exemplify what happens when children fail to develop empathy and the ability to relate to or to respond to other people.

Because all psychiatric drugs impair brain function in global ways, including the frontal lobes, they also impair empathy and the overall ability to relate. As a result, all psychiatric drugs will exacerbate a child or teen's underlying lack of development in empathic relationships. These children will improve if medication is withdrawn and replaced with caring, patient, informed engagement from the adults in their lives, both at home and in school or treatment facilities.

> Diagnoses and drugs give parents, teachers, and children alike the destructive idea that the children are defective and cannot learn from us to control their behavior and to fulfill their lives.

A Child Diagnosed With Asperger's

Jimmy's case illustrates that with help from their parents, children can learn to control bizarre behaviors, and that drug-induced tardive dyskinesia (TD) is often dismissed as just one more sign of the child's mental condition.

Three months before coming to my office, 9-year-old Jimmy was diagnosed with Asperger's disorder by a child psychiatrist and started on olanzapine (Zyprexa) 5 mg/day. His parents, both busy and dedicated professionals, noticed that their son became lethargic and that the "spark" was missing from his eyes.

Suspecting the medication, they brought him to me for further evaluation. His "weird" behaviors were diminished by the Zyprexa but "so was Jimmy himself," his mother told me on the phone.

Jimmy had always been a fretful child with quirky behaviors who was shy and at times, anxious, but he was very bright, could become warm and cuddly, and made friends with other children. He did well in school.

During the initial session, his parents readily admitted that they had been very preoccupied with their careers in the first 2 or 3 years of Jimmy's life and that he had spent a great deal of time in day care. We conducted this conversation in Jimmy's presence, and at times, I directed remarks to Jimmy, such as "It's wonderful that your parents realize that you didn't get enough attention when you were very small," and "It sounds like they want to change and give you more attention now."

At one point, Jimmy started grimacing and acting childish. I pointed out to him, "That kind of weird behavior makes other people feel uncomfortable, but it gets attention. I want to help you act in ways that will get you the kind of attention you will really like without having to do that weird stuff."

Jimmy was unfazed by my remarks, but his parents were startled and perhaps offended. "All the other doctors said he couldn't control himself. He has a disorder."

At this point, Jimmy ran behind the couch where his parents were sitting. From there, he made faces at the ceiling. Jimmy's parents became embarrassed and reprimanded him to no effect.

I said, "Jimmy, I know you can control your behavior. I've seen lots of kids who behave like you, and they learn to control their behavior. And of course, they're much, much happier and get along so much better when they stop behaving in childish and weird ways."

> Children old enough to talk are old enough to listen and can benefit from direct, honest, and caring communication about controlling their behavior. Very short explanations suffice, followed by instructions on how to behave better.

After talking with his parents for a while, I coaxed Jimmy from behind the couch and asked him to sit on the hassock right next to me. I started a discussion about how much time he spent with his father, and Jimmy quickly replied, "Not enough!" With coaching from me, his dad agreed it would be a good idea to spend more time with his son.

I observed, "Dad, I'm sure it's hard for you when he acts so weird, making faces, hiding, and the like."

Unaccustomed to speaking the truth to his son about his behavior, his Dad shrugged.

"I'm sure it's tough," I said.

Jimmy was glued to the conversation, sitting on the hassock, and occasionally, I reached over to pat his shoulder, which he accepted with a small grin. He was now behaving entirely normally.

I told Jimmy, "It's great to see you acting normally—I mean, like any other kid. You're very intelligent, and despite the way you behave, you get good grades. You're really a handsome kid. You've got a great smile when you're not grimacing," I laughed. "You won't have any trouble getting good attention for the real you—the boy who doesn't have to act weird anymore."

After we'd finish a very good exchange with each other, Jimmy ended it by making faces.

I laughed, "I love you Jimmy, you're so full of life, but that weird stuff has got to stop today. From now on, your parents are going to tell you every time to stop, and when you do stop, they'll give you attention. But when you act weird, you'll get no attention, except a reminder to stop."

The next time Jimmy grimaced and moved his body oddly, his dad on his own said in a friendly manner, "Nah, no more of that, Jimmy. Now, let's talk about what you and I are going to do together this weekend."

> In our current society, the most common source of problems in boys is DADD—dad attention deficit disorder.

Toward the end of the session, we further discussed having normal expectations for Jimmy's behavior at all times. Jimmy would no longer be told he had a disorder; he would be told he had to learn to relate in a positive fashion with people. From now on, Jimmy would be able to get attention simply by asking for it but always in a normal and respectful manner.

Before he left, his dad tried to wiggle out from the coming Saturday's commitment with his son because he had to travel. Jimmy instantly started making odd motions with his arms and hands.

"Stop everything," I announced gently. "Look what just happened."

"Yeah," Jimmy observed, "You see, he doesn't really want to spend time with me."

His mother spoke up for the first time in a firm voice, "Your dad has bad habits, Jimmy, just like you do. And I should have done what the doctor's doing a long time ago." "Manny," she addressed her husband, "It's time to take charge of your relationship with your son. And Jimmy, it's time for you to take charge of yourself. I've got high expectations for both of you and for me. Jimmy, we're going to do this together as a family."

I had noticed during the session that Jimmy had frequent bouts of eye blinking that lasted for nearly a minute at a time. Although the previous psychiatrist had told the family that this was just "nerves" and "more Asperger's behavior," it is a very common early sign of TD. Other than the blinking, my TD examination was negative.

At the end of the session, Jimmy and his parents enthusiastically expressed their mutual desire to stop Jimmy's medication completely. Because the exposure was limited to 3 months, I did not expect a severe withdrawal reaction in the child and recommended that they reduce the medication to 5 mg every other day for a week until they next saw me. I explained that the dose reduction would also help in evaluating Jimmy for TD because the antipsychotic drugs tend to mask the overt symptoms while they cause the underlying disorder. I also gave them my private phone numbers and urged them to check with me in 3 days.

I explained that during this withdrawal period Jimmy's parents should spend enough time with him in the morning before school and at dinner to make sure he was doing well. Then, at least one parent should spend time with him before bed.

I also brought up the possibility of getting Jimmy a cell phone, so that he could call them at lunch break as well. "I think you'll get to like being in touch as much as possible, so much so, you might just want to keep it up even after the withdrawal period is over."

A few days after the first session, Jimmy's mother phoned to ask if we should give him medication to help him sleep during the withdrawal, but I reminded her of the new principle that Jimmy deserved a lot more genuine attention—that he needed his parents not pills. She spent extra time with her son over the next few nights until he fell asleep. Contrary to her fears, he did not "take advantage" and demand her increased attention every night. They made a ritual of one parent visiting with Jimmy every night at bedtime, and he returned to sleeping well.

Except for a few nights of difficulty falling asleep, Jimmy had no significant withdrawal problems after stopping the medication. Within 2 weeks, the blinking symptoms disappeared. He seemed "more alive" to his parents.

Over the next several sessions, Jimmy's behavior improved dramatically. Within 3 months, there was nothing at all odd in Jimmy's behavior, and his relationship with his parents was much improved. Teachers, other parents, and children also noticed the difference. After those few months, I rarely saw Jimmy while I worked with his parents.

TD will often abate if the offending medication is stopped soon after recognition of the symptoms. Children are especially likely to completely recover if the drugs are quickly stopped. Prescribers, therapists, and other clinicians who work with children and adults taking antipsychotic drugs need to know how to identify potential symptoms of TD.

I continued for a year in couples therapy with Jimmy's parents, focusing on their own needs for attention and love within their relationship. They learned to carve out time for each other, became more accustomed to engaging in meaningful conver-

> Psychiatric medication often replaces genuine relationships in families. Entire families can end up on medication when the issues could have been handled with relative ease in family therapy.

sation, and learned how to better fulfill each other's needs for intimacy, love, mutual support, and fun. During this time, Jimmy became less and less a topic of conversation because he was doing so well. He was enjoying school and conflicts at home were ordinary.

Ten Years of Unwarranted Medication

The case of Maryanne describes the withdrawal of a 16-year-old from multiple medications after 10 years of exposure.

Maryanne was 16 years old and entering the 11th grade when her single mother brought her to me because of increasing concerns about her seeming "over-drugged." In addition, Maryanne's mother was shocked when her daughter's psychiatrist told them at the most recent visit that he only needed to see Maryanne "once a year" because she was doing so well on her various medications.

Maryanne's father had disappeared when Maryanne was an infant. At age 6, unlike her older sister, Maryanne seemed "spoiled" and difficult to discipline. Her sophisticated mother took her to a well-known psychiatrist who specialized in psychopharmacology. She was placed on sertraline (Zoloft) and then suffered what her mother called "a very bad behavioral reaction to the drug," with crying and severe temper tantrums. The psychiatrist explained that Maryanne's "paradoxical reaction" indicated an underlying bipolar disorder. He placed her on the mood stabilizer divalproex sodium (Depakote).

Over the next several years, Maryanne was prescribed increasing amounts of drugs to control her "moodiness." For the past 2 years—since age 14—she had been taking four adult psychiatric medications: (1) the sedating mood stabilizer divalproex sodium (Depakote) 1,500 mg daily, (2) the sedating older antidepressant amitriptyline (Elavil) 50 mg at night for sleep, (3) the highly stimulating newer antidepressant bupropion XL (Wellbutrin XL or extended release), and (4) the very potent antipsychotic drug aripiprazole (Abilify) 10 mg daily.

On the initial phone call, Maryanne's mother told me that she had successfully reduced her daughter's Abilify to 10 mg/day about 6 months earlier. When she then tried to stop the 10 mg, within 2 days, her daughter withdrew emotionally into "a dark place," retreating into her room, and refusing to relate to anyone. However, Maryanne seemingly did well when she only missed a day of Abilify, as occasionally happened by mistake.

Still on the phone, I discussed the risk of TD, made an appointment for them, and recommended that Maryanne skip the evening dose of Abilify on the day before she came to see me. That would help to bring out any symptoms of TD that the drug might be masking.

I met Maryanne and her mother in the waiting room, and we decided that I would begin by seeing the teenager by herself. Maryanne and I talked for 45 minutes and then her mother joined us for an equal amount of time.

Maryanne was the younger of two girls, and her older sister was now living at college. Maryanne's mother described her younger daughter as a "moody kid" with an occasional day or two feeling blue every month or so, often in relation to her period. She would also have occasional times of "exuberance" about her social life and sports, with a tendency to "act silly" at times.

These brief "episodes" were quite unlike her mother or older sister's more sober behavior. They both had "steady temperaments" and "serious academic minds."

Maryanne had become seriously "depressed" only on the occasion when her mother had attempted to stop the Abilify. She had several friends at school and an active social life, enjoyed sports, but got only passing grades.

From her mother's viewpoint, Maryanne could be "obstinate," "not listen," and act "sassy." In the session, her mother became embarrassed when Maryanne displayed the spunk of a normal teenager.

With her mother observing, I took several minutes to examine Maryanne for TD. Her tongue, when at rest in her mouth and on extension, quivered. In addition, the sides of her tongue curled upward making a cup-like shape. The abnormality was obvious enough for her mother to recognize, although neither of them had been previously aware of it. I explained to Maryanne and her mother that this was a typical early sign of TD, but because I found no other definitive signs of the disorder, it might go away some time after the medication was stopped.

In addition, Maryanne had a moderate tremor of her hands, which worsened when she stood and extended her arms. I explained that the tremor was probably because of drug toxicity rather than TD.

Maryanne was unaware of feeling sedated. She thought, "I'm just clumsy with my hands," and she thought the tremor was "nerves." None of her symptoms seemed to bother her very much, and she did not seem very distressed by my discussion of her condition.

In contrast to her mother and the description of her older sister, she had the kind of spirit that lit up a room. Despite the medication effects, she radiated enthusiasm, and I was not surprised that she had friends and was able to play sports.

Like most patients on heavy medication, Maryanne was medication spellbound by the drugs and therefore felt little concern about the adverse effects.

I told Maryanne that I liked her very much and that I thought she would thrive as we reduced the medication. I explained that most adults would be unable to function at a normal level while taking this drug regimen and that it was a tribute to Maryanne's physical and mental strength that she radiated so much energy and only on occasion seemed "drugged."

I reassured Maryanne's mother that her daughter was a wonderful young woman. I explained she was temperamentally different from her mother and sister, but she was entirely normal. Each of them grinned broadly, enormously relieved and greatly encouraged by what her mother called "the best psychiatric evaluation imaginable."

Maryanne and her mother were worried about stopping Abilify "cold turkey." She had already missed a day of 10 mg, so we decided to have her take 10 mg every other day for the next week, and then if all went well, we would stop it. We arranged for brief daily telephone contacts for the period of the taper.

One week later, Maryanne came with her mother for the second time. A quick TD examination showed no change in her condition. Maryanne said she felt ready to stop taking the drug, and her mother agreed. I reminded them that she might still have a withdrawal reaction, including a flair-up of abnormal movements as her body reacted to the absence of the drug.

Maryanne spent the second half hour of our session without her mother, talking about her life at home and at school. At school, a girl had written her a "mean" note. Maryanne was surprised at my opinion that the girl was probably jealous of her. She had no idea what a vibrant and intelligent youngster she was. Other than wishing her mom wasn't always judging her behavior and spending too little "fun time" with her, she had no complaints at home.

Before the session was over, Maryanne told me that she had smoked marijuana 2 years earlier as a freshman to "cool out" her emotions, and that she was more depressed at that time than her mother or anyone else realized. I discussed the importance of her not taking any additional psychoactive substances.

Maryanne volunteered that she would like to tell her mother about our conversation, and we invited her in from the waiting room for the last few minutes. Maryanne's mother handled the disclosure of marijuana in a caring manner and was grateful for my straight talk with her about avoiding all psychoactive substances.

The next week, no longer taking Abilify, Maryanne felt much more alert and realized that she had been very slowed down by the drug.

> Patients often realize in retrospect that their psychiatric drug was suppressing their mental and emotional functioning.

Three weeks later, Maryanne came in again with her mother, who said that Maryanne was keeping up with her school work for the first time ever. Maryanne said she had gained some confidence from our last conversation and instead of turning down a date with a classmate she admired, she decided to accept it. She felt she was "ready to make better choices." I told her how proud of her I was—that it was very rare for a teenager to make such remarkable changes so quickly.

With Maryanne and her mother together, we discussed which of the next three drugs to begin tapering. Maryanne said she had no problems sleeping and didn't think she would have insomnia if we stopped the evening dose of amitriptyline. Also, I pointed out, she was taking 1,000 mg of her 1,500 mg of divalproex sodium at night and that would also continue to sedate her at bedtime even if we stopped the amitriptyline. We decided to cut the drug in half from 40 mg to 20 mg.

One week later, Maryanne and her mother both said she was doing better, and we agreed to stop the amitriptyline. We reviewed Maryanne's progress and once again, I talked with Maryanne alone, mostly about respecting and developing her considerable abilities.

In subsequent sessions, Maryanne said that she had become so accustomed to a doctor giving her pills to control her emotions that she had had little sense that she could be in charge of her feelings. Consistent with that, she didn't think about planning ahead. Before working with me, Maryanne had been trying to get used to the idea that she was "bipolar" and would have limitations for the rest of her life. I told her unequivocally that she had nothing whatsoever wrong with her and that she was in fact gifted with a very strong brain that had refused to be blunted by the heavy load of drugs. She liked this very much.

Two weeks after stopping the amitriptyline, we decided to drop one of her three 500 mg Depakote (divalproex sodium) tablets at night. I had originally suggested that we might want to reduce her stimulating antidepressant, bupropion, because we had already stopped some of her sedating drugs. But she felt strongly that the Depakote was in fact making her feel "droopy." As we reduced her medications, she was becoming more aware of their adverse effects.

One week later, Maryanne arrived with her mother, who said they needed to come into the session together. In the car on the way to my office, Maryanne had just told her mom that she "forgot" to take her nighttime divalproex sodium 1,000 mg for 3 days in a row when she had an overnight on the weekend. Her mom was annoyed and a little scared.

I suggested to Maryanne's mother, "Take a look at Maryanne. How does she look?" The question seemed to awaken her mom. "She looks beautiful. And I was thinking on the way over, before she told me, that she seems so much brighter and cheerier and more playful. It was like I was beginning to see my little girl again," she cried.

We agreed that Maryanne would take the morning dose of divalproex sodium (Depakote) for 3 days and then stop entirely. I reminded them that the main risk during withdrawal from the drug was seizures, but because she did not have a seizure disorder, that was unlikely.

I expressed concern that without the sedating Depakote, the bupropion XL 150 mg might produce increased irritability, emotional instability, or even mania—but my concerns were ameliorated by how well Maryanne was doing.

I spent some time alone with Maryanne. When I gently asked her about missing the drug doses, she admitted that "maybe I forgot them on purpose." I said I understood her eagerness to get off the medications because she was feeling better and better, but I'd feel safer if she followed my instructions. She promised to do so.

At the next visit, mother and daughter had decided it was time to reduce her bupropion XL 150 mg. To facilitate this, I prescribed bupropion tablets 50 mg three times a day. Because these were not extended release, I instructed Maryanne to take one at breakfast and two at dinner after school. Because the drug can be very stimulating, I didn't want her taking one too close to bedtime.

> Patients who have been warned about the dangers of psychiatric medications will, at times, make decisions to reduce or stop the drugs without consulting with the clinician. The clinician should avoid generating conflict and instead use it as a teaching moment about the risks and the need for cooperation.

I explained that once she was stable on the new dosing schedule, we could begin reducing the drug 50 mg at a time to see if she could tolerate it. I reviewed again the potential problems of withdrawal. "Crashing" was the most likely problem, along with fatigue, but a paradoxical euphoria and even mania was possible. As always, I urged them to call me at the very first sign of any emotional or behavioral change that concerned them.

We spent the remainder of the session together talking about what it would take for Maryanne to turn around her still lackadaisical study habits to have one good semester to show colleges next year. She felt she was doing very well emotionally, enjoying school, and no longer looking or feeling at all drugged. She still had a gross tremor, however, that the teacher noticed when she was handling apparatus in chemistry class.

Over the next 3 weeks, Maryanne withdrew from the bupropion 150 mg at the rate of 50 mg/week. She felt she was getting "tired out" toward the end, so we reduced the last week at 50 mg every other day. Otherwise, it was uneventful.

After 10 years on psychiatric drugs, 16-year-old Maryanne managed to withdraw from four psychiatric medications in about 4 months without any serious setbacks along the way. This success was caused by her youth, her physical and personal strength, a very supportive mother, and good therapeutic rapport.

I evaluated Maryanne for TD one more time toward the end of her treatment. Despite my hopes for a complete remission, her tongue remained moderately abnormal. Hopefully, she will never experience any functional deficits from this continuing disorder, but it reflects damage to the basal ganglia of the brain that could worsen in later years. I reminded her to avoid any and all drugs in the future that could cause abnormal movements, including drugs sometimes prescribed for the flu, such as Compazine (prochlorperazine) and Reglan (metoclopramide).

At the end of a successful school year, Maryanne and her mother felt she no longer needed therapy.

Prescribers need to be aware of the many severe adverse effects caused by antipsychotic drugs, to routinely check for them, to withdraw youngsters as quickly as possible, and to avoid starting them on these drugs in the first place.

Maryanne's case may seem very unusual in several ways. First, a 16-year-old is diagnosed at age 10 with bipolar disorder because of an adverse drug reaction to an antidepressant drug that she should not have been given. The correct diagnosis was a sertraline-induced mood disorder with manic features (irritability). Second, she was prescribed multiple adult drugs over the years, culminating in polydrug therapy with four medications. Third, at no time did she suffer from a serious diagnosable psychiatric disorder. Fourth, her prescriber failed in multiple ways to provide adequate care. Fifth, the "problem" was not in the youngster but in her mother's initial difficulty in dealing with Maryanne's exuberance.

In reality, Maryanne's case is not unusual. This scenario is common throughout this country and reflects a tragic tendency to prescribe drugs to children, to misinterpret adverse effects as the unmasking of mental illness, and to fail to provide proper individual counseling and family therapy.

Provided they have a supportive and responsible family, most children can easily be removed from psychiatric drugs with the provision of counseling and, most importantly, family therapy.

KEY POINTS

▪ Responsible, caring parents are the key to successfully withdrawing children from psychiatric medication, just as they are the key to their children's successful growth and development.

▪ Children can usually be withdrawn with relative ease from psychiatric medications as long as responsible parents are involved and willing to work on improving their child-rearing skills and their parent–child relationship.

▪ Children who suffer exclusively from ADHD-like symptoms are especially easily withdrawn from medication, provided that their parents are willing to improve their disciplinary and overall parenting skills.

▪ Most children and youth who have a history of manic-like symptoms have developed them as an adverse reaction to antidepressants or stimulants and will do very well with medication-free therapy.

▪ Children diagnosed with Asperger's or autism need especially intensive, informed caring from the adults in their lives, not only in the family but also in the school or other institutional setting. Psychiatric drugs suppress the ability to feel empathy and to relate and make it even harder for these children who are socially impaired to mature in their social capacities.

▪ Children old enough to talk are old enough to listen and can often be helped through direct conversation and guidance in cooperation with concerned and responsible parents, who are also working on improving the quality of their family life.

▪ Even after prolonged exposure to multiple psychiatric drugs, children and youth can often be withdrawn with relative ease if they have a stable family with at least one responsible parent who is willing to learn new and improved approaches to relating with the child.

CHAPTER 19

Concluding Thoughts for Prescribers, Therapists, Patients, and Their Families

The emphasis in this book on psychiatric drug withdrawal inevitably raises questions about the effectiveness of therapy without drugs. There is a long history and considerable scientific literature on treating even patients who are very disturbed without resorting to medication. My own career began as a college volunteer nearly 60 years ago, working closely with state mental hospital patients who were severely impaired, and that positive experience informed my development as a psychiatrist and psychotherapist. Prescribers and therapists who embrace a person-centered collaborative approach to therapy and to medication withdrawal will find it professionally gratifying and will help many patients and their families.

When patients cannot find a psychiatrist who is willing to reduce or stop their medication, with the aid of this guidebook, they may be able to collaborate with a primary care doctor or nurse practitioner, as well as a therapist, toward their goal of medication-free living.

For those patients who continue to suffer from lingering adverse drug effects long after drug withdrawal, it is important to realize that as unique human beings, you retain the ability to live principled and loving lives beyond any previous expectations.

A LONG HISTORY OF MEDICATION-FREE TREATMENT

Some individuals described in this book were psychotic during the period of withdrawal and then improved without medication, confirming that people who are very disturbed can be treated with psychotherapy in a person-centered collaborative approach. Although it is in danger of being lost to memory and to clinical practice, there is a long history and extensive literature demonstrating how to treat psychiatric patients without resorting to drugs. This includes outpatients and hospitalized patients meeting the diagnostic criteria for manic episodes and schizophrenia (for an overview, see Breggin, 2008a, pp. 425–457).

During the era of moral therapy in the 18th and 19th centuries, retreats or hospitals were established, especially in Great Britain, which treated the full range of psychiatric patients according to the "moral" principle of kindness, caring, Judeo-Christian ethical and spiritual encouragement, and healthy living. In retrospect, these drug-free facilities did at least as well in treating patients who are disturbed as modern hospitals do today (Bockoven, 1963). Quakers led in the development of long-lasting and effective treatment havens. Samuel Tuke's (1813) book-length treatise described how the staff was taught to treat patients with kindness, respect, and patience, and how patients were helped through moral persuasion based on religious and ethical principles to calm their spirits and appeal to their reason, even in the individuals who are most disturbed (Tuke, 1996). Tuke specifically rejected the medical treatments of his time as causing more harm than good. In many ways, moral therapy was very similar to the person-centered collaborative approach.

In more recent times, American psychiatrist Loren Mosher developed Soteria house, a home-like residential setting for treating individuals diagnosed with a first episode of schizophrenia. In some of his many published studies, none of the patients were given medications, and in others, a small fraction was medicated (Mosher, 1996; Mosher & Bola, 2004; Mosher & Burti, 1989). In controlled clinical trials in which patients were randomly assigned to a mental hospital ward or to Mosher's Soteria house, the drug-free patients in Soteria house did at least as well as the patients who were hospitalized and medicated. The Soteria patients suffered less stigmatization and humiliation, felt more empowered, and escaped the many adverse effects associated with antipsychotic medication.

For many years in Western Lapland, Finland, a mental health team has responded to every first episode of severe psychiatric disturbance with a family intervention in the home, along with psychotherapy (Seikkula, 2006; Seikkula et al., 2003). The program is called "The Open Dialogue Approach" to emphasize how the treatment team interacts freely with each other and with the family. Psychosis is viewed as a family phenomenon rather than an individual disorder. Medications are not the first choice and are rarely prescribed and then almost always for only a short period. The program has been so successful that overall unemployment and disability have been dramatically reduced in the community. So few patients now remain psychotic for the 6 months required for a diagnosis of schizophrenia that schizophrenia as a diagnosis is disappearing in the region.

Many clinicians have also described the successful treatment of patients who are psychotic with individual or family psychotherapy (Breggin, 1991, 1997b; Karon, 2005; McCready, 1995, 2002). Until the recent balkanization of psychiatry as a biologically based specialty, clinicians frequently treated the full spectrum of patients with psychotherapy.

In my experience, success in treating first episode psychosis depends to a great deal on the cooperativeness of the family. Much as I have described regarding withdrawing patients who are disturbed from multiple psychiatric drugs, treating people who are acutely psychotic as outpatients requires a supportive family that is willing to take responsibility for improving communications and relationships with each other, including the designated patient. With or without attempt at medication withdrawal, treating patients who have been on multiple psychiatric drugs for many years and who usually remain dependent on their families is very difficult because these families are so often very distressed and conflicted.

MY FORMATIVE STATE MENTAL HOSPITAL EXPERIENCE

The first of the key points at the end of Chapter 1 is central to the person-centered approach: "Empathy, honest communication, and patient empowerment lie at the heart of the person-centered approach."

Empathy is suppressed when healthcare providers are taught

> These principles of *empathy, honesty,* and *empowerment* are the essence of any helping or healing approach to another human being. Unfortunately, they are easily lost or suppressed in the training of mental health professionals.

to think diagnostically, quickly pigeonholing the individual into one or another conveniently tailored category, instead of seeing the person's individuality and uniqueness, personal strengths, essential worth, and need for understanding.

Honesty is corrupted in the training process when professionals are encouraged to act as if they know more than they do; when in reality, their experience and wisdom may fall far short of that of their patients. They may never learn that their real strength lies in their capacity to offer a safe environment, and to care and understand, rather than to impose authority.

Empowering individuals to make their own choices and direct their own paths becomes a threatening concept to those professionals who are taught to diagnose, to enforce conformity to the therapy, and above all else, to emphasize medication compliance.

Nearly 6 decades ago, I unexpectedly found myself thrust into the corrupt heart of the mental health system, a state mental hospital. I was a wide-eyed young college freshman, appalled by the calamitous conditions under which the patients lived and motivated to try with all his might to make things better. I began with a great gift in my initial efforts to help some of the most despairing and overwhelmed people on earth. The gift was . . . that I had no mental health training.

Being untrained, not looking at people through the psychiatric lens and not treating them with psychiatric authority, I had to develop whatever basic human skills I possessed to try to help these abandoned and oppressed souls. Untrained as I was, there seemed nothing else to do other than to approach the patients *as I would want to be approached*—with care and concern, with a desire to get to know them, and with a commitment to finding out what it was they needed and wanted, and how I could help them get it. Spontaneously, I was doing "person-centered therapy."

I first began working intensively with patients in the fall of 1954, when I was an 18-year-old Harvard college freshman volunteering at a nearby state mental hospital called Metropolitan State. Eventually, I became the director of the Harvard-Radcliffe Mental Hospital Volunteer Program, and it became the center of my college experience. I spent many hours each week during the school year, as well as two full summers, working in a vast, oppressive institution from which relatively few people were ever released.

From the moment I set foot into Metropolitan State, I was appalled by how abused and humiliated the patients were by the authoritarian and sometimes violent staff, and by the abysmal and even sickening living conditions. It reminded me of my Uncle Dutch's description of liberating a concentration camp at the end of World War II.

As I grew more familiar with what was going on in the hospital, I was struck by the use of brain-damaging "treatments," including insulin coma, electroshock, and lobotomy. I reacted with disbelief when told by the doctors that these treatments "killed bad brain cells." Not yet a student of the brain, it took little sophistication to realize the unlikelihood of such an explanation.

The chlorpromazine (Thorazine) tidal wave that swept over state mental hospitals in the mid-1950s had not yet arrived in the backwaters of Metropolitan State. As a result, many of the patients remained full of life and were able to express and to share their feelings of loneliness, abandonment, despair, and anguish. It was possible to relate to them as persons. I was deeply moved by how starved they were for caring human contact, and how eagerly they embraced any kindness or interest that we, as volunteers, offered them.

Some of the patients at Metropolitan State—they were really inmates—were obviously very disturbed or "crazy," but they were often grateful for our unexpected presence in their lives and became calmer and more social when around us. At no time was a volunteer ever threatened or injured by a patient, even when working on the "violent wards," where I spent most of my time.

Everywhere we went in the hospital, we were greeted with heartfelt warmth. It was clear to me that there was no essential difference between "me and them," except perhaps in the luck of the draw that I had been spared some of the worst that life deals out. I did not feel superior to them. I felt, "There but for the grace of God go I."

Nowadays, a student visiting or working in any acute or long-term mental health facility will be misled into thinking that "mental patients" inherently lack feeling about their lives or living conditions. In reality, they are medicated into this seeming obliviousness. Students trained in modern mental health facilities cannot learn what the person is really like beneath the drug-induced apathy and indifference.

In the second year of my volunteer work—my sophomore year of college—I developed a volunteer case aide program in which each of 15 students, including myself, was assigned "our own patient" to visit on a weekly basis. Supervision was limited to occasional group meetings with a skilled and empathic social worker. It seemed obvious that the most important thing we could offer these people was care and even love, provided we respected boundaries and did nothing to take advantage.

Some staff expressed fears we would harm the patients, so we were assigned to chronic inmates whom they felt were beyond help and perhaps beyond harm. These souls were variously designated "back ward patients" and "burnt out schizophrenics," and they had not as yet been subdued with chlorpromazine.

The widespread use of antipsychotic drugs would eventually create a more docile and submissive inmate population, but the drugs were not responsible for the later emptying of the state mental hospitals, which did not take place for another decade or more after the drugs arrived (Breggin, 1983, pp. 61–65; Scheper-Hughes, 1978; Scull, 1977). Political changes, not treatment changes, led to so-called deinstitutionalization, which involved the states shifting the financial burden from themselves to the federal government.

In the new case aide program, we, as volunteers, were working with largely drug-free patients. This meant we could fully relate to them as persons. To everyone's astonishment, in the first year of the college volunteer case aid program we were able to help 11 of the 15 patients assigned to us to return home or to find improved placements in the community. In

In the 1960s, psychiatric patients became eligible for federal disability payments for the first time. No longer responsible for their financial support, the states summarily turned out tens of thousands of state hospital inmates. Their lives were not improved, with most ending up in bleak nursing homes and board and care homes—or on the streets.

a 1–2 year follow-up, only three returned to Metropolitan State. There was no need for a placebo control group to prove the effectiveness of our efforts because hardly any patients from these wards were ever discharged from the hospital.

The program drew national attention and media coverage and was so successful that it was praised as an important innovation in mental health by the Joint Commission on Mental Illness and Mental Health (1961, pp. 90–91; quoted in International Center for the Study of Psychiatry and Psychology [ICSPP], 2009, p. 54). The report of that Presidential Commission, called *Action for Mental Health*, was the last psychosocially oriented document to be issued by National Institute of Mental Health (NIMH) or organized psychiatry. The future focus of the mental health establishment would be on cooperative efforts with the pharmaceutical industry to promote biochemical explanations and drugs.

Each volunteer in our volunteer program had his or her own personal approach to relating to patients, some adopting a "therapeutic" approach and some a more social or companionable approach. We tried to interact with our patients in a spontaneously caring and even loving manner. As volunteer case aides, we tended to do whatever seemed useful, from helping patients obtain eyeglasses, nicer clothes, or needed dental care to reestablishing relationships with their families. The patients benefitted from a combination of practical attention to their needs and genuine caring for them as people. This combination remains the best approach to helping people who are emotionally disabled. As I have previously written, "I learned how basic human relationship could revive, and even restore, the lives of the most chronically disturbed patients, even those who had experienced years of abuse in a state mental hospital" (Breggin, 2008a, p. 437).

Out of this intensive 4-year experience, I decided to pursue a career as a psychiatrist based on two principles—that biological psychiatric treatments can do more harm than good and that the patients can benefit dramatically from caring human relationships that attend to their basic needs and help them to feel valued.

Still a student at Harvard and a premedical student, I worked with mental health leaders and groups in several states to promote volunteer programs. Great enthusiasm was shown for this innovated human services approach to helping people who are emotionally disturbed and disabled in long-term hospitals.[1]

---

[1] I also began my first book, *College Students in a Mental Hospital*, which became jointly authored by additional volunteer leaders after I graduated (Umbarger, Dalsimer, Morrison, & Breggin, 1962). The book specifically spoke of caring as central to the healing process.

As a result of my experience, including the enthusiastic welcoming of our case aid program by leaders in psychiatry, I envisioned myself becoming a psychosocially oriented psychiatrist devoted to improving the delivery of psychological and social services. But when I finished my medical and psychiatric training 8 years later in 1966, followed by 2 years as a full-time consultant with the NIMH, the psychiatric landscape was already being transformed for the worse. Psychosocial approaches were being expurgated from a purified biological psychiatry. The profession was becoming so biologically oriented that it would no longer tolerate caring, nonmedical psychotherapeutic approaches, especially for patients seen as seriously mentally ill. So instead of stay-

Because my experience in the mental health field began with very disabled and dependent people, it was apparent that many patients required a great deal more help than traditional one-to-one psychotherapy. They needed a collaborative team approach involving support, guidance, and, at times, monitoring by informed and caring adults. A person-centered collaborative approach was at the heart of the volunteer case aide program and provides the best therapy for individuals who, for many different reasons, may be unable to take care of themselves. This includes dependent children and adults, people who are emotionally and cognitively disabled, and patients whose judgment may be impaired by psychiatric medication or medication withdrawal.

ing at NIMH or accepting a full-time post at a university, I went into private practice, offering the kind of approach I value—individual, couples, and family therapy, including children.

As it turned out, my private practice would provide me sustained satisfaction and energy to this very day, as private practice can still do for professionals who take a person-centered approach. Instead of burnout at age 76, I am enjoying my work as much as ever. There is no burnout when the therapist adopts a person-centered approach. Doing person-centered therapy means getting to know people intimately within a safe environment, having people share their deepest feelings with you, finding ways to empower their lives, knowing you must be at your best as a person every hour you spend with them, and looking forward to being with people you care about. What is there to burnout about? As I sometimes tell my patients, "Even on a bad day, it's impossible for me to feel depressed or crazy when I'm working with you because I have to be thinking about you and your needs. If you can learn to do that for the people around you, you'll never get depressed or crazy again."

Eventually, I could not ignore how the escalating use of psychiatric medication was harming millions of patients, and how my colleagues were largely unaware of the hazards. In 1983, I wrote *Psychiatric Drugs: Hazards to the Brain*, and soon patients began seeking me out specifically for medication-free treatment, often involving drug withdrawal.

I developed a specialty in clinical psychopharmacology with emphasis on evaluating adverse drug effects and offering help with drug withdrawal. It became clearer and clearer to me that by embracing drugs and electroshock, psychiatry was suppressing and destroying the personhood of their patients. Exactly the opposite of a person-centered approach, biological psychiatry was a person-suppressing approach.

Since the beginning of my private practice in 1968, I have refrained from starting my own patients on psychiatric drugs, and I let potential patients know this before they make their first appointment. The only exception is an occasional prescription for sleeping medications during a crisis or during withdrawal. Some patients come to see me on medications and then decide that they do not want to withdraw from them, and often, we can find a way to work together, holding out the goal of eventually stopping the drugs.

I treat the complete spectrum of patients, including patients who are actively psychotic, provided that they can come to my office. If patients are independent and high functioning, I conduct person-centered individual, couples, or family psychotherapy. I use the person-centered *collaborative* approach described in this book with children, with adults who are emotionally disabled and dependent, and with anyone undergoing a difficult withdrawal. A person who is hallucinating or deluded is no less a person than anyone else and will often respond more quickly than others to a glimmer of hope that the new person in the room actually cares and might possibly be trusted.

> Many clinicians may not feel comfortable treating patients who are disturbed or disturbing without resort to psychiatric drugs. Hopefully, this guide for a person-centered collaborative approach to medication withdrawal will prove useful even to those who do not fully share my critical assessment of psychiatric medications and my emphasis on psychotherapeutic approaches. Whatever the clinician's orientation, there can be no doubt that many patients are given too many drugs in too large doses over too long periods.

CONCLUDING THOUGHTS FOR PRESCRIBERS AND THERAPISTS

If you are a prescriber who has little time or inclination to offer psychotherapy, you will find that teaming up with one or more good psychotherapists will enormously enhance the services that you provide to your patients. Any time a prescriber determines that a patient is suffering from sufficient emotional distress to benefit from medication, that same patient should be encouraged to try counseling or psychotherapy.

Drugs by themselves are rarely the answer to anyone's emotional problems and frequently undermine a patient's determination or motivation to take charge of his or her own life in new and creative ways.

As I've documented in earlier chapters, all psychiatric drugs have serious long-term adverse effects and tend to produce chronic brain impairment (CBI). If at all possible, it is best to recommend psychotherapy before recommending medication.

When the prescriber views the therapist as a partner who participates fully in the medication and withdrawal process, the patient will receive the best care. The informed therapist should feel free to discuss every aspect of medication treatment with patients and their families, including informing them about risks associated with medication while helping to monitor adverse effects during treatment and withdrawal. As the clinician who most often sees the patient, the therapist will usually be in the best position to identify adverse drug effects before they become serious or life threatening. Because the therapist is most familiar with the patient and the family, the therapist is best able to help the patient and family make ongoing decisions about continuing medications or withdrawing from them.

Therapists should not be required or feel obliged to promote "medication compliance." Medication compliance is antiquated in an era when patients have complete access to drug information and possess the right to decide whether or not to take psychoactive medication.[2] Respect for patient autonomy and self-determination is ethically required and therapeutically indispensable.

Prescribers can no longer assume the role of medical doctors or nurse practitioners working in isolation prescribing for patients who then depart the office to dutifully take their drugs. It's simply unrealistic. On their own, patients commonly modify the doses of their drugs or stop taking them altogether. They often make these decisions by themselves precisely because they fear that their prescriber will disapprove of their wishes, especially regarding stopping drugs.

There is a vast field of professional opportunity for prescribers and therapists who wish to help patients minimize their medication use and who will sympathetically respond to a patient's desire to take less medication or no medication at all. As I suggested earlier in this chapter, a practice of person-centered therapy will remain invigorating and never lead to burnout.

Prescribers are usually inundated with work and typically must stay abreast of complex information about multiple drugs at once. Because of time limitations, prescribers often work from memory or refer to very brief lists of adverse effects in a digital handbook. By contrast, some

---

[2]Individuals subjected to outpatient or inpatient commitment can lose their right to reject medication. Forced medication is not therapy. It is coercion and should have no place in mental health practices (Breggin, 1991).

patients spend hours looking up the adverse effects of the few drugs they are taking. As a result, patients (and their families) often know much more than their prescribers about adverse effects and withdrawal effects of the specific drugs they are taking. The modern prescriber will best serve patients by working together with therapists, patients, and their significant others or families, especially during difficult drug withdrawals.

Although few of us have been trained to implement a person-centered collaborative approach, the process can flow easily from our concern for the best interests and needs of our patients. If we work as professionals to empathize with our patients and their families, we will find ourselves pursuing a person-centered collaborative approach.

Only when we focus on our patients' wishes, values, and choices can we best serve their needs and interests. Only when we fully collaborate among ourselves as prescribers and therapists, and with our patients and their families, can we be sure that we are doing everything we can to be helpful, especially in difficult cases where the patient is likely to be temporarily impaired by dose changes and drug withdrawal.

CONCERN FOR THE PATIENTS AND THEIR FAMILIES

In the last few years, there has been a changing perspective on the part of patients and their families involved in treatment with psychiatric medications. Many patients and families feel wounded by their experience with prescribers and therapists. They feel they have been pushed into taking psychiatric drugs. They find themselves ushered through an assembly line of medication checks. They believe that their complaints about adverse drug effects have been ignored. Every mental health professional seems to push medications on them, and none seem to consider the reasonableness of limiting exposure to these potentially toxic substances or seeking other approaches.

The mental health landscape may not be quite that universally bleak, and some prescribers and therapists are becoming skeptical about freely dispensing drugs and more willing to communicate honestly and to collaborate with their patients and families. Patients nonetheless remain hard-pressed to find anyone to help them withdraw from drugs in a rational manner with supportive therapy. My hope is that this guide will be useful in bringing together prescribers,

Too often, patients and their families cannot find a psychiatrist to help them through drug withdrawal. Using this guidebook as a model approach, they may be able to enlist a primary care physician or nurse practitioner, along with a therapist, in their medication withdrawal program.

therapists, patients, and their families who wish to be involved in a person-centered collaborative approach.

For those of my colleagues who make the person-centered collaborative approach a part of their clinical practice, an increase in professional satisfaction is guaranteed. Nothing is more satisfying than seeing the good effect of this kind of cooperative approach on the lives of our patients and their families.

My greatest concern is for patients—and their families—who have been injured by exposure to psychiatric medications and who may not fully recover after withdrawal. Recovery from injury to the brain and nervous system can take place at a much slower pace than injury to other organ systems, such as the skin, muscles, or gastrointestinal system. Many patients take many months to recover from lingering adverse effects, such as fatigue, memory and other cognitive problems, or odd sensations in their skin. Some patients may take several years or more for additional or complete recovery. Patience is required, coupled with a realization that despite these injuries, people can go on to live very full lives.

As human beings, we are more than what happens to our brains and our bodies. Whether we view ourselves as souls, spirits, or simply unique and valuable individuals, we can find the strength to live ethical and loving lives, even in the presence of an injured brain or compromised mental function. My wish for you is to find the confidence and dedication to live an even better life than you ever anticipated or imagined.

Bibliography

Aarskog, D., Fevang, F. O., Klove, H., Stoa, K. F., & Thorsen, T. (1977). The effect of stimulant drugs, dextroamphetamine and methylphenidate, on secretion of growth hormone in hyperactive children. *Journal of Pediatrics, 90*(1), 136–139.

Adderall XR. (2010). *Medication guide.* Rockville, MD: U.S. Food and Drug Administration. Retrieved from http://www.fda.gov/downloads/Drugs/DrugSafety/ucm085819.pdf

Addonizio, G., Susman, V. L., & Roth, S. D. (1986). Symptoms of neuroleptic malignant syndrome in 82 consecutive inpatients. *The American Journal of Psychiatry, 143*(12), 1587–1590.

Adityanjee. (1987). The syndrome of irreversible lithium effectuated neurotoxicity. *Journal of Neurology, Neurosurgery, and Psychiatry, 50*(9), 1246–1247.

Adityanjee, Munshi, K. R., & Thampy, A. (2005). The syndrome of irreversible lithium-effectuated neurotoxicity. *Clinical Neuropharmacology, 28*(1), 38–49.

Akinbami, L. J., Liu, X., Pastor, P. N., & Reuben, C. A. (2011). *NCHS Data Brief: Attention deficit hyperactivity disorder among children aged 5–17 years in the United States, 1998–2009.* Retrieved from Centers for Disease Control and Prevention website: http://www.cdc.gov/nchs/data/databriefs/db70.htm

Al Banchaabouchi, M., Peña de Ortíz, S., Menéndez, R., Ren, K., & Maldonado-Vlaar, C. S. (2004). Chronic lithium decreases Nurr1 expression in the rat brain and impairs spatial discrimination. *Pharmacology, Biochemistry and Behavior, 79*(4), 607–621.

Alehan, F., Saygi, S., Tarcan, A., & Gurakan, B. (2008). Prolonged neonatal complications after in utero exposure to fluoxetine. *The Journal of Maternal-Fetal & Neonatal Medicine, 21*(12), 921–923.

American Academy of Pediatrics. (2011). *AAP expands ages for diagnosis and treatment of ADHD in children.* Elk Grove Village, IL: Author.

American Psychiatric Association. (1980). *Diagnostic and statistical manual of mental disorders* (3rd ed.). Washington, DC: Author.

American Psychiatric Association. (1990). *Benzodiazepine dependence, toxicity, and abuse: A task force report of the American Psychiatric Association.* Washington, DC: Author.

American Psychiatric Association. (1992). *Tardive dyskinesia: A task force report of the American Psychiatric Association.* Washington, DC: Author.

American Psychiatric Association. (2000). *Diagnostic and statistical manual of mental disorders* (4th ed., text rev.). Washington, DC: Author.

Andrews, P. W., Kornstein, S. G., Halberstadt L. J., Gardner, C. O., & Neale, M. C. (2011). Blue again: Perturbational effects of antidepressants suggest monoaminergic homeostasis in major depression. *Frontiers in Psychology, 2,* 159. doi: 10.3389/fpsyg.2011.00159

Angell, M. (2004). *The truth about drug companies: How they deceive us and what to do about it.* New York, NY: Random House.

Antonuccio, D. O., Danton, W. G., DeNelsky, G. Y., Greenberg, R. P., & Gordon, J. S. (1999). Raising questions about antidepressants. *Psychotherapy and Psychosomatics, 68*(1), 3–14.

Ashton, H. (2002). "The Ashton Manual." Benzodiazepines: How they work and how to withdrawal. Retrieved on June 12, 2012 from http://www.benzo.org.uk/manual/.

Asscher, A. W. (1991). Dear doctor/dentist/pharmacist: Withdrawal of triazolam [Letter]. London, UK: Committee on Safety of Medicines.

Aursnes, I., Tvete, I. F., Gaasemyr, J., & Natvig, B. (2005). Suicide attempts in clinical trials with paroxetine randomised against placebo. *BMC Medicine, 3,* 14. doi: 10.1186/1741-7015/3/14

Bahrick, A., & Harris, M. (2008). Sexual side effects of antidepressant medications: An informed consent accountability gap. *Journal of Contemporary Psychotherapy, 39,* 135–143. doi: 10.1007/s10879-008-9094-0

Baldessarini, R. J., Tondo, L., Ghiani, C., & Lepri, B. (2010). Illness risk following rapid versus gradual discontinuation of antidepressants. *The American Journal of Psychiatry, 167*(8), 934–941.

Barker, M. J., Greenwood, K. M., Jackson, M., & Crowe, S. F. (2004). Cognitive effects of long-term benzodiazepine use: A meta-analysis. *CNS Drugs, 18*(1), 37–48.

Barnes, T. R., & McPhillips, M. A. (1995). How to distinguish between the neuroleptic-induced deficit syndrome, depression and disease-related negative symptoms in schizophrenia. *International Clinical Psychopharmacology, 10*(Suppl. 3), 115–121.

Barnhart, W. J., Makela, E. H., & Latocha, M. J. (2004). SSRI-induced apathy syndrome: A clinical review. *Journal of Psychiatric Practice, 10*(3), 196–199.

Baughman, F., Jr., & Hovey, C. (2006). The ADHD fraud: How psychiatry makes "Patients" out of normal children. Victoria, BC: Trafford Publishing.

Beck, M. (2011, August 9). Confusing medical ailments with mental illness. *Wall Street Journal. Health Journal,* p. 1.

Bergman, H., Borg, S., Engelbrektson, K., & Vikander, B. (1989). Dependence on sedative-hypnotics: Neuropsychological impairment, field dependence and clinical course in a 5-year follow-up study. *British Journal of Addiction, 84*(5), 547–553.

Bhidayasiri, R., & Boonyawairoj, S. (2010). Spectrum of tardive syndromes: Cinical recognition and management. *Postgraduate Medical Journal, 87*(1024),132–141.

Birzele, H. J. (1992). Benzodiazepine induced amnesia after long-term medication and during withdrawal. *European Review of Applied Psychology, 42*(4), 277–282.

Blumenthal, J. A., Babyak, M. A., Doraiswamy, P. M., Watksin, L., Hoffman, B. M., Barbour, K. A., . . . Sherwood, A. (2007). Exercise and pharmacotherapy in the treatment of major depressive disorder. *Psychosomatic Medicine, 69*(7), 587–596.

Bockoven, S. (1963). *Moral treatment in American Psychiatry.* New York, NY: Springer Publishing.

Bola, J., Lehtinen, K., Cullberg, J., & Ciompi, L. (2009). Psychosocial treatment, antipsychotic postponement, and low-dose medication strategies in first-episode psychosis: A review of the literature. *Psychosis, 1,* 4–18.

Borcherding, B. G., Keysor, C. S., Rapoport, J. L., Elia, J., & Amass, J. (1990). Motor/vocal tics and compulsive behaviors on stimulant drugs: Is there a common vulnerability? *Psychiatry Research, 33*(1), 83–94.

Borgwardt, S. J., Smieskova, R., Fusar-Poli, P., Bendfeldt, K., & Riecher-Rössler, A. (2009). The effects of antipsychotics on brain structure: What have we learnt from structural imaging and schizophrenia? *Psychological Medicine, 39*(11), 1781–1782.

Brahams, D. (1991). Triazolam suspended. *Lancet, 338*(8771), 938.

Breggin, P. (1962). *The college student and the mental patient. In College Student Companion Program: Contribution to the social rehabilitation of the mentally ill.* Rockville, MD: National Institutes of Mental Health.

Breggin, P. (1979). *Electroshock: Its brain-disabling effects.* New York, NY: Springer Publishing.

Breggin, P. (1980). Brain-disabling therapies. In E. Valenstein (Ed.), *The psychosurgery debate: Scientific, legal and ethical perspectives* (pp. 467–505). San Francisco, CA: Freeman.

Breggin, P. (1981a). Disabling the brain with electroshock. In M. Dongier & D. Wittkower (Eds.), *Divergent views in psychiatry* (pp. 247–271). Hagerstown, MD: Harper & Row.

Breggin, P. (1981b). Psychosurgery as brain-disabling therapy. In M. Dongier & D. Wittkower (Eds.), *Divergent views in psychiatry* (pp. 302–326). Hagerstown, MD: Harper & Row.

Breggin, P. (1983). *Psychiatric drugs: Hazards to the brain.* New York, NY: Springer Publishing.

Breggin, P. (1989a). Addiction to neuroleptics? [Letter]. *The American Journal of Psychiatry, 146*(9), 560.

Breggin, P. (1989b). Addiction to neuroleptics: Dr. Breggin replies [Letter]. *The American Journal of Psychiatry, 146,* 1240.

Breggin, P. (1990). Brain damage, dementia and persistent cognitive dysfunction associated with neuroleptic drugs: Evidence, etiology, implications. *Journal of Mind and Behavior, 11,* 425–464.

Breggin, P. (1991). *Toxic psychiatry: Why therapy, empathy and love must replace the drugs, electroshock, and biochemical theories of the "new psychiatry."* New York, NY: St. Martin's Press.

Breggin, P. (1992). A case of fluoxetine-induced stimulant side effects with suicidal ideation associated with a possible withdrawal syndrome ("crashing"). *International Journal of Risk & Safety in Medicine, 3,* 325–328.

Breggin, P. (1993). Parallels between neuroleptic effects and lethargic encephalitis: The production of dyskinesias and cognitive disorders. *Brain and Cognition, 23*(1), 8–27.

Breggin, P. (1997a). *Brain-disabling treatments in psychiatry.* New York, NY: Springer Publishing.

Breggin, P. (1997b). *The heart of being helpful.* New York, NY: Springer Publishing.

Breggin, P. (1998a). Analysis of adverse behavioral effects of benzodiaz-epines with a discussion of drawing scientific conclusions from the FDA's spontaneous reporting system. *Journal of Mind and Behavior, 19,* 21–50.

Breggin, P. (1998b). *Risks and mechanism of action of stimulants. In NIH consensus development conference program and abstracts: Diagnosis and treatment of attention deficit hyperactivity disorder.* Rockville, MD: National Institutes of Health.

Breggin, P. (1999a). Psychostimulants in the treatment of children diag-nosed with ADHD, Part I: Acute risks and psychological effects. *Ethical Human Sciences and Services, 1,* 13–33.

Breggin, P. (1999b). Psychostimulants in the treatment of children diag-nosed with ADHD, Part II: Adverse effects on brain and behavior. *Ethical Human Sciences and Services, 1,* 213–242.

Breggin, P. (1999c). Psychostimulants in the treatment of children diag-nosed with ADHD: Risks and mechanism of action. *International Journal of Risk and Safety in Medicine, 12,* 3–35.

Breggin, P. (2000a). The NIMH multimodal study of treatment for attention-deficit/hyperactivity disorder: A critical analysis. *International Journal of Risk & Safety in Medicine, 13,* 15–22, 2000.

Breggin, P. (2000b). *Reclaiming our children: A healing plan for a nation in crisis.* Cambridge, MA: Perseus Books.

Breggin, P. (2001a). *The antidepressant fact book.* Cambridge, MA: Perseus Books.

Breggin, P. (2001b). MTA study has flaws. *Archives of General Psychiatry, 58*(12), 1184.

Breggin, P. (2001c). *Talking back to Ritalin,* (rev. ed.). Cambridge, MA: Perseus Books.

Breggin, P. (2002a). Fluvoxamine as a cause of stimulation, mania, and aggression with a critical analysis of the FDA-approved label. *International Journal of Risk & Safety in Medicine, 14,* 71–86.

Breggin, P. (2002b). *The Ritalin fact book.* Cambridge, MA: Perseus Books.

Breggin, P. (2003). Suicidality, violence and mania caused by selective sero-tonin reuptake inhibitors (SSRIs): A review and analysis. *Ethical Human Sciences and Services, 5,* 225–246.

Breggin, P. (2005). Recent U.S., Canadian and British regulatory agency actions concerning antidepressant-induced harm to self and others: A review and analysis. *Ethical Human Psychology and Psychiatry, 7,* 7–22.

Breggin, P. (2006a). Court filing makes public my previously suppressed analysis of Paxil's effects. *Ethical Human Psychology and Psychiatry, 8*(1), 77–84.

Breggin, P. (2006b). Drug company suppressed data on paroxetine-induced stimulation: Implications for violence and suicide. *Ethical Human Psychology and Psychiatry, 8,* 255–263.

Breggin, P. (2006c). How GlaxoSmithKline suppressed data on Paxil-induced akathisia: Implications for suicide and violence. *Ethical Human Psychology and Psychiatry, 8,* 91–100.

Breggin, P. (2006d). Intoxication anosognosia: The spellbinding effect of psychiatric drugs. *Ethical Human Psychology and Psychiatry, 8,* 201–215.

Breggin, P. (2006e). Recent regulatory changes in antidepressant labels: Implications for activation (stimulation) in clinical practice. *Primary Psychiatry, 13,* 57–60.

Breggin, P. (2008a). *Brain-disabling treatments in psychiatry: Drugs, electroshock, and the psychopharmaceutical complex* (2nd ed.). New York, NY: Springer Publishing.

Breggin, P. (2008b). *Medication madness: True stories about mayhem, murder and suicide caused by psychiatric drugs.* New York, NY: St. Martin's Press.

Breggin, P. (2010). Antidepressant-induced suicide, violence, and mania: Risks for military personnel. *Ethical Human Psychology and Psychiatry, 12,* 111–121.

Breggin, P. (2011a). *Empathic therapy: A training film.* [DVD]. Available from http://www.breggin.com

Breggin, P. (2011b). *Prozac turned teen into murderer. Psychiatric drug facts.* Retrieved from http://www.breggin.com/index.php?option=com_content&task=view&id=295

Breggin, P. (2011c). Psychiatric drug-induced chronic brain impairment (CBI): Implications for long-term treatment with psychiatric medication. *International Journal of Risk & Safety in Medicine, 23*(4), 193–200.

Breggin, P., & Breggin, G. (1994). *Talking back to Prozac: What doctors aren't telling you about today's most controversial drug.* New York, NY: St. Martin's Press.

Breggin, P., & Breggin, G. (1998). *The war against children of color: Psychiatry targets inner city youth.* Monroe, ME: Common Courage Press.

Breggin, P., & Breggin, G. (2008). Exposure to SSRI antidepressants in utero causes birth defects, neonatal withdrawal symptoms, and brain damage. *Ethical Human Psychology and Psychiatry, 10,* 5–9.

Breggin, P., Breggin G., & Bemak, F. (Eds.). (2002). *Dimensions of empathic therapy.* New York, NY: Springer Publishing.

Breggin, P., & Stern, E. M. (Eds.). (1996). *Psychosocial approaches to deeply disturbed patients.* New York, NY: Haworth Press.

Brill, H. (1959). Postencephalitic psychiatric conditions. In S. Arieti (Ed.), *American handbook of psychiatry* (pp. 1163–1174). New York, NY: Basic Books.

Brown, P., & Funk, S. C. (1986). Tardive dyskinesia: Barriers to the professional recognition of an iatrogenic disease. *Journal of Health and Social Behavior, 27*(2), 116–132.

Brumm, V. L., van Gorp, W. G., & Wirshing, W. (1998). Chronic neuropsychological sequelae in a case of severe lithium intoxication. *Neuropsychiatry, Neuropsychology, and Behavioral Neurology, 11*(4), 245–249.

Buchsbaum, M. S., Wu, J., Haier, R., Hazlett, E., Ball, R., Katz, M., . . . Langer, D. (1987). Positron emission tomography assessment of effects of benzodiazepines on regional glucose metabolic rate in patients with anxiety disorder. *Life Sciences, 40*(25), 2393–2400.

Burton, T. (2011, July 5). Pfizer drug tied to heart risks. *Wall Street Journal,* p. B3.

Carlezon, W. A., Jr., & Konradi, C. (2004). Understanding the neurobiological consequences of early exposure to psychotropic drugs: Linking behavior with molecules. *Neuropharmacology, 47*(Suppl. 1), 47–60.

Carpenter, W. (1977). The treatment of acute schizophrenia without drugs. *American Journal of Psychiatry, 134,* 14–20.

Cassels, C. (2011). *Prescription stimulant use in kids with ADHD still rising.* Retrieved from Medscape Medical News: Psychiatry website: http://www .medscape.com/viewarticle/750713

Castellanos, F. X., Giedd, J. N., Marsh, W. L., Hamburger, S. D., Vaituzis, A. C., Dickstein, D. P., . . . Rapoport, J. L. (1998). Quantitative brain magnetic resonance imaging in attention-deficit hyperactivity disorder. *Archives of General Psychiatry, 53*(7), 607–616.

Cavanagh, J., Smyth, R., & Goodwin, G. M. (2004). Relapse into mania or depression following lithium discontinuation: A 7-year follow-up. *Acta Psychiatrica Scandinavica, 109*(2), 91–95.

Chouinard, G., Annable, L., Mercier, P., & Ross-Chouinard, A. (1986). A five-year follow-up study of tardive dyskinesia. *Psychopharmacology Bulletin, 22*(1), 259–263.

Chouinard, G., & Chouinard, V. A. (2008). Atypical antipsychotics: CATIE study, drug-induced movement disorder and resulting iatrogenic psychiatric-like symptoms, supersensitivity rebound psychosis and withdrawal discontinuation syndromes. *Psychotherapy and Psychosomatics*, 77(2), 69–77.

Chouinard, G., & Jones, B. D. (1980). Neuroleptic-induced supersensitivity psychosis: Clinical and pharmacologic characteristics. *The American Journal of Psychiatry*, 137(1), 16–21.

Ciompi, L., Dauwalder, H. P., Maier, C., Aebi, E., Trütsch, K., Kupper, Z., & Rutishauser, C. (1992). The pilot project "Soteria Berne." Clinical experiences and results. *British Journal of Psychiatry. Supplement*, (18), 145–153.

Coupland, C., Dhiman, P., Morriss, R., Arthur, A., Barton, G., & Hippisley-Cox, J. (2011). Antidepressant use and risk of adverse outcomes in older people: Population based cohort study. *BMJ (Clinical Research ed.)*, 343, d4551.

Crane, G. (1973). Clinical psychopharmacology in its 20th year. *Science*, 181, 124–128.

Croen, L. A., Grether, J. K., Yoshida, C. K., Odouli, R., & Hendrick, V. (2011). Antidepressant use during pregnancy and childhood autism spectrum disorders. *Archives of General Psychiatry*, 68(11), 1104–1112.

Csoka, A. B., & Shipko, S. (2006). Persistent sexual side effects after SSRI discontinuation. *Psychotherapy and Psychosomatics*, 75(3), 187–188.

Deakin, J. B., Rahman, S., Nestor, P. J., Hodges, J. R., & Sahakian, B. J. (2004). Paroxetine does not improve symptoms and impairs cognition in frontotemporal dementia: A double-blind randomized controlled trial. *Psychopharmacology*, 172(4), 400–408.

de Girolomo, G. (1996). WHO studies in schizophrenia: An overview of the results and their implications for the understanding of the disorder. In P. Breggin & E. Stern (Eds.), *Psychosocial approaches to deeply disturbed persons* (pp. 213–231). New York, NY: Haworth Press.

de Montigny, C., Chaput, Y., & Blier, P. (1990). Modification of serotonergic neuron properties by long-term treatment with serotonin reuptake blockers. *The Journal of Clinical Psychiatry*, 51(Suppl. B), 4–8.

Deniker, P. (1970). Introduction of neuroleptic chemotherapy into psychiatry. In F. Ayde & B. Blackwell (Eds.), *Discoveries in biological psychiatry* (pp. 155–164). Philadelphia, PA: Lippincott.

Dorph-Petersen, K. A., Pierri, J. N., Perel, J. M., Sun, Z., Sampson, A. R., & Lewis, D. A. (2005). The influence of chronic exposure to antipsychotic medications on brain size before and after tissue fixation: A comparison of haloperidol and olanzapine in macaque monkeys. *Neuropsychopharmacology, 30*(9), 1649–1661.

Drug advertising in the Lancet. (2011). *Lancet, 378*(9785), 2.

Drug facts and comparisons. (2012). St. Louis, MO: Wolters Kluwer Health, Inc.

Dwyer, D. S., Lu, X. H., & Bradley, R. J. (2003). Cytotoxicity of conventional and atypical antipsychotic drugs in relation to glucose metabolism. *Brain Research, 971*(1), 31–39.

Ebert, D., Albert, R., May, A., Merz, A., Murata, H., Stosiek, I., & A (1997). The serotonin syndrome and psychosis-like side-effects of fluvoxamine in clinical use—an estimation of incidence. *European Neuropsychopharmacology, 7*(1), 71–74.

El-Mallakh, R. S., Gao, Y., & Jeannie Roberts, R. (2011). Tardive dysphoria: The role of long term antidepressant use in-inducing chronic depression. *Medical Hypotheses, 76*(6), 769–773.

Emslie, G. J., Heiligenstein, J. H., Wagner, K. D., Hoog, S. L., Ernest, D. E., Brown, E., . . . Jacobson, J. G. (2002). Fluoxetine for acute treatment of depression in children and adolescents: A placebo-controlled randomized clinical trial. *Journal of the American Academy of Child and Adolescent Psychiatry, 41*(10), 1205–1215.

Firestone, P., Musten, L., Pisterman, S., Mercer, J., & Bennett, S. (1998). Short-term side effects of stimulant medication are increased in preschool children with attention-deficit/hyperactivity disorder: a double-blind placebo-controlled study. *Journal of Child and Adolescent Psychopharmacology, 8*(1), 13–25.

Fisher, C. M. (1989). Neurological fragments. II. Remarks on anosognosia, confabulation, memory, and other topics; and an appendix on self-observation. *Neurology, 39*(1), 127–132.

Flashman, L. A., Amador, X., & McAllister, T. W. (2011). Awareness of deficits. In J. M. Silver, T. W. McAllister & S. C. Yudofsky (Eds.), *Textbook of traumatic brain injury* (2nd ed., pp. 307–323). Washington, DC: American Psychiatric Publishing.

Foley, D. L., & Morley, K. I. (2011). Systematic review of early cardio-metabolic outcomes of the first treated episode of psychosis. *Archives of General Psychiatry, 68*(6), 609–616.

Food and Drug Administration. (1992). New Halcion labeling. *Medical Bulletin, 22*(1), 7.

Food and Drug Administration. (1995). *A MedWatch continuing education article.* Rockville, MD: Staff College, Center for Drug Evaluation and Research, Food and Drug Administration.

Food and Drug Administration. (2004). *Determination that Serzone (nefazodone hydrochloride) was not withdrawn from sale for reasons of safety or effectiveness.* Rockville, MD: Author. Retrieved from http://www.federal register.gov/articles/2004/10/26/04-23857/determination-that-serzone-nefazodone-hydrochloride-was-not-withdrawn-from-sale-for-reasons-of

Food and Drug Administration. (2005). *Information for healthcare professionals: Pemoline tablets and chewable tablets (marketed as Cylert).* Rockville, MD: Author. Retrieved from http://www.fda.gov/Drugs/DrugSafety/PostmarketDrugSafetyInformationforPatientsandProviders/ucm126461

Food and Drug Administration. (2009). *Suicidal behavior and ideation and antiepileptic drugs.* Rockville, MD: Author. Retrieved from http://www.fda.gov/Drugs/DrugSafety/PostmarketDrugSafetyInformation forPatientsandProviders/ucm100190.htm

Freeman, M. P., Mischoulon, D., Tedeschini, E., Goodness, T., Cohen, L. S., Fava, M., & Papakostas, G. I. (2010). Complementary and alternative medicine for major depressive disorder: A meta-analysis of patient characteristics, placebo-response rates, and treatment outcomes relative to standard antidepressants. *The Journal of Clinical Psychiatry, 71*(6), 682–688.

Gallanter, M., & Kleber, H. D. (Eds.). (2008). *The American Psychiatric Publishing textbook of substance abuse treatment* (4th ed.). Washington, DC: American Psychiatric Publishing.

Gardiner, H. (2009, March 10). Doctor's pain studies were fabricated, hospital says. *The New York Times.* Retrieved from http://www.nytimes .com/2009/03/11/health/research/11pain.html?pagewanted=print

Gentile, S. (2010). On categorizing gestational, birth, and neonatal complications following late pregnancy exposure to antidepressants: The prenatal antidepressant exposure syndrome. *CNS Spectrums, 15*(3), 167–185.

Ghaemi, S. N., Ostacher, M. M., EI-Mallakh, R. S., Borrelli, D., Baldassano, C. F., Kelley, M. E., . . . Baldessarini, R. J. (2010) Antidepressant discontinuation in bipolar depression: A systematic treatment enhancement program for bipolar disorder (STEP-BD) randomized clinical trial of long-term effectiveness and safety. *The Journal of Clinical Psychiatry, 71*(4), 372–380.

Giedd, J. N., Castellanos, F. X., Casey, B. J., Kozuch, P., King, A. C., Hamburger, S. D., & Rapoport, J. (1994). Quantitative morphology of the corpus callosum in attention deficit hyperactivity disorder. *The American Journal of Psychiatry, 151(5)*, 665–669.

Gilbert, A. R., Moore, G. J., Keshavan, M. S., Paulson, L. A., Narula, V., Mac Master, F. P., . . . Rosenberg, D. R. (2000). Decreased thalamic volumes of pediatric patients with obsessive-compulsive disorder who are taking paroxetine. *Archives of General Psychiatry, 57(5)*, 449–456.

Gill, S. S., Bronskill, S. E., Normand, S. L., Anderson, G. M., Sykora, K., Lam, K., . . . Rochon, P. (2007). Antipsychotic drug use and mortality in older adults with dementia. *Annals of Internal Medicine, 146(11)*, 775–786.

Gitlin, M. J., Swendsen, J., Heller, T. L., & Hammen, C. (1995). Relapse and impairment in bipolar disorder. *The American Journal of Psychiatry, 152(11)*, 1635–1640.

GlaxoSmithKline. (2006, May). Important prescribing information. (Dear Healthcare Professional letter). [About clinical worsening and suicide in adults taking Paxil]. Philadelphia, PA: Author.

Glazer, W. M., Morgenstern, H., & Doucette, J. T. (1993). Predicting the long term risk of tardive dyskinesia in outpatients maintained on neuroleptic medications. *The Journal of Clinical Psychiatry, 54(4)*, 133–139.

Goeb, J. L., Marco, S., Duhamel, A., Kechid, G., Bordet, R., Thomas, P., . . . Jardri, R. (2010). [Metabolic side effects of risperidone in early onset schizophrenia]. *Encephale, 36(3)*, 242–252.

Goldberg, E. (1985). Akinesia, tardive dysmentia, and frontal lobe disorder in schizophrenia. *Schizophrenia Bulletin, 11(2)*, 255–263.

Goldberg, J. F., & Truman, C. J. (2003). Antidepressant-induced mania: An overview of current controversies. *Bipolar Disorder, 5(6)*, 407–420.

Goodnough, A. (2011, September 14). Abuse of Xanax leads a clinic to halt supply. *The New York Times*. Retrieved from http://www.nytimes.com/2011/09/14/us/in-louisville-a-centers-doctors-cut-off-xanax-prescriptions.html?_r=1&hpw

Goodwin, F. K., & Jamison, K. R. (1990). *Manic-depressive illness*. New York, NY: Oxford University Press.

Grant, I., Adams, K. M., Carlin, A. S., Rennick, P. M., Lewis, J. L., & Schooff, K. (1978). The collaborative neuropsychological study of polydrug users. *Archives of General Psychiatry, 35*, 1063–1074.

Grant, P. M., Huh, G. A., Perivoliotis, D., Stolar, N. M., & Beck, A. T. (2012). Randomized trial to evaluate the efficacy of cognitive therapy for low-functioning patients with schizophrenia. *Archives of General Psychiatry, 69*(2), 121–127. doi:10.1001/archgenpsychiatry.2011.129

Grauso-Eby, N. L., Goldfarb, O., Feldman-Winter, L. B., & McAbee, G. N. (2003). Acute pancreatitis in children from valproic acid: Case series and review. *Pediatric Neurology, 28*(2), 145–148.

Grignon, S., & Bruguerolle, B. (1996). Cerebellar lithium toxicity: A review of recent literature and tentative pathophysiology. *Thérapie, 51*(2), 101–106.

Gualtieri, C. T., & Barnhill, L. J. (1988). Tardive dyskinesia in special populations. In M. E. Wolf & A. D. Mosnaim (Eds.), *Tardive dyskinesia: Biological mechanisms and clinical aspects* (pp. 137–154). Washington, DC: American Psychiatric Press.

Haddad, P., Anderson, I., & Rosenbaum, J. (2004). Antidepressant discontinuation syndromes. In P. Haddad, S. Dursun & B. Deakin (Eds.), *Adverse syndromes and psychiatric drugs: A clinical guide* (pp. 183–206). Oxford, England: Oxford University Press.

Hales, R. H., Yudofsky, S. C., & Gabbard, G. O. (Eds.). (2008). *The American Psychiatric Publishing textbook of Psychiatry* (5th ed.). Washington, DC: American Psychiatric Publishing.

Halpern, R. (2011, October). Radio interview on pain management. The Dr. Peter Breggin Hour on the Progressive Radio Network. Retrieved from http://www.progressiveradionetwork.com/the-dr-peter-breggin-hour

Hamer, M., David Batty, G., Seldenrijk, A., & Kivimaki, M. (2011). Antidepressant medication use and future risk of cardiovascular disease: The Scottish Health Survey. *European Heart Journal, 32*(4), 437–442. doi:10.1093/eurheartj/ehq438

Hammad, T., Laughren, T., & Racoosin, J. (2006). Suicidality in pediatric patients treated with antidepressant drugs. *Archives of General Psychiatry, 63*(3), 332–339.

Harrow, M., & Jobe, T. H. (2007). Factors involved in outcome and recovery in schizophrenia patients not on antipsychotic medications: A 15-year multifollow-up study. *The Journal of Nervous and Mental Disease, 195*(5), 406–414.

Heinrichs, R. (2011, September 16). *Her majesty the queen and C.J.P (Citation#2011 MBPC 62)*. Winnipeg, Manitoba. Retrieved from http://breggin.com/index.php?option=com_content&task=view&id=295

Henry, C., Sorbara, F., Lacoste, J., Gindre, C., & Leboyer, M. (2001). Antidepressant-induced mania in bipolar patients: Identification of risk factors. *The Journal of Clinical Psychiatry, 62*(4), 249–255.

Ho, B. C., Andreasen, N. C., Ziebell, S., Pierson, R., & Magnotta, V. (2011). Long-term antipsychotic treatment and brain volumes: A longitudinal study of first-episode schizophrenia. *Archives of General Psychiatry, 68*(2), 128–137. doi:10.1001/archgenpsychiatry.2010.199

Hoehn-Saric, R., Lipsey, J. R., & McLeod, D. R. (1990). Apathy and indifference in patients on fluvoxamine and fluoxetine. *Journal of Clinical Psychopharmacology, 10*(5), 343–345.

Hosenbocus, S., & Chahal, R. (2011). SSRIs and SNRIs: A review of the discontinuation syndrome in children and adolescents. *Journal of the Canadian Academy of Child and Adolescent Psychiatry,* 20(1), 60–67.

Howland, R. H. (1996). Induction of mania with serotonin reuptake inhibitors. *Journal of Clinical Psychopharmacology, 16*(6), 425–427.

Howland, R. H. (2010a). Potential adverse effects of discontinuing psychotropic drugs. *Journal of Psychosocial Nursing and Mental Health Services, 48*(9), 11–14.

Howland, R. H. (2010b). Potential adverse effects of discontinuing psychotropic drugs. Part 1: Adrenergic, cholinergic, and histamine drugs. *Journal of Psychosocial Nursing and Mental Health Services, 48*(6), 11–14.

Howland, R. H. (2010c). Potential adverse effects of discontinuing psychotropic drugs. Part 2: Antidepressant drugs. *Journal of Psychosocial Nursing and Mental Health Services,* 48(7), 9–12.

Howland, R. H. (2010d). Potential adverse effects of discontinuing psychotropic drugs. Part 3: Antipsychotic, dopaminergic, and mood-stabilizing drugs. *Journal of Psychosocial Nursing and Mental Health Services, 48*(8), 11–14.

Hyman, S. E., Arana, G. W., & Rosenbaum, J. F. (1995). *Handbook of psychiatric drug therapy* (3rd ed.). New York, NY: Little Brown.

IMS Health Incorporated. (2011a). *Top-line market data.* Retrieved from IMS Health Incorporated website: http://www.imshealth.com/portal/site/ims/menuitem.5ad1c081663fdf9b41d84b903208c22a/?vgnextoid=fbc65890d33ee210VgnVCM10000071812ca2RCRD&vgnextfmt=default

IMS Health Incorporated. (2011b). *Top therapeutic classes by prescriptions.* Retrieved from IMS Health Incorporated website: http://www.imshealth.com/deployedfiles/ims/Global/Content/Corporate/Press%20Room/Top-line%20Market%20Data/2010%20Top-line%20Market%20Data/2010_Top_Therapeutic_Classes_by_RX.pdf

IMS Health Incorporated. (2011c). *Top 20 U.S. Pharmaceutical products by dispensed prescriptions*. Retrieved from IMS Health Incorporated website: http://www.imshealth.com/deployedfiles/ims/Global/Content/Corporate/ Press%20Room/Top-line%20Market%20Data/2010%20Top-line%20 Market%20Data/2010_Top_Products_by_RX.pdfIMS

International Center for the Study of Psychiatry and Psychology. (ICSPP) (Eds.). (2009). *The conscience of Psychiatry: The reform work of Peter R. Breggin, MD*. Ithaca, NY: Lake Edge Press.

Institute for Safe Medication Practices. (2011). *QuarterWatch: 2010 (Quarter 3). New signals for liraglutide, quetiapine and varenicline*. Retrieved from http:// www.ismp.org/QuarterWatch/default.asp

Inuwa, I., Horobin, R., & Williams, A. (1994). A TEM study of white blood cells from patients under neuroleptic therapy. ICEM 13 Paris [International Congress of Electron Microscopy], (pp. 1091–1092).

Ioannidis, J. P. (2011). Excess significance bias in the literature on brain volume abnormalities. *Archives of General Psychiatry*, *68*(8), 773–780.

Iyer, S., Naganathan,V., McLachlan, A. J., & Le Couteur, D. G. (2008). Medication withdrawal trials in people aged 65 years and older: A systematic review. *Drugs & Aging*, *25*(12), 1021–1031.

Joint Commission on Mental Illness and Mental Health. (1961). *Action for mental health: Final report*. New York, NY: Basic Books.

Joukamaa, M., Heliövaara, M., Knekt, P., Aromaa, A., Raitasalo, R., & Lehtinen, V. (2006). Schizophrenia, neuroleptic medication and mortality. *The British Journal of Psychiatry*, *188*, 122–127.

Juurlink, D. N., Mamdani, M. M., Kopp, A., & Redelmeier, D. A. (2006). The risk of suicide with selective serotonin reuptake inhibitors in the elderly. *The American Journal of Psychiatry*, *163*(5), 813–821.

Karon, B. P. (2005). Recurrent psychotic depression is treatable by psychoanalytic therapy without medication. *Ethical Human Psychology and Psychiatry*, *7*, 45–56.

Keitner, G. I. (2005, October 1). Family therapy in the treatment of depression. *The Psychiatric Times*, *27*(11), 40–42. Retrieved from http://www .psychiatrictimes.com/print/article/10168/52636?printable=true

Kennedy, D. L., & McGinnis, T. (1993). Monitoring adverse drug reactions: The FDA's new MedWatch program. Rockville, MD: U. S. Food and Drug Administration.

Kessler, D. A. (1993). Introducing MEDWatch. A new approach to reporting medication and device adverse effects and product problems. *The Journal of the American Medical Association*, *269*(21), 2765–2768.

Kilbourne, A. M., Ignacio, R. V., Kim, H. M., & Blow, F. C. (2009). Datapoint: Are VA patients with serious mental illness dying younger? *Psychiatric Sevices, 60*(5), 589.

Kim, H. S., Yumkham, S., Choi, J. H., Kim, E. K., Kim, Y. S., Ryu, S. H., & Suh, P. G. (2006). Haloperidol induces calcium ion influx via L-type calcium channels in hippocampal HN33 cells and renders the neurons more susceptible to oxidative stress. *Molecules and Cells, 22*(1), 51–57.

King, R. A., Riddle, M. A., Chappell, P. B., Hardin, M. T., Anderson, G. M., Lombroso, P., & Scahill, L. (1991). Emergence of self-destructive phenomena in children and adolescents during fluoxetine treatment. *Journal of the American Academy of Child and Adolescent Psychiatry, 30*(2), 179–186.

Kirsch, I. (2010). *The emperor's new drugs: Exploding the antidepressant myth*. New York, NY: Basic Books.

Kirsch, I., Deacon, B. J., Huedo-Median, T. B., Scoboria, A., Moore, T. J., & Johnson, B. T. (2008). Initial severity and antidepressant benefits: A meta-analysis of data submitted to the Food and Drug Administration. *PLoS Medicine, 5*(2), e45.

Kirsch, I., Moore, T. J., Scoboria, A., & Nicholls, S. (2002). The emperor's new drugs: An analysis of antidepressant medication data submitted to the U.S. Food and Drug Administration. *Preventive & Treatment, 5*(23). Retrieved from http://www.journals.apa.org/prevention/volume5/pre0050023a.html

Konopaske, G. T., Dorph-Petersen, K. A., Pierri, J. N., Wu, Q., Sampson, A. R., & Lewis, D. A. (2007). Effect of chronic exposure to antipsychotic medication on cell numbers in the parietal cortex of macaque monkeys. *Neuropsychopharmacology, 32*(6), 1216–1223

Konopaske, G. T., Dorph-Petersen, K. A., Sweet, R. A., Pierri, J. N., Zhang, W., Sampson, A. R., & Lewis, D. A. (2008). Effect of chronic psychotic exposure to astrocyte and oligodendrocytic numbers in macaque monkeys. *Biological Psychiatry, 63*(8), 759–765.

Kripke, D., Langer, R., & Kline, L. (2012). Hypnotics' association with mortality or cancer: a matched cohort study. *British Medical Journal Open, 2*(1). doi:10.1136/bmjopen-2012-000850

Krystal, J. H., Rosenheck, R. A., Cramer, J. A., Vessicchio, J. C., Jones, K. M., Vertrees, J. E., . . . Stock, C.; for Veterans Affairs Cooperative Study No. 504 Group. (2011). Adjunctive risperidone treatment for antidepressant-resistant symptoms of chronic military service-related PTSD: A randomized trial. *The Journal of the American Medical Association, 306*(5), 493–502.

Kwon, P., & Lefkowitz, W. (2008a). Neonatal extrapyramidal movements. Neonatal withdrawal due to maternal citalopram and ondasentron use. *Pediatric Annals, 37*(3), 128–130.

Kwon, P., & Lefkowitz, W. (2008b). Poor neonatal adaptation in term infant. Fluoxetine toxicity. *Pediatric Annals, 37*(3), 131–133.

Lacasse, J. R., & Leo, J. (2011). Serotonin and depression: A disconnect between the advertisements and the scientific literature. *PLoS Medicine, 2*(12), e392.

Lagace, D. C., & Eisch, A. J. (2005). Mood-stabilizing drugs: Are their neuroprotective aspects clinically relevant? *The Psychiatric Clinics of North America, 28*(2), 399–414.

Lagnaoui, R., Bégard, B., Moore, N., Chaslerie, A., Fourrier, A., Letenneur, L., . . . Moride, Y. (2002). Benzodiazepine use and risk of dementia: A nested case-control study. *Journal of Clinical Epidemiology, 55*(3), 314–318.

Lambert, N. (2005). The contribution of childhood ADHD, conduct problems, and stimulant treatment to adolescent and adult tobacco and psychoactive substance abuse. *Ethical Human Psychology and Psychiatry, 7*, 197–221.

Lattimore, K. A., Donn, S. M., Kaciroti, N., Kemper, A. R., Neal, C. R., Jr., & Vazquez, D. M. (2005). Selective serotonin reuptake inhibitor (SSRI) use during pregnancy and effects on the fetus and newborn: A meta-analysis. *Journal of Perinatology, 25*(9), 595–604.

Latuda. (2010, November). Complete prescribing information. Retrieved from http://www.latuda.com/LatudaPrescribingInformation.pdf

Leber, P. (1992). Postmarketing surveillance of adverse drug effects. In J. Lieberman & J. Kane (Eds.), *Adverse effects of psychotropic drugs* (pp. 3–12). New York, NY: Guilford.

Leff, J., & Berkowitz, R. (2006). Working with families of schizophrenic patients. In P. Breggin & E. Stern (Eds.), *Psychosocial approaches to deeply disturbed persons* (pp. 185–211). New York, NY: Haworth Press.

Lehtinen, V., Aaltonen, J., Koffert, T., Räkköläinen, V., & Syvälahti, E. (2000). Two-year outcome in first-episode psychosis treated according to an integrated model: Is immediate neuroleptisation always needed? *European Psychiatry, 15*(5), 312–320.

Levin, A. (2011, May 8). Brain volume shrinkage parallels rise in antipsychotic dosage. *Psychiatric News*, p. 1.

Lieberman, J. A., & Stroup, T. S. (2011). The NIMH-CATIE schizophrenia study: What did we learn? *The American Journal of Psychiatry, 168*(8), 770–775.

Lieberman, J. A., Stroup, T. S., McEvoy, J. P., Swartz, M. S., Rosenheck, R. A., Perkins, D. O., . . . Hsiao, J.; for the Clinical Antipsychotic Trials of Intervention Effectiveness (CATIE) Investigators. (2005). Effectiveness of antipsychotic drugs in patients with chronic schizophrenia. *The New England Journal of Medicine, 353*(12), 1209–1223.

Littrell, J., & Lyons, P. (2010a). Pediatric bipolar disorder: An issue for child welfare. *Children and Youth Services Review, 32*(7), 965–973. doi:10.1016/j.childyouth.2010.03.021

Littrell, J., & Lyons, P. (2010b). Pediatric bipolar disorder: Part I—Is it related to classical bipolar. *Children and Youth Services Review, 32*(7), 945–964. doi:10.1016/j.childyouth.2010.03.020

Ljung, R., Björkenstam, C., & Björkenstam, E. (2008). Ethnic differences in antidepressant treatment preceding suicide in Sweden. *Psychiatric Services, 59*(1), 116–117.

Loring, D. W. (2005, September 1). Cognitive side effects of antiepileptic drugs in children. *Psychiatric Times, 22*(10), 1–10. Retrieved from http://www.psychiatrictimes.com

Lucire, Y., & Crotty, C. (2011). Antidepressant-induced akathisia-related homicides associated with diminishing mutations in metabolizing genes of the CYP450 family. *Pharmacogenomics and Personalized Medicine, 4*, 65–81.

Malberg, J. E., Eisch, A. J., Nestler, E. J., & Duman, R. S. (2000). Chronic antidepressant treatment increases neurogenesis in adult rat hippocampus. *The Journal of Neuroscience, 20*(24), 9104–9110.

Marks, D., Breggin, P., & Braslow, D. (2008). Homicidal ideation causally related to therapeutic medications. *Ethical Human Psychology and Psychiatry, 10*, 134–145.

Marks, I. M., De Albuquerque, A., Cottraux, J., Gentil, V., Griest, J., Hand, I., . . . Tyrer, P. (1989). The "efficacy" of alprazolam in panic disorder and agoraphobia: A critique of recent reports. *Archives of General Psychiatry, 46*(7), 668–672.

Mastronardi, C., Paz-Filho, G., Valdez, E., Maestre-Mesa, J., Licinio, J., & Wong, M. L. (2011). Long-term body weight outcomes of antidepressant-environment interactions. *Molecular Psychiatry, 16*(3), 265–272.

Matheson Commission. (1939). *Epidemic encephalitis. Etiology, epidemiology, treatment. Third report of the Matheson Commission.* New York, NY: Columbia University Press.

Mathew, R. J., & Wilson, W. H. (1991). Evaluation of effects of diazepam and an experimental anti-anxiety drug on regional cerebral blood flow. *Psychiatric Research, 40*(2), 125–134.

Mayes, S. D., Crites, D. L., Bixler, E. O., Humphrey, F. J., II, & Mattison, R. E. (1994). Methylphenidate and ADHD: Influence of age, IQ and neurodevelopmental status. *Developmental Medicine and Child Neurology, 36*(12), 1009–1007.

McCall, M., & Bourgeois, J. A. (2004). Valproic acid-induced hyperammonemia: A case report. *Journal of Clinical Psychopharmacology, 24*(5), 521–526.

McClelland, R. J., Fenton, G.W., & Rutherford, W. (1994). The postconcussional syndrome revisited. *Journal of the Royal Society of Medicine, 87*(9), 508–510.

McCready, K. (1995, Summer). What heals human beings? Technology or humanity—There's a choice! [Report from the Center for the Study of Psychiatry and Psychology]. *Rights Tenet: Newsletter of the National Association for Rights Protection and Advocacy (NARPA)*, p. 3.

McCready, K. (2002). Creating an empathic environment at the San Joaquin Psychotherapy Center. In P. Breggin, G. Breggin & F. Bemak (Eds.), *Dimensions of empathic therapy* (pp. 67–78). New York, NY: Springer Publishing.

McIntyre, M. (2011, September 17). Judge agrees Prozac made teen a killer. *Winnipeg Free Press*, p. 1.

Medco. (2011). *America's state of mind. Medico health solutions.* Retrieved from http://medco.mediaroom.com/

Meeks, T. (2010). Drugs, death and disconcerting dilemmas: An overview of antipsychotic use in older patients. *Psychiatric Times, 27*(2), 17–22.

Mejia, N. I., & Jankovic J. (2005). Metoclopramide-induced tardive dyskinesia in an infant. *Movement Disorders, 20*(1), 86–89.

Mejia, N. I., & Jankovic, J. (2010). Tardive dyskinesia and withdrawal emergent syndrome in children. *Expert Review of. Neurotherapeutics, 10*(6), 893–901.

Metadate CD. (2011). *The physicians' desk reference* (pp. 3260–3264). Montvale, NJ: PDR Network.

Miller, R. (2009). Mechanisms of action of antipsychotic drugs of different classes, refractoriness to therapeutic effects of classical neuroleptics, and individual variation in sensitivity to their actions: Part II. *Current Neuropharmacology, 7*(4), 315–330.

Minessota Community Measurement. (2010). *Health care quality report.* Retrieved from http://mncm.org/site/upload/files/2010_Disparities_Report_FINAL.pdf

Moncrieff, J. (2006). Why is it so difficult to stop psychiatric treatment? It may be nothing to do with the original problem. *Medical Hypotheses, 67*(3), 517–523.

Moncrieff, J. (2007a). *The myth of the chemical cure: A critique of psychiatric drug treatment.* Hampshire, UK: Palgrave Macmillan.

Moncrieff, J. (2007b). Understanding psychotropic drug action: The contribution of the brain-disabling theory. *Ethical Human Psychology and Psychiatry, 9,* 170–179.

Moore, T. J., Furberg, C. D., Glenmullen, J., Maltsberger, J. T., & Singh, S. (2011). Suicidal behavior and depression in smoking cessation treatments. *PLoS ONE, 6*(11), e27016. doi:10.1371/journal.pone.0027016

Moore T. J., Glenmullen J., & Furberg, C. D. (2010). Prescription drugs associated with reports of violence towards others. *PLoS ONE, 5*(12), e15337. doi:10.1371/journal.pone.0015337

Moreno, C., Laje, G., Blanco, C., Jiang, H., Schmidt, A. B., & Olfson, M. (2007). National trends in the outpatient diagnosis and treatment of bipolar disorder in youth. *Archives of General Psychiatry, 64*(9), 1032–1039.

Morishita, S., & Arita, S. (2003). Induction of mania in depression by paroxetine. *Human Psychopharmacology, 18*(7), 565–568.

Mosher, L. R. (1996). Soteria: A therapeutic community for psychotic persons. In P. R. Breggin & E. M. Stern (Eds.), *Psychosocial approaches to deeply disturbed persons* (pp. 43–58). New York, NY: Haworth Press.

Mosher, L., & Bola, J. (2004). Soteria-California and its American successors: Therapeutic ingredients. *Ethical Human Psychology and Psychiatry, 6,* 7–23.

Mosher, L., & Burti, L. (1989). *Community mental health: Principles and practice.* New York, NY: W. W. Norton & Company.

Myslobodsky, M. S. (1986). Anosognosia in tardive dyskinesia: "Tardive dysmentia" or "tardive dementia"? *Schizophrenia Bulletin, 12*(1), 1–6.

Myslobodsky, M. S. (1993). Central determinants of attention and mood disorder in tardive dyskinesia ("tardive dysmentia"). *Brain and Cognition, 23*(1), 88–101.

Naik, G. (2011, August 10). Mistakes in scientific studies surge. *Wall Street Journal, Health,* p. 1.

Nasrallah, H. A. (2007). The roles of efficacy, safety, and tolerability in antipsychotic effectiveness: Practical implications of the CATIE schizophrenia trial. *The Journal of Clinical Psychiatry, 68* (Suppl. 1), 5–11.

Navari, S., & Dazzan, P. (2009). Do antipsychotic drugs affect brain structure? A systematic and critical review of MRI findings. *Psychological Medicine, 39*(11), 1763–1777.

Newman, T. B. (2004). A black-box warning for antidepressants in children? *The New England Journal of Medicine, 351*(16), 1595–1598.

Nurse's drug handbook. (2012). Montvale, NJ: PDR Network.

Parks, J., Svendsen, D., Singer, P., & Foti, M. E. (Eds.). (2006). *Morbidity and mortality in people with serious mental illness.* Alexandria, VA: National Association of State Mental Health Program Directors Medical Directors Council.

PAXIL®. (2011). *Tablets and oral suspension. Prescribing information.* Retrieved from http://us.gsk.com/products/assets/us_paxil.pdf.

Perlis, R. H., Ostacher, M. J., Patel, J. K., Marangell, L. B., Zhang, H., Wisniewski, S., . . . Thase, M. E. (2006). Predictors of recurrence in bipolar disorder: Primary outcomes from the Systematic Treatment Enhancement Program for Bipolar Disorder (STEP-BD). *American Journal of Psychiatry, 163*(2), 217–224.

Physicians' desk reference. (2011). Montvale, NJ: PDR Network.

Pies, R. (2011, July 11). Psychiatry's new brain-mind and the legend of the "chemical imbalance." *Psychiatric Times.* Retrieved http://www.search-medica.com/resource.html?rurl=http%3A%2F%2Fwww.psychiatrictimes.com%2Fblog%2Fcouchincrisis%2Fcontent%2Farticle%2F10168%2F1902106%3F_EXT_4_comsort%3Dnf&q=Pies&c=ps&ss=psychTimesLink&p=Convera&fr=true&ds=0&srid=5

Pigott, H. (2011). STAR*D: A tale and trail of bias. *Ethical Human Psychology and Psychiatry, 13*(1), 6–28.

Pigott, H. E., Leventhal, A. M., Alter, G. S., & Boren, J. J. (2011). Efficacy and effectiveness of antidepressants: Current status of research. *Psychotherapy and Psychosomatics, 79*(5), 267–279.

Pittman, G. (2010). ADHD drugs have no long-term effects: Study. Retrieved from A.D.D. Resource Center website: http://www.addrc.org/adhd-drugs-have-no-long-term-growth-effects-study/

Pratt, L., Brody D., & Gee, Q. (2011, October). Antidepressant use in persons aged 12 and over: United States, 2005–2008. *NCHS Data Brief, 76,* 1–8

Prien, R. F., Levine, J., & Switalski, R. W. (1971). Discontinuation of chemotherapy for chronic schizophrenia. *Hospital & Community Psychiatry, 22*(1), 4–7.

Proal, E., Reiss, P., Klein, R. G., Mannuzza, S., Gotimer, K., Ramos-Olazagasti, M. A., . . . Castellanos, F. X. (2011). Brain gray matter deficits at 33-year follow-up in adults with attention-deficit/hyperactivity disorder established in childhood. *Archives of General Psychiatry, 68*(11), 1122–1134.

Rapoport, J. L., Buchsbaum, M. S., Zahn, T. P., Weingartner, H., Ludlow, C., & Mikkelsen, E. J. (1978). Dextroamphetamine. Its cognitive and behavior effects in normal prepubertal boys. *Science, 199*(4328), 560–563.

Rappaport, M., Hopkins, H. K., Hall, K., Belleza, T., & Silverman, J. (1978). Are there schizophrenics for whom drugs may be unnecessary or contra-indicated? *International Pharmacopsychiatry, 13*(2), 100–111.

Read, M. (2002). Long acting neuroleptic drugs. In D. Heard (Ed.), *Zoological restraint and anesthesia*. Ithaca, NY: International Veterinary Information Service. Retrieved from http://www.ivis.org/special_books/Heard/read/IVIS.pdf

Reinblatt, S. P., & Riddle, M. A. (2006). Selective serotonin reuptake inhibitor-induced apathy: A pediatric case series. *Journal of Child and Adolescent Psychopharmacology, 16*(1–2), 227–233.

Riddle, M., King, R., Hardin, M., Scahill, L., Ort, S., Chappell, P., . . . Leckman, J. (1991). Behavioral side effects of fluoxetine in children and adolescents. *Journal of Child and Adolescent Psychopharmacology, 3*, 193–198.

Rosebush, P. I., & Mazurek, M. F. (1999). Neurologic side effects in neuroleptic-naive patients treated with haloperidol or risperidone. *Neurology, 52*(4), 782–785.

Sackeim, H. A., Prudic, J., Fuller, R., Keilp, J., Lavori, P. W., & Olfson, M. (2007). The cognitive effects of electroconvulsive therapy in community settings. *Neuropsychopharmacology, 32*(1), 244–254.

Sannerud, C., & Feussner, J. (2000). Is Ritalin an abused drug? Does it meet the criteria for a Schedule II substance? In L. Greenhill & B. Osman (Eds.), *Ritalin theory and practice* (pp. 24–42). New York, NY: Mary Ann Liebert Publishers.

Sansone, R. A., & Sansone, L. A. (2010). SSRI-induced indifference. *Psychiatry (Edgemont), 7*(10), 14–18.

Sarchet, P. (2011). Harvard scientists disciplined for not declaring ties to drug companies. Retrieved from Nature News Blog, Nature.Com website: http://blogs.nature.com/news/2011/07/Harvard_scientists_disciplined.Html

Scheper-Hughes, N. (1978). Dilemas in deinstitutionalization: A view from inner city Boston. *Journal of Operational Psychiatry, 12*, 90–99.

Schildkrout, B. (2011). *Unmasking psychological symptoms: How therapists can learn to recognize the psychological presentation of medical disorders*. Hoboken, NJ: Wiley.

Schmauss, C., & Krieg, J. C. (1987). Enlargement of cerebral fluid spaces in long-term benzodiazepine abusers. *Psychological Medicine, 17*(4), 869–873.

Schooler, N. R., Goldberg, S. C., Boothe, H., & Cole, J. O. (1967). One year after discharge: Community adjustments of schizophrenic patients. *The American Journal of Psychiatry, 123*(8), 986–995.

Science Daily. (2006). *Simple lifestyle changes may improve cognitive function and brain efficiency.* Retrieved from http://www/sciencedaily.com/releases/2006/05/060522150621.htm

Science Daily. (2011a). *Patients who use anti-depressants are more likely to suffer relapse, researcher finds.* Retrieved from http://www.sciencedaily.com/releases/2011/07/.110719121354.htm

Science Daily. (2011b). *Tricyclic anti-depressant medication use liked to increased risk of heart disease.* Retrieved from http://www.science daily.com/releases/2010/11/101130230850.htm

Scull, A. (1977). *Decarceration: Community treatment and the deviant: A radical view.* Englewood Cliffs, NJ: Prentice Hall.

Sears, M. (2010). *Humanizing health care: Creating cultures of compassion with nonviolent communication.* Encinitas, CA: PuddleDancer Press.

Seikkula, J. (2006). Five year experience of first-episode nonaffective psychosis in open-dialogue approach. *Journal of Psychotherapy Research, 16,* 214–228.

Seikkula, J., Alakare, B., Aaltonen, J., Holma, J., Rasinkangas, A., & Lehtinen, V. (2003). Open dialogue approach: Treatment principles and preliminary results of a two-year follow-up of first episode schizophrenia. *Ethical Human Sciences and Services, 5*(3), 163–182.

Sherrod, R. A., Collins, A., Wynn, S., & Gragg, M. (2010). Dissection dementia, depression and drug effects in older patients. *Journal of Psychosocial Nursing and Mental Health Services, 48*(1), 39–47.

Shipko, S. (2002). Serotonin reuptake inhibitor withdrawal: Out of the frying pan and into the fire. *Ethical Human Sciences and Services, 4,* 83–91.

Shulman, K. I., Sykora, K., Gill, S., Mamdani, M., Bronskill, S., Wodchis, W., . . . Rochon, P. (2005). Incidence of delirium in older adults newly prescribed lithium or valproate: A population-based cohort study. *The Journal of Clinical Psychiatry, 66*(4), 424–427.

Silver, J., Yudofsky, S., & Hurowitz, G. (1994). Psychopharmacology and electroconvulsive therapy. In R. Hales, S. Yudofsky & J. Talbott (Eds.), *The American Psychiatric Press handbook of psychiatry* (2nd ed.). Washington, DC: American Psychiatric Press.

Sinclair, L. (2011, October 21). Stimulant use for ADHD continues to rise among teens. *Psychiatric News*, p. 1(continued on 25).

Singh, S., Loke, Y. K., Spangler, J. G., & Furberg, C. D. (2011). Risk of serious adverse cardiovascular events associated with varenicline: A systematic review and meta-analysis. *Canadian Medical Association Journal*, *183*(12), 1359–1366. doi:10.1503/cmaj.110218

Sivertsen, B., Omvik, S., Pallesen, S., Bjorvatn, B., Havic, O. E., Kvale, G., . . . Nordhus, I. H. (2006). Cognitive behavioral therapy vs zopiclone for treatment of primary insomnia in older adults: A randomized controlled trial. *The Journal of the American Medical Association*, *295*(24), 2851–2858.

Small, G. W., Silverman, D. H., Siddarth, P., Ercoli, L. M., Miller, K. J., Lavretsky, H., . . . Phelps, M., (2006). Effects of a 14-day healthy longevity lifestyle program on cognition and brain function. *The American Journal of Geriatric Psychiatry*, *14*(6), 538–545.

Smith, J. (2011, August 2). SSRIs may not be safer than tricyclics in elderly. *Clinical Psychiatry News*. Retrieved from http://www.clinicalpsychiatrynews.com

Smith, J. M., Kucharski, L. T., Oswald, W. T., & Waterman, L. J. (1979). A systematic investigation of tardive dyskinesia in patients. *The American Journal of Psychiatry*, *136*(7), 918–922.

Sparhawk, R. (2011). In bipolar disorder beyond 10 weeks of treatment, the term antidepressant is a misnomer. *The Journal of Clinical Psychiatry*, *72*(6), 871.

Splete, H. (2011, September 11). Antipsychotics linked to metabolic syndrome spike in children. *Clinical Psychiatry News*. Retrieved from http://www.clinicalpsychiatrynews.com/single-view/antipsychotics-linked-to-metabolic-syndrome-spike-in-children/934df78c22.html

Spurling, G., Mansfield, P., & Lexchin, J. (2011). Pharmaceutical company advertising in the Lancet. *Lancet*, *378*(9875), 30.

Stern, S., & Lemmens, T. (2011). Legal remedies for medical ghostwriting: Imposing fraud liability on guest authors of ghostwritten articles. *PLoS Medicine*, *8*(8), e1001070. doi: 10.1371/journal.pmed.1001070

Strattera. (2011). *Physician's desk reference*. Montvale, NJ: PDR Network.

Subcommittee on Attention-Deficit/Hyperactivity Disorder; for the Steering Committee on Quality Improvement and Management. (2011). ADHD: Clinical practice guideline for the diagnosis, evaluation, and treatment of attention-deficit/hyperactivity disorder in children and adolescents. *Pediatrics*, *128*(5), 1007–122.

Sundell, K. A., Gissler, M., Petzold, M., & Waern, M. (2011). Antidepressant utilization patterns and mortality in Swedish men and women aged 20–34 years. *European Journal of Clinical Pharmacology, 67*(2), 169–178. doi:10.1007/s00228-010-0933-z

Suppes, T., Baldessarini, R. J., Faedda, G. L., & Tohen, M. (1991). Risk of recurrence following discontinuation of lithium treatment in bipolar disorder. *Archives of General Psychiatry, 48*(12), 1082–1088.

Swanson, J., & Castellanos, F. (1998). *Biological bases of attention deficit hyperactivity disorder: Neuroanatomy, genetics, and pathophysiology. In NIH Consensus Development Conference program and abstracts: Diagnosis and treatment of attention deficit hyperactivity disorder* (pp. 37–42). Rockville, MD: National Institutes of Health.

Swanson, J. M., Elliott, G. R., Greenhill, L. L., Wigal, T., Arnold, L. E., Vitiello, B., . . . Volkow, N. D. (2007a). Effects of stimulant medication on growth rates across 3 years in the MTA follow-up. *Journal of the American Academy of Child and Adolescent Psychiatry, 46*(8), 1015–1027.

Swanson, J. M., Hinshaw, S. P., Arnold, L. E., Gibbons, R. D., Marcus, S., Hur, K., . . . Wigal, T. (2007b). Second evaluation of MTA 36-month outcomes: Propensity score and growth mixture model analyses. *Journal of the American Academy of Child & Adolescent Psychiatry, 46*(8), 1003–1014.

Swartz, M. S., Stroup, T. S., McEvoy J. P., Davis, S. M., Rosenheck, R. A., Keefe, R. S., . . . Lieberman, J. A. (2008). What CATIE found: results from the schizophrenia trial. *Psychiatric Services, 59*(5), 500–506.

Tata, P. R., Rollings, J., Collins, M., Pickering, A., & Jacobson, R. R. (1994). Lack of cognitive recovery following withdrawal from long-term benzodiazepine use. *Psychological Medicine, 24*(1), 203–213.

Teller, D. N., & Denber, H. C. (1970). Mescaline and phenothiazines: Recent studies on subcellular localization and effects upon membranes. In A. Lajtha (Ed.), *Protein metabolism of the nervous system* (pp. 685–698). New York, NY: Plenum Press.

Tetrault, J. M., & O'Connor, P. G. (2009). Management of opioid intoxication and withdrawal. In R. Ries, D. Fiellin, S. Miller & R. Saitz (Eds.), *Principles of addiction medicine* (pp. 589–606). Philadelphia, PA: Lippincott, Williams & Wilkins.

Thase, M. E. (2011). Antidepressant combinations: Widely used, but far from empirically validated. *Canadian Journal of Psychiatry, 56*(6), 317–323.

Tost, H., Braus, D. F., Hakimi, S., Ruf, M., Vollmert, C., Hohn, F., & Meyer-Lindenberg, A. (2010). Acute D2 receptor blockade induces rapid, reversible remodeling in human cortical-striatal circuits. *Nature Neuroscience, 13*(8), 920–922.

Tuke, S. (1996). *Description of the retreat.* London, UK: Process Press. (Originally published 1813).

Turner, E. H., Matthews, A. M., Linadartos, E., Tell, R. A., & Rosenthal, R. (2008). Selective publication of antidepressant trials and its influence on apparent efficacy. *The New England Journal of Medicine, 358*(3), 252–260.

Uhde, T. W., & Kellner, C. H. (1987). Cerebral ventricular size in panic disorder. *Journal of Affective Disorders, 12*(2), 175–178.

Umbarger, C., Dalsimer, J., Morrison, A., & Breggin, P. (1962). *College students in a mental hospital.* New York, NY: Grune & Stratton.

University of Rochester Medical Center. (2011). *Anti-depressants boost brain cells after injury in early studies.* Retrieved from http://www.urmc .rochester.edu/news/story/index.cfm?id=3173

U.S. Department of Health and Human Services (2009, September 2). Justice department announces largest health care fraud settlement in its history. Pfizer to pay $2.3 billion for fraudulent marketing. *HHS News Release.* Retrieved from http://www.hhs.gov/news/press/2009pres/09/20090902a.html

Uzun, S., Kozumplik, O., Jakovljević, M., & Sedić, B. (2010). Side effects of treatment with benzodiazepines. *Psychiatria Danubina, 22*(1), 90–93.

Valenstein, M., Kim, H. M., Ganoczy, D., McCarthy, J. F., Zivin, K., Austin, K. L., . . . Olfson, M. (2009). Higher-risk periods of suicide among VA patients receiving depression treatment: Prioritizing suicide prevention efforts. *Journal of Affective Disorders, 112*(1–3), 50–58.

Van Haren, N. E., Schnack, H. G., Cahn, W., van den Heuvel, M. P., Lepage, C., Collins, L., . . . Kahn, R. S. (2011). Changes in cortical thickness during the course of illness in schizophrenia. *Archives of General Psychiatry, 68*(9), 871–880.

Verbanck, P. (2009). [Drug dependence on benzodiazepines and antidepressants]. *Revue Médicalle de Bruxelles, 30*(4), 372–375.

Verdoux, H., Cougnard, A., Thiébaut, A., & Tournier, M. (2011). Impact of duration of antidepressant treatment on the risk of occurrence of a new sequence of antidepressant treatment. *Pharmacopsychiatry, 44*(3), 96–101.

Verrotti, A., Greco, R., Latini, G., & Chiarelli, F. (2005). Endocrine and metabolic changes in epileptic patients receiving valproic acid. *Journal of Pediatric Endocrinology & Metabolism, 18*(5), 423–430.

Wamsley, J. K., Byerley, W. F., McCabe, R. T., McConnell, E. J., Dawson, T. M., & Grosser, B. I. (1987). Receptor alterations associated with serotonergic agents: An autoradiographic analysis. *The Journal of Clinical Psychiatry, 48*(Suppl.), 19–25.

Wegerer, V., Moll, G. H., Bagli, M., Rothenberger, A., Rüther, E., & Huether, G. (1999). Persistently increased density of serotonin transporters in the frontal cortex of rats treated with fluoxetine during early juvenile life. *Journal of Child and Adolescent Psychopharmacology, 9*(1), 13–24.

Weiden, P. J., Mann, J. J., Haas, G., Mattson, M., & Frances, A. (1987). Clinical nonrecognition of neuroleptic-induced movement disorders: A cautionary study. *The American Journal of Psychiatry, 144*(9), 1148–1153.

Whitaker, R. (2010). *Anatomy of an epidemic: Magic bullets, psychiatric drugs, and the astonishing rise of the mental illness in America.* New York, NY: Crown Publishers.

Whitely, M. (2011*). Speed up & sit still. An informative website.* Retrieved from http://speedupsitstill.com

Whitfield, C. (2010). Psychiatric drugs as agents of trauma. *International Journal of Risk and Safety in Medicine, 22*, 195–207.

Whitfield, C. (2011). *Not crazy: You may not be mentally ill.* Muse House Press/Pennington.

Wide, K., Winbladh, B., & Källén, B. (2004). Major malformations in infants exposed to antiepileptic drugs in utero, with emphasis on carbamazepine and valproic acid: A nation-wide, population-based register study. *Acta Paediatrica, 93*(2), 174–176.

Wilens, T. E., Biederman, J., Kwon, A., Chase, R., Greenberg, L., Mick, E., & Spencer, T. J. (2003). A systematic chart review of the nature of psychiatric adverse events in children and adolescents treated with selective serotonin reuptake inhibitors. *Journal of Child and Adolescent Psychopharmacology, 13*(2), 143–152.

Wittchen, H. U., Jacobi, F., Rehm, J., Gustavsson, A., Svensson, M., Jönsson, B., . . . Steinhausen, H. C. (2011). The size and burden of mental disorders and other disorders of the brain in Europe 2010. *European Neuropsychopharmacology, 21*(9), 655–679.

Wolfe, J. (2011). ADHD diagnoses continue their upward spiral. *Psychiatric News, 46*(20), 17.

Wongpakaran, N., van Reekum, R., Wongpakaran, T., & Clarke, D. (2007). Selective serotonin reuptake inhibitor use associates with apathy among depressed elderly: A case-control study. *Annals of General Psychiatry, 6*, 7. Retrieved from http://www.annals-general-psychiatry.com/contents/6/1/7

Woods, S., Morgenstern, H., Saksa, J., Walsh, B., Sullivan, M., Money, R., Hawkins, K., Gueorguieva, R., & Glazer, W. (2010) Incidence of tardive dyskinesia with atypical versus conventional antipsychotic medications: a prospective cohort study. *Journal of Clinical Psychiatry, 71*, 463–474.

Wu, C. S., Wang, S. C., Chang, I. S., & Lin, K. M. (2009). The association between dementia and long-term use of benzodiazepine in the elderly: Nested case-control study using claims data. *The American Journal of Geriatric Psychiatry, 17*(7), 614–620.

XANAX® XR CIV. (2011). *Complete prescribing information.* Retrieved from http://labeling.pfizer.com/ShowLabeling.aspx?id=543

Yu, X. (2011, July 2). Three professors face sanctions following Harvard Medical School inquiry. *The Harvard Crimson,* p. 1.

Zarrouf, F., & Bhanot, V. (2007). Neuroleptic malignant syndrome: Don't let your guard down yet. *Current Psychiatry, 6*(8), 89–95.

Zhao, Z., Zhang, H. T., Bootzin, E., Millan, M. J., & O'Donnell, J. M. (2009). Association of changes in norepinephrine and serotonin transporter expression with the long-term behavioral effects of antidepressant drugs. *Neuropsychopharmacology, 34*(6), 1467–1481

Zhou, L., Huang, K. X., Kecojevic, A., Welsh, A. M., & Koliatsos, V. E. (2006). Evidence that serotonin reuptake modulators increase the density of serotonin in the forebrain. *Journal of Neurochemistry, 96*(2), 396–406.

Zoler, S. (2011, January). Pediatric admissions doubled in 10 years. *Clinical Psychiatry News,* pp. 1–3.

Appendix: Psychiatric Medications by Category

PART I: ANTIDEPRESSANTS

Selective Serotonin Reuptake Inhibitors (SSRIs)

Celexa (citalopram)
Lexapro (escitalopram)
Luvox (fluvoxamine)
Paxil (paroxetine)
Prozac and Sarafem (fluoxetine)
Zoloft (sertraline)

Other Newer Antidepressants

Cymbalta (duloxetine)
Effexor (venlafaxine)
Pristiq (desvenlafaxine)
Remeron (mirtazapine)
Symbyax (Prozac plus Zyprexa, an antipsychotic drug)
Viibyrd (vilazodone)
Vivalan (viloxazine)
Wellbutrin and Zyban (bupropion)

Older Antidepressants (Partial List)

Anafranil (clomipramine)
Asendin (amoxapine; warning: neuroleptic dopamine blocker)
Desyrel (trazodone)

Elavil (amitriptyline)
Norpramin (desipramine)
Pamelor (nortriptyline)
Parnate (tranylcypromine)
Sinequan (doxepin)
Surmontil (trimipramine)
Tofranil (imipramine)
Vivactil (protriptyline)

PART II: STIMULANTS AND ATTENTION DEFICIT HYPERACTIVITY DRUGS (ADHD)

Addictive, unless otherwise indicated.

Classic Stimulants

Adderall, Adderall XR (amphetamine mixture)
Desoxyn (methamphetamine)
Dexedrine (dextroamphetamine)
Focalin, Focalin XR (dexamethylphenidate)
Ritalin, Metadate, Methylin, Concerta, Daytrana (methylphenidate)
Vyvanse (lisdextroamphetamine)

Others

Cylert (pemoline; no longer available)
Intuniv (guanfacine, long-acting, not addictive)
Nuvigil (armodafinil; not approved for ADHD)
Provigil (modafinil; not approved for ADHD)
Strattera (atomoxetine; not addictive; warning: very stimulating; suicide risk)

PART III: SEDATIVE, HYPNOTIC, AND ANXIOLYTIC DRUGS (TRANQUILIZERS AND SLEEPING AIDS)

Addictive, unless otherwise indicated.

Benzodiazepine Antianxiety Drugs (Tranquilizers)

Ativan (lorazepam)
Klonopin (clonazepam)
Librium (chlordiazepoxide)
Serax (oxazepam)
Tranxene (chlorazepate)
Valium (diazepam)
Xanax (alprazolam)

Other Antianxiety Drugs

Miltown (meprobamate)
BuSpar (buspirone; not addictive)

Benzodiazepine Sleeping Aids

Dalmane (flurazepam)
Doral (quazepam)
Halcion (triazolam)
ProSom (estazolam)
Restoril (temazepam)

Non-Benzodiazepine Sleeping Aids

Ambien (zolpidem)
Intermezzo (zolpidem sublingual tablets),
Lunesta (eszopiclone)
Rozerem (ramelteon; not addictive)
Silenor (doxepin; not addictive, a sedative antidepressant)
Somnote (chloral hydrate)
Sonata (zaleplon)

Barbiturate Sleeping Aids

Butisol (butabarbital)
Carbrital (pentobarbital and carbromal)
Seconal (secobarbital)

PART IV: ANTIPSYCHOTIC DRUGS (NEUROLEPTICS)

Newer (Novel or Atypical) Antipsychotics

Abilify (aripiprazole)
Clozaril (clozapine)
Fanapt (iloperidone)
Geodon (ziprasidone)
Invega (paliperidone)
Latuda (lurasidone)
Risperdal (risperidone)
Saphris (asenapine)
Seroquel (quetiapine)
Symbyax (Zyprexa plus Prozac)
Zyprexa (olanzapine)

Older Antipsychotic Drugs

Asendin (amoxapine, approved and marketed as antidepressant)
Etrafon (Elavil plus Trilafon)
Haldol (haloperidol)
Loxitane (loxapine)
Mellaril (thioridazine)
Moban (molindone)
Navane (thiothixene)
Prolixin (fluphenazine)
Serentil (mesoridazine)
Stelazine (trifluoperazine)
Taractan (chlorprothixene)
Thorazine (chlorpromazine)
Tindal (acetophenazine)
Trilafon (perphenazine)
Vesprin (triflupromazine)

Neuroleptics Used for Other Medical Purposes

Compazine (prochlorperazine)
Inapsine (droperidol)
Orap (pimozide)
Phenergan (promethazine; weak neuroleptic effects)
Reglan (metoclopramide)

PART V: LITHIUM AND OTHER DRUGS USED AS MOOD STABILIZERS

Depakote (divalproex sodium; antiepileptic drug)
Equetro (extended-release carbamazepine; antiepileptic drug)
Lamictal (lamotrigine; antiepileptic drug)
Lithobid, Lithotabs, Eskalith (lithium)

Off-Label or Unapproved Mood Stabilizers

Catapres (clonidine; antihypertensive drug)
Neurontin (gabapentin; antiepileptic drug)
Tegretol (carbamazepine; antiepileptic drug)
Tenex (guanfacine; antihypertensive drug)
Topamax (topiramate; antiepileptic drug)
Trileptal (oxcarbazepine; antiepileptic drug)

Index

Abilify. *see* aripiprazole

abject humiliation, therapist handling of patient feelings, 182

abnormal movements, in antipsychotic drug withdrawal, 125

activation or stimulation, in antidepressant withdrawal, 121

Adderall/Adderall XR. *see* amphetamines

addiction. *see* drug abuse and dependence

adverse drug effects
  acute, 43
  antidepressant drugs, 57–72
  antipsychotic (neuroleptic) drugs, 39–56
  benzodiazepines, other sedatives, and opiates, 85–97
  chronic brain impairment, 19–38
  examples of delayed recognition of, 15–16
  lithium and other mood stabilizers, 99–108
  medication spellbinding, 109–116
  stimulant drugs, 73–84
  time to occurrence, 16
  varied sources of information on drugs, 17–18

affective dysregulation. *see* emotional worsening

aggression, stimulant treatment and, 81

agitation, benzodiazepine withdrawal, 125

akathisia, 16, 40

alpha-adrenergic rebound, in antipsychotic drug withdrawal, 125

alprazolam, 17, 26–27, 85, 88–89, 125, 147
  chronic brain impairment, 21
  interdose symptoms, 89
  intoxication, 91
  long-term exposure, 92–94
  mania and, 91
  SSRI combination, 91

Ambien. *see* zolpidem

American Academy of Pediatrics, 74

amitriptyline, 17, 57, 122

amphetamines, 77, 80, 126–127
  see also list of Stimulants and Attention Deficit Hyperactivity Drugs in the Appendix
  overdosage, 81

Anafranil. *see* clomipramine

anger, medication spellbinding, 111

anosognosia, in chronic brain impairment, 22–23, 28–29

antidepressants, 12–13, 15, 96. *see also* list of "Antidepressants" in the Appendix
  bipolar disorder, 61–62
  brain dysfunction and cellular abnormalities, 60–61

CPSIA information can be obtained
at www.ICGtesting.com
Printed in the USA
LVHW011921010419
612564LV00017B/275

9 780826 108432